THE POLITICS OF *RAPE*

The Victim's Perspective

Diana E. H. Russell

STEIN AND DAY/*Publishers*/New York

First Stein and Day paperback edition, 1975
First published in 1975
Copyright © 1974 by Diana E. H. Russell
Library of Congress Catalog Card No. 73-90697
All rights reserved
Designed by Ed Kaplin
Printed in the United States of America
Stein and Day/*Publishers*/Scarborough House
Briarcliff Manor, N. Y. 10510
ISBN 0-8128-1860-1

"A shocking and revealing book."

—*Texas Banner*

"Ms. Russell's interviews (and those of her associates) are notable for their sensitivity to the less tangible human and political issues involved in this ultimate act of aggression."

—*Publishers Weekly*

"A definitive book about rape and its victims ... Offers important suggestions to all women threatened by rape."   —*Grinnell Register*

"A painful, enlightening, and most important book."   —*Cosmopolitan*

*In the hope that understanding rape
from the victim's perspective may
facilitate the eradication of rape*

CONTENTS

Rape and Society

ACKNOWLEDGMENTS

This book could never have been written without the help of a large number of people. Virginia Behrens, a student at Mills College, where I teach, was the person who first responded with enthusiasm to my idea of interviewing rape victims for a book. Her support at that time was very important to me, as was our sharing the excitement and headaches of the first interviews.

Next, I wish to thank Anne Stevens and Renée Green, also students at Mills College, who became interviewers early in the study. They helped in getting black women to participate. Anne Stevens also read through the second draft of the manuscript, and provided me with critical feedback on how she as a black woman reacted. In addition, some paragraphs Anne wrote were directly incorporated into the concluding comments of chapter 15.

Doris Balabanian, a student at UC Berkeley, became the fifth interviewer. She and I did most of the interviewing, and her contribution was absolutely indispensable. Cameron Smith kindly allowed me access to her interviews of rape victims, one of which is published in this book. I also appreciate Deborah Dietz's permission to include two or three paragraphs from her unpublished paper on rape.

Phyllis Pacin accepted the laborious task of typing most of the taped interviews and produced a really expert transcript. I am very grateful for her contribution. Laurie Tempkin assisted greatly with library research, Xeroxing articles, and in numerous other ways. And Christine Cavanaugh, Barbara Seid, Janis Miyamoto, Patricia Raley, Eulalia Watkins, Betty Lee, and Sylvia Joyner helped with typing.

Jack Fremont not only contributed a chapter to the book, but read two of the earlier drafts and made extensive editorial and substantive suggestions. I believe the book is substantially better for his help, and his belief in the importance of the research was also very valuable to me.

The editorial and substantive suggestions of Arlene Daniels have also been indispensable. The promptness with which she returned draft after draft was impressive, and her encouragement at all stages of the research was much appreciated. I have also benefited from the advice and help of Howie Becker, Kent Rush, Molly Wilcox, Rebecca Hazelwood, and Ruth Balden.

Carol Murray, Barbara Fagan, and Darlene Cole read parts of the book. All of them gave me encouragement and helpful suggestions, particularly for the last chapter on solutions. Barbara Fagan and Margaret Stone, by permitting me to expand on their bibliography, help provide readers with a more comprehensive list of further readings and research sources on rape. In addition, some of Barbara's ideas were directly incorporated into the chapter on solutions.

I am grateful to Shirley Fisher of McIntosh and Otis for her interest in my work on rape at an early stage and for finding a publisher for me. And I am indebted to Mary Solberg, my editor at Stein and Day, for the work she did on the manuscript.

I am also grateful to the committee on faculty research grants at Mills College for contributing $1,600 to this research, and to Bay Area Women Against Rape (BAWAR) for allowing me to include their advice to women in the Appendix.

Most of all I would like to thank the rape victims who volunteered for this study. This book would obviously not have been possible without their willingness to be interviewed. Many found the interview painful, and some might find it painful once again to see their experience in print, and to hear people talk about it. Since the bulk of the book consists of the 22 accounts of rape victims, it seems reasonable that a percentage of what profits may accrue from this book should be given to them.[1] The remainder of the profits will go to those who contributed most to this book without remuneration, and to rape crisis centers that try to help rape victims and educate the public about the problem.

It is not possible to mention all the other women, mostly feminist, many of whose names I do not know, whose thinking has contributed to the analysis, interpretation, and conclusion of this book. Without their input, often unconscious for both them and myself, this book would be a much poorer one. In this sense, I see it very much as a collective enterprise, even though I cannot name everyone in the collective.

The names of the rape victims and all people mentioned in their interviews have, of course, been changed. Other small but immaterial changes have sometimes been made in order to protect the anonymity of the rape victims.

---

1. I have only been able to recontact 14 of the 22 rape victims. Unless the remaining 8 women contact me, I shall not be able to give them their share of the profits, if such there be. They should contact me at P.O. Box 9947, Mills College, Oakland, CA 94613. Should I not hear from them one year after the publication of this book, I shall donate their share to a rape crisis center.

Introduction

"Who's supposed to be on trial here?" Gillian Jones, exasperated and bewildered, put the question at the end of a day of testifying at what she had previously thought was the trial of Jerry Plotkin. According to Ms. Jones, Mr. Plotkin, a San Francisco jeweler, together with another man, had forced her at gunpoint into his car, taken her to his swank apartment where two other men waited, and the four men raped her and forced her to commit other sexual acts.[1] On the day that Ms. Jones, a twenty-three-year-old secretary, complained that she appeared to be the one on trial, she had been subjected to numerous questions about her present and past sex life, the sex life of her lover, and even the sexual play of her two children.

Ms. Jones, like millions of other Americans, was not at that time having a monogamous relationship with a man. Irrelevant as this was to establishing whether or not Ms. Jones was raped by Jerry Plotkin, his attorney's chief line of attack was to try to show that she had a background of promiscuity and emotional instability. At the same time, the bulk of Plotkin's defense consisted of "admitting that he frequently picked up girls in bars, that he frequently took them to his apartment, and that sexual relationships frequently ensued." So, whereas Ms. Jones's multiple sexual relationships were used as damning evidence against her claim to having been raped, Mr. Plotkin's multiple relationships were apparently supposed to suggest that he was less likely to be a rapist.

Following Ms. Jones's appearance on the witness stand, a group of women handed out a leaflet, "Rape in the Courtroom," on the steps of City Hall, near where the trial was taking place. The leaflet attacked Mr. Plotkin's attorney for introducing, and the judge and prosecutor for allowing, evidence about Ms. Jones's sex life:

> There can be no clearer example of women's real place in this society [the leaflet declared]. When a person is robbed, the robber is put on trial. When someone is murdered, the murderer is tried. But when a woman is raped, it is the woman and not the rapist who

1. *San Francisco Chronicle*, April 15 and 17, 1971. To protect the victim from any unwanted publicity, a pseudonym is used.

is put on trial. . . . If she can be shown to have any sexual history, the rapist must be acquitted, for by their definition it is then no rape at all. For a woman to allow herself to be a sexual person, to enjoy her sexuality in her own way in her own time, is for her to lose all protection from being forced to commit sexual acts with any man at any time.

The protest had no impact on the outcome of the trial. After three days of deliberation, the jury acquitted Mr. Plotkin. According to the newspaper account, it was the rereading of Ms. Jones's testimony regarding her sex life that convinced the undecided of Plotkin's innocence. One might wonder what motivation a sexually free woman might have for falsely accusing an unknown man of rape when the odds of getting a conviction are so heavily weighted against her.

In the course of attending and protesting this trial, my awareness about rape changed. I began to get some notion of how much more widespread rape was than I had realized. Prior to this time I had met only one woman who had said that she had been raped. During the course of our demonstration, several women passersby stopped and said that they had been raped, but had not reported it because of the treatment they anticipated in court. In addition, several of my sister picketers told me that they had been raped, or knew of women who had been.

Attending the trial, then, began the destruction of some myths about rape that I shared with most other people. For example, I had seen rape as an extremely sadistic and deviant act, which could be performed only by crazy or psychopathic people. I carried around in my head a picture of rape that involved a strange man jumping out of the bushes and attacking and raping a solitary woman on her way home late at night. The notion of rape by a lover or friend or colleague just hadn't occurred to me. I also imagined that rape victims would be young women who would fit common cultural standards of attractiveness.

Throughout my life, I had personally taken numerous risks in going out with men I didn't know at all well, or walked home alone at all hours of the night. For some reason, I credited myself for having been lucky. Buried deep in me was the notion that rape was something that didn't happen to a "good" woman like me.

The idea of collecting women's accounts of their rape experiences occurred to me during the trial as the most obvious way of correcting my own and others' ignorance. It also seemed a way of enabling the victims, most of whom keep the ugly experience to themselves, to feel less isolated. Finally, it seemed to me that this would be a good first step toward achieving change in the treatment of rape victims.

Before embarking on this study, I went through the literature on rape to discover if my ignorance about rape could be cured by knowledge of available research findings. I was appalled to find how common it is for clinicians and researchers (usually male) to assume that rape victims enjoy being raped. Only this week I received a letter from an associate consulting editor of *Medical Aspects of Human Sexuality* inviting me to answer a question sent by a physician for publication in the journal: "In cases of forcible rape what percent of the victims experience orgasm?"

The interviews in this book emphatically contradict the prevalent view of male authors, clinicians, and doctors, that women enjoy being raped. They provide real evidence on the basis of which to judge the validity of some of the established views on rape by giving serious attention to the feelings of rape victims, including many who did not report their rapes, and by relating rape to the society at large.

RAPE DEFINED

The law defines rape as sexual intercourse with a female, not the wife of the perpetrator, accomplished without the consent of the female. Hence the law denies that wives can be raped by husbands, or that men can rape men, or that women can rape women or men. It also differentiates forced vaginal penetration from forced oral or anal penetration, and from cases in which a man forces a woman to masturbate him or uses his mouth, hand, or some foreign object to penetrate her instead of his penis.

For the purposes of this book I decided to concur with the legal definition in some respects but not in others. I defined rape as intercourse imposed on a female against her wishes where her wishes are known to the rapist or where she expresses her wishes forthrightly, verbally, and/or physically. I also include cases where, by virtue of being unconscious, drugged, asleep, or in some comparable state, the woman is in no position to consent to the act. "Intercourse" must involve some penetration, but not necessarily ejaculation, and anal or oral penetration by the penis is also regarded as rape, as is forcible intercourse imposed by a husband on his wife.

THE STATISTICS OF RAPE

Even within the strictest legal definition of rape, official statistics on the incidence of reported rape show dramatic increases. Of course, it cannot be definitely known whether this increase is indicative of a similar increase in unreported rape, which constitutes the vast majority of cases. It could be simply that more women are reporting rape each year, and that the incidence is not really rising at all. Perhaps the influence of the ideas of women's liberation make victims more inclined to report the crime since women are increasingly rejecting the notion that rape victims are responsible for what happened to them, and more women wish the rapist to be punished. In addition, women may be developing a greater sense of responsibility toward others who might be raped if a rapist is not reported.

However, it could also be argued that the women most affected by the women's movement are more aware of the unfair treatment rape victims are likely to receive and therefore less likely to report it. In this series of interviews the more politically conscious women often did not report rape.

Besides the increase in violent crimes in general, there are other factors that may account for the increase in the rape rate. More women are rejecting unofficial curfews and male chaperones. They are walking alone at night, hitchhiking, going to places of entertainment alone or with other women.

There is also some male backlash caused by women's growing desire to be more independent of men. This painful period of transition is a time of tremendous misunderstanding and hostility between the sexes. Rape is the way some men express their hostility to women. More threatened male egos may mean more rape. In the short run, the more women who break out of the traditional female role and assert themselves in new ways, the more threatened male egos there are.

The ninety women willing to be interviewed for this book were obtained through word of mouth, advertising in the Berkeley women's newsletter, and notices on some local community and college bulletin boards. Several of the victims were personal friends or acquaintances of the five interviewers. All interviews were taped.

Although the chief concern of this book is to educate people about rape from the victim's perspective, one chapter on rape from the rapist's perspective is included. Just as I think it is crucial for women to interview rape victims, it seemed important for a man to interview rapists. I was fortunate that Jack Fremont wanted to make this investigation.

The Victim

"The fear of sexual assault is a special fear: its intensity in women can best be likened to the male fear of castration."
—Germaine Greer, "Seduction Is a Four Letter Word"

"There are nights when cold fear suddenly comes over me as I sit alone in my house. I know that I will carry this fear as long as I live. Six years ago I was the victim of an attempted rape in these very rooms, and I can never forget the horrifying sensation of helplessness a woman feels when pitted against a powerful, sex-crazed deviate. I would prefer any kind of quick, clean death to another sordid struggle with such a man."
—Gladys Denny Shultz, "Society and the Sex Criminal"

" 'What was the defendant wearing?' That was Mr. Freeman's lawyer.
'I don't know.'
'You mean to say this man raped you and you don't know what he was wearing?' He snickered as if I had raped Mr. Freeman.
'Do you know if you were raped?' "
—Maya Angelou, *I Know Why the Caged Bird Sings*

ONE

The Trauma of Rape

Throughout the following year, whenever I
worked in the garden, I had a little holster, and
I kept a gun on my hip. I was so afraid of being
surprised again.

This is the case of Ms. X, a fifty-five-year-old white woman who teaches elementary school.[1] Ms. X refused to give her name even to the interviewer. Her insistence on total anonymity highlights her continuing fears about being identified as a rape victim. Interestingly, however, Ms. X said that it was a great relief to have the opportunity to talk to someone about her experience and she hoped that other women might learn from her experience to protect themselves better.

Ms. X has four grown children and was divorced two years prior to being raped. She said the divorce was "very mutual and friendly. . . . We were growing in different directions, and so there was no big trauma." She said she had previously had "total trust in men." Ms. X was forty-eight when she was raped seven years ago. In all these years, she had previously told only one person about the experience.

Ms. X: My boys were in the army, my girl was at college, and I lived alone. I live in the mountains at the end of a road which is completely blind. None of my neighbors can see up that road, so someone could park up there, and no one would ever know it. Apparently the man who raped me had been following me and watching my habits for a long time. He had probably tried the door on several occasions, but fortunately it was locked.

It was a Sunday morning around noon. I had gone up the road to get the newspaper and had come back into the house and was reading the paper.

1. Ms. X was interviewed by Cameron Smith, a doctoral student at the University of California at Santa Cruz, for a study that she is doing on rape victims.

Then I went into the bathroom. I opened the door to the bathroom from my bedroom, and he was standing there with a gun. I just froze. I went into shock.

He kept me prisoner for two nights and two days. With a gun at my head, he made me call my school district on Monday to tell them I was sick. I tried to get out of the bathroom window once, but he caught me. When he slept he kept a tight grip on me so that if I just moved he would arouse and hit me for trying to escape. The first night I didn't sleep at all.

INTERVIEWER: Could you describe him?

Ms. X: He looked like he had been a boxer, a professional fighter. He had scars on his eyebrows, his cheekbones, and his nose. He had very little hair on his body. I think he was probably part American Indian. But he had a lot of white blood too. I imagine he was in his forties. He was not well educated, but he had a very quick clever intelligence.

He was very sadistic. His sexual assaults went on constantly, and I was forced into perverse activities—the whole ugly mess—gagging, choking, vomiting. He cleverly didn't black my eyes or leave marks. There were some bruises from where he threw me into furniture, but mainly he would twist my arm and choke me. I found that if I fought him very hard, he came to orgasm more quickly, and it was over for a while, which shows his sadism. I was wondering, "What can I do to get out of this horror?" I would try to submit, thinking, maybe that would get it over with, but I found that it infuriated him if I submitted without fighting him.

INTERVIEWER: So did you fight?

Ms. X: Yes, I did.

INTERVIEWER: Did he tell you anything about himself?

Ms. X: Not a thing. But he kept threatening to kill me if I did certain things, like if I got to the phone, or tried to escape. He said he had to do what he had to do. He kept saying that. "I have to do this." With my background in psychology, I thought, here's a real sexual psychopath.

He said, "I don't want to kill you, but if you do these things, I'll have to kill you." He said that several times.

INTERVIEWER: Did he ask you any questions?

Ms. X: No. I tried to talk to him, but he would not talk. And I found that he didn't have any wallet, so that I couldn't get his license or any other kind of identification. I couldn't do anything! He made me feed him what I had in the house. I had very little, and I had no money, but he wasn't interested in money apparently.

INTERVIEWER: Do you think he'd done this before with other women?

Ms. X: I'm sure he had. He was so expert at immobilizing a woman. He knew exactly what to do. Up until this time, I had believed that rape was impossible if a woman didn't want to be raped, that it could only happen to a woman who submits. But I found out how a woman can be totally immobilized. He was a heavy man. He was probably two hundred pounds, and very strong. He would lie on one side of my body, pinning down one leg and one arm, and he'd get his other arm up under my knee, and he'd be twisting my other arm, so that I just couldn't move. He would do it three or four, maybe five times, and then he would sleep. I did escape once from his grip, and I got some clothes on, and I was heading out of a window as quietly as I could, but he caught me.

INTERVIEWER: What was going through your head?

Ms. X: I felt that I was outside my body, watching this whole thing, that it wasn't happening to me, it was happening to somebody else. It was a strange feeling, absolutely unreal. I was terrorized, but it's very hard to describe the shock of what was happening. At first, I went into a state of shock where I just shook and shook and shook and shook and shook. And I was freezing cold. Just freezing cold. And he kept the gun on me all the time. He showed me the bullets in case I should think it unloaded.

Then after two days, he was gone. I didn't even know he was gone. Monday night he disappeared as quickly as he came.

INTERVIEWER: Had you ever seen him before?

Ms. X: Never.

INTERVIEWER: Do you think he had been drinking?

Ms. X: Not at all, although he looked for liquor in the house. I didn't have any. When I realized he was gone, I wanted to pour Lysol all over me. I wanted to be cleansed. I took a bath, and then I thought about calling the police. And I thought no, I can't do that. It's too much of a horror story. People would look at me differently. If it's so horrible to *me*, it must be horrible to other people. I don't want anybody to know what happened to me. I thought that they would see me differently if they knew about it.

INTERVIEWER: Why?

Ms. X: Because I thought that other people thought the way I had thought, that this couldn't happen to a woman who didn't want it, or allow it.

INTERVIEWER: You really felt that a woman couldn't be raped?

Ms. X: Yes. Can you imagine? I really believed that. So I assumed that if I told people, they would think I had consented, because they would think as I had thought before I had the experience. Also, I remember reading something that stuck in my head about how you have to press charges, and you have to go to court, and you have to do all this stuff. I just couldn't do it.

I'm basically a rather retiring person, and the thought that I would have to be in a roomful of people who knew what had happened to me made me sick.

INTERVIEWER: Were there any other reasons you didn't want to report the rape?

Ms. X: Well, I think prison would be no place for a man of that age, a psychopath. I don't think psychiatric care could help a man like that.

It would have been marvelous had I known a woman police officer I could talk to, if I had known that it would be confidential, and that I would be treated like a person who did not want to be raped. I never flirted with men, I didn't act seductive in any way. I wasn't interested at the time. I was trying to survive financially, pouring myself into my work, and if I had known I'd be treated like a decent human being, I would have been happy to report it.

INTERVIEWER: Have you ever had any dealing with the police?

Ms. X: Never, except that I always drive too fast, and I'm always looking in the rear-view mirror. My kids have never been in trouble. Prior to this I had had an incredibly smooth life.

INTERVIEWER: So, what did you do next?

Ms. X: I called my friend, because I knew I couldn't go to school the next day. I didn't know how long it would be before I could face people. She came up to the house and stayed with me, and I poured the whole thing out to her, and we cried together, and held each other. She never told her husband because she said she knew his attitude toward me would change. He also thought a woman couldn't be raped.

After I had called my friend, I said, "Will you stay here and answer my phone, so that if anybody calls from the school department and wants to know how I am, you can say I have the flu, and that you're taking care of me." Then I went straight down to the nearest town, and into the sporting goods store, and I bought a forty sentinel gun and a small Browning automatic. Incidentally, I told the man who raped me that I was going to do this. I told him that I would kill him if he ever came back, and I know I would. And that was a shock to me, to know that this peaceful person who had never known anything but love was capable of killing a human being. But I knew that I could. I know I would kill him.

INTERVIEWER: Did you ever see him again?

Ms. X: I was sitting in the living room one night about six months later. There's nothing out there, so I don't draw the drapes. I was sitting there watching television, and something caught my eye, a flash like a match on the steps outdoors. It was very dark, and I looked at it, and then I saw the glow of a cigarette, and I watched it. And I thought, he's there. I felt that it was he.

So I went and got my forty sentinel pistol. It's a large one, and I set it in a very obvious place right beside me on the couch. And I thought, if I act afraid, I'm dead. I'm going to let him know I'm not afraid, and then I'll kill him. And then he left. He never tried to get into the house.

INTERVIEWER: What were your feelings when sitting there with your gun?

Ms. X: I was frightened inside. My heart was pounding, but I was very cool in appearance. I acted unconcerned. I think he might have thought he could pull the whole scene again, but since I was well armed, I think he was afraid. On a couple of occasions later, I saw cigarettes that had been stamped out on the steps, and at that time I didn't smoke at all. Throughout the following year, whenever I worked in the garden, I had a little holster, and I kept a gun on my hip. I was so afraid of being surprised again.

INTERVIEWER: You didn't move?

Ms. X: No. I guess I'm stubborn. I decided this man isn't going to drive me away from the environment I love. I'm not going to let this thing that happened to me change my life that much, that I have to lose what I worked for and love.

INTERVIEWER: Would you have liked to kill him?

Ms. X: No, I wouldn't like to kill him. But I *would* kill him if he attacked me again. I wouldn't like to kill any human being.

INTERVIEWER: So what did you do after talking to your friend?

Ms. X: I stayed home and kind of healed. Then I went to school Friday. It was very hard. Very hard.

INTERVIEWER: Did you have bad dreams after the rape?

Ms. X: Oh, yes. And I would relive it. It became almost an obsession. I thought I was being punished for something. And I kept wondering, why did this happen to me? What have I done that this thing would happen?

INTERVIEWER: Did you blame yourself?

Ms. X: I was trying to find ways to blame myself. Trying to think, what did I do? What brought this on? Later I knew that this was ridiculous, because I hadn't done anything, and it had just happened.

INTERVIEWER: Did you have to take tranquilizers?

Ms. X: Oh, yes.

INTERVIEWER: Did you go to a doctor?

Ms. X: Yes, but it wasn't until weeks later. I didn't want to go to my own doctor because he was a personal friend of mine. So I couldn't go to him. I asked one of the teachers that I had known in the district. She didn't work in my school, but she had lived a more worldly life than I had, and was more experienced in many ways. So I asked her about a doctor I could go to for a VD check, and she recommended one. I wasn't worried about pregnancy or anything like that, because I was unable to be pregnant.

The rape was a trauma in so many ways, I can't tell you. He injured me so badly. There was blood, lots of blood, all the time.

All through the time he was there, and then afterwards, there was a heavy discharge, a bloody discharge, and that's what scared me. I thought, gee, maybe I have venereal disease. I went to a doctor who I never saw before or since, and he made a joke of it as though I was a really hot number. He acted as though I was a swinger or a prostitute. I didn't tell him I'd been raped. I just said that I had had relations with a man I didn't know, and that I was worried.

He really thought it was hilarious. He was joking, "Wow! You must be something else!" It made me sick. It made me even sicker when he said, "No, you don't have any venereal disease, but stay away from those rough ones." Another bad thing was that he examined me without the presence of a nurse. The nurse went out, and he shut the door, which was very odd. That's never happened to me before. Also, he acted seductive.

INTERVIEWER: Could you tell me more about him?

Ms. X: I imagine he was in his fifties. He belonged to the American Medical Association and was supposed to be respectable. So this experience made me glad I hadn't told anybody else about it. It reinforced all my fears. The only relief was that I didn't have VD.

In talking with friends and people after it happened, I tried to find out their attitudes toward rape, and it too reinforced what I had previously thought. They all think that rape isn't really possible. So there was no way to break out of the guilt.

INTERVIEWER: Did you seek counseling?

Ms. X: I wanted to so badly! I was so tempted! I knew some good counselors, and I would even be on the phone sometimes to call a counselor, but I never was able to do it. I would come so close, because I badly wanted to talk it out, but I couldn't do it. I'd just say, deal with it yourself. Cope with it in your own way. I found out that I am very strong, which surprised me. I wondered if all the protective, loving bringing up that I had had made me strong.

I learned to cope with the obsession by myself. I'd start to fall asleep at night, and the whole thing would come back. Also, I had a number of headaches. Tranquilizers don't do much for me but depress me, so I just took simple medicine. But I would get so discouraged. Sometimes I would get very depressed. I'd think, I'm never going to get this out of my head. When is this garbage going to get out of my head? Because I could be in the most harmonious situation, and bang, there it was again. It was like a flash, and then I'd have to just wrench it away again.

INTERVIEWER: Did it affect your attitude toward men?

Ms. X: I'm afraid it did. About three years later I was approached by a professor at X College, and he wanted to take me out. I knew he was a wonderful, fine man, but I was so nervous that I shook the whole time. I was a lousy date because I was so tense. I just couldn't be with a man. The only men I could be with and be comfortable were my sons and my son-in-law.

Dealing with men, even on a business level, was very difficult. Finally, I got to be very objective, and I got over most of it, but if I was alone with a man or he came to the house to pick me up for a date, I was really shaky. I kept telling myself, why, you idiot, why are you like this? Stop it. Relax. But I couldn't.

INTERVIEWER: Did you ever tell anybody else?

Ms. X: No. Just that one woman friend. And I never mentioned it to her again. Strangely, it embarrassed her. I tried one time to bring it up again when I was feeling that I wanted to talk it out again, and I could see that it embarrassed her, so I shut up. I thought, well, I'm not going to lay all this heavy stuff on her again. It isn't fair to her.

INTERVIEWER: So you never told your children?

Ms. X: No. But I'm fine now. I can relate to men easily now, and I don't get uptight. I haven't had any sexual relationships since that time. But I think I could now.

INTERVIEWER: Do you think that your being raped affected this?

Ms. X: I had not been having any sexual relations with my husband for about five years before we were divorced, and I hadn't had any after the divorce either.

INTERVIEWER: So that makes it fourteen or fifteen years since you had sexual relations voluntarily. What are some other ways in which the rape affected you?

Ms. X: I couldn't lock myself into the car I had at that time, and so I carried this little Browning automatic whenever I drove. It made me feel guilty and frightened, and I swore that when I got another car, I'd be sure I'd get one that I could lock on the driver's side. Otherwise, when you stop at a stop sign at night it's risky.

We have a joke in my family and with my friends about how I lock everybody in. I lock myself in, and I've done it so much that it's a habit now, an absolute habit. I do it automatically, so when somebody tries to go out to the car to get something, the door's locked. And they say, "Oh, mother locks in her guests. Once you get into this house, you never get out. She doesn't want anybody to leave," and we just laugh about it.

Before, the only time I locked up was at night, and when I was ready for bed, I checked all the doors. But that's really silly, because if you're there alone, anybody can walk in at other times, which I found out. That man was clever. He had watched me to find out what my patterns were. And he saw me go up and get the paper, and he knew that that door wasn't locked.

I went through a bad period where I was too paranoid. I was carrying the gun, and I knew I couldn't always live with a gun on my hip whenever I was working in the yard, so I decided to be very careful about locking doors. I still have a gun at home, and it's loaded, and I will always have a gun.

The trauma of Ms. X's rape experience was deep and long lasting. Three years later she trembled with fear when she went out with a man. Now, seven or eight years later, she still locks her guests in. For over a year, she felt she had to be armed to go out in the garden or drive her car.

Ms. X's experience illustrates the impossible position in which the myth that women cannot be raped places rape victims. To the extent that friends and acquaintances, employers and clients, believe the myth, to that extent victims have to deal with incredulity should they choose to talk about their experiences. Ms. X has been imprisoned by that myth.

When even a highly respectable "privileged" woman like Ms. X chooses this kind of solitary confinement rather than face people's reactions to her experience, something is incredibly amiss in our society.

TWO

The Virgin and the Whore

I went with one of them, and we went to some
dark desolate place, and they said, "This is it.
You better fuck or get out!" Their line was,
"Well, you're not a virgin anyway."

In Western societies, there are still "good girls" and "bad girls," virgins and
whores. And male behavior toward females generally depends on which of
the two labels females are perceived to deserve. A "good girl" deserves a
male's "best behavior," though attempts are constantly made to turn a
"good girl" into a "bad girl."

Loss of virginity, particularly at a young age, can evoke in males a "no
holds barred" approach. The girl becomes a whore, and only a sucker
would treat a whore well. Because a whore is seen as "bad," conscience can
be suspended. A sexually active male can see himself as decent while seeing
the females with whom he has sex as bad. The influence of this double
standard persists in spite of the "sexual revolution."

Perhaps the most tragic aspect of the good girl–bad girl dichotomy is the
extent to which women accept the labels. The good girl prides herself on
being virtuous, though the price may be sexual deprivation and repression,
and the bad girl often cannot escape the stigma attached to activities many
men openly boast about.

Rosalind Cohen comes from an upper-middle-class Jewish background.
Married for fourteen years, she has four children. She was gang-raped when
she was fifteen years old, seventeen years ago. Although she did tell a few
people about the experience some time ago, only recently has she felt able to
talk about it fully. Before, the feeling of shame was too great.

"I used to think it changed me in other people's eyes if they knew," she
said, "but now I feel I am still the same Rosalind I was before we started
talking." Ms. Cohen's involvement in the women's movement appears to

have brought about the change. Meeting other women who were able to talk about their rape experiences was particularly helpful.

In talking about her experience of rape, Ms. Cohen found it necessary to give background information. I have included much of it because I think it illustrates very dramatically what the costs of a sexual double standard can be, and how it can relate to rape.

ROSALIND COHEN: The first time I had intercourse was with a boy who told me he wasn't going to do it. I was fifteen. We were making out in somebody's basement, and it led to his fingering my vagina and that sort of thing. He said he wanted to put his penis inside me. I said, "No, I've never done it before." He said, "I won't put it all the way inside. I'll just put it outside."

I didn't think it was the right thing to do, but he assured me that he liked me a lot and all of that crap. I liked him a lot. He was the first boy that I had ever had this big kissing and hugging romantic thing with. So I said he could put his penis next to me. But he kept pushing it further and further, and then there was this awful pain. But I didn't know it was inside of me. I kept thinking it wasn't, because he kept telling me it wasn't. Young girls are very naive about what's really going on. I just didn't know.

When I got home I saw that I was full of blood, so I figured it out. The bleeding was from inside. I had thought that the pain was from him pressing against my hymen, that it was just so resistant that it wasn't allowing him to get inside. I had kept sort of moving back, and he kept moving up, and I kept moving back. Why I endured this, God knows. But I did, because I wasn't into sticking up for my rights or speaking out. I never had done that.

INTERVIEWER: What did you feel about losing your virginity?

Ms. COHEN: I think at the actual time of discovery of the blood I was quite shocked that I had actually done it. But other than that, I can't remember any particular feelings. I know I had some, but I can't remember.

My mother caught on that something was going on. She didn't like this boy I was seeing because he had tattoos and looked like a gangster. She got in touch with his family, and I don't know what she said, but I couldn't see him anymore. So I was kind of pissed off at my mother and pissed off at this whole interrupted sexual thing. I think I was ready for some sexual life.

Then this friend told me about these guys she had met in the movies. She said if I went to the movies with her, I could meet them too, and so I did. These guys were in a gang. They were very exciting to me because they were big, strong, tough gangsters. The first time I met them, they were sitting in the movies, and she was giving one of them a hand job. This really appealed to me because of the forbidden, secret aspect.

One night when she went out with one of them, she got me to go along. I went with one of them, and we went to some dark desolate place, and they said, "This is it. You better fuck or get out!" Their line was, "Well, you're not a virgin anyway," which they soon ascertained. So I had intercourse with one of them that time.

I kept going out with this guy and my friend, and every time I went out with him, something would happen, and his friends would come along, and they would pull some kind of thing like, "You gotta fuck with all of us or you gotta get out of the car." I don't know why I did it, I've never figured it out. A lot of times we would be drinking, and I'd be very drunk, but I guess there was also some kind of an appeal in it to me. I never enjoyed the sexual acts themselves, but I always *thought* I would enjoy them.

INTERVIEWER: How did you see these experiences at the time?

Ms. COHEN: Well, I'm not sure. I had a lot of self-hatred at the time, and whenever I did have intercourse, I always felt pretty guilty. I felt that I was doing an awful thing I couldn't stop myself from doing, and that I was an awful person because of it. I lived in an environment where girls who did this were called whores. I had to keep it all a very big secret, but that was really how I saw myself.

INTERVIEWER: Did you want to have intercourse?

Ms. COHEN: Yes, I wanted it physically. If I would be kissing a boy, I would feel these really strong urges to go on. The actual intercourse itself was like me lying there passively, and the guy doing his thing, and it was never a pleasure. From the moment of penetration, it was not a pleasure.

INTERVIEWER: On the occasions when there was more than one guy, how did you feel?

Ms. COHEN: There was some kind of excitement, not in the sex, but in being wanted. It sounds very silly to me now, but there must have been a need. I must have felt that somebody liked and wanted me.

The rape occurred with all of these guys and all of their friends. One day when I was sitting out in front of a friend's house, a couple of them pulled up in a car and said, "Come on, get in the car." I had a feeling that it was going to be one of those group sex deals, and I really didn't want to do it, but I was afraid of them. I was also really afraid that they might tell my other friends what was going on. So I got into the car with them.

They drove me to some place in their neighborhood, which was far from my neighborhood. They took me into a house they called their clubhouse. There was a trap door leading to a basement below where there were beds. They pulled off all my clothes, and I remember screaming and protesting and saying, "Let me go," but to no avail. The whole day was spent with guys coming in and going out and coming in and going out. There were a lot of them. I couldn't count how many.

INTERVIEWER: How did this experience compare with the others you described?

Ms. COHEN: With the other experiences I always thought that the one guy liked me. I guess I thought that he was sort of my boyfriend. I remember one time talking them out of it and crying and becoming hysterical and screaming and carrying on so that it was too much for them. But I didn't often, and I don't know why. Not that it was a lot of times that I'd have sex with a couple of other people.

But this time was different in that this was not with my boyfriend. I didn't want to go. I was afraid not to go because I was afraid that they would tell my friends. From the time I got near them, I knew that something terrible was going to happen, but there was just no way out.

I thought maybe it would be a couple of guys and that I could get out of there, but it wasn't just a couple. It was at least twenty. I tried to run out, but they just barred me from leaving. They held me down. Also they would lie and say, "Well, a couple of us, and then you can go." After every time I would carry on and say, "Let me go. Please let me go."

INTERVIEWER: Did all the others watch?

Ms. COHEN: I can't remember. I've repressed a lot of it.

INTERVIEWER: Did everybody who came into the basement rape you?

Ms. COHEN: I have a feeling there were more people there than raped me.

INTERVIEWER: Were you afraid for your life?

Ms. COHEN: I was afraid of getting beat up. I've been beaten up enough by my brother to know that men are stronger than women, and I'm terrified of being hit. But I don't think I ever thought I'd be killed.

After it was all over, they said I could go, and I went upstairs to get my clothes. I was naked with all these guys there, and they started tormenting me and telling me I had to dance to get my clothes. You can imagine how humiliating it was to be naked in a roomful of men who were giving me orders to dance.

INTERVIEWER: Did you do it?

Ms. COHEN: No. I screamed and cried and became hysterical.

INTERVIEWER: How did they react to that?

Ms. COHEN: They loved it. They just laughed and tormented me more until somebody took pity on me. It was one of the boys who was supposedly my friend who took pity on me and took me to the bathroom and gave me my clothes. Somebody else decided that what they were doing was really pretty disgusting, and they should let me get out of there. He said he would take me home. I said I didn't want him to take me home, I just wanted to get out of there and get home myself. He assured me it wasn't safe for me to walk in that neighborhood alone. I would be grabbed again by the rest of his gang, and it would happen again. Apparently girls are not allowed to walk in that neighborhood without being grabbed off the street and raped. I found this out later when I talked to somebody who came from there.

INTERVIEWER: From your description it seems as if their clubhouse was a rape den.

Ms. COHEN: Yeah, it was.

INTERVIEWER: Were the rapes physically painful?

Ms. COHEN: Oh, yes. It was physically painful and I was physically repulsed. And I did a lot of crying and begging to let me get up and go.

INTERVIEWER: What did you feel afterward?

Ms. COHEN: Utter disgust. And utter fear.

INTERVIEWER: Were you afraid that they would get you again?

Ms. COHEN: Yeah.

INTERVIEWER: Did you see them again?

Ms. COHEN: No. Fortunately our neighborhoods were quite separated. They would have had to come out of their way looking for me.

The one who drove me home warned me, "If you get pregnant, it's tough shit on you. Don't you ever dare bring us to court, because we'll all say that you fucked us because you wanted to. You won't be able to get anybody in trouble." That was warning number one. No court in the world will ever convict anybody of paternity if you were fucked by twenty guys. I have a friend who brought one of her boyfriends to court when she was pregnant. He brought a lot of his friends to court, and he got off, because his friends said they slept with her, when in fact, they hadn't. Warning number two was, "If you ever see me or any of us on the street, you better run away fast."

INTERVIEWER: This was the guy who took pity on you?

Ms. COHEN: Yeah. He was very nice to me. He bought me a hamburger or something on the way home. I can't remember if I ate it, but he insisted on stopping. I was just sitting there, not talking to him at all, but he was being very solicitous. The threats didn't come till he actually got two blocks from my house and let me out. It was as if he had to do that. His image of himself as a big bad guy was at stake. He couldn't break down and be nice.

INTERVIEWER: Were you afraid of pregnancy?

Ms. COHEN: No. Pregnancy had no reality to me. It was something they suggested. I never had used any contraceptives. I was very lucky I didn't get pregnant, because then I would have had to tell my parents.

INTERVIEWER: What happened after you arrived home?

Ms. COHEN: In those days I lived out on the street as much as I could. My friends were on the street. They all had wondered what had happened to me after I was driven away by the two men in the car. I made up a story. I was quite a mess, disheveled and sweaty and wrinkled and rumpled. I told them that they had roughed me up and sort of punched me around, and they accepted that.

INTERVIEWER: Did the experience affect your behavior afterward in any way?

Ms. COHEN: Oh, I'll say it did! In ways that I'm just fathoming now. In the first place, I didn't have any more sexual escapades after that time. I was horrified by the whole thing, horrified that people would find out. I remember coming home from school every day and sneaking from the bus to my house in mortal fear that I'd see them. I felt I was living this double life. This thing had happened to me, and I couldn't tell anybody. I had to maintain my innocence and virginity and that sort of thing with my friends.

I wouldn't go near boys very much anymore, except for very innocent little things, like kissing and hugging. I started getting drunk a lot. That satisfied my need to do something bad, my juvenile delinquent need. And I got arrested a few times with some friends for doing little silly things. I was a very angry person.

INTERVIEWER: Do you know what about?

Ms. COHEN: I was angry at my mother and my brother. It seems to me in some way that my mother was implicated in all this. You see, the weird thing was that when I had intercourse, I kept thinking about my mother. I knew that she was all mixed up in it. My mother was a very sexually repressed person. She always accused me of doing all the things I was doing, but I denied it. She lived in deadly fear of me doing these things. I fulfilled her fear for her.

INTERVIEWER: Did the experience affect your feelings about yourself?

Ms. COHEN: I guess I hated myself even more than I had before.

INTERVIEWER: Did it change your attitude to men?

Ms. COHEN: I've never thought much of men. My thing about men goes way back to my childhood and my brother, my brother showing me pornographic things when I was eight, my brother molesting me when I was nine. I mean, I had a lot of sexual knowledge.

INTERVIEWER: How old was he then?

Ms. COHEN: Fourteen.

INTERVIEWER: And what form did the molesting take?

Ms. COHEN: First he wanted me to watch him masturbate. Then he wanted me to masturbate him. I think he wanted me to blow him, but I didn't do that. And he wanted to have intercourse with me, but I didn't do that. But I may have let him put his penis next to me.

His favorite was me masturbating him, and then he would come in a little glass and show me how much there was. All this was happening when I was supposed to be a young innocent child. And I knew there was a great discrepancy in my life there. He threatened me that I better not tell my mother, or else he'd kill me. I told her anyway, but she knew that he meant he would kill me if she let him know that I told her. So she could never do anything about it.

INTERVIEWER: So you told her, but she didn't do anything?

Ms. COHEN: Right. My brother was always sort of mentally deranged and very violent, and when he went on one of his insane rampages, he was very scary. He could beat my mother up. He could certainly beat me up, which he did many times. She feared for my life.

She worked, and there were many hours when she wasn't home and we were. So she could do nothing. She just sat back and let him do all these things to me. I would say, "I don't want to do it, I don't like it." He would promise me that I could have this record or that coveted thing. And I would say, "OK," and then he would do whatever he was going to do, but he wouldn't let me have the record. I wanted my brother to like me, and I always kept hoping if I did it this time, he'd give me the thing, and he'd like me. But he never did.

I told my brother about my other sexual experiences once. I thought he would be pleased. After all, it was my brother who introduced me to sex. He taught me every dirty word there was, and every act that there was between a man and a woman. So I thought he would be very pleased. He got all the information out of me, and then he started a campaign of torturing me and calling me a whore.

INTERVIEWER: At what age did this happen?

Ms. COHEN: Sixteen. A few months after the rape.

INTERVIEWER: Was he the only person you told?

Ms. COHEN: No, I told somebody else a year later. He was a real boyfriend, who I slept with. After the rape I only slept with two boys before I got married. When we finally broke up, this boyfriend was so angry with me for breaking up that he called up my brother, and he started telling him all about the things I had told him. So I got to feel that you shouldn't tell anybody anything.

INTERVIEWER: How did your boyfriend react to you telling him about the rape?

Ms. COHEN: He was really concerned. He really cared at the time.

INTERVIEWER: How long did your brother continue to call you a whore?

Ms. COHEN: Until I left home. I was driven out by this name calling. He would call me these names over and over again when no one else was home, knowing that I couldn't tell my mother. If I told my mother, she would say,

"Well, what do you care if he calls you that?" He knew that he had me by the so-called balls. He did other things to torment me, but that was the worst torment of all.

INTERVIEWER: What's your relationship with him like now?

Ms. COHEN: We have no relationship. Since I left home when I was eighteen, we've never spoken.

When I met my husband shortly after this—I was eighteen—I told him I was a virgin. I wasn't about to tell anybody the truth anymore. So I passed myself off as a virgin, and he believed it. I put on a proper show for him the first time we slept together.

INTERVIEWER: Of pain?

Ms. COHEN: Uh-huh. He was very drunk, so it made it easier.

INTERVIEWER: Did you ever tell him?

Ms. COHEN: Many years later.

INTERVIEWER: How did he react?

Ms. COHEN: He started punching me in the head. He was horrified.

INTERVIEWER: Why did you tell him?

Ms. COHEN: The guilt became unbearable. I couldn't stand passing myself off as a person that wasn't me. Last summer I told a friend who had been my friend at the time what had really happened that day, and she was horrified. She said, "Why didn't you tell me?" And I said, "How could I have told you when you would have called me the same names that you always called everybody else? You made it impossible for me to tell you."

INTERVIEWER: Did you think of reporting the rape to the police?

Ms. COHEN: There was no question of doing that.

INTERVIEWER: Did you even think about it?

Ms. COHEN: No. Because I didn't want my parents to know.

INTERVIEWER: How do you think they would have reacted?

Ms. COHEN: I don't know. I thought my mother would probably scream and become hysterical and call me a whore.

INTERVIEWER: Was that the worst thing you could be called?

Ms. COHEN: Sure. I mean that's the total depersonalization, defining you as this object. You have no personality, hopes, dreams, or ambitions. You're just a whore.

INTERVIEWER: Do you regret in any way the way you handled the situation when you were raped?

Ms. COHEN: Once I was in their hands, so to speak, there was no other way I could have acted. There was no getting out of it.

INTERVIEWER: What about getting into it?

Ms. COHEN: I don't know why I got into the car. That preoccupied me for months later. Why did I get into the car? Why didn't I ask my friends to help me? I went over a whole lot of things like this, but I've done a really good job of forgetting. I've been trying to let it come out lately, because it did happen, and it was an important part of my life. But it wasn't until recently that it was acceptable to talk about it, so unfortunately I just can't bring it all back.

INTERVIEWER: Can you think of any solutions to the rape problem?

Ms. COHEN: I think that the only solution would be for men to be put in jail forever, because rape to men is a joke. They know they won't be caught, they won't be prosecuted. If they knew they couldn't get away with it, fifty percent of it would stop immediately, and then we'd have just fifty percent to deal with. We can change society, but we're not going to change it very quickly. But we *can* change the *penalty* for rape quickly, and we *can* get one hundred percent conviction for every rape case. I think that would change a lot of people's heads around.

Guys joy riding out for the night, it's great. They'll pick up a girl, and they'll bang her, and she isn't going to tell, and they know she won't. And they know that the judge probably won't convict them.

INTERVIEWER: What's your reaction to people who think that rape is usually provoked?

Ms. COHEN: I get very hostile and I want to kill them.

In spite of the fact that I knew a lot of the people who raped me, it *was* rape. I did *not* ask for it! I did *not* wish it! I did *not* bring it on myself! So when people say that, I get very, very hostile. Because no matter who you are or what you've done, that's not something that you're asking for. There may be a whole lot of psychological problems when we end up allowing ourselves to be sexually abused, but that's not what we *wanted*. I believe we're just truly taken advantage of.

The experiences Ms. Cohen describes dramatically illustrate the damaging effects of the double sexual standard, and how this standard bolsters a rape mentality.

Accepting her relationship with her brother at least to the extent of wanting him to like her, Ms. Cohen got in touch with her sexuality, something girls are not supposed to do. "Whenever I did have intercourse," she said, "I always felt pretty guilty. I felt that I was doing an awful thing I couldn't stop myself from doing, and that I was an awful person because of it." Like her brother, who tormented her for sexual behavior to which he had not only introduced her, but which he apparently saw as quite acceptable for himself, Ms. Cohen had also internalized the double standard.

Perhaps Ms. Cohen's perception of herself as "bad" explains why she was attracted to "bad" people who treated her harshly and confirmed her feelings about herself. It is one thing for a girl to have sex, including casual sex, because she likes it, and it is quite another thing to have it out of self-hatred or rebellion against a mother whose notions of sex as dirty have been internalized. Certainly, the lack of pleasure in Ms. Cohen's sexual relations with boys comes out starkly.

At the same time, it would probably be difficult for a sexually free girl to find teen-age boys who do not adhere to a double standard. This was the second double bind that Ms. Cohen was in. Males demanded that she be sexual, which she wanted to be, and then punished her for it.

Characterizing women as good and bad also alienates them from one another. In this instance, Ms. Cohen feared that if her mother found out about the rape, she too would see her daughter as a whore. She also believed that her best girl friend would have called her a whore had she been told of the rape. This alienation contrasts sharply with the solidarity among men.

Perhaps it is not so surprising that with the males together, and the females divided, it took Ms. Cohen fifteen years to tell a woman that she had been raped.

THREE

Good Girls Get Raped, Too

The only thing that changed was the notion
that it could never happen to me. I never really
understood before how girls got raped.

The notion that "it could never happen to me" indicates an internalization
of the good girl–bad girl dichotomy. "Rape only happens to bad girls. I am a
good girl, so it can't happen to me." In the course of these interviews I came
across this way of thinking again and again.

Daphne Fujimoto, a Japanese-American woman, was twenty-two when
she was raped, so she wasn't required to be a virgin in order to be classified as
good. Cultural stereotypes of Japanese women tend to place them in the
"good" category. They are seen as nice, sweet, docile, passive, obedient, and
pure. In addition, Ms. Fujimoto was raped by a black man, and she felt that
the racial stereotypes held by the district attorney and the police of black
men as violent and oversexed played an important part in the considerate
and sympathetic treatment they gave her. Had her rapist been a middle-
class white, he might have evoked male loyalty and made the police think
twice before classifying her as good.

Ms. Fujimoto was raped five months prior to being interviewed. She is
single, a recent college graduate, and the product of a middle-class home.

DAPHNE FUJIMOTO: I met Joe two years ago in an English class. We had
gone out about three or four times when he asked me if I wanted to go on a
picnic the next weekend with some other members of our rhetoric class. I
told him that I didn't think that I got along with him that well, and so I
didn't think I should see him again.

But he persuaded me to go out with him to have a drink and talk it over,
and then persuaded me to go to the picnic by emphasizing that it was a class

reunion. He said that if I didn't want to spend time with him, I could spend time with his friends. I thought, "Oh, that's good, that's safe."

When the day came, he picked me up, and we went to get the groceries, and then I asked him, "Well, where are we going to meet the others?" He said, "Oh, I forgot to tell you. They aren't coming." I was angry because I didn't want to go with him in the first place, but I didn't say anything because I thought it would be rude.

We went out to a beach, and we had barbecued spareribs and spent the day there. When it was time to go, he wanted to know if he could kiss me. I said OK, and so we kissed once. He really liked it, and he thought I was a very sensuous person. On the way back, we stopped at a friend's house in San Francisco. He was away, but his roommate, the girl he's living with, was there. She invited us in for drinks, and I had more than I could handle. Joe got drunk too. But we were having a good time because I liked this girl. Her name was Lucy Mason. I really liked her company more than anyone I had seen for a long time.

But I got so drunk, I went to the bathroom, and threw up, and then I almost blacked out. Joe wanted to leave around nine o'clock, but I didn't feel like going anywhere. I said, "Wait half an hour until I sober up." But he wanted to leave right away, though he was kind of drunk too. I insisted that we stay until we had coffee or something to get more sober. I didn't think he was in any condition to be driving, and I wasn't in any condition to be walking around.

Lucy served us tea, and then Joe started getting kind of obnoxious. He started to say that I had deceived him like all the other women he had known. Before that, he said how sincere I was, and how special I was, and that I was different.

On the way home he started swearing at me. I asked him to take me home. He said no, he wasn't going to take me home, he was going to go home to his place first to take a shower. I said, "Well, why can't you drop me off first?" He wouldn't do that. So I planned to walk home as soon as we got out.

But like a fool, I said to myself, I should be more considerate and help bring the stuff up to his apartment. You know, after a picnic there's a lot of junk. So I went up to his apartment and brought some stuff into the kitchen. He came in behind me, and he closed the door. I thought he was going to change his mind and be nice enough to give me a ride home. I was such a fool.

He put his stuff down, put on a record, and I began to see that he really wasn't interested in going on the road again. Then he approached me, and he tried to force himself on me. He tried to kiss me, and I said, "No, Joe.

No." And he kept trying to force himself on me, and I kept saying no, and then he picked me up and sort of swung me on the couch, and before I knew it, he had taken my pants off. Just like that. I couldn't believe it. It was like he was an expert at it, like he'd practiced it many times.

And then he got on top of me and said that he wanted to make love with me. I said I didn't want to. He said that if I would just let him do it once, he would get up and let me go. I kept saying no, no, no, no, no, no. But he took his pants off and said that he wouldn't hurt me. I thought he *was* going to hurt me. I thought he was going to kill me or something. I guess I was really hysterical then in a rational sort of way, because I wasn't screaming or anything. The reason I didn't scream was that I thought that he would beat me up or really hurt me if I did. So I submitted. When he finally let me up, he went to the bathroom.

He had kept saying things like, "Well, why don't you just stay here tonight?" And, "After tonight can we continue to have this kind of a relationship?" So I didn't think he was going to let me go. When he got up, I was preparing to run away, but he was looking straight at me. He had the bathroom door open, and he was sitting on the toilet taking a crap. I asked him if I could get a drink of water, because the kitchen was right near the front door.

I was stark naked. I walked toward the kitchen, but instead of going in, I went through the front door. I ran across the hall to the apartment across the way, because I had heard people coming in and out of there, and I just hoped to God they were home. I pounded on the door with all my might, and I screamed at the top of my lungs, "Let me in, let me in. He tried to rape me. He raped me." A tall black guy came to the door, and as soon as he opened it, I rushed in. Joe had just come out of his door, and he was coming after me. There was a girl there, and I ran into her arms.

Joe tried to follow me. The guy that came to the door tried to fend him off, but he had a hard time doing it, so he asked the girl, Jane, to help him. She ran to the kitchen, got a kitchen knife, and started brandishing it in the air as if she were going to attack him with it. So finally Joe said, "OK, OK, OK. Just leave me alone," and he went back to his apartment. Then the guy that answered the door started to try to break into Joe's apartment to go after him, and in the meantime, they phoned the police.

The police came to question Joe, and they questioned me. They took me down to the hospital for a test. After that, they brought me to the police station, and I filled out a report there. Then I went home. Joe was put in jail for the weekend.

INTERVIEWER: Did you ever see Joe again?

Ms. FUJIMOTO: I saw him once from a bus, but that was it.

INTERVIEWER: He never came back to bother you?

Ms. FUJIMOTO: No. I made it very clear, and the inspector made it very clear to him, that if he hassled me in any way by making phone calls or coming to my house, I could have him arrested for disturbing the peace.

INTERVIEWER: Could you describe the degree to which you resisted?

Ms. FUJIMOTO: When he approached me, trying to force kisses on me, I tried to push him away. He allowed himself to be pushed away a few times, but then after that, he wouldn't have any more of it. That's when he threw me on the couch, and grabbed my pants, and ripped them off. When he was on top of me, I tried to push him off, but he was so heavy I couldn't move him.

The main resistance I offered was verbal. I pleaded with him for ten minutes. I said, "Please, Joe, don't. Please, please, don't!" I was pleading with him, almost crying, but he'd just wait until I would stop, and then he would try again. And I would plead and plead and plead with him. I wasn't screaming. I was not yelling. But he was dead set on what he was going to do.

INTERVIEWER: Did you scream at all?

Ms. FUJIMOTO: No, I didn't. His reaction was so extreme, I thought he was crazy enough to kill me after he raped me. I couldn't see any reason for him to rape me because I didn't think that I had led him on in any way. I had made it very clear to him that I wasn't in love with him, and that I didn't want a physical relationship with him, and that I didn't even think I could get along with him.

INTERVIEWER: Why do you suppose he raped you?

Ms. FUJIMOTO: He said that he was very much attracted to me, and that he thought that I was a very good person. I think his motivation was just to have sex with me, and when I refused to go home when he wanted to go home, I think he felt that I had insulted his manhood, that I preferred to be with a woman instead of him. And he felt deceived too, so I think it was a type of retaliation.

INTERVIEWER: Why did he feel deceived?

Ms. FUJIMOTO: I didn't do what he wanted right at the moment he wanted it. For example, he wanted to leave Lucy's place. He really wanted to leave. He was quite persistent. That's when he got angry, when I wouldn't leave. See, I think he had a stereotype of Japanese women, that they are submissive and docile and would cater to his every whim. But I didn't.

INTERVIEWER: Could you describe Joe physically?

Ms. FUJIMOTO: He's from twenty-four to twenty-seven years old, and he's black, a light-skinned black. He's a big guy, about five feet nine or ten, very stocky, and extremely heavy. I think he could be a hundred and eighty to two hundred pounds. He was an undergraduate and wanted to be a law student.

INTERVIEWER: Could you describe the amount of force he used?

Ms. FUJIMOTO: I tried to push him away, but when I realized that I couldn't push him away if he didn't want to be pushed, I got very frightened. When he threw me on the couch, I knew I didn't have a chance, and I just wondered how I was going to get out of the situation. The look in his eyes, that's what scared me! It was very menacing, and he looked so moody, like some sort of maniac. It convinced me I shouldn't do anything more to try to get away.

INTERVIEWER: Who did you tell afterward?

Ms. FUJIMOTO: Everyone in that apartment across the hall knew about it. And the police. And the people at the hospital. And then the people at my house found out about it. I told them.

INTERVIEWER: How did these different people react?

Ms. FUJIMOTO: The people across the hall rose to my defense immediately. The black guy who came to answer the door went so far as to fend Joe off physically. He was willing to get into a fight to do that. And they were all very sympathetic to me.

The police who came were extremely sympathetic from the moment I saw them to the last dealings I had with them. They were very patient in their tone of voice, the questions they asked, the gestures they made. I guess a lot of it was because I was so hysterical at the time. I was shaking and trembling and crying, and I couldn't speak very clearly.

But also I think a lot of it was because of the stereotype of me as a Japanese girl, and my assailant as a black man. Joe's a very intelligent person, but when I talked to the D.A., who was also extremely sympathetic to me, he said, "Well, I don't know how smart this guy is, but—" assuming that he really wasn't very smart. The doctor at the hospital was kind of routine, very mechanical.

INTERVIEWER: What exactly happened in your dealings with them?

Ms. FUJIMOTO: When they arrived at the apartment I had escaped to, they asked me about what had happened. I told them, and they made sure I had all my possessions before I left the apartment. One of the policemen was very warm and tried to be soothing. He was very, very kind. He took me to the hospital, and he told me where to go. He was very attentive and understanding, and after that he took me to the police station, and he got me tea and made sure that I had everything I needed. Then he took me home in the morning, because it took a long time to write down the report of what had happened.

INTERVIEWER: So you were there all night?

Ms. FUJIMOTO: Yeah, I was there all night. A policewoman wrote what had happened. I read the report she had written, and she asked me to sign it. But I couldn't agree to it, because to me it didn't convey enough of how I felt about it, nor of what had actually transpired, not just physically, but emotionally and mentally. And the policeman had said this statement would be very important if I were to press charges. So the woman said that I could write it up myself if I wanted to. I told her I would, and I wrote up this sixteen-page report.

The police were very impressed with it. It took until about six in the morning to do it. Then the policeman took me home. He gave me his card, and he said I should call him if I ever needed any help. He was so kind, I couldn't believe it.

I had heard the police give people who have been raped a really hard time saying that it was their fault, that they were just a prostitute anyway, and that they were asking for it. But I got just the opposite. It was like the royal carpet treatment.

INTERVIEWER: How far did the case get?

Ms. FUJIMOTO: They told me to go see the D.A., so I went Monday morning as soon as I could. We sat down and talked for two hours. We discussed the pros and cons of my pressing charges, and we finally decided that it really wouldn't be worth my while, since I was going to Japan, and it would go past September before the proceedings were over.

The inspector who was guarding Joe came in also, and he too was very sympathetic with my case. The D.A. was too. They felt that I was a very kind, sensitive, and intelligent person, who had been assaulted by this terrible, unfeeling, crude black man. They were very indignant, more indignant than I was, that I had been raped. They were just totally affronted. I couldn't completely relate to their sympathy for me. It was just so deep. It was a moral outrage to them.

INTERVIEWER: So you didn't press charges because you were going to Japan?

Ms. FUJIMOTO: No, there were other reasons. It's very difficult to win a rape case. And the background in this incident was not in my favor. I had gone to his apartment a couple of times to have dinner, and I had gone out with him, and so in the jury's eyes, it would look as if a relationship was developing. It was foolish on my part to continue to see him, but I was under the assumption that people could be friends, if not lovers. They pointed out to me how naive I was, and how I should be much more careful. So after about two hours of weighing the pros and cons, we decided it would be best if I didn't press charges because there wasn't enough substantive evidence to have an easy case, and it would really be hard on me.

INTERVIEWER: Did the experience affect any of your attitudes toward men? Men in general or black men specifically?

Ms. FUJIMOTO: I'm a lot more careful now about who I go out with, and under what circumstances I allow myself to be in their company, who I invite over to my house, and whose house I go over to.

I'm not sure whether it has affected my attitudes toward black men. My experiences with black men have been pretty negative all along, except for one or two. I realize that not every black man is going to rape me. That's outrageous. But I'm more cautious around black men now.

INTERVIEWER: Did the experience affect any of your attitudes or feelings toward sex?

Ms. FUJIMOTO: No.

INTERVIEWER: Toward yourself?

Ms. FUJIMOTO: No.

INTERVIEWER: Did you learn anything about yourself that you didn't know before?

Ms. FUJIMOTO: Yeah. I'm too wishy-washy about guys. I should have called it to a halt long before.

INTERVIEWER: What kinds of emotions did you feel during and after the rape?

Ms. FUJIMOTO: During the rape I was deeply frustrated because I was powerless. I wanted to kill him, but I couldn't. And I was afraid. I also felt anger, extreme anger that I was in this helpless position and subjected to such an experience.

INTERVIEWER: Did you feel guilty or responsible in any way for the rape?

Ms. FUJIMOTO: I didn't feel guilty. And responsible? For the rape? How could I be responsible for the rape?

INTERVIEWER: Because you went into his house of your own accord.

Ms. FUJIMOTO: Hell, no! It wasn't my fault at all! Not an ounce of it!

INTERVIEWER: How upsetting would you say the experience was? Would you say it was traumatic?

Ms. FUJIMOTO: It was very traumatic, in a strange way. Things that are traumatic you think will last a lifetime. They will come back to haunt you and sort of eat away at you through your daily life. During the rape I was very rational. I was calculating how I could get out of this as soon as possible without getting hurt. But as soon as I left his apartment, I became hysterical. It was as if while I was just addressing myself to the present moment, I could continue to be rational. But as soon as I left his apartment and started pounding on the door, my mind just flipped out. I was totally panicked, and when I panicked, that's when it became traumatic. And that's when I went into hysteria. I was screaming and trembling from the top of my head to the bottom of my toes.

When the police came I was still really shaky, but by the time I wrote the sixteen-page report, I was pretty calm. And I was very rational for the next three days. I said, well, you just have to take it in stride. Things happen to you in life that aren't pleasant, but you have to roll with the punches. I did that for three days.

But on the third day, in the evening, I started crying hysterically. I cried for about two hours straight. It was the most violent crying that I had ever undergone. I was crying and crying, and it wasn't, you know, like sniffling or sobbing. It was wailing.

INTERVIEWER: Do you still feel traumatized by it even though it happened five months ago?

Ms. FUJIMOTO: No, I don't. I don't feel it at all. Well, hardly at all. Other things which were much less traumatic affect me more now. Maybe I've just repressed it. I don't think about it anymore.

INTERVIEWER: Did your experience of rape change your thinking about rape at all?

Ms. FUJIMOTO: The only thing that changed was the notion that it could never happen to me. I never really understood before how girls got raped. Also, I always thought that they got raped on the street, walking in the dark. It was surprising to me that I would get raped in the apartment of a friend—well, not a friend, but an acquaintance.

INTERVIEWER: Did you perceive it as rape at the time?

Ms. FUJIMOTO: Definitely. And I made it very clear to him that what he was doing was raping me. I said, "Do you realize what you're doing? You're *raping* me!" I told him direct so he would know what the hell he was doing, in case he wasn't aware of it.

INTERVIEWER: What advice would you give to other women on how to handle a rape situation if it were to happen to them?

Ms. FUJIMOTO: I would tell them not to resist, if they don't think they can overcome the person physically, and if they know they'll get physically hurt if they do resist.

INTERVIEWER: Would you handle the situation you were in in the same way if it were to happen again?

Ms. FUJIMOTO: Yes. The reason it's not traumatic for me now is that I didn't get beat up. I wasn't subjected to any physical violence per se. I didn't get hit in the face, I didn't get slapped around, and I didn't get thrown around that much. I think that's what I wanted to avoid more than anything.

I wasn't concerned about losing my virginity, because I wasn't a virgin. The thing I was most interested in at that time was my own personal security, physical and mental. I figured that if I got pregnant, I could always get an abortion. So what I did was resist as much as I could verbally. People have told me that I should have resisted more physically. Some people have said that if I had, he wouldn't have thought it worth the trouble.

INTERVIEWER: How do you feel about people telling you that?

Ms. FUJIMOTO: Well, I think that everyone's got their own opinions. I think it's much better to be physically raped than mentally raped. It's much better to get it over and done with, and not be traumatized for the rest of your life.

INTERVIEWER: Do you have any ideas as to why men rape?

Ms. FUJIMOTO: I think a lot of rape has to do with the man's image of himself as a sexual soldier. He has to go out and win his battles, make his conquests. And I think a lot of it has to do with society's conditioning about how sexual a man should be, and what it means to be able to make it with a woman, and also the restrictions that this society places on sex. It's almost schizophrenic. It's bound to lead to some kind of frustration.

Ms. Fujimoto is the only woman interviewed who reported to the police a rape that was perpetrated by someone with whom she had a dating relationship.

It is very unusual in circumstances like these for a woman to be regarded as "good" rather than "bad" and, hence, to be believed. It was probably not merely because she seemed to them to be a nice, sweet Japanese girl, nor that her rapist seemed to them a stupid, unfeeling, crude black man, but that her panic aroused the protective impulse of the police as well as the stranger into whose arms she ran. In addition, there were witnesses to attest that a man had tried to follow her into their apartment. Finally, the rapist was caught right away. All these factors resulted in what is, unfortunately, an uncommonly gentle police reaction.

Ms. Fujimoto's advice that rape victims should not physically resist unless they believe they can overcome the rapist is quite widely shared and even more widely followed by rape victims. Unfortunately, passive submis sion usually makes it much more difficult to press charges, and some rape victims feel very upset with themselves afterward if they reacted submissively.

Before she was raped, Ms. Fujimoto subscribed to two widely held myths about rape: first, that it is very difficult, even if possible, for a woman to be raped, and second, that the rapist would be unknown to her, not a friend. Prior to a rape experience, most victims, not surprisingly, subscribe to the same myths about rape as everyone else.

FOUR

Females as Prey

I felt like I'd brought out the worst in these men just by being an available female body on the road. I felt like if I hadn't been on the road, these men would have continued in their good upstanding ways, and that it was my fault that they'd been lowered to rape me.

Women often take responsibility when men treat them as prey. This isn't just an odd female quirk. The attitude is deeply entrenched in the thinking of men, as well. Women are taught to make themselves attractive to men. Those who don't are ignored by men or incur their displeasure. But if they become victims of sexual assault, they are immediately suspected of collusion. No man is ever guilty. If he did something bad, it must have been invited.

Consciously or unconsciously, most women alter their behavior to lessen the possibility of being attacked. Some dress drably, look straight ahead when walking, never speak with strangers, do not hitchhike, do not travel alone, do not walk alone at night. Women are taught to distrust and to be wary from the time they are very young. Girls are encouraged to stay indoors, while boys are sent out to explore the world.

Some girls, like Carla Stewart, rebel and suffer the consequences. She was raped on eight different occasions. Why, after being raped once, then again and again, Ms. Stewart did not change her behavior, in this case hitchhiking, is often the only question asked in such a case. The fact that this vulnerable and naive fourteen-year-old girl was raped six times within two weeks while hitching across the country raises other questions: Why are females prey? And is the prey really responsible for predatory behavior?

INTERVIEWER: How old were you when you were raped?

CARLA STEWART: I was fourteen. I'd been raped three or four times before, but this was to me the most scary rape of my life. My first rape had been just a few days earlier, and I was a virgin when it happened. I had very little conception of what sexual intercourse was all about until I was actually raped. I didn't really know that the penis was placed in the vagina until it actually happened, and I didn't know what he was doing or why he was doing it or anything about it. He appeared to be enjoying himself while he was doing it, and this totally flabbergasted me because I was feeling nothing but hurt and pain. I suppressed it because it was just too much to handle at the time.

INTERVIEWER: You said this first rape happened only a few days before the most scary one?

Ms. STEWART: Right.

INTERVIEWER: But it was your fourth rape?

Ms. STEWART: Right.

INTERVIEWER: You were raped every day?

Ms. STEWART: Just about every day. I was on the road for a little less than two weeks altogether, and I was raped six times during the whole time on the road.

INTERVIEWER: Have all your rapes been when you were hitchhiking?

Ms. STEWART: Yes, all of them.

INTERVIEWER: Would you like to tell me about the most scary one when you were fourteen?

Ms. STEWART: I was living in Nebraska at the time, with my parents, and it was summertime, and I decided to run away from home for about the third time. So I did, and this rape occurred between Nebraska and Denver, Colorado. I'd been on the road about seven days, and I hitchhiked the whole way. Although I'd been raped three times before this, I'd pushed them out of my mind.

When these two men picked me up, I looked upon them as individual human beings, not men who were capable of raping me. I was very naive and dumb. I got into the car, and told them that I was headed for California, and they promised to take me as far as they were going, which was about twenty-five miles.

I was sitting between them, and they immediately started touching me and making comments about my body. I was thin, very, very sunburned, very tattered and dirty. I had no clothes but a torn blouse and a pair of shorts. All my other clothes had been lost, and I was barefooted. We stopped at a liquor store, and they bought some beer, and they made me drink some beer. I had never drunk any before, and I didn't like it, but I did it to please them. I took a swallow or two, and it made me sick.

They told me what I needed was a bath and some sleep, and so they would take me to their house and give me the opportunity to do this. I began to become afraid then, and the memories of my past rapes started pushing up. But I ignored them, and decided that that was what I really needed, so I went along with them. We went down a long, long dirt road, and eventually all the houses disappeared, and there were just empty fields, and we came to a shack in the middle of an empty field.

We went inside, and it was empty and deserted and old and musty smelling, and there was no furniture except for an old bed in one of the bedrooms. They took me to the bathroom, and they told me to take a bath. I started undressing, and there was no lock on the bathroom door, so they wandered in, and they started to help me undress. I pushed them away, and I tried to push them out of the bathroom, but it didn't work. They dragged me into the bedroom and raped me on that old bed.

After they'd finished, they asked me which one I liked better, and I told them I liked the one that took the quickest. They told me they were going to go out and get some of their friends and bring them back to the shack, and we were all going to have a party, and the men were going to pay them for going to bed with me. So I was getting really scared, and I envisioned myself being trapped in that house the rest of my life, because they apparently felt that they'd come across something really good. They'd been planning to leave the state because the sheriff was after them for petty theft and things like that, and they'd been living on stolen chickens and vegetables from the farms around, and now they had a way of making money.

I was really scared. I started doing some really fast talking, and I told them that before I did any more fucking, I would have to get drunk. They said, "You stay here. We'll go out and get you some beer, and you can get drunk that way." I told them, "No, I have to be in a bar, with the music and the low lights and the atmosphere."

So finally we all got back in the car and drove to a little bar, and we got out and went inside. As soon as we got in, I told the bartender that these men were holding me against my will. They turned around and started laughing at me. And the bartender told me that if it was true, I should get out of there right then and there, and that he would watch the men, and I was to get out of the state and never come back. So I ran out the door and ran down the road, and I escaped.

INTERVIEWER: What were the men like? Can you describe them?

Ms. STEWART: They were in their early thirties, they were white, and they were very crude, loudmouthed, typical beer-drinking hillbilly type men. They had an old beat-up car, and very few possessions.

INTERVIEWER: Why do you suppose they raped you?

Ms. STEWART: I feel that's the way they related to all women, as potential rapes. And as I was alone, female, very desperate, and in need of whatever they could give me, they just took advantage of me.

INTERVIEWER: Do you suppose they had that in mind as soon as they picked you up?

Ms. STEWART: I'm sure they did.

INTERVIEWER: Did you tell the police?

Ms. STEWART: No. I've been raped altogether eight times in my life, and I've never told the police about any of them.

INTERVIEWER: Why didn't you tell the police in this case?

Ms. STEWART: Because I was a runaway and a minor. The police would probably send me right back home, and I didn't want to go.

INTERVIEWER: Did you resist in any way at any time?

Ms. STEWART: I didn't resist because I was afraid for my life. I felt I had to give in and humor them, or they would probably kill me or beat me up.

INTERVIEWER: What about when you were in the car before they got to their shack?

Ms. STEWART: I kept hoping that they were sincere, although I really suspected they weren't. I kept clinging to this belief that all men are really good and society makes them evil, and that when they meet with another really good human being, this brings out the good in them—all this philosophical bull shit.

INTERVIEWER: Who did you tell afterward?

Ms. STEWART: I didn't tell anybody about this until I was eventually sent back home. Then I told my brother about it, but nobody else.

INTERVIEWER: How did he react?

Ms. STEWART: He didn't believe me. He thought it was a fantastic story I'd made up. I didn't tell anyone else until several years later.

INTERVIEWER: Did the experience affect your behavior in any way?

Ms. STEWART: It made me more wary of men. I was more careful from then on who I got into a car with. If I didn't like the looks of the men, I didn't get into the car, whereas before I'd get into the car with anybody who stopped.

INTERVIEWER: How about in situations besides hitchhiking?

Ms. STEWART: I still clung to this belief that all men are basically good, and I didn't let it affect my attitude toward men. I still looked upon them as better than women, and what I was supposed to be looking for in life, a man.

Recently when I began reviewing the past rapes, I've begun to get really angry. I'm even beginning to look upon every fuck as a rape. I'm really angry at all men. I'm gradually disassociating myself from men, and eventually I want to have as little as possible to do with even the men friends that I now have.

INTERVIEWER: Did the experience affect any of your attitudes toward yourself?

Ms. STEWART: After each rape I felt dirty and disgusting, and I really hated myself for having allowed myself to get raped. I thought I was really dumb, really stupid to have fallen again for a man's lies. I felt like I'd brought out the worst in these men just by being an available female body on the road. I felt like if I hadn't been on the road, these men would have continued in their good upstanding ways, and that it was my fault that they'd been lowered to rape me.

But now I see there was nothing else I could have done in the situation, and it wasn't my fault.

INTERVIEWER: How upsetting would you say the experience was?

Ms. STEWART: At the time it wasn't that upsetting. I forgot about it as soon as it was over.

INTERVIEWER: Was it at all traumatic for you?

Ms. STEWART: I wouldn't say traumatic. It was a source of shame and humiliation at the time of happening, but after it was over, I really suppressed it so well. Maybe in a few years when I've really gotten my anger at a more intensified level, it might turn out to be traumatic.

INTERVIEWER: Were these men forceful?

Ms. STEWART: Very forceful and very rough. They slapped me around. They held my arms down. They were even going to sit on me, but I told them that wasn't necessary.

INTERVIEWER: Did they threaten you in any way?

Ms. STEWART: They didn't threaten me, but I have been in rapes where I was threatened.

INTERVIEWER: What emotions did you feel during and after the rape?

Ms. STEWART: During the rape I totally divorced myself from the here and now. I concentrated on the scenery outside the window, and I just pretended that it wasn't happening to me. After it was over, I was aware of pain and dirtiness in my body, and I was hurt in my pride and confused about why they had raped me and why they were laughing at me and making fun of my body and taunting me. And I was also very sure that God was watching the whole thing and shaking his head and saying what a horrible person I was for allowing myself to get raped.

INTERVIEWER: Did you feel any contempt or hate or anger toward them?

Ms. STEWART: No. I forgave them immediately. I felt like it was all my fault that I'd been raped. I said, well, they're men. They just can't help themselves. That's the way men are.

INTERVIEWER: Do you regret in any way the way you handled the situation?

Ms. STEWART: I regret the way I ran away from home so ill prepared. But I don't feel there's anything I could have done about the rape, because I was totally without anything. All I had was the clothes on my back.

INTERVIEWER: Does this apply to the other rapes too?

Ms. STEWART: Well, I feel I could have prevented my first rape.

INTERVIEWER: How did it happen?

Ms. STEWART: Well, I was wandering around Omaha, trying to find a way to get out. It was in the middle of the city, and two men saw me wandering around, and they started following me in their car. At that time I was still very flattered by any attention paid to me by men. So I got into the car with them and almost immediately they took me to their apartment and raped me. I feel I could have got out of that. I feel like I could have just said, "No thanks. I don't want a ride," because I still had some clothes and money at the time.

INTERVIEWER: Are there any other rape experiences that you would like to talk about?

Ms. STEWART: My most recent rape happened last year outside of Portland, Oregon, when I was hitchhiking back from there to Berkeley. This was also with two men. I was wandering around Portland trying to find the freeway. I'd never been there before, and I was totally lost, and it was about midnight. These two men in a car started following me around, and I ignored them at first, but somehow they started to pen me in. Trying to get away from them was taking me deeper and deeper into the slum area. It was very scary, so I asked them if they knew where the freeway was, and they told me to get into the car, and they would take me there. Before I'd gotten in, they said, "What's the matter? You think we're going to rape you or something?" And I said, "Yes, I do think that," and they said, "No, we won't rape you. We promise we won't rape you." So finally I got in the car. I was very tired. I hadn't slept in about forty-two hours. I'd hitchhiked up from Berkeley the day before, and I hadn't had any sleep since. I hadn't had anything to eat since. I had barely even had a chance to rest or sit down, so I was really spaced, and I decided to chance it. We went about twenty-five miles down the road, and then they turned off on a dark road, and they said, "Have you ever been beat up before?" I said no, and they said, "Well, if you don't get in the back seat and take your clothes off, we're going to beat you up." So I got in the back seat, and they raped me, one at a time, and then they threw me out of the car, and they said, "Don't turn around or you'll get shot." So I didn't turn around. Then when they got back up to the freeway, they turned around, and they said, "You just got the clap." And then they drove away. I got back to Berkeley a few days later, and it turned out that I did have the clap.

INTERVIEWER: What were your impressions of their motives?

Ms. STEWART: I feel they were just taking advantage of me because I was alone and available. That's just the way men relate to women. If they're alone and available, well, use them. And it's nothing perverted. It's just their normal way of relating to women. It's just an everyday occurrence. If they've got the chance, they'll take it.

INTERVIEWER: Could you describe them?

Ms. STEWART: Well, these two men were in their early twenties. They were white. They looked like city kids, and they were very drunk. They had bottles all over the car. It was a brand-new car. It could have been their parents'. They could have been brothers or cousins. They looked very much alike. They were friendly enough. They offered me money and cigarettes and food, but I didn't take any.

INTERVIEWER: What advice would you give to other women on how to avoid being raped?

Ms. STEWART: I think it's really hard. I guess the best thing is just to have nothing to do with men. Ignore them totally. Hitchhiking alone is sometimes necessary. I feel like all the hitchhiking I've done, which is about nine thousand miles altogether, was absolutely necessary. I didn't have any friends, male or female, who could have hitchhiked with me, so that was the only way I could go.

INTERVIEWER: Is there any other advice you would give about how to handle a rape situation?

Ms. STEWART: If it's one man, a woman can fight back. I've been raped mostly by men in pairs, and then it's almost impossible to fight back. The only thing I could have done was to surrender so that they wouldn't harm me any more.

INTERVIEWER: Can you think of any solutions to the rape problem?

Ms. STEWART: Changing the whole social attitude toward women is the only answer. When men stop looking at women as potential lays, a lot of rape will stop.

Ms. Stewart's casualness about what many would consider horrendous experiences is one of the most remarkable aspects of this case.

If it is seen as in men's nature to rape, then it becomes too easily the female's responsibility not to give them the opportunity. And then the only control the woman has over what happens to her is to stop taking risks. But if doing what one wants to do in life means one must risk becoming a victim then one must accept the consequences. Allowing oneself to get too upset would only make life harder.

Being casual and accepting was Ms. Stewart's way of handling an unpleasant choice. For her, it seemed more important to get away from home than it was to avoid getting raped. Since this was her choice, her anger was muted.

It is widely believed that a person's taking responsibility for what happens to her is the first step in seeing that unpleasant things stop happening to her. However, taking personal responsibility for things that are not one's responsibility, like being a rape victim, is indicative of self-hatred, and self-hatred is the biggest block to change. In Ms. Stewart's case, for example, her taking personal responsibility for the rapes did not help her. ("I forgave them immediately. I felt like it was all my fault that I'd been raped.")

Rape victims have to stop blaming themselves. This won't prevent rape, but it may help women like Ms. Stewart not to accept it as passively and repeatedly as she did.

Like many victims who have been raped in hitchhiking situations, Ms. Stewart continued to hitch. Systems of public transportation in this country are often inadequate, and hitchhiking means being mobile. Similarly, many people who have cars cannot imagine how they could manage without them, and they continue to drive in spite of the dangers of driving cars, and even if they have had accidents. Indeed, it would be seen as a psychological hang-up if they didn't.

For those who see public transportation as an alternative for hitchikers, it should be pointed out that using public transportation can be very dangerous for women who are alone at night. They must walk to and from the stop, and sometimes wait a long time in an unsafe place for the transportation to arrive.

Yet, the standard reaction to women hitchhikers, particularly those who continue to hitch after having been raped, is that they are asking for it, or at the very least, that they couldn't care about being raped all that much. Otherwise, they wouldn't keep taking the risk by hitching. But why is it that people do not argue that drivers who have automobile accidents are similarly "asking for it" or don't mind having accidents all that much, if they continue to drive afterward?

FIVE

Females as Cunts

So now I've got the impression that there's no such thing as a man who's really sensitive to women. They just look at women like they're cunts.

Ms. Stewart was constantly preyed upon by men who were strangers to her. With Alicia Gomez the process of depersonalization went a step further. She was preyed upon by acquaintances and friends. First she was raped by her baby sitter's husband at the age of four. The second time, a date raped her when she was fourteen. Her third experience was at the hands of a friend of her woman friend's father. In the fourth and most traumatic of all her experiences, Ms. Gomez was raped by a close friend, a political comrade who was a "revolutionary" and whom she had helped a great deal. It was after this experience that she expressed the feeling that men look at women as nothing more than cunts.

Many women who have been politically active in causes other than women's liberation have shared Ms. Gomez's experience of finding themselves comrades by day, albeit in a position of envelope addressers and phone answerers, and cunts by night. A woman who is not seen as the property of a particular man is especially subject to this treatment. Many women have opted out of radical movements because they find that at night their most basic rights, control over their own bodies and recognition as whole human beings, are often not recognized by men they had believed to be their brothers. The view that women's oppression is not as important as racial oppression and that women should therefore put aside their struggle until the other struggles have succeeded is very common and seems to be a logical extension of sexism itself. Radical women must struggle to raise less privileged men to the position of the more privileged men. And then? *Then* women can start working on their own oppression. Meanwhile, their place is prone, and their power is pussy power.

Ms. Gomez is a twenty-year-old Chicana who has been separated from her husband for three years. She has no children.

INTERVIEWER: You told me that the last rape was the most traumatic. Did you know the man at all?

ALICIA GOMEZ: I knew him for about two months before it happened. Carlos was from Chicago. He was political, and he considered himself a revolutionary. When him and his brother first came from Chicago, I tried to help them because I was from Chicago too. I used to watch his son. We used to have good discussions about politics and different movements.

Me and my sister and my girl friends thought that this was one man who was really a straight guy, who was really sensitive to women's feelings. He had told me that he had been an alcoholic before, and I guess he was having some problems, so he started drinking again.

One night he came over to my house kind of late. He didn't act like he was drunk, but then he sat down, and he started talking to me and my sister, and I noticed he had a bottle of whiskey in his back pocket. He started drinking, but I didn't realize how smashed he was. He didn't come on to me sexually or emotionally, but he started coming on to my sister. He was trying to kiss her, and he was falling on her. I got mad and started screaming at him. I told him to get out of my house and to leave my sister alone. At first he refused to leave. But finally after arguing with him and screaming at him, he left. He was outside my door, banging on it, pleading for me to let him in. I was getting tired of hearing him bang at the door and screaming my name out. It had gotten pretty late. It was about two o'clock in the morning, so I decided to try to take him home.

I went out the door, and I said, "Come on." He said, "Where are you going?" I said, "Come on. Just come on." So I started walking, and he followed me, and I walked him all the way to his house, which was about a mile. When we got to his house, I said, "Well, here you are. You're at home." Then he said, "Where you going?" I said, "I'm going home," and he said, "Oh, no, you're not. Come on, stay a little while." I said, "No, I'm going to go home. It's late."

So then he picked me up and threw me over his shoulder. He took me up the stairs and into his house. His little boy, who was staying in the house by himself, opened the door, and he looked at his father, and he said, "Daddy, where have you been?" I looked at Carlos with disgust, and I said, "What's wrong with you? Didn't you see the way José looked at you?" His little boy was just standing in the doorway looking at him. So I said, "Come on, let's go in the house," because I figured he wasn't going to let me go anyway. Every time I tried to go down the stairs, he kept stopping me.

I went into the house, and I sat down on the couch, and I started thinking to myself, well, how am I going to get out of this one? So I said, "Can I have a drink of water?" He went to the kitchen to get the drink of water, and I ran for the door and tried to get out. But he said, "Oh, no, you don't," and he grabbed the door and locked it. Then he took his son in his room. I guess he was trying to put him to bed.

I went into the kitchen real quietly, and I tried to open the back door, but I couldn't get the damn door open, and he got there before I could open it. I wasn't familiar with the house, so I didn't know how to get out fast enough. So there we were in this kitchen. I think the light was out. Anyway, he said, "Come on, why don't we go in my room." I said, "Come on, let's be reasonable," and then I started getting mad. I said, "Look, you don't know when somebody doesn't want you, do you?"

He started getting closer and closer to me, and he backed me up against an ironing board. I picked up the iron, and I was holding it in my hand, and I said, "Look," I said, "if you don't let me out that door, I'm going to hit you with this iron." And he said, "Go ahead and hit me." I thought and thought about it, but, I don't know why, I just couldn't do it. So I put it down.

Then he grabbed me, and he said, "Come on, we're going into my room." I ran across to the other side of the room. I knew what was coming now, I knew I was going to be raped, so I thought, I'll try something new. So I pretended like I'd passed out. I just fell to the floor. I thought, if he's going to rape me, I'm not going to move. He's going to have to drag me in there. I just stayed there on the floor, and at first he got scared. I guess he was confused because he was so drunk. He went to his room, and he said, "José, Alicia's sick. Something's wrong." Then he came back to the room, and he said, "OK, now. If you're kidding, you better get up." I just stayed there. I didn't move. He started dragging me out of the kitchen by my feet. As he was dragging me, my blouse was sliding up, and he laughed to himself, and he said, "Oh, come on, don't do that, Alicia. You're starting to look sexy."

He dragged me into his room. His son was in Carlos' bed, but there was a mattress on the floor. José was awake. "What are you doing?" he asked his father. José was about five years old. Carlos said, "Oh, go to sleep, José. Something's wrong with Alicia. She's sick. She's going to spend the night." His son wasn't even asleep when he started taking off my clothes. I didn't move. I stayed there like I was knocked out. I didn't move one muscle. He took off all my clothes, and he raped me, and I just laid there like a rag doll. When he was finished, he just went to sleep.

When he went to sleep, I got up, and I got my clothes on. I was scared to death that he was going to wake up, or that his son was going to wake up, so I did everything slowly. I got dressed, and I looked around his room, hating him, and I thought, I want to do something to him. I looked around his room, and I saw this gun. I thought, oh, this must mean something to him. I'll take this. So I put it in my coat pocket. And I went into the bathroom, and I got a razor blade, and I cut his telephone wire as close to the wall as I could. I wanted some kind of revenge.

I could only find one shoe, so I was looking around the house for my other shoe, but I was very nervous that he might wake up. I found an old pair of cowboy boots. I don't know what size they were. They were big, though. I put my shoe in my coat pocket, and I put on the cowboy boots, and I went out the door, and I walked home. I really felt shitty. It must have been around four or four-thirty in the morning. I was walking across the railroad tracks, and I had these great big cowboy boots on, and I turned my collar up, and I felt like I just hated everything around me. I felt like I could relate to being a lesbian. I felt like I wanted to be one, and that's what the world had made me. I just hung my head down and walked home.

When I got home, I woke my sister up, and I told her what had happened. I sat down, and we cried about it. I told my sister about cutting his telephone wires, and that I was scared he was going to come back because he was going to find his gun missing.

Sure enough, about three hours later, a car pulled up outside. Before he came, we had talked about what we would do. I had a shotgun in my house, and I told her, "If he comes back, I'm going to shoot him." She said, "Oh, don't shoot him. You'll go to prison." I said, "Well, if he tries to break the door down, I'm going to shoot him. That's legal. If he doesn't try to break in, we'll just scare him."

He came up the stairs, and he knocked on the door, and he said, "Alicia, Alicia, I'm worried about you. You were sick." I said something like, "Look, motherfucker, get away from my door, or I'm going to blow your brains out." And he just laughed, I guess because he didn't think I was serious. So my sister went over to the door, and she pulled the curtain away from the door, and I was a few feet away, holding the shotgun. He looked in the door, and he saw the shotgun, and he jumped back. He stood there at the door for a long time, trying to get me to open the door.

At first he was afraid, but then I guess he didn't think that I would shoot him. So when he started banging on the door and shaking the door, I said, "That's right. Open the door. Break it. That's all I want you to do. Break it and make it legal." Then I told my sister to go next door to call the police. So she went next door, and she woke up the old man there, and he called the police. But Carlos left before the police got there.

INTERVIEWER: What did you tell the police when they got there?

Ms. GOMEZ: I just told them that there was this guy that I knew, and that he was drunk and he was bothering me. I was scared to report him.

INTERVIEWER: Did you see him any time after that?

Ms. GOMEZ: Yeah. At school there was a Young Lords' movie, and I was sitting alone in the auditorium when he came in. He was on the other side of the room. He saw me, and I saw him, but we didn't say anything to each other.

INTERVIEWER: Why do you think he wanted to rape you?

Ms. GOMEZ: I think he was drunk, for one thing. And I think there was something wrong with him mentally.

INTERVIEWER: Did you feel guilty or responsible in any way for what happened?

Ms. GOMEZ: Do you mean had I come on to him? No, not at all.

INTERVIEWER: How did it affect your behavior afterward?

Ms. GOMEZ: Well, my attitude toward men has changed a lot. I thought this guy was one guy that was really sensitive to women, and he turned out to be completely the opposite. So now I've got the impression that there's no such thing as a man who's really sensitive to women. They just look at women like they're cunts. As far as my sexual behavior, all through my life when I've supposedly been making love with a man, sometimes I flash back on when I was raped, and get this real nasty feeling, and I want to push the guy off of me.

INTERVIEWER: What did you feel during and after he raped you?

Ms. GOMEZ: Disgust. A little bit of fear. Contempt. Hate. Anger.

INTERVIEWER: Why did you decide not to report the rape to the police?

Ms. GOMEZ: Because police are men. I don't think they are going to be able to relate to the experience. They're not going to be sensitive. They're not going to really care. They've probably done it themselves.

INTERVIEWER: Do you regret in any way the way you handled the situation?

Ms. GOMEZ: No, I think the way I handled it this time was about the best. By falling down on the floor and being completely submissive, I didn't get beat up.

INTERVIEWER: Do you think he would have beaten you up?

Ms. GOMEZ: Sure. And I was really glad that when he did come back, I had the courage to hold the gun up to his face.

INTERVIEWER: What advice can you give to other women on how to handle a rapist?

Ms. GOMEZ: I'd like to see a bunch of women get together and beat the shit out of the dude. I think if women did that, men would think twice about raping a woman.

INTERVIEWER: How many women do you know personally who have been raped?

Ms. GOMEZ: Just about every woman I know. Even my mother. I asked her about it. She's been raped twice. It surprised me because she never said anything about it before that.

INTERVIEWER: Will you tell me now about being molested when you were four years old?

Ms. GOMEZ: Well, I don't remember very much about it. My mother was working, and she used to take my sister and me to a baby sitter. It was a family, a man and a woman and their sons. I don't remember how many sons there were. The woman used to take us into a bedroom and put us in bed with her husband, and he used to molest us.[1]

INTERVIEWER: This happened every time you went?

Ms. GOMEZ: Just about. I can remember being afraid. I can remember their sons. I don't remember how old they were, but they were pretty big. I can remember them hanging me out of the apartment window by my feet and saying if I ever told, they'd drop me. I can also remember my mother going to their house and being mad, but I wasn't too sure what was going on. And I can remember being in the hospital with doctors or police asking me all kinds of questions.

INTERVIEWER: Did the police ever do anything about this man?

Ms. GOMEZ: I don't know.

INTERVIEWER: Would you say it was a traumatic experience for you?

Ms. GOMEZ: I think so, but all through my life I have tried to push it out of my mind.

INTERVIEWER: How old were you the next time you were raped?

Ms. GOMEZ: Fourteen. I was at that age where I thought I knew everything, and so I went out with this big-time gang leader. He took me out to eat and to a show, and then him and his friends and I drove to the park. Him and I got out of the car, and we walked through the park. Then he said, "Lay down under the bush." I tried to talk to him. I said, "Oh, we don't want to do that." I said, "Why don't we go to my house, and we can be there by ourselves, and everything will be nice," and all this shit. I thought that if I got home, I could run in the door and lock it. But I wasn't able to talk my way out of it.

I can remember I was still trying to when this police car came up, and the

1. Ms. Gomez consistently spoke of this as a rape experience, except here where she refers to it as "molesting." It may be relevant that the interviewer for some reason used the word molestation rather than rape. Unfortunately, the interviewer did not try to get further clarification.

policeman said to me, "Is this guy bothering you?" I can remember struggling in my mind, should I tell him or shouldn't I? I decided not to because I was afraid. I figured that if I did tell him, this guy would come after me. So he told me to lay down under this bush. I was afraid that he would beat me up. All kinds of things were running through my mind of how I could get out of this. But I didn't get out of it. He raped me behind the bush.

Afterward I got up and he got up, and he said, "I hope you're not mad at me," or something. And I said, "Oh no, I'm not mad at you." So then he said, "Well, I guess I'll walk you home." I said, "Oh yeah, sure. Walk me home." When we got to my house, he said, "Well, when can I see you again?" I said, "Oh, here's my phone number," and I gave him a phony number.

INTERVIEWER: Did you ever see him again after that?

Ms. GOMEZ: No.

INTERVIEWER: Did you report this rape to the police?

Ms. GOMEZ: No. If I had reported it, I know that I could have gotten killed.

INTERVIEWER: Did you feel at all guilty or responsible for the rape?

Ms. GOMEZ: No, but I think I was pretty naive to go out with this guy in the first place.

INTERVIEWER: Could you describe him?

Ms. GOMEZ: He was black, and he was a flashy dresser, and he was pretty old. He was around twenty or twenty-one, and he was pretty big.

INTERVIEWER: Who did you tell afterward?

Ms. GOMEZ: I told my sister. And my boy friend came over, and I told him. Naturally he got mad because I had gone out with somebody else, and so he called me a whore. I got mad, and I went in the kitchen, and I got a knife, and I told him I was going to kill him for saying that. His friend who was with him tried to stop me.

When they got the knife out of my hand, I ran out of the house. I was living near the lake, and I ran all the way to the beach and into the water. My boy friend and his friend and my sister ran after me. I didn't know they were following me, though, until they came in the water after me.

INTERVIEWER: Was this rape very traumatic for you?

Ms. GOMEZ: Yes, it was. When I thought about it, it made me sick. When it came into my mind, I tried to push it out.

INTERVIEWER: Do you regret in any way the way you handled the situation?

Ms. GOMEZ: Yes, I do. I was so naive that I didn't realize that I was going to be raped. I think I should have run, you know, just took off. I think I should have told the cop. No, on second thought I don't think I should have told him, because something would have happened to me.

INTERVIEWER: How did you feel during and after the rape?

Ms. GOMEZ: I felt embarrassment, shame, and disgust. And I felt guilty because I felt that I shouldn't have gone out with anybody except my boy friend. And hate. I hated the guy.

INTERVIEWER: Did this experience affect any of your attitudes toward men?

Ms. GOMEZ: Like I said before, when I make love with a guy, I think about when I was raped, and I get disgusted.

The third time was when I was nineteen. I went to Tijuana with my girl friend from Oakland. We went to downtown Tijuana to go party. She had lived in Tijuana before, and so she was showing me around. We went to different night clubs, and we went dancing. Then we met a friend of her father's, this older man. She was all excited about seeing him and everything. She hadn't seen him since she was a little girl, and I guess she was really impressed with him. She said that he would give us a ride home. I guess my girl friend was interested in him.

She was sitting in the front with this guy, and I was sitting in the back with his friend. I didn't know my way around Tijuana, and I thought we were going home. But then I asked her, "Where are we going?" And she said, "Oh, they're going to go over to a friend's house first, then they're going to take us home." I said, "Well, I think we should go right away because it's getting late and your father's going to be worried about you." And she said, "Oh, no, no. That's OK." Both of these guys were pretty drunk.

We stopped at a store, and when we got out of the store I went up to my girl friend and said, "Look, let's take a cab home. These guys are pretty drunk, and they're not driving too good." She said, "No, I don't want to," and she started giggling. I said, "What's so funny?" And she said, "Oh, he gave me some reds." I said, "You're stupid, man. What did you drop some reds for? Are *they* doing reds?" She said, "Yeah." And I said, "Oh, man!"

I tried to talk her into taking a cab again, but she didn't want to. I didn't want to leave her because she was a good friend of mine, so I stayed with her, and we got back in the car. They drove over to a motel. I was the only one who wasn't high. Then her father's friend said, "Let's go in here and talk for a little while." I said, "No. Let's go." I started getting mad at my friend. I said, "Come on. Let's go." And she said, "No. They just want to talk to us for a little while. Come on." Then she told them, "Aw, there's something wrong with her. She doesn't want to come." So he said to me, "Here, I'm going to go get a room so we can talk." And I said, "Talk? You guys don't want to talk!" I said to my friend, "Come on. You can see that they don't want to talk. Don't be stupid. Let's go."

So anyway, they got the room. I didn't want to leave her alone because I didn't think it would be right for me to leave her by herself. So we went into this room. I went to the bathroom, and when I came out my girl friend and this other guy had left. I went to the door, and the door was locked. And there was me and her father's friend in the room. I said, "I better leave." He said, "No, you're not leaving," and he wouldn't let me out the door. He could only speak Spanish, and I could only speak English, and so it was almost impossible to try to talk my way out of it.

Then he started hitting me. He knocked me across the room. I tried to fight. I said, I'm going to fight my way out of this, which I tried to do. I tried to push him away, and I tried to pick up something to hit him with.

INTERVIEWER: Did you scream?

Ms. GOMEZ: Yes. I was yelling at him at the top of my voice. But he was a lot stronger than me. I realized this when he hit me across the room. There wasn't any way I was going to be able to fight my way out of it. I'd just get beat up more. So I said, "Oh, yeah, OK."

Afterward I got up. He was asleep. When you take reds and you go to sleep, it's a real hard, solid sleep. I saw two watches, and I took them, and I took a wallet for revenge. I put the things in my pocket, and I left the room, and I started walking. I walked all the way through the border, all the way into San Diego. And then I started hitchhiking, and I hitchhiked all the way to Oakland.

INTERVIEWER: Did you feel guilty and responsible at all?

Ms. GOMEZ: I felt guilty for leaving my girl friend there. Responsible? No, I didn't feel responsible.

INTERVIEWER: Did you report the rape to the police?

Ms. GOMEZ: No.

INTERVIEWER: Why not?

Ms. GOMEZ: For one reason, I couldn't speak Spanish.

INTERVIEWER: Do you regret in any way the way you handled the situation?

Ms. GOMEZ: Yeah. I think that I should have gone to this girl's father and told him what had happened. And I should have known what was going to happen. I should have grabbed my friend by the hand and started walking away.

INTERVIEWER: What did you feel during and after this rape?

Ms. GOMEZ: Anger, disgust, contempt, and hate. I felt pretty hopeless too, you know. I felt like, oh shit! This is what life is all about. It's going to be like this for the rest of my life.

INTERVIEWER: Did all of these rapes affect your attitudes or feelings toward yourself?

Ms. GOMEZ: Well, I've thought, four times! That's a lot, you know. Maybe there's something wrong with me. But when I think about that, I remember that I was four years old the first time and what could I have possibly done? How *could* it have been me?

INTERVIEWER: So you don't feel bad toward yourself?

Ms. GOMEZ: Sometimes when I think about them, I feel nasty. I feel kind of dirty. I think it was a scummy experience, and I have scummy scars on me from this happening to me.

If rape is a product of sexist values, then one would expect the incidence of rape to be high among Chicanos. According to Ms. Gomez, most of the women she knows have been raped, including her mother, who was raped twice. Three of Ms. Gomez's rapes were by Chicano men. Whether or not their attitudes and behavior are at all indicative of cultural norms, Ms. Gomez seems to see rape as a grisly fact of life.

Ms. Gomez found her last rape experience the most traumatic, and the one before the least, despite the violent treatment at the hands of the latter rapist. Some of the least violent rapes can be the most traumatic. Carlos's raping her was particularly upsetting because she regarded him as a friend whom she trusted and believed to be "sensitive to women's feelings." Learning that such a man can be a rapist was obviously more disillusioning than discovering this about an acquaintance.

While many rape victims express a desire for revenge, Ms. Gomez is one of the few interviewed who acted it out by taking Carlos's gun and cutting his telephone wires and taking two watches and the wallet of the older man who raped her. It is interesting that while Ms. Gomez was unable to throw the iron at Carlos to defend herself against rape, she claimed to want to kill him after she returned home and said she would shoot him if he gave her the opportunity to do it legally. Her apparently inconsistent behavior might be explained by suggesting that fear was the predominant feeling before the rape while anger took over after it.

When a woman is a victim of several rapes, people are even more inclined to blame her. Ms. Gomez was able to reject such responsibility, but many women react very differently.

SIX

The Stigma of Being Raped

> For a couple of weeks after that I wouldn't go to school because I was so embarrassed about what had happened to me.... I felt like people would say, "Look at her. She's been raped," and they'd look at me like I was some kind of whore.

In a culture that values female virginity, the rape victim is considered impure, "spoiled goods." If she were innocent she wouldn't have been raped. Tragically, the victim often feels this about herself. For Roxanne Watson, whose experience is the subject of this chapter, this was the case. Even in a very supportive environment, when family and friends reacted sympathetically, and the police treated her reasonably well, she felt stigmatized at the age of ten, ashamed rather than angry about being a rape victim.

Both Ms. Stewart and Ms. Cohen were afraid they would be regarded as whores as a result of being raped. But why would a rape victim fear being seen as a whore? Presumably because of the myth that women who do not really want to be raped cannot be raped. Therefore the rape victim must be whore material even if she isn't getting paid for it.

This feeling of being stigmatized is a major reason many women do not want to report their experiences to the police. Ms. Watson, for example, was not willing to press charges and felt it necessary to lie to her schoolmates about it. (She said she'd been beaten up. There's no shame in that!)

Ms. Watson, a fifteen-year-old girl of Filipino descent, was raped five years ago.

ROXANNE WATSON: It was Tuesday in November. I was ten years old, and I had picked up my little sister, who was five, from the baby sitter's. We were coming back, and I decided to take the park because it was a short cut to our house, and I saw this guy. He was about sixteen. He was black and really rough looking, really, really repulsive. I said, "I hope he doesn't start making any cracks when we walk by." I looked down, and I held my sister's hand, and we were walking past, and he said, "Have you seen my little sister?" I said no.

We started walking past him, and he said, "Hey, come here. I've got a gun in my pocket, and if you don't come, I'm going to blow your ass off." I looked at my little sister, and thought about running, but I knew that she wouldn't be able to follow me if I ran. Then he said, "I'm going to count to three, and if you don't come here, I'm going to blow your ass off." I didn't know what to do. He started counting, and I didn't know whether to run, or to scream, or whether to go forward.

So he counted, "One. Two," and I go, "Oh, no!" I looked at my sister, then I walked up to him, and he said, "Come on, follow me, I want to show you something." My first reaction was, oh, man, he killed somebody. He's going to show me a body. He started going through the bushes, and I had to help my little sister.

We got to these bushes which were real low, and I had to scoot down, and so did he. My sister was in back of me, and he said, "Take off your panties." I wouldn't do it, so he pulled them down and told me to sit down, and I did. He pulled his pants down and his underwear, and he told me to raise up my legs and bend my knees. I didn't know what was happening. I was so scared. He said, "Don't scream, and don't cry, and everything will be all right." He got down, and he started pushing his penis into me. I don't remember how it felt. It wasn't very hard, and I don't know exactly if he got it into me or not, but I remember all the time I wanted to get away.

I was thinking of when we would call the police, because I knew I was going to tell the police, even though he said, "You're not going to tell anyone." I said, "No, no, I won't tell nobody!" But I thought, "Maybe I can get some information out of him, and help to catch him." So I started asking him questions. I asked, "Where do you live?" And he said, "I live in Hunter's Point." I asked him his name and he said, "Ricky," and I said, "Isn't that a nickname?" He said, "No, that's my name." I didn't believe him, but then I kept on talking to him just because of a lack of anything better to do.

I asked him, "Were you in the riots at Hunter's Point? I heard there were some riots there." He said, "Yeah, and I went to jail." I don't remember exactly what other questions I asked him.

I kept on thinking about how I was going to get away. After a bit, I couldn't take any more. I started crying, and my little sister was really scared, and she said, "Roxanne, don't cry." I stopped crying. And then he said something about there being some kind of a discharge coming out of me. And he said, "When we finish, I'm going to make you lick it up." And I said no! And later he said, "After I finish with you, I'm going to do it to your little sister too," and I said, "No, you won't! No, you won't! Because I'll scream my head off if you do!" He said, "OK, OK. I won't."

I pulled up my pants, and I said, "You go out first." And so he went out, and I grabbed my little sister's hand, and I ran. I ran through the back yard, and I jumped over the fence. We ran upstairs, and I came into the kitchen, and my mother was there. I was shocked, you know, and just sitting there when all of a sudden I started crying. My sister said, "No, Roxanne, don't cry, don't cry, don't cry. She's going to find out." She was still worried about the guy, you know.

I wanted to tell my mother, but I kept on crying and crying. She said, "What happened? What happened?" I didn't know what the word for it was, and so I said, "Well what happened was there was this guy in the park, and he pulled down my pants, and he pulled down his pants." Then I started crying again, and then she started crying, and she called the police, and she said, "I'd like to report a rape." I cried for a really long time.

The police came and asked me a bunch of questions: how old I was and what he looked like and what he was wearing. I described him to them. I said, "He's really, really big. He's about sixteen and sort of husky, and he has a really big nose and thick lips and short hair." They asked me, "Well, did he kiss you?" and I said, "Yeah, he did." And the cop said, "Well, how did it feel? Was it gentle?" I said, "No, it was sickening!" I turned away and started crying again, because I couldn't understand how he could ask if his kiss was gentle when he was raping me.

They told me to change clothes because they wanted to inspect them. So I changed my clothes, and they said, "Come on, we're going to go look around for him." So I got in the back seat, and we went down to the park. I stayed in the back seat, and the police went out, and they asked all the kids around there, "Has anybody seen a guy of such-and-such a height? Because he raped the little girl inside the car." I remember they were coming up to the car and looking at me like I was some kind of animal. And I turned my face, and I hid in my mother's arms, because I didn't want them to see me.

Then the police said, "Well, you have to get inspected by the doctors." So we went up into the building. I remember there was a doctor and two nurses. They made me lift my knees again, and they examined me. It hurt really bad. They said they had to test to see if I was really raped or not. I didn't understand why they were doing it, but I said, "Well, OK." It really, really hurt. The nurse gave my mother a sleeping pill to give me because I was jittery. I wouldn't eat anything, and I was really, really nervous.

Then they took me up to look at some pictures. I must have gone through ten racks, and I didn't see anybody that looked anything like him.

Then some plainclothes men took me down to the gym to see if he was down there. I went in, and I saw these people from my school, these two guys who had basketball practice, and also two other guys who lived up the street. They asked me, "What are you doing down here? What are you doing?" I didn't want to tell them because I was afraid of what they might say, so I didn't say anything to them. I was so embarrassed. We went home, and my parents gave me a sleeping pill.

For a couple of weeks after that I wouldn't go to school because I was so embarrassed about what had happened to me. I didn't feel really responsible, but it was just that this guy had done this to me, and I was so young, you know. I felt like people would say, "Look at her. She's been raped," and they'd look at me like I was some kind of whore. I was afraid to go to school. I didn't tell anybody what had happened. I just said I was beat up. Even to my closest friends at school I wouldn't say anything about what had happened.

INTERVIEWER: Did they catch the guy?

Ms. WATSON: Yeah, about a week later. They didn't want me to know, because they wanted me to identify him. They told my mother they had caught a guy who fit the description and admitted to it. The plainclothes man came to my house, and me and my cousin and my mother went down to the police station. During the car ride he asked me, "Well, can you tell me what happened?" I was afraid to say anything. I didn't want to say any more. I was sick and tired of being questioned.

We got down there, and there was a room full of guys. I had been down there once before when they had only one guy, and I had looked through a one-way mirror so that I got to see him, without him seeing me, but he wasn't the one. This time it was a roomful of fifteen or twenty guys, and they were all black, and all could have fit the description.

The plainclothes man said, "Come on, we're going in the room, and you can look at them." I said, "No, I can't go in there. If he's in there and he sees me, he's going to want to kill me or something because I reported it." He said, "No, he won't," and I said, "Can I look through the door? Can I look through the window in the door?" So he said, "I guess that's OK, but if you don't see him, then we're going to have to bring you in for a closer look."

First I took the top row, and I looked at each one really carefully. They were all looking at something on the other side of the room. I don't know what it was. There was one guy, he was dressed all in black, and he was staring straight at me. I stepped back and wasn't sure what to say because if I reported him and he was still looking at me, then he might try and hurt me sometime later. My mother said, "Well, do you see him?" I said, "Yeah," and I pointed him out, and I said, "It's that one in the black."

I was scared because I had reported him and I didn't know what he would say. But then I was happy to have him not on the loose, and to know he'd been caught.

INTERVIEWER: Was there a trial?

Ms. WATSON: No. They said I could go up for a trial, but I would have to testify. The fact that I would have to be telling this in front of other people scared me. I said no, I wouldn't do it. And my mother said, "Well, OK, you don't have to do it if you don't want to. All we need do is sue him." I said, "No, no, I don't want to do it," because I didn't want to have other people know about it.

INTERVIEWER: So do you know what happened to him?

Ms. WATSON: I think he got sentenced to a mental institution because he had some kind of disturbance.

INTERVIEWER: Did you ever tell any of your friends?

Ms. WATSON: I told my closest friends. One of my friends was so shocked. She just couldn't believe it. And another friend was really, really hurt because she felt with me. Then the day after it happened, my cousin came over. We were really close, but I didn't know how she would react. My mother had told her, but I didn't know whether to talk about it with her or not. I said, "Well, do you want me to tell you about it?" and she said, "Only if you want to." So I did, and she was really nice about it.

My mother was really, really hurt by it too because she felt for me. But she was mad at my grandmother because my grandmother kept babying me and would do all kinds of things for me because of what happened. My mother said, "This is something that has happened, but we can't baby her and treat her like that just because it has happened. It happened, and now it's over, and there's nothing we can do about it."

And then I told my stepfather. He didn't know what to say to me. He said, "Baby, I'm sorry." He looked at me like, "What can I do?" and he was ready to kill the guy. He wanted to go out and find him and destroy him. All he could feel was this physical violence toward him.

I told my boy friend about it, and he didn't know what to say either. He told me later, "I didn't know what to say. I felt sick inside. I wanted to kill him. I wanted to hurt him so bad though I didn't even know him."

INTERVIEWER: So then nobody that you told ever blamed you?

Ms. WATSON: No, not at all.

INTERVIEWER: Do you think that it has affected your attitude toward boys or men?

Ms. WATSON: A lot. I get this feeling of being scared of teen-agers who are really acting bad, and those who try to be the greatest lover of them all and are forceful. Older men who don't have girl friends or wives really scare me. I don't want to get near them. It also has affected my choice of men now. I want somebody who is very gentle and very slow and not aggressive, not trying to prove his masculinity, only trying to make it out equally between us.

INTERVIEWER: Do you think that it's affected you at all sexually?

Ms. WATSON: No, I don't think that it's affected me that way. It hasn't because I was so young. I really didn't relate it to a sexual act. It's more like somebody was doing something forceful more than sexual.

Ms. Watson's experience is unusual in that while she was being raped she knew she was going to report it to the police. Her foresight in trying to get information about her rapist while in a frightening situation is remarkable in light of her age. It is also unusual for a rapist to be caught, and her foresight probably played a part in his apprehension.

The reasonable way the police treated Ms. Watson might have resulted from her young age and the fact that her rapist was black. In addition, her mother reported it right away. But in spite of the comparatively sympathetic treatment, she still felt alienated by it.

Her mother's respect for her, in allowing her to decide whether or not to press charges, perhaps explains why Ms. Watson was able to tell her mother she was raped. Many children, afraid they'll be blamed or punished, do not tell their parents. She was fortunate to have a mother who believed her and who did not hold her responsible in any way. Many children cannot depend on such respect and trust.

Ms. Watson's stepfather and boy friend both wanted to kill her rapist. This reaction is very common on the part of males who are close to women who have been raped. Women rarely express the same sentiment. This attitude among men may be explained by the fact that many men unconsciously see women as men's property, so that for one man to rape another's woman is deeply insulting and humiliating for the man.

According to the masculine mystique, a man must protect his female property. To fail as a protector is to fail as a man. The only way for a man to rescue his image in this situation is to be willing to be violent toward the interloper. Rape can therefore be seen as a way of getting back at men as well as women, easier than attacking men directly because women are easier to victimize and much less likely than men to strike back.

For Third World men an additional factor in their desire to kill the rapist of "their" women may be their feeling of impotence in this society. They have come to expect unfair treatment from white institutions, so they have to rely on their own actions if they and those near and dear to them are to experience any kind of justice.

The Rapist

"Those men were the most normal men there (San Luis Obispo prison). They had a lot of hang-ups, but they were the same hang-ups as men walking the street."
—Alan Taylor, parole officer, quoted in
The Rape Handbook

"If it wasn't what she wanted why had she darkened her eyes with cosmetics? Why? Lips painted, shaved legs. I'll never believe they aren't inviting us to do whatever we want to do."
—Evan S. Connell, Jr., *The Diary of a Rapist*

SEVEN

No Right to Say No

> He said that what attracted him to me was the
> fact that I had my own mind, that I wasn't
> submissive, but at the same time all he wanted
> to do was to crush it out of me.

Jean Michel, a twenty-four-year-old white woman, described herself as having been a hippie housewife until she left her husband nearly four years ago. Both she and her husband, Don, came from middle-class families. Ms. Michel was nineteen when she was raped five years ago. The rapist was her husband.

Many women who are raped by their husbands do not perceive that they are victims of rape. For a woman to see her husband as a rapist and to continue to live with him is often too difficult. Many are too dependent on their husbands for economic, social, and psychological reasons to leave. One solution for these women is not to see forcible intercourse as rape. Another more common adaptation is to give up the right to say no, to be always sexually available, regardless of her wishes.

When a woman handles the situation in the latter way, her husband, technically speaking, is not a rapist, because she is not resisting him. It could be argued that such a woman is too oppressed to be raped. Many wives do not feel they have the right to say no any more than the law does. Others believe they have this right, but they find it more traumatic to resist and be defeated.

While many "hippie" men reject the traditional male role as breadwinner and the cultural stereotype of masculine appearance by wearing long hair and nontraditional clothing, they do not reject the traditional female role, nor the sexist notion that males should dominate females. Indeed, Ms. Michel's opinion that hippie men are even more concerned about their masculinity than so-called straight men is probably true. Hippie "chicks," as they are invariably called, are often seen as the communal property of men rather than the private property of a single man, as is common in the straight world.

JEAN MICHEL: We had been married for a very short time, but had been living together for about two years. We got married when I was six-months pregnant.

We lived in an apartment in New York, and there were two young girls downstairs who were friends of ours. One of them was very broke and decided to do a porno movie. She asked if I minded if Don, my husband, would be her stud. I really did mind, but I wanted to be a good sport. I was on a good hippie wife trip. Don was a really *macho* stud type, so he was very excited about doing it.

He went down, and they did some shots. The girl, Amanda, came back upstairs and asked if I would come down. I said I would, but that I didn't want to get involved in it. I took my month-old daughter with me. I went because I was very jealous. Don liked to taunt me with how he wanted a nice young lay. By this time there were several other people there, and they all wanted to do a big orgy trip, but they were all scared of it too. It was more talk than action.

I was in the back room, nursing my daughter with my shirt off, and my husband came in and said, "Come on in and join us." I was really very much dominated by him at the time, and I couldn't quite refuse. I didn't want to appear uptight and embarrassed, so I went into the other room to watch.

Don grabbed me and started cajoling me, "Let's have a good fuck scene. Nobody else will do it." I said no, no, no, no, I didn't want to do it, so he forced me. He took my clothes off. There were about six or seven people there. It was a very gross scene. Everybody was really appalled, but nobody would do anything to stop him. I fought him as much as I could. I tried to keep my legs closed and kept pushing him off. But I didn't actually attack him or slug him. It still sickens me, revolts me.

INTERVIEWER: Why do you think no one intervened?

Ms. MICHEL: I don't know what the situation would have been if I had really screamed. Perhaps somebody would have done something. But Don was making it into a big joke. "This is what we're here for, isn't it?" he said. But it wasn't what I was there for. It's what he was there for. There were two other men there. One was a revolting skag freak [heroin addict]. The other was a photographer who obviously wasn't going to interfere with anything. He was taking stills of us.

INTERVIEWER: What did you say to your husband?

Ms. MICHEL: I cried, and I kept saying, "I don't want to do this stuff. Don't! I'm not kidding." I probably laughed, but it was hysterical laughter.

He was really enjoying it. He was into the whole *macho* trip of thinking that women want to be raped, and he couldn't understand what the big objection was.

INTERVIEWER: Do you think it was obvious that you were upset?

Ms. MICHEL: People would have to be purposely putting blinders on not to know that I was upset. I wasn't sobbing, but I was crying out and saying no. I was just classically humiliated and embarrassed.

INTERVIEWER: Had he ever tried to force you in your private love making?

Ms. MICHEL: No. As a matter of fact, there wasn't very much sex between us at all at the time. My daughter was a month old, and I was up nursing her all night. I didn't get much sleep. I was in the middle of prolonged postpartum blues.

What happened was horrible. I left him not long after that. It's been over five years, and I still haven't really gotten over it. But mainly I'm concerned at what it is in me that allowed that to happen.

INTERVIEWER: What did he actually say before he raped you?

Ms. MICHEL: I can't remember his exact words. The sense of it was, "Come on, baby. What's wrong?" But he was forcing me.

INTERVIEWER: Do you think he really thought you wanted to do it, or do you think he wanted a rape scene?

Ms. MICHEL: I think he wanted a rape scene, but he had to pretend in his head that I really wanted it, or at least give that appearance to the other people.

INTERVIEWER: What happened immediately afterward?

Ms. MICHEL: I got up quickly and got dressed, went in the other room, got my daughter, and went upstairs to our apartment. I was pretty hysterical. Then I went to another woman's apartment and told her what had happened, but only very sketchily. I didn't feel that safe with her. I mean I liked her, but there really wasn't any support between us other than the fact that we were two oppressed women who didn't really recognize the causes of our oppression. I cried, and she held me. Then I said, "Oh, I've got to go back and take care of Ginny. I think her diapers need changing." So I was pretty much alone, and I just sat in the apartment while they were downstairs continuing their pseudo-orgy.

INTERVIEWER: Did you tell her that you had been raped?

Ms. MICHEL: I didn't face that it was rape then. I said that Don had fucked me in front of a lot of people, or something like that.

INTERVIEWER: Did you perceive it as rape at the time?

Ms. MICHEL: I knew that I had been raped, but somehow I thought that it was partially my fault, that I had brought it upon myself. I thought that I shouldn't have gone there, and that I should have known that Don was pig enough to do something like that, though I certainly didn't anticipate it.

INTERVIEWER: Were you surprised at his doing it?

Ms. MICHEL: Yeah, I was. I cried for a while afterward, but not for very long. I suppressed it. After that, I broke out in hives. I've had hives only twice, and both times it's been purely psychosomatic. It lasted about two weeks.

INTERVIEWER: How did the people in the room react?

Ms. MICHEL: I was really blind to them. Nobody said anything that I can remember. The two young girls worried me. One of them is since dead from serum hepatitis, which she got from shooting heroin. She was fresh in from the suburbs, and I think the scene really freaked her. I didn't go back down.

INTERVIEWER: So your husband stayed there?

Ms. MICHEL: Yeah. While I was dressing, he just said, "Give me a joint," and, "Who's next?" or some asinine thing like that.

After a while he came up and asked me to come back down again, and he was telling me about what a great scene was going on. And then he came back in a couple of hours. Afterward, he was very disgusted by the whole thing, not because he had raped me, but because nobody could really get it on, in his terminology.

When I had come down the first time before the rape, he was sitting there with his clothes off, and there was another woman next to him who was massaging his penis, and he was fondling her, and I think that he wanted to fuck everybody there, and the whole thing never happened. I don't know why they didn't. This one woman was obviously ready to, but Don said that he had been repulsed by her in some way.

INTERVIEWER: How did you and he relate when he came back to the apartment?

Ms. MICHEL: I didn't make any accusations at him or anything like that. I was very withdrawn. I slept alone.

INTERVIEWER: Did he seem concerned at all about how you felt?

Ms. MICHEL: No. But the next day the rape provoked an argument which resulted in his beating me. Then I had the hives, so I went to the doctor, who wanted me to see a shrink, which I did. But I couldn't keep seeing the shrink because my husband was jealous of him, and he made it too difficult for me to go, so I stopped.

Things went from bad to worse. I don't know how long it would have taken me to get out of it if my mother hadn't had a heart attack. Just before I left to be with my mother, I overheard some other people in the building saying, "God, how can Jean stay with him?" And another older woman said,

"Well, she must be a masochist." I thought, "Wait a minute. They're talking about me. I'm *not* a masochist. What am I doing here?"

After splitting, I saw that I could get out of the situation. I got some perspective on it. It was just being away from him that did it. I never discussed it. In fact I didn't even tell my mother that I was leaving him until later. I was gone a month. Don tried to convince me that everything had changed, so I went back for three days, but I didn't unpack my suitcases. We got into a fight about that, and so, when he went out to a baseball game, I left.

INTERVIEWER: Who did you tell about the rape aside from the woman who lived above you?

Ms. MICHEL: I've told very few people. I don't think I ever told my sister. That's who I went to after that. I told one man that I lived with a year or so ago and I've mentioned it kind of casually every once in a while with other women. But I haven't really discussed it thoroughly with anyone before.

INTERVIEWER: How did the man you were living with react?

Ms. MICHEL: Oh, he cried. He is a very loving, open person, and he said, "I hope he never comes out here to visit. I'd probably kill him."

INTERVIEWER: Why do you think you told so few people?

Ms. MICHEL: Just talking about it brings back this incredible sense of humiliation that's really heavy. I'm very good at suppressing my anger and sadness, but I'm having trouble not crying right now. If I let it out, it won't stop, and I just can't deal with it.

INTERVIEWER: So humiliation was the predominant feeling at the time you were raped?

Ms. MICHEL: Yeah.

INTERVIEWER: What else did you feel?

Ms. MICHEL: There was probably some anger, but I was very good at not dealing with anger and just turning it into sadness or depression. Still, I wanted to choke him, but he had my arms pinned back.

INTERVIEWER: What about later?

Ms. MICHEL: Well, in our day-to-day living I was not in touch with much anger. Eventually I became as violent as he was, but not as strong. I mean he didn't only hit me. He bit me and tore my hair. I have a scar on my arm from where he bit a hole out of it one time. The only way to end the beating situation was to become submissive, so it could go on for hours and hours and hours until I couldn't take it any longer, and I'd end up on the floor a sobbing heap, and then he would continue kicking at me for a while. Then he would pick me up and brush the tears away and tell me how sorry he was. And he'd ask me to stay in so that people wouldn't see the black eye and bruises. Another trip he laid on me was how heavy it was for him to deal with his guilt about beating me.

I guess I got beaten up so much because I wouldn't submit to him. It was always the old turnaround, "If you didn't provoke me, this wouldn't happen." I wasn't passive while he was hitting me. I tried to defend myself, but he was definitely stronger than I was. The situation was totally unbearable. It took me a while to split because I'd just given birth to my daughter, and I didn't know where to go or what to do, and I didn't have any money.

· INTERVIEWER: Did you marry him because you were pregnant?

Ms. MICHEL: Yeah. I tried to pretend otherwise at the time, but that was pretty much it. Things were pretty idyllic for about six months, and then they progressively got worse, and I knew when I was pregnant that I shouldn't marry him, and I shouldn't stay with him. But I kept making excuses for him. The beatings got worse when I was pregnant. I kept hoping that when the baby was there, the reality of it would change him.

INTERVIEWER: Why do you think you stood for the beatings?

Ms. MICHEL: I don't think I would have, if I hadn't been pregnant. I would have been gone very fast. I didn't know I was pregnant until I was almost four months pregnant. I never suspected it because I had been told I was infertile and my periods were always irregular. I was having morning sickness and sleeping all the time, so I finally got clued in. And it was just too heavy to split and have the baby alone.

INTERVIEWER: Had he beaten you before you were pregnant?

Ms. MICHEL: Yeah, but it wasn't the same.

INTERVIEWER: Not as heavy?

Ms. MICHEL: No. And it got more frequent.

INTERVIEWER: Can you say how frequently?

Ms. MICHEL: Oh, there would be a violent argument probably once a week. But I wouldn't get so badly beaten up that it could be seen once a week. I probably had a black eye a month.

INTERVIEWER: Why did you feel you couldn't leave when you were pregnant?

Ms. MICHEL: I was scared. I didn't have any money. I couldn't work. We were on welfare. My husband was declared psychologically unfit for work, which is actually true. He can't stand having a boss, is what it boils down to. He's a highly intelligent person. He's a good poet, and I don't say that lightly, but he's shiftless, and he's totally fucked up.

INTERVIEWER: Why do you think he raped you?

Ms. MICHEL: Just to prove what a big stud he was. The obvious Freudian interpretation is that he's really unsure of his masculinity, which I know he is. He has to prove it constantly. The worst beating I ever got was when I told him he wasn't a man, he was a boy—which he is.

INTERVIEWER: Why was he insecure about his masculinity?

Ms. MICHEL: I think a lot of it had to do with his size. He's quite short, five feet, five inches maybe, and I guess he's pretty effeminate looking. He has delicate features, he's very thin. He is from a middle-class family, but he used to hang around with what they called the greasers or the hoods. That was a definite choice of his. It wasn't what his friends were doing. He chose those friends.

INTERVIEWER: I'd like to get some idea of the impact the rape had on you. Was it just like another bad beating?

Ms. MICHEL: There's something worse about being raped than just being beaten. It's the final humiliation, the final showing you that you're worthless and that you're there to be used by whoever wants you. In general, I think rape is a political act on the part of the man. He used to boast about it to his friends!

INTERVIEWER: About raping you?

Ms. MICHEL: Yeah. We went, shortly after that, before I left him, to his sister's wedding in Boston. And he was boasting about raping me to Jim, the young man his mother was living with. I think even in front of his mother.

INTERVIEWER: Did he call it rape?

Ms. MICHEL: Yeah, he did. He called it rape. He said, "I forced her in front of a group," and he gave the background of the situation. Of course he didn't say I didn't want to be there in the first place.

INTERVIEWER: How did they react?

Ms. MICHEL: Jim was appalled, but he was used to humoring Don. Shortly after that there was a very violent fight between us. Don hit me in the middle of a parking lot in front of his mother and Jim. They had to hold him back, if you can believe it. Don had been boasting about raping me just before he hit me. Jim's main concern was to get Don away from me so I could get myself together, and he did that by humoring Don.

INTERVIEWER: Did he brag about the rape to anybody else besides his mother and her lover?

Ms. MICHEL: I think he probably did, but not when I was around. He would have his male friends come over, and they would get so stoned they couldn't move out of their chairs. I would always leave the room and close the door. I vaguely remember him making comments about it to them. But he was always making comments that humiliated me in one way or another, talking to them about this or that chick he wanted to make, and things like that.

Don appalled everyone, although they didn't know the full horror of it.

I think that even the men that he would talk to were appalled at the way he treated me. But in their roles as men, they weren't allowed to show that. A couple of them who were obnoxious when they were around him were very sympathetic to me when he wasn't around.

INTERVIEWER: Did the rape affect your sexual relationship with Don at all?

Ms. MICHEL: No. I was very, very insecure in our sexual relationship. He wanted it that way I think. He wasn't sleeping with me. He was staying up all night, and I very much wanted to sleep with him. We had sex very rarely. I only had an orgasm with him once or twice. There wasn't any more or less sex after the rape.

INTERVIEWER: About how often did you have sex?

Ms. MICHEL: Once every couple of weeks, or once every month.

INTERVIEWER: Why do you think it was that rare? Did he have a low sexual drive?

Ms. MICHEL: No, it wasn't that. It was that he was looking for fresh game. I was his house frau by that time, his baby's wet nurse. We made love a lot at first. But later he used to masturbate in the morning after I got up, rather than make love to me. He told me that he couldn't stand making love to me because I didn't come. He would try to blame me for this, but I think it nagged at him. He was an inconsiderate lover. It was a slam, bam, thank you, ma'am, kind of trip.

INTERVIEWER: Did he sleep with other women?

Ms. MICHEL: No, he didn't sleep around. It was all talk. The only time he slept with anyone else, and I know it for sure, because he would love to tell me about it if he had, was the night my baby was born. He told me the next day. It was with that young girl, Amanda, who lived downstairs.

And it was just before or just after the rape that we went to a party, and he was very much on the make with a sixteen- or seventeen-year-old girl. I spent the whole time hanging onto the baby while he was trying to come on to this girl. He spent our last money sending her some flowers because he had insulted her virginal innocence or something. Anyway, he didn't sleep with her, but he tried as hard as he could. He also encouraged me to sleep with other men. One time he actually tried to set up a little thing, a wife swap. Neither of the wives went along with it, but the two men thought they had it all arranged.

INTERVIEWER: How did you react to his interest in girls?

Ms. MICHEL: I couldn't complain, because that would bring on another violent attack.

INTERVIEWER: Did you ever try to change his sexual behavior?

Ms. MICHEL: No. I felt very insecure, too. I'd been with four or five guys before I went with Don. I'd never come with them either, so I was beginning to wonder if I was frigid. But even if I had known what I needed in order to come, I probably wouldn't have been able to tell him.

INTERVIEWER: How was he when you first met?

Ms. MICHEL: He was very gentle, worrying, considerate, poetic, and I really fell for it. I can't remember when it changed. It was all very gradual.

INTERVIEWER: Do you think Don came to hate you?

Ms. MICHEL: He denies that. After all these years of being separated from him, he still wants me to come back and live with him. He claims that he loves me more than he's loved anyone else. The only thing I can figure out is that I didn't totally submit, and because I didn't submit, I got the worst beatings of anyone he's ever lived with. He felt very ambivalent. He said that what attracted him to me was the fact that I had my own mind, that I wasn't submissive, but at the same time all he wanted to do was to crush it out of me.

Anyway I did go back and meet him at his mother's house in Boston for Christmas a year and a half or so after we'd been apart. He didn't beat me then, but the arguments were just as insane, and he did pin me to the wall so I would listen to what he had to say, and he did insult me. And he didn't sleep with me as much as I wanted him to.

INTERVIEWER: Why were you tempted to go back?

Ms. MICHEL: Because he was so ardent in his wooing. I loved him, whatever that means. I missed him. I wanted Ginny to have a father, and I kept hoping. I really wanted to believe that he had changed.

INTERVIEWER: Did the rape affect your feelings about yourself at all?

Ms. MICHEL: Yeah, it did. I felt very dirty. I felt the humiliation. I felt filthy, used. For the longest time I couldn't think about it. I would just totally freak out. I can think about it a little more now, but it was terrible.

INTERVIEWER: Did the rape change your feelings about Don?

Ms. MICHEL: I guess it did. I'm contradicting myself. I originally said that I thought I knew he was capable of that, but I guess I didn't really. Afterward, I hated him more. But I really internalized it more than doing anything against him.

INTERVIEWER: And what is your opinion of hippie men?

Ms. MICHEL: They're superpigs!

INTERVIEWER: They are more *macho* than nonhippie men?

Ms. MICHEL: Yeah. But Don is different than the run-of-the-mill hippie man. He never liked the word. He certainly didn't like to be called a hippie. He considered himself above that and intellectually superior to it.

INTERVIEWER: How traumatic would you say the rape was for you?

Ms. MICHEL: Very traumatic. I haven't begun to deal with it, and I'm not sure that I ever will be able to. I keep wishing there was some way I could work through this rage that I have about it, but I don't see any way to do it. I don't have much faith in psychiatry. I started to be in a group, but I really felt that I might have just totally dominated the whole group if I began to let any of this stuff come out.

INTERVIEWER: Regarding the rape situation, do you regret the way you handled it?

Ms. MICHEL: Yeah.

INTERVIEWER: How would you—

Ms. MICHEL: Kick him in the balls! Of course, if I had done that, I would have had the shit beaten out of me.

INTERVIEWER: You still wish that you had done it?

Ms. MICHEL: Yeah. He threatened to come out here this summer, and I went through a very heavy scene where I realized that I really wanted to kill him. Here's this man calling me on the phone, wondering why I can't have a civil conversation with him, when what I want to do is strangle him!

Except for a gang rape, Ms. Michel is the only woman interviewed who was raped in front of a group of people. Usually this would be dangerous since nonparticipants could become witnesses. In this case, however, rape was legal, since the law does not recognize rape within marriage.

Don appears to suffer from a severe case of *machismo* (an exception is his apparent lack of hypersexuality). He was unfit for employment because he could not tolerate any authority over him. Other examples of his *macho* qualities are legion: his need to dominate his wife; his preference for young "chicks"; his concern with sexual conquest (his wife became sexually uninteresting to him once she was conquered); his selfishness in sexuality ("it was a slam, bam, thank you, ma'am" approach to sexual relations); his blaming her for his inadequacy as a lover; his need to prove his sexual potency to other men; his desire to appear a stud; his preoccupation with his small stature and effeminate appearance; his preference for hanging around with "greasers" when growing up; his violence toward his wife. One of the most telling manifestations of his *machismo* was the severe beating he gave his wife when she said that "he wasn't a man, he was a boy."

The rape was fully in keeping with the rest of Don's behavior. While his *machismo* was extreme, it was not so extreme that one can simply dismiss it as sick. Elements of it are far too widespread in husband-wife (and, more generally, male-female) relationships to be dismissed as aberrant. Wife beating, after all, is pretty common. So is sex as conquest.

Can we dismiss Ms. Michel as a masochist who wanted the humiliation and brutality that she got? She was indeed dominated, mistreated, and hurt, but it seems clear that she did not get pleasure out of these experiences. She explicitly denied doing so and clearly regarded her marriage as a very unhappy one.

Many women have such a low sense of self-worth that they don't feel they can expect to be, or insist on being, treated as equal, worthy people. Labeling them as masochists obscures the fact that many women's feelings of worthlessness are socially induced, and saying that they get pleasure out of some degree of domination or pain is a way of sanctioning their oppression.

The use of the word *masochist* also obscures the fact that a person's feeling of self-worth can change. With Ms. Michel, for example, it appears first to have diminished. After repeated blows to her self-esteem, she could not even complain about being raped, but finally, on getting away from her husband for a while, her feelings of self-worth appear to have revived, and she gained sufficient self-esteem to reject her husband.

EIGHT

Lovers Rape, Too

> He'd spent the whole day telling me I was dis-
> gusting, he hated the sight of me, I was ugly, I
> was really repulsive, he had no respect for me,
> he thought I was really awful—and then he
> wanted to fuck!

Wives cannot report their husbands if they are raped by them, but technically, a woman can report a lover. However, very few do. Victims who are
raped by their lovers are unlikely to be believed, and collusion on the part of
the victim is usually suspected.

Susan Gage didn't even face the fact that her lover, Norman, had raped
her until six months afterward. If the rapist is, or has been, a lover, the
feeling of betrayal is invariably much greater than if he is an acquaintance
or a stranger.

Ms. Gage was twenty years old when she was raped by her lover. It was
two years ago.

SUSAN GAGE: I had been living with Norman for a year and a half, and we
were in love with each other. We went on a vacation, and we were out in the
mountains with a couple of friends of his. We dropped acid, and it was very
powerful. We were running around the side of this mountain, and I started
having a really bad time because I was having all these memories from my
childhood that I didn't want to look at. They were scaring me, so I started
getting kind of shaky. I needed somebody to be with me, just to take my
mind off my own mind. So I turned to Norman, but he was really disgusted
to see me so freaked out. At one point, while we were tripping together, I
was tagging along behind him asking him to just be with me and take care of
me, and he spat in my face. It got worse and worse psychologically. The
memories were bad enough, but to have my own lover spit in my face and
tell me that I was disgusting and really a shit for bumming him out was more

than I could handle. I got more desperate, and the more desperate I got for some humanity, the more disgusted he became.

We came back out of the mountains to these people's house, and everybody there was strange to me except for him. He was all I had, and he just kept telling me how disgusting I was, and that he could hardly wait to get away from me, and that he wished he could just kick me out. He told me that I was the ugliest person, and that he hated me, and that I was disgusting and repulsive and terrible. I was afraid of everything at that point. I was really, really in bad shape psychologically.

By the end of the day I was getting myself together, though I was still kind of paranoid. We were in the house visiting with these people, but we were going to sleep in the back of a Volkswagen bus. He told me to get outside and go to bed or something, so he wouldn't have to look at me. I went down to the bus, but I was afraid to be alone, so I came back up to the house, and he got really mad at me because I wouldn't stay away. But he went back down to the bus with me. I just wanted to go to sleep, but I didn't want to be alone. I was hoping that he would at least stay with me until I fell asleep or something.

Well, it wasn't what he had in mind. It really shocked me because he wanted to fuck. I said, "No, I don't want to." He'd spent the whole day telling me I was disgusting, he hated the sight of me, I was ugly, I was really repulsive, he had no respect for me, he thought I was really awful—and then he wanted to fuck! I said no, I didn't want to fuck with anybody who thought I was the most repulsive, hateful thing on the earth. But he started shoving and knocking me down and pulling my clothes off. And every time I said no, he shoved me down and hit me. He'd never been violent with me before.

I was already so psychologically destroyed that I didn't know what to do. I was in a totally strange place, and he was all I had, and he was my only way of getting back to my home. I tried to resist, but he was getting more and more violent. Then he just turned me over on my stomach and fucked me in the ass. It was really gross. He'd never done that before. I thought that he loved me, you know. I felt really bad.

INTERVIEWER: What happened afterward?

Ms. GAGE: He told me he never wanted to see me again. As soon as we got back home, that was it. We drove across the country, and it was like a bad dream the whole way home. I really felt like I was on my own and if I didn't watch out for myself, anything could happen.

The next night after that he wanted to fuck me again. I said no. I was in good enough shape then that I would have fought him, and he knew it. He just wanted to get his rocks off in me even though he found me disgusting. I couldn't believe it. When we got back, I was really depressed. I felt if this is love, then I don't believe in anything anymore.

I decided that I would stay in the house I was living in with him before. Two of my friends were living there and I had no place else to go. It was a nice place to live, and it was good paying the rent with other people beçause it wasn't so expensive.

Once we got back to town and I wasn't so freaked out any more, he decided that I was attractive again and he wanted to stay with me. I guess he didn't mind my company so much once I had myself together, and I wasn't asking anything from him. And so we stayed together. Afterward, it was so painful to remember that I repressed it. I never told any of my friends about it. I kept it inside of me. I just pretended that it didn't happen.

I lived with Norman another six months after that. But even though I didn't admit to myself that it had happened, it poisoned my mind. I couldn't be happy after that, and no matter how well things were going, I still wasn't satisfied. I thought I'd spend a month away from him with one of my girl friends. I got to talking to her one night, and it all came out.

When I said it out loud, I really flipped out. I had really never reacted to it the way I should have, because I loved him and I couldn't believe that it happened. But when I said it out loud, I started to get really mad. I went wild when I realized that it had really happened, and soon after that I left him. I couldn't take it once I said it out loud.

INTERVIEWER: What do you think his motivation was in raping you?

Ms. GAGE: I think I really scared him when I was freaking out, because I asked him for help, and he knew that I was in desperate need, and it's scary to have somebody be desperate when they want something from you. Maybe he knew he couldn't help me, and it probably freaked him out to realize that I was asking for something human and he couldn't give it. By raping me, I think that he was trying to prove to himself that he was in control of the situation and that he was superior to the situation somehow.

INTERVIEWER: Did it affect your attitudes toward men?

Ms. GAGE: Yeah. When you live with somebody a year and a half and you trust him, and something like that happens, you know you're just not going to trust anybody that much again. And before that I thought he was a special guy. I had gotten into women's liberation and had been thinking about what male chauvinists are, and I had thought that he was a little out of the ordinary because he was sensitive to me. And I thought he was trying to change. But after that, man, I don't care how sensitive a guy is, I'm not trusting him!

INTERVIEWER: Did it affect your attitudes towards sex?

Ms. GAGE: I just turn to ice if anybody gets near my ass. And a long time after that, I thought I wasn't going to be interested in men any more as sexual partners. I'm sleeping with a guy now though who is really nice to me, but I'm just waiting for him to do something to treat me like a piece of shit.

INTERVIEWER: Did it affect your attitude toward yourself?

Ms. GAGE: After it happened I felt really cynical and like I was always going to be passive. And I felt about as low as I could feel, and like I was never going to be anywhere else but low. I felt all the things that he said to me. That I was ugly. That I was disgusting. It all affected me. I felt after that that if I ever had a family, if I ever had children, I didn't want them growing up in a world that would affect them the way this one had affected me.

So I got more into politics after that. And after I talked to my girl friend about it, I felt really, really bad that it had taken me so long to react to it. It took me six months after it happened before I would face it and leave, before I would react the way I should.

INTERVIEWER: Then do you regret the way you handled the situation?

Ms. GAGE: I don't really expect that I could have reacted any differently at the time of the rape, because my brain was like Jello or mashed potatoes. But I should have faced it after that, like the next day, or the next week. I really should have killed him. I should have screamed and yelled and told everybody, and I should have left him right then and there. I should have kicked his ass first.

INTERVIEWER: What advice would you give to other women regarding how to avoid being raped?

Ms. GAGE: To avoid being raped means to not be anywhere where men are, unless you've got a bodyguard or something. I mean, if I get raped by my own lover, who's supposed to be protecting me from other people raping me, what can I say? Don't associate with men.

INTERVIEWER: How many women do you know personally who have been raped?

Ms. GAGE: I don't know a lot of women, but people that I've personally talked to about it, I'd say about eight, and some of them were raped more than once.

The degree to which Ms. Gage was able to repress her experience, together with her anger and hatred of Norman, is a lesson in how oppression can work. Despite the fact that her boyfriend violated her when she was highly vulnerable, her major reaction initially was to hate herself.

Telling her girl friend what had happened enabled Ms. Gage to get in touch with her anger and stop internalizing it so much. The fact that talking to a sympathetic friend could have such an impact on her feelings reveals the power of talking about one's oppression in a supportive situation. It also shows how isolation from such support can serve to keep one oppressed, but unable to see that oppression.

The words "love" and "making love" convey the way we want to see such relationships and acts. But sometimes the reality is that of "making hate," and "hate" would be a more valid description of the relationship. Although Ms. Gage saw Norman as just wanting "to get his rocks off," his rape seems to have had less to do with sex than with his desire to express his contempt toward her and to defile and hurt her. His raping her anally made it a double rape. Not only did she not want to have sex with him at that time, but he also forced her to have sex in a way that was painful and outside of their usual "love-making" practices.

Conversations with many women suggest that the desire of some men to have anal intercourse may come from a need to break in a new kind of virgin. It can be hard to find a vaginal virgin in some circles, but still relatively easy to find a woman who hasn't had anal intercourse. In addition, many women don't enjoy it, or actively hate it, so it can be a good way of expressing hostility toward us.

NINE

Some of Our Best Friends Are Rapists

The first rape was one where I was really trying hard to be friends with this person, and for a long, long time I had a bitterness because I felt I had been used.... I felt John had abused my friendship as well as my body, and for a while I really felt kind of crippled from the experience.

It has already been pointed out that in cases of rape by friends, it is usually assumed that the victim colludes in her own victimization. It is frequently suggested that the word "rape" be confined to cases where the woman is raped by a stranger and that another word be invented for cases in which the woman is raped by a friend, acquaintance, lover, or husband. While the relationship between rapist and victim is an important variable, emphasis on it as the key distinction is debatable. The experience of Helen Rawson, the subject of this chapter, together with the experiences related in the two previous chapters, contradicts the notion that rape by a friend, lover, or husband is less traumatic than rape by a stranger. Ms. Rawson felt doubly wronged.

"Collusion" denotes agreement or conspiracy. A victim's collusion in her own rape means that she cooperates or agrees to being raped, which would seem to render the word "rape" meaningless. And for rape between friends automatically to be suspect on grounds of collusion seems very much in error. While Ms. Rawson now feels that she was naive to have looked for the best in her friends rather than to have suspected the worst, naiveté neither invites nor deserves rape. Using the relationship between rapist and victim as *the* basic distinction between rape experiences can perpetuate rather than shatter the myth of collusion.

Ms. Rawson is thirty-four years old. She is single, black, and lives alone. Unemployed at the time she was interviewed, she describes her origins as lower class, but she herself enjoys a middle-class life-style. She is talented and well educated (with an M.A.), a woman who prefers mundane part-time work so that her creative energy is free primarily for painting. She was twenty-one when she was raped the first time.

HELEN RAWSON: The story is a difficult one to tell, because it reflects so much on my stupidity, although I can understand it in terms of my being socialized to be stupid. I still feel the guilt common to women who've been raped.

I was raped by a friend. It was at a time in my life when I was very concerned with love conquering everything. You must accept people and show them that you trust them, despite the fact that they've done nothing trustworthy. You must help them to appreciate themselves. I forget how I met this man, but he was a friend of other friends of mine, as well as being my own friend.

This guy was aspiring to be a playwright, and I can recall my boyfriend, Dick, and I going out one night and reading John's play with other people. He seemed to be more than unusually distressed at that time. Reflecting on the situation, I imagine he's probably an unusually distressed person, even now. Misfit would probably be the best word for this individual. He was very shy, very self-effacing, and obviously in need of ego bolstering.

At that time I was living in an apartment with a roommate who went home to San Jose every weekend, so the apartment was mine on the weekends. One day during the week, on a Tuesday, I think, John walked me home. The apartment was part of an old home that had been converted into units, and so there we were in the downstairs hallway, and I was trying to get my key out of my purse to open the door. It was two or three in the afternoon. We were right at my front door inside the building, when he tried to subdue me. There was an overstuffed chair there, and I remember falling back on that.

My reaction at the time was, "Oh, my God, you're causing a scene." I really didn't think he was going to rape me, but I thought he might push the situation to the point where I might have to scream. I am a person who hates scenes!

I was strong enough, or his intention was weak enough, that I was able to get out of his grip and out the front door. I talked to him outside, and I probably sounded like a mother talking to a child, "Now, that's just not the right thing to do, John! I've been very friendly with you. Is this how you treat me in return?" But the full impact did not register with me. Anyway, he talked and looked hangdog.

He said he was having some kind of problem defining himself as a male.

Of course, my response was that you don't define yourself in violent ways like that. Forcing yourself on someone does not prove that you're anything except despicable. So he cooled off, and I cooled off, and I went back into my apartment.

It was either on a Friday or a Saturday night that he called up. He knew my boyfriend was out of town, and he also knew my roommate was out of town, and he said, "Helen, I would like to see you in a certain environment." He wanted to take me to a honky-tonk, and it sounded pretty exciting to me. In fact, even now somebody could probably get me out of my house if they were going to take me to some unusual kind of place.

I was still playing the role of the understanding, show-that-you-accept-people-even-though-they-have-problems kind of woman. Also I was a little bored confronting the weekend without my boyfriend. So he came over. He had something in a package, and he said he had to put it in the refrigerator, and he wanted to leave it there and pick it up on the way back. I said fine. We went to the honky-tonk, and as I recall, we really did not dance together much, but I had a ball. In fact, I had such a ball that it might have contributed to what subsequently happened because the air was charged with a kind of wild uninhibitedness.

At one point I was dancing with two men, neither of them John. John was watching. It was a rough environment. If I heard anybody get angry at somebody else, I would have probably made an immediate beeline for the door, because there was no telling what was going to be flashed—guns, knives, anything.

John was amazed and kind of delighted that I had entered that environment and immediately become a part of it, far more so than he had. I can recall on the way home, when he stopped for gas, he made some comment that had overtones of threat, if one were to look at it closely. He said there was something suggestive about the way I was dancing with the men.

We got home, and this is where the cleverness of his plan becomes apparent. He'd left something in my refrigerator, so of course he had to come in, and he went to get it. I remember standing in the hallway to the kitchen. Because I had had a good time that night, I was saying something innocuous, but full of spirit about it, and the next thing I know, I've been struck, and I've hit the floor.

It just happened. There was no warning. It was just, wham! And then he's on top of me, his knee digging into my thigh, and he has one arm twisted behind my back, and he's saying, "I don't want to hurt you. I don't want to hurt you. Don't scream. Relax and I won't hurt you." It was just a matter of a few seconds before he'd ripped my pants off, and then he entered me very rapidly.

I had the feeling that I could get seriously hurt if I screamed. I had an entirely different feeling this time from the time I was in the hall, where he really didn't use his full force. It was controlled coercion then. This time it was obviously not controlled. I couldn't remember ever being knocked down by anybody. I was really stunned, and my arm was hurting.

So when he said, "I don't want to do anything to you. Don't scream," I took his advice. Also, I had been listening to my mother talk to women, and eavesdropping on all those women's conversations, and the wisdom that I had gleaned from them was that if you see no way out, relax, and hopefully you get away with your life. So all of this was playing in my mind. Anyway, the actual entering of my body and ejaculating took place quite rapidly. Somehow, he got sperm all over my skirt.

When it was all over, he just sort of lay there, and then did the classic thing of apologizing. "I've never done this before. Forgive me." At that point, I was unsure how to react. I was not sure whether he'd got his equilibrium back yet. What he was doing was trying to get sympathy. Since I had been such a damn fool earlier, I guess he thought maybe he could get sympathy for the rape too. But it wasn't forthcoming, and I was finally telling him to "get the hell out of here," and that I was going to call the police. Then he started back toward me, and he said, "I'm going to rip the phone out of the wall if you touch it." I said, "OK. Just get the hell out. Just go, go." So he went.

Within a week I told my boyfriend. He had intercourse with me, and it was very painful. John had entered at the wrong angle, and I was either actually ripped or pretty well chafed down there, so intercourse was very hard and very painful. I explained this to my boyfriend, and besides, I had nobody else to talk to. Dick knew this fellow pretty well, so he didn't go into one of these oh, you-asked-for-it things. I mean he realized that this fellow was sick, and had problems, although his initial reaction was to go and beat him up.

He did go down to John's house, but John wouldn't open the door and come out. Dick eventually took me to the Berkeley Police Station, and the officer made it very clear what he thought would happen if it went to court, and what I had to be prepared for, and by the time he'd explained all that, we said forget it. I didn't get the feeling that he was trying particularly to discourage me. I did have the feeling, though, that he was trying to make it very realistic to me. He said, "I want you to know what you're getting into, because you will have to testify, and you will have to make these things public. And sometimes women just don't feel up to it when it gets to that stage." So we didn't press charges.

John tried to call me a couple of times after that, and he tried to speak to me on the street, but I ignored him.

I've sufficiently overcome a lot of my feeling about it. I guess it's from what's been happening with women's lib over the past three years. I see myself now more as a victim of role playing than anything else.

INTERVIEWER: What effect did the rape have on you?

Ms. RAWSON: Intercourse was painful for about two weeks. I resented tremendously the way I had been used. It was like, "I'll use you to wipe my penis off on, and unload onto you, and that's that."

I think it affected my attitude toward men. From a very early age I've been very sensitive to the sexual caste system in this society, so there's always been a latent kind of hostility, a going along with the program because I saw no alternative. To buck it meant a kind of death. What the rape did was to bring to the surface certain hostilities toward men and to sharpen them, but also, because it involved somebody I had really tried to befriend, it gave me a wariness about people in general.

INTERVIEWER: Did you need to talk about it?

Ms. RAWSON: I felt so shitty and so guilty and so stupid that after divulging it to Dick, and then going to the police station and having to confront a stranger with it, I think that dried up most of my need to talk about it. I think it would have probably been very good for me to have had a couple of sessions with a shrink since my ego had been damaged, and I didn't want to carry around a good deal of hate toward men as a result of my experience, but I didn't see one.

INTERVIEWER: So you felt guilty and angry?

Ms. RAWSON: The anger I felt was directed mainly at myself, but I also felt anger whenever I came near John. In fact, the last time I saw him was about five years ago, which would place it about seven years after the incident, and I can remember well the anger I still felt then. And the times that he called on the phone, he got slammed up on. But the bulk of the anger was directed toward myself.

INTERVIEWER: Is this still the case?

Ms. RAWSON: No. What I would really like to do is stomp him in the ground.

INTERVIEWER: Do you have fantasies of doing that?

Ms. RAWSON: Yes, I try to exorcise a good deal of my hostilities through fantasy. One thing I'd like to do, that I especially wish I could have done at the time, is to have subdued him in some way. This will sound gruesome, but I would have loved to cut off his penis and put it in his mouth like a stuffed pig. At the time, though, I was pretty inhibited about this sort of thing. I thought it wasn't a nice thing to think. Oh, but since then!

I did get angry when I was telling him to get out of my apartment, because I felt even more misused to have somebody deceive me, brutalize me, rape me, and then hang around trying to get my forgiveness, and trying to use me as some kind of shrink. It seemed like there was no end to the insensitivity. I recall getting angry, but I can also recall trying to keep it in check, because I still didn't know what he might do.

There was another time that I got raped too. It was by someone I had met on campus and really liked. Both of these guys [John and Graham] are campus people, by the way—your "better folk"! They were both students.

INTERVIEWER: Were they white or black?

Ms. RAWSON: They were black.

INTERVIEWER: About how old were they?

Ms. RAWSON: John was at least three years older than I was. Graham was also older by a couple of years. He was a relative of somebody who was prominent in Africa, and that's how I met him. I was very interested in Africa at that time. Graham was an exciting personality. He had a lot of drive and dynamism, was seemingly always cheerful. We saw a lot of each other on campus, and so eventually we agreed to get together sometime.

When I talked to him before I first went out with him, the conversation was pretty direct regarding what we both anticipated. I anticipated going to bed with him the night I went out with him, but what happened was that I felt ill that night. I went out, but I told him I had a dreadful headache. At the door, I said, "Look, Graham, I'd really wanted to go to bed with you tonight, but I'm just feeling so lousy. I'd be bad for you, and I wouldn't enjoy it. Can't we make it another time?" He should have realized that he was not talking to somebody who was stringing him along. Our relationship had been very direct and, I would say, adult.

INTERVIEWER: How old were you at this point?

Ms. RAWSON: I think I must have been twenty-four or twenty-five. Let me emphasize that up until that point, I had thought Graham was interesting and exciting.

I had opened my front door, and Graham came in. I said something like, "Come and let's have coffee, and we'll talk, because I feel kind of finky, finking out like this." There was a long hallway from my front door. And the next thing I remember was being in the hallway and being up against the wall, and this man was all over me.

I'm saying, "But look, Graham, it's just a matter of a day or two." It's pretty apparent after a few seconds that Graham has no intention of recognizing the fact that I'm not up to it. His attitude seems to be, "Tough." And I've got a losing battle against the wall. I'm pushing him, but obviously I'm not going to overcome him. I realized I was losing the battle, my pants were coming down.

I imagine I could have screamed and hollered. I didn't, because of an inhibition about scenes. I'm slowly overcoming it with age, but it was there. Also, I'm not convinced screaming and hollering is protection.

I also recall having the feeling that I'm not going to give this jerk the satisfaction of beating me in a fight, damn it. I could see that my struggling was exciting to him. I'd seen that before in men, but nobody before had pushed it like Graham. So I said, "OK, Graham, look, let me get my diaphragm on, because I don't want to get pregnant from something like this." He let me do that, and then I just lay there, and he came in. If you look at it from a time point of view, I got rid of him faster than had we struggled more.

I was totally turned off, but he came very rapidly. What enjoyment a creature could get out of what he did is beyond my imagination, but you know, it's possible that he really did enjoy himself. I can't put myself in his position. He certainly wasn't like John. He did not see himself as a rapist. He had no apologies. It was just brass all the way. What is so funny is that he couldn't figure out why I wouldn't go out with him afterward. He never understood.

INTERVIEWER: How did you explain it to him?

Ms. RAWSON: I recall sharing very few words with him after that. We had certain common political interests, and our paths crossed, and I was civil. But my reaction was more, "You *know* why I'm not going out with you," rather than to give him any lengthy explanation.

INTERVIEWER: But he didn't seem to know?

Ms. RAWSON: No. Actually that incident may have been a blessing, because I may have gone on with illusions about him for a long time, and then got shafted even worse. From talking to other people about him, evidently he's not a person to be trusted. He doesn't function with the usual kinds of restrictions in personal relationships.

INTERVIEWER: Why do you think he raped you?

Ms. RAWSON: I think what was going on in his head was, "Me, Graham, horny. You, woman!" I have a feeling that the same thing might have occurred even if we didn't have an understanding that we were going to bed before we went out.

When I think back on it, it makes me so furious that he cared so little about us as a relationship, because I really had looked at him in terms of a sustained relationship, and he certainly killed it that night. You can't have friends who will say, "You've got a headache? Well, tough shit, I'm going to use you anyway, and I don't care if you appreciate it or not."

INTERVIEWER: Did you tell anybody about what happened?

Ms. RAWSON: No, I don't recall telling anybody. In fact, this is the first time I've really discussed in detail either of these things, because they left me with a feeling of being used like so much toilet paper.

The first rape was one where I was really trying hard to be friends with this person, and for a long, long time I had a bitterness because I felt I had been used in more than one way in that case. I felt John had abused my friendship as well as my body, and for a while I really felt kind of crippled from the experience.

With Graham, the handwriting was there. He was the shafting kind of person. Somehow the second experience left less deep scars and was easier to write off.

INTERVIEWER: You mentioned having fantasies of retribution against John. Did you have these kinds of fantasies in relation to Graham too?

Ms. RAWSON: I tend to have a lot of fantasies about men, period. I feel raped by men in many ways.

INTERVIEWER: Do you feel the hatred of men that has built up is largely due to these rape experiences, or do you feel that it is due to other bad experiences with men?

Ms. RAWSON: I think they're all connected. The anger is probably very deep because it's had to be repressed for so long. People tend to see you as weird if you're not going along with the established program. So there's a long residue of anger. I think the rapes tended to focus it, and made me deal consciously with my anger, but they just happened to be a more nitty-gritty form of the rape that goes on constantly in this society.

I've gotten my anger fairly well under control now. But it hasn't really been tested, because I don't have to go out every day to a job, and I don't have to deal with the subtle insults that you have to put up with when you're working with men. Also I don't have to deal with the fact that even though I think I am more capable than most of my bosses have been, I'll never have the opportunity to be in their position. I mean there's a kind of anger that wells up from all that.

INTERVIEWER: Do you relate to men now?

Ms. RAWSON: Yes, I relate to men. One of my warmest friends is a male, but it's clear to me that the reason I didn't marry him, say, twelve years ago, was because, regardless of how warm, sweet, humane, intelligent, and all the wonderful things he is, he was still a male chauvinist pig. There were certain roles he expected of me.

INTERVIEWER: Are all men like that, in your experience?

Ms. RAWSON: Yes, I have to say that *all* men are male chauvinist pigs!

INTERVIEWER: What do you think the solutions are to the rape problem?

Ms. RAWSON: Unfortunately, I hurt my back about two years ago, so I haven't learned my judo and karate, but if it weren't for my back I certainly would know it backward and forward. I think there should be women's groups patrolling various areas and women's groups for rape victims.

But ultimately, I am the kind of person who wants to know that I can depend on myself. I have a thirty-eight that is purse size, and I know how to use it, and I would not feel too much compunction about wiping out somebody who was attacking me. In fact, I would probably enjoy doing it, for all the times I didn't do it in the past.

Also I keep my door heavily locked, and I am on the third floor. I try to avoid as many risky situations as I can. When I go out in the world, I'm usually not wearing anything that anybody could consider suggestive. So I'm trying to attract as little attention as possible.

I avoid being in certain unpleasant places, but I don't really think that I should have to avoid it. I think I should be able to function freely in this world.

Many would not regard Ms. Rawson's experience with Graham as rape. Her relative lack of resistance, combined with her being able to insert a diaphragm to protect herself from pregnancy, doesn't fit the "classic" definition. However, the classic definition of rape would seem to apply only to a minority of cases. Ms. Rawson clearly did not want to have intercourse with Graham, she was direct in telling him that, and none of her actions suggested otherwise. There are many ambiguous or borderline cases, but Ms. Rawson's does not appear to be one of them.

Many men think "no" is just a show of resistance from a "good" girl or woman. They are not always wrong. Ms. Rawson, however, was very explicit with Graham, for example, about wanting to sleep with him but not feeling up to it on that particular occasion.

John, in contrast to Graham, appears to have perceived his act as rape. It seems that he knew Ms. Rawson would not have sex with him voluntarily, since she had a sexually exclusive relationship with Dick. Apparently, however, he felt she provoked him. In the dating game it is common for men to expect sex in return for taking a woman out and footing the bill. Perhaps he felt sex was due him after he had provided Ms. Rawson with the opportunity to have "such a ball."

While this way of thinking doesn't always lead to rape, it often leads to pettier forms of assault. In dating situations many women are made to feel exploitative if they don't reciprocate with sex at the end. Yet if the woman offers to pay half the bill or insists on it, many men take this as an attack on their masculinity.

Some people like to think that a woman who is confident and assertive and who carries around a don't-mess-with-me attitude toward men won't be bothered. While passivity and submissiveness may make women more rapable, it is a mistake to think that any woman is invulnerable to rape. Ms. Rawson is a very strong woman who earnestly rejects the traditional submissive female role. But this did not, and does not, make her invulnerable to rape and other forms of male harassment.

All the precautions Ms. Rawson takes also demonstrate the political impact of rape. Few people enjoy living in an armed camp with curfews, but women who live alone are often forced to place such restrictions on themselves.

TEN

Give It to Me, Bitch,
or I'll Rape You

He felt that women oppressed him because he needed them
badly, and they were always playing games with him like going to
his house and then saying no. . . . Then he started telling me he
could understand how men sometimes go out and rape women.

"Rape is caused by male anger at female sexism," asserted an angry man on a
call-in radio show. Women who take pains to look attractive to men and
evoke their sexual interest, but who then refuse, as he saw it, to "follow
through" bring rape on themselves.

Many men share this attitude, though most of them draw the line before
rape. Men and women have different perspectives on dating and sex, though
it appears that women understand the male perspective better than men
understand the female perspective. This is to be expected since it is in
women's best interests to know and understand men, much the same way as
it behooves the slave to know and understand the master. Rachel Gold
appears to have had more understanding of her rapist than he appears to
have had of her.

Ms. Gold is a nineteen-year-old, single, white woman who comes from a
middle-class background. She was eighteen when she was raped, nine
months before this interview.

RACHEL GOLD: I was hitchhiking from campus to home every day, and
Fred picked me up. He was black, about twenty-eight years old. He rode a
huge motorcycle, and when he asked me for my telephone number, I gave it
to him.

At that time this male-dominated society had me convinced, as it has
most women convinced, that there is something wrong with a woman who
doesn't want to relate to men, or at least that if there's nothing wrong with

/ 97

the woman, she must simply have run into the wrong men, and should therefore keep trying to find the right ones. This was an absurdity, since I had known many men but had only loved women. It had nothing to do with the particular men I knew but rather with the fact that all men are extremely oppressive and unlovable. But since men's emotional lives depend upon women's remaining brainwashed and powerless, they put a lot of effort into it and have been pretty successful.

So I gave Fred my number. A week later, he asked me to go out with him for a drink. He came by my house and picked me up in a big fancy car with two kids in the back seat. He told me they were his kids and that he had been married and divorced or separated. His laundry was in the back seat, and he said that he had to wash it. It was a real innocent-looking scene.

I got into the car, and we went to his former house, where I met his wife. He dropped off his kids, and then we went to the laundromat to do his laundry. We put his laundry in and went around the corner to the Green Bear for a glass of wine. All this time I was really impressed by his attempt at being honest with me, and so I trusted him. Unfortunately, rape is a completely honest act for men, so honesty is really no grounds on which to trust them.

Fred had been brought up in an upper-middle-class black home in New York and had assimilated into the white culture. After we had a glass of wine and his laundry was done, we got in the car, and he took me up to where he lived. He was renting a room in the basement of someone's house. We went into his apartment and sat down.

When I went in, I didn't think he might attack me, and I don't think he had thought of it either. He turned on some music and wanted to dance, and I thought that was strange. I wasn't used to going to a man's apartment anyway, but I was even less used to having them want to dance. So he started dancing with me, and he started kissing me.

In my previous experiences when I had let men do any sexual things at all, immediately they would want to go to bed with me, and there would be a big conflict about it. So I said, "Look, I don't want to kiss you," and he said, "Why not?" I said, "I don't want to go to bed with you, and so I don't want to do anything that will lead you on in any way. I really don't want any sexual involvement." He tried to kiss me again, and I said no, and he said OK.

We sat down on a couch, and he started telling me about how it had been months since he'd been able to get together with a woman, and he was really frustrated, and a whole long sob story about how he just couldn't make it. I was compassionate. I was saying, yeah, how terrible. It got heavier and heavier. I was talking about how sexually fucked up our whole society was, and he was talking about how frustrated he was, and how he would come home from work and go right to sleep and wake up at three in the morning and go out and ride his motorcycle, because he felt so frustrated sexually.

He told me that he felt that women were in total control of the sexual situation because they had the choice to fuck a man whenever they wanted and whoever they wanted, whereas a man had to go around and find someone willing. He had no understanding of the fact that a woman's opportunity to fuck a man whenever she wants isn't necessarily desirable for women, and that men actually are in control since, as holders of the power positions in society, they are able to push upon women a male-oriented definition of sexuality, a definition which they have the physical and legal power to enforce upon any rebellious women.

Another thing he said was that he couldn't just fuck anyone. It had to be someone he was attracted to. He felt that women oppressed him because he needed them badly, and they were always playing games with him like going to his house and then saying no. There he was, a man who had the physical power to lock me up and rape me, without any real threat of societal punishment, telling *me* that *I* was oppressive because I was a woman! Then he started telling me he could understand how men sometimes go out and rape women.

I started thinking, oh, God. I don't know why I didn't think it before then. He was telling me a story of someone who had raped a woman, and I said, "I'd like to go home now." He got up, ran to the door, and bolted it. Then he turned around and grabbed me and started to pull off my shirt. I was trying to fight him off, but he was a lot stronger than me. He pushed me down on the couch and tried to pull my clothes off.

I was crying and shaking, and I was saying, "Please, don't. Please, don't." All I could think of to do to get him away from me was to poke him in the eyes, but I couldn't do it! I just couldn't do that, even if it meant being raped.

INTERVIEWER: Why couldn't you do it?

Ms. GOLD: I'd never done anything as gruesome as poking someone's eyes out before. I just couldn't do it, which in some ways I felt good about at that time because I didn't really want to be able to do that to someone. But also, I thought that if I hurt him not quite enough and then tried to run, that he would be so angry that he'd really hurt me badly. He looked at me and said, "Don't make me hurt you," as though I was, by not giving in to him, forcing him to rape me. That's how he justified the whole thing. He kept saying women were forcing him to rape them by not being there when he needed them.

At first I was out of control of my emotions, I was shaking and crying, but then I thought that if I kept on doing this, he'd leave me alone. The only tactic that I could use was to be so frightened that he couldn't do it. I said, "Just a minute. Let me sit up. Let me sit up," and he let me. I tried to talk him out of it. I tried to talk him into at least letting me go that night and then maybe I would see him again. Anything to get out of there! But he said, "I won't let you leave here, because I don't think you'll ever come back. But if you will just get in bed with me, I promise you that I won't do anything to you, if you're still so frightened." He said, "What I really want is a warm body. It's not the sex I need so much as the affection."

I felt that there was very little I could do, and so I got in bed with him. He started trying to kiss me again, and I said, "Look, I don't want you doing this." He looked at me and said, "I'm sorry," rolled over and fell asleep. I couldn't get out of the bed without crawling over him and waking him up, and then the door was bolted. I thought, well, maybe he isn't going to hassle me anymore.

I lay there about five hours, sleeping half the time and awake half the time. He had to go to work in the morning at seven o'clock, so when his alarm clock rang, I thought, oh, good, it's all over now. I can go home. He turned off the alarm and started to kiss me, but he knew right away that I was feeling the same way as the night before. Then he just got on top of me. He wasn't going to mess around anymore, because he knew that it wasn't going to do any good. I said, "Wait a minute! What are you doing? I thought you weren't going to do anything!" He said, "Look, I gave you all night to calm down, to start feeling better, to start being affectionate to me, and you haven't changed at all." Like, now you're going to get it!

There was nothing I could do at that point. I was in bed. He had made me strip the night before, so I didn't have any clothes on. He entered part way into me and started pumping. He was looking at me, and in my very coldest voice I said, "I *wish* that you would go away." Before he could come or anything, he said, "Oh, shit!" He sat up and said, "All right. I won't bother you anymore if you promise that you will see me again." I couldn't believe that he thought I would see him again, but in order to get away as soon as possible, I said, "Yes. OK. Anything." We got dressed, he drove me home, and he went to work.

INTERVIEWER: When he said, "Oh, shit," was he angry with himself or with you?

Ms. GOLD: Both. He wanted, and I think even expected, me to make everything all right in the morning, like I was going to be calmed down, and I was going to be able to fuck him, and everything was going to be nice. When he realized that that wasn't the case, he got angry and disgusted.

I felt as though he wanted to punish me for that, to show me he cared less about me and how I felt about it, whereas the night before it was important to him that I felt all right about it. If I had responded, I don't think he would have been disgusted with either of us, but because I didn't respond, he was disgusted with me and disgusted with himself for having done it. I got the feeling that it made him really dislike himself.

I was totally freaked out. I didn't even feel like it was all his fault. I felt like it was my own fucked-up sexuality as well as his, that it was the effect society had on both of us that had caused the whole thing.

INTERVIEWER: How did you feel that your sexuality contributed to what happened?

Ms. GOLD: At the time I was pretty confused since I had been told all my life that I should want to be involved with men and I was feeling the opposite. I had gone to bed with a man once before, had felt it to be no big deal, and didn't particularly want to do it again. I was still feeling that there was something wrong with not liking men, that I had a fear of men that should be overcome. As a result, I felt at the time that my sexual "fears" and confusion must have had something to do with the rape.

Looking back on it, I can see that my sexuality was fine. My confusion was part of the brainwashing that all women experience, and the only part it played in the rape was that it got me to go out with him, which I should never have done in the first place. The general thing in Berkeley is that when a man you don't know walks up to you on the street or picks you up hitchhiking and asks you for your phone number and asks you out, it's because he wants to go to bed with you. But I didn't realize this then.

Also, I told him how I felt about my limited sexual experience with men, and his line was, "Well, how do you know?" It's the kind of thing that a lot of men say, "All you need is one good fuck, and then everything will be all right. You'll like men." Also, his reaction was that, since I had slept with at least one man, it was all right for him to rape me. I would have been somehow more justified in my refusal if I hadn't slept with anyone.

INTERVIEWER: Since you weren't a virgin you had nothing to lose?

Ms. GOLD: Yeah. I felt also that my extreme fear, being paralyzed with shaking and crying, was part of my fear of the whole sexual thing anyway, and in a lot of ways that reaction made him continue, because it made him feel he was getting a response, and he just wanted to keep going with it.

Now I feel that he was much more responsible than I felt at that time. Then I felt that if I could have done something different, responded to him differently, been less compassionate, it might have been better. But the whole time, even afterward, I felt that not only had he fucked me over, but that he had been fucked over societally, and so he was oppressed as well as I was. Now I think that's a bunch of bull shit, and I allow myself to feel a lot more hostility toward him.

At the time of the rape I felt that some abstract unisexual blob called society subjects both men and women to bad conditioning as they grow up, so that by the time they are adults they are too messed up to relate in a real way.

I see it differently now. That abstraction, "society," is controlled by men. They hold the positions of power in society's major institutions, and they have physical control of the streets as well. It is they who impose their rape mentality upon *us*. When they say that we oppress them they are complaining about whatever meager resistance we may put up against being totally squashed by them.

INTERVIEWER: How forceful was Fred?

Ms. GOLD: The very first time that he threw me down on the couch and got on top of me, that was the only time that I really put up as much struggle as I could. He used all of his strength, and he was very forceful and kept me down. That was when I realized how much stronger he was than I. And that was the only time that he had to be that forceful.

INTERVIEWER: So you gave up after that?

Ms. GOLD: Yeah. When I was in bed with him we didn't get into a physical struggle because after that I knew that trying to fight him off was hopeless. I preferred to be calmer about it than be kicking and screaming and still having to submit.

INTERVIEWER: Could you say anything more about your impression of Fred's motivation?

Ms. GOLD: I still believe he was being honest with me. What he did came out of the combination of extreme frustration and the feeling that unless he could successfully have sex with a woman, he wasn't a man. It was like he *had* to have that sexual desire. He needed to need sex in order to feel he was a man.

He never really talked about the way women oppressed him in biological terms at all. It was all in terms of how much he wanted them. I got similar impressions when I saw him afterward. I think he felt sincerely bad that he had done the whole thing, yet he still expected to see me again. He had said, "I'll leave you alone right now if you'll see me again," as though, of course, I'd see him again, because he was only doing what he needed to do.

He called me up a couple of days after it happened, and he asked me how I felt. I told him I felt shitty and disgusted with him, and with myself and with the whole world, which I did, and that I didn't really feel good about seeing him, and that I wouldn't ever see him again in private.

Later I received from him a cartoon in the mail of a man in a business suit carrying a briefcase being held up by a poor man. The poor man was saying, "Will you please give me all your money so that I don't have to rob you?" What Fred was trying to say to me was, "If only a woman would give herself to me, I wouldn't have to force her."

I ran into him on the street about a month after that. He said, "What did you think of the cartoon?" I said it didn't make any sense to me, because I felt that in saying that, the man was forcing the thing just as much as if he was doing it in the first place. Fred said, "Oh, yeah." He told me that he had seen several women since he had seen me, and that they had all given him "a lot of women's liberation stuff" that he didn't understand and told him that he was a male chauvinist pig. He said he would like to talk to me about it so he could understand it, because he had a lot to work through. I said, "I really don't want to talk to you about it," and he said OK, and that was it for that time.

The last time I saw him he stopped me on the street, and we got into a little discussion in which I let him know that I didn't have a place to live and didn't have much money. He said, "Listen, do you still feel hostile toward me? Do you still feel angry toward me?" I said, "I sure do!" He said, "Oh. Well, listen, there is a vacant room in the duplex, and I was thinking that the place could use some fixing up. Maybe you could work fixing it up every once in a while, and you could live there for free, and we could break even, so to speak." I just looked at him and said, "First of all, I wouldn't live anywhere near you, and second of all, what you did is not the kind of thing you can break even for," and I left.

Afterward I realized that he saw me and probably all women as whores. He could do anything to us and just make up for it with money or some other kind of payment, like a place to stay. And if we don't see it that way, then we are hurting him.

INTERVIEWER: Why did you stop on the street when he told you to?

Ms. GOLD: I had a split reaction. One was strong anger and hostility, and the other was fear, because when I'm in a position with a man where he can physically overpower me, I'm afraid.

INTERVIEWER: Do you think that he perceived himself as a rapist at all?

Ms. GOLD: No, I don't.

INTERVIEWER: Do you think that he perceived what he did to you as rape?

Ms. GOLD: Probably not.

INTERVIEWER: How do you think he saw it?

Ms. GOLD: That's hard to say. He thought I should have done it with him of my own free will, so he probably felt justified in forcing me to do it. I know that somehow he felt bad about it afterward. His whole attempt to "break even" shows that even much later he felt some kind of guilt. I think probably most of his guilt comes from the fact that his behavior caused me to reject him, and that was hard on his ego.

INTERVIEWER: Do you think that when he took you to his apartment, he was planning to make it with you?

Ms. GOLD: Yeah.

INTERVIEWER: Do you think that if you weren't willing, he had contemplated raping you?

Ms. GOLD: No. I think that he assumed he'd make it with me.

INTERVIEWER: Can you go back to the incident and try to think of your feelings at the time?

Ms. GOLD: I really was just overcome with fear. I was more afraid of being raped violently than of anything else. Of course, forced intercourse is always a violent thing, but less scary than a kicking, screaming kind of scene I wasn't prepared for. It was so confusing and so quick at first that it was much more frightening then, though I wasn't really afraid of him physically harming me or killing me or anything like that. His intentions really were not to hurt me at all, and I would have been no use to him at all if I were hurt.

But the most frightening thing was, I'd never been in a position before where it was made so clear to me that I was totally powerless, physically anyway, in the presence of another person who was going to use me. Just being put in that helpless situation was really frightening. The act of rape was an enforcement of his power against my will.

I felt humiliated and foolish because I had trusted him. I think that I didn't allow myself to feel hatred because it's not "nice." Instead I internalized my anger and felt shitty about myself. I think it would have been much healthier for me to allow myself to feel and express the hatred which I internalized and covered with compassion.

INTERVIEWER: Do you think that he had done this with other women?

Ms. GOLD: No, I think it was the first time that he had done that.

INTERVIEWER: It seems that he really couldn't quite carry through with it.

Ms. GOLD: Right. He actually pulled out. It wasn't that he lost his erection and couldn't, but that he decided he didn't want to go through with it.

INTERVIEWER: Do you think the rape affected your behavior in any way?

Ms. GOLD: It affected my immediate life by making me feel as though the entire world was perverted, and I didn't really want to deal with anybody, especially men, for a while. I ended up going through a period of getting drunk a lot, and things like that.

About a month after that I decided I had really been kidding myself in thinking I should relate to men. I had been pushing myself into it, but I really didn't want to have anything to do with them, and I never have. I realized at the same time that I'd been repressing all the positive feelings I had for women, and I decided that that was crazy, and I was going to allow myself to feel these feelings. I had already been involved with a woman, but I had not accepted that I was gay. But about a month after the rape, I decided that I really was, and that what I wanted was to be with women. I don't think that the rape made it happen, although because of the time sequence, I have to say that it probably contributed to my ability to say no to men, and to see how men really treated me most of the time. At that point I decided not to give out my telephone number and not be afraid.

I see now that there's an assumption made by men that I will not reject them, and that assumption made me feel as though I shouldn't, which doesn't make sense at all, especially now that I'm really not interested in deep involvements with them.

INTERVIEWER: Did your experience of rape change your attitude to yourself at all?

Ms. GOLD: It intensified my feelings of confusion, and it made me feel as though I needed to hurry up. It was much more important to get things together right away and know where I stood, know how I felt, and stop bullshitting around. I felt generally worse about myself, but that didn't last too long. Within a couple of months, I got rid of feeling I was fucked up and ended up feeling a lot better.

INTERVIEWER: Did it change your attitude toward sex at all?

Ms. GOLD: Maybe a little about sex with men. But I see sex with men and sex with women as totally different. It confirmed some of my ideas about sex with men, which played a part in my decision not to have sex with them. Sex, for men, is totally oriented toward the man's orgasm and isn't successful unless it involves intercourse and orgasm, which is ridiculous, because sex to me is a much more sensual, much more emotional experience. It doesn't just involve one particular spot on the body getting excited and aroused, and then it's over, and it's either a success or a failure.

INTERVIEWER: Did it affect your view of men in general?

Ms. GOLD: I don't really think it changed things that much. I think that all it did was to confirm ideas that I had about the societal conditioning of men and of women. All it did emotionally was to make me a little bit more hesitant to have anything to do with men, especially sexually. On the other hand, I had men friends at the time, and I didn't feel any differently about them or look at them any differently after the experience.

INTERVIEWER: Did that hesitancy you felt apply to white men as much as black men?

Ms. GOLD: Yes. Because I really didn't think of him that much as a black man as opposed to a white man.

INTERVIEWER: Did you tell anyone afterward?

Ms. GOLD: Yeah. The first person I told was Kathy, the woman who had been my lover, the woman I had lived with for a little while. She was my closest friend and as soon as it got late enough to call, I called.

I was living with one woman and three men, and one of the men in the house was a real close friend of mine. I saw him downstairs and told him I had had a really bad experience, but I couldn't tell him what had really happened because I felt he wouldn't understand. Even though he was a close friend, and someone I felt was sensitive, which is a feeling I don't get from a lot of men, I felt that he, as a man, could not understand. I asked him whether he felt that men were naturally more horny than women were, because I was trying to understand what had happened and why it had happened.

INTERVIEWER: Did he try to get you to tell him?

Ms. GOLD: No, he didn't. He wasn't very responsive.

INTERVIEWER: What was Kathy's reaction?

Ms. GOLD: She was compassionate and very caring and she made me feel a lot better. She helped me to feel more secure after being very frightened. I didn't tell other people for a while. After it became less of an emotional thing for me to talk about, I was able to tell other friends. It was hard at first, and then after a while it just became a story that almost could have happened to someone else, because I had told it and told it.

INTERVIEWER: How have people reacted?

Ms. GOLD: I can't remember that many reactions because I didn't get too many strong reactions in any direction. Mainly people don't know what to say. They've responded well in the sense that they've tried to feel for me, but they didn't say very much about it. Responses that bothered me came from friends who want me to be heterosexual, like, "Shit. Here goes another experience for her that will make her afraid of men, and make her pull away from men." But even those reactions were compassionate reactions.

The main way that I can differentiate reactions is between gay women and some particularly conscious nongay women, and straight women and men. The gay women and the conscious women were able to help me to understand the experience so that I didn't feel so shitty about it, whereas the women who are not that conscious, especially heterosexual women and men, made me feel as though it was terrible but yet that's the way it is—reality is terrible.

I told a straight woman about it the other day, and she told me that she thought that to a certain degree it had to be my fault. She wasn't saying that I necessarily wanted to be raped, but she thought it was my fault for putting out vibrations of fear. She believed that if you feel fear, a man is much more likely to attack you than if you come across as strong and able to defend yourself. I felt strange getting that reaction.

INTERVIEWER: It's interesting that this is pretty much what you said you felt about it yourself.

Ms. GOLD: The thing is, there was so much time before he did anything, so much talking. We must have had a forty-five-minute discussion about the whole sexual situation before he did anything. I guess it's possible that no matter what I said or no matter what went on in those forty-five minutes he would have done it, but for some reason, maybe because it's been told to me so often, I feel as though there may have been some other way that I could have dealt with it to change the situation. I don't know so much whether it was because of my feeling of fear, but my main reaction was compassion for him. I thought at the time that this would stop him from doing anything. I thought that a colder reaction would make him more able to rape me.

INTERVIEWER: Did you think about reporting it to the police?

Ms. GOLD: I thought about it the day after the morning that he took me home. There were two problems. One was that even if they convicted him I didn't think there was anything that they would do to change him. And the second thing was that I thought there was no way that I could prove that he had raped me. So I felt pretty helpless. The thing is that the police and the courts make it nearly impossible to take any action against someone in a case like this, which is probably why so many rapes go unreported.

INTERVIEWER: Did other people advise you on this?

Ms. GOLD: The only person I talked with about whether I should report the rape was Kathy, who was the first person I told about it. She saw both the pros and the cons of reporting it. First she thought that I should, and then when I told her why I didn't think I should, she said, "Yeah, you're probably right, I guess." So I never did report it.

INTERVIEWER: If you were in the same situation again, would you handle it differently?

Ms. GOLD: That's hard to say, because I could never get in that particular situation again. First of all, even the way that I talk with men now is different. When I talked to them in the past, there was always a question in my mind about a sexual relationship, and now it is not in my mind at all. I've talked to men who've gotten to know me about this, and they sense now that there's no question of a sexual relationship with me.

If I somehow were in that position again, the only thing that would be different now would be my way of understanding it, and my way of dealing with him, which would be much less compassionate and much less confused, which would give me a feeling of more confidence, and I think I'd probably be calmer.

INTERVIEWER: Do you have any views on why men rape?

Ms. GOLD: I suspect that most men at one time or another in their lives force intercourse on a woman, psychologically or physically. If they don't do it directly, then they do it indirectly by perpetuating the myth that women like to be raped. Every man, whether or not he rapes women, is in some way emotionally dependent on his power. Rape flows naturally from this. When rape is blamed on "incompatible socialization" of males and females, it seems as though no one is particularly responsible other than the abstract "society."

INTERVIEWER: Do you see rape as much worse than physical assault, or do you see it as equivalent?

Ms. GOLD: I see rape as being worse in that it doesn't come from a need for money and it doesn't come from total insanity either. Whatever it is that causes someone to hit someone else is horrifying in a different kind of way. Rape seems to be so imbedded in our society. It seems just a natural outcome of the way that men are. And that is a really frightening thing.

INTERVIEWER: Do you have any ideas about solutions?

Ms. GOLD: Ultimately, the only solution is to eliminate all the men! If women could live in separate societies, that would be a step in the right direction, but male imperialism would never allow us to do that.

As far as temporary solutions go, I think that the particular kind of situation I was in can be avoided by not relating to men, which I intend to do for other reasons anyway. But that really doesn't solve the problem by any means, since a woman's deciding not to relate to men doesn't mean that they won't attempt to force her to relate to them.

I think that women learning self-defense and forming defensive as well as retributive rape squads could improve the situation some, but these really wouldn't be any kind of solution, because women will still have to feel fear and paranoia whenever they walk down the street. In order to make any real improvements, we have to take power from men. We need to take action which threatens them. If women continue to patronize men and betray themselves for men, we will continue to be powerless.

I'm hoping soon to learn some kind of self-defense, which is something I never wanted to do before, because I felt that learning some form of self-defense like karate was walking around with a weapon, and I didn't like having to walk around feeling that way. But now I'm willing to do that.

Ms. Gold provides a vivid portrait of her rapist and of the incompatible needs of males and females. While many males are interested in more than sexual relationships and many women want to limit their relationships to sex only, by and large far more men than women look merely for sex. This is especially true of young men at the height of their sexual capacity.

Ms. Gold also mentions what I believe to be one of the socialized differences between male and female sexuality that leads to frustrations between women and men: the genital orientation of many men, along with their orgasm fixation. Sex for her, and for most women, "doesn't just involve one particular spot on the body getting excited and aroused, and then it's over, and it's either a success or a failure."

Ms. Gold's rapist felt that her choice to go out with him necessarily implied her sleeping with him. Ms. Gold did not. Rape was the consequence of her not obeying his rules.

Women have expectations and rules too. A common expectation is that sex will lead to a more intimate relationship or greater commitment. But when the man does not follow these rules or expectations, he cannot be physically coerced into doing so.

Rather than poke Fred's eyes and possibly hurt him seriously, Ms. Gold allowed herself to be raped. She made a decision many women make, particularly relatively protected, middle-class women, who have been trained all their lives not to be violent. Accepting blame to the extent she did, particularly right after the rape, and her understanding of her rapist are also fairly common female responses to rape.

Intimidated by men's physical strength, in the past Ms. Gold "would just play along," at least when in a position with a man in which he could physically overpower her. The popular view is that men's greater physical strength no longer plays a role in perpetuating male domination in modern industrial societies, but it may be a more important factor than many realize in interpersonal relations between males and females.

Being able to defend ourselves is only half the battle. Being willing to defend ourselves is the other half. Unlearning to not fight is equally as important as learning to fight.

ELEVEN

Some Rapists Think They're Lovers

He wanted me to have an orgasm. When I finally figured out that he wouldn't come until I did, I just pretended that I had an orgasm.

What reward does a rapist get for rape? He takes quite a risk for something many can readily get for comparatively little money. The pleasure must be in the taking. Some rapists appear to prefer the woman to fight back, since a willing or even submissive woman presumably takes away from the feeling of power and conquest. Challenge makes the victory so much sweeter. This kind of rapist doesn't need to try to win the woman emotionally.

Other rapists appear to want to turn the woman on physically, as well as win her emotionally. It is still a power trip, but it expresses itself in a different way. Many of the victims reported that the men who raped them saw themselves as lovers, not rapists. Various explanations account for this peculiar attitude. Some rapists staunchly believe that women want a forceful man who won't accept their no at face value. They are unable to hear her protests for what they are. Others simply believe that women like to be raped.

Still others think that if a woman is stimulated in "just the right way" she will enjoy it. The conquest may seem more important if the rapist believes he has turned the woman on physically, particularly if it is against her will. Getting the victim to respond physically may also alleviate the rapist's guilt feelings.

The man who raped Janet Mathews did not perceive himself as a rapist. He kept asking her out on dates afterward, and assumed a paternalistic role toward her (he was concerned about her dropping out of school). He also wanted her to have an orgasm before he was able or willing to come himself. Ms. Mathews was the only victim interviewed who mentioned faking orgasm, but because of the vulnerable and frightening position they are in, many victims pretend to go along with the rapists' expectations. For example, some victims do not let them know that they see themselves as having been raped and agree to go out with their rapists later with no intention of doing so. A few victims actually go out with their rapists-who-think-they're-lovers, since they too see themselves as conquered property. This is especially likely if the victim was a virgin.

Ms. Mathews was nineteen years old when she was raped, and she was in the middle of her second year at one of the UC campuses. She is twenty-two now.

JANET MATHEWS: I was sitting in a sociology class, and my TA [Teaching Assistant] came up and sat next to me. He started talking to me during the lecture, and since he was witty I talked with him. Afterward I went with him to an outdoor coffee house on campus. We sat with the professor and talked. It was really interesting, except for one strange occurrence. John, the TA, hated dogs, and he kicked a dog while we were there That made me wonder a little about him.

He offered me a ride back to my dorm, which was about a half mile away, and I accepted because he was an interesting fellow and a TA. Everyone was my age at school, and it was nice to talk to somebody who was older. John was probably in his thirties. We were driving along when he suggested we go to a particular park. I liked the park, so I agreed. It's a huge park, and nobody else was there. We kept talking about sociology and the ways sociology is applied and what you can do with it after you graduate.

John had a brace on his foot that I had never noticed before. He kept doing things like hanging on trees and showing how strong he was. He picked up sticks and kind of thrashed them around.

It was four o'clock in the afternoon, getting toward sunset. We were still talking about sociology, you know, really academic stuff. We got to this lookout point, and he started talking about my sexuality and asking me how many guys I'd kissed. I said to myself, "Oh, God, what's this guy trying to do?" He really had me spooked at this time because he kept doing all these strange things on the side.

He kept coming up to me, and I kept moving away. I wasn't playing coy, I remember that distinctly. He tried to kiss me, and I moved away from him, but he kept coming after me, and he had a stick in his hand, and he said, "You know, you have to let me kiss you." Just from what he had done, I realized that I'd better let him kiss me.

INTERVIEWER: Were you scared of him?

Ms. MATHEWS: I was a little frightened by him because I'd never been with a fellow who did so many weird things to try to show he was masculine. He kept chinning himself on branches. And the cruelty that I'd noticed when he was kicking the dog came out. His whole facial expression changed. I suggested that we leave. I said I had to get back because I was living with my sister and her husband and we had dinner at five.

He grabbed me by the hand and said, "OK, let's go." I walked along behind him, and then he tried to take me off the path and down into a more secluded area. I said, "Now wait a second." He kept grabbing me, and it was frightening because he was really, really strong. And he kept picking up sticks and thumping the ground. I got really frightened, and then I panicked and started to run up the hill.

I was all dressed up. I was wearing heels and a skirt, and I couldn't get away. He grabbed me by the leg and dragged me down into this little place. The park was deserted, and it was ten miles away from town or from anywhere that I could get to. So there wasn't any point in yelling or screaming. Before this point he had been trying to go through a normal seduction scene, but he didn't try anymore.

He still had the stick in his hand, and I can't remember exactly what he said, but he was intimating that he would hit me with it. He got on top of me and held me with one hand, and he had the stick in the other hand like he was going to hit me.

Then he dropped the stick and started grabbing at my clothes. He didn't take my clothes off. He just pushed up my skirt and dragged down my underwear. I had panty hose on, and he pulled them down. I kept pulling my clothes back up every time he grabbed me. Then he got my arms behind my back, so after struggling for a while I decided, well, just let him screw me, you know. I used my strength to struggle against him, but I realized he was a TA, *my* TA, the guy who gave me grades, and to struggle too much would just blow it for me in the class.

INTERVIEWER: Was the class very important to you?

Ms. MATHEWS: Yeah. It was my major. The social climate at this place was free love and all that stuff. I was in a hip crowd, and I was supposed to give in to guys. It was sort of the social mores. But this guy was so cruel. With any other guy, I could have talked him out of it or said, "Come on, let's wait, this is really a bad time, I'm all dressed up," and pretended that there would be some other time when we could do it.

But John wouldn't take any of that. He started telling me how pretty I was. He said he was married, and he didn't exactly say that he was a good lover, but that he understood women. In fact, he was vicious.

He thought he was making love to me. He fondled me, stroked my sides, and grabbed his hands around my lower back. But he never took my clothes off other than pulling my underwear down, and he just pulled his pants down.

INTERVIEWER: Was it painful for you?

Ms. MATHEWS: I was tight, but it didn't hurt very much. He wasn't violent. He was trying to seduce me.

INTERVIEWER: How quickly did he come?

Ms. MATHEWS: Not at all quickly. He kept jabbing at me. He wanted me to have an orgasm. When I finally figured out that he wouldn't come until I did, I just pretended that I had an orgasm. Then he came. I stroked his hair and told him what a good lover he was, just to get him away from me and convince him to take me home. I wanted to get this thing over as soon as possible and get out of there and not have him hurt me.

After it was over, we walked back to his car. He drove me to school, and I got my car, and then I drove home.

INTERVIEWER: What kind of contact did you have with him afterward?

Ms. MATHEWS: He phoned me and tried to get together again with me. He'd come and sit next to me in class and talk with me.

INTERVIEWER: How did you feel about him then?

Ms. MATHEWS: I hated him, but I was very much afraid of him. I decided to drop out of school. You know, having a teacher rape you is the last straw. He kept phoning me and asking me to come over to his office and talk to him. One night I went over to his office with a girl friend because he kept demanding that I do so, and he threatened to come over to my house if I didn't.

So I went over there and told him I was going to drop out of school and go home. He got really upset about that. I just stopped going to class to avoid seeing him, and I told everybody that if he ever phoned, I wasn't home.

INTERVIEWER: Did you ever see him again?

Ms. MATHEWS: Whenever I saw him, I'd avoid him. He was still a TA there when I left.

INTERVIEWER: Who did you tell afterward?

Ms. MATHEWS: I told a close girl friend of mine the next day. She was really promiscuous, and to her it was like nothing had happened. She was used to that sort of thing herself. Her reaction frightened me, and I didn't want to talk about it. It made me feel stupid that I could have gone out to a park with a guy I didn't even know. I didn't have a boyfriend at the time so there was no male to talk to who could get irate.

INTERVIEWER: Who was the next person you told?

Ms. MATHEWS: My fiancé, about a year later. He got really mad and wanted to kill the guy.

I realized the way my girl friend reacted was the way all of my peers would have reacted, that I had really just done something stupid. I got the feeling that's what happens to girls. There's no way to buck it. I became very callous after that and started taking advantage of men.

The fact that it was socially acceptable for me to be taken advantage of and that nobody was going to get upset about it when I was so upset made me feel really very, very cold toward men. I'd seduce them, but I'd never nave an orgasm. I went through a whole castrating thing. I played strong female and got these nice young boys to love me, and then I'd dump them. I was mean towards men for a long time.

INTERVIEWER: Did it affect your behavior in any other way?

Ms. MATHEWS: I became a little more cautious before putting myself in a position where I'd be alone with a man. I stopped dressing up. I used to wear suits to school, but I stopped wearing them, and stuck to my blue jeans. I'm sure that part of the problem was that I had made myself attractive, and my hair had been down. So I started wearing my hair back all of the time. I didn't want men to see me as a female. I didn't want to attract a rapist.

INTERVIEWER: How did you feel about changing like this?

Ms. MATHEWS: It made me really sad. It made me withdraw and become much more secretive about my behavior. And I took more drugs and stuff like that.

INTERVIEWER: Did you feel at all revengeful?

Ms. MATHEWS: No. I felt mad at the world and at men, but not in an overt vengeful way. I just thought, "Wow, if this is the way it's going to be, I'm not going to play the part."

INTERVIEWER: Did you perceive it as rape at the time?

Ms. MATHEWS: Yeah.

INTERVIEWER: Did you say that to him?

Ms. MATHEWS: No.

INTERVIEWER: Have your feelings changed about it since it happened?

Ms. MATHEWS: I realize I could have avoided the whole situation if I had had a little more smarts. I was stupid enough to stay with him, and to get myself into a situation where I could be taken advantage of. Now I know how to maneuver my way around.

INTERVIEWER: Do you feel now that you would fight back more?

Ms. MATHEWS: I couldn't have in that situation. I tried, I struggled, but I realized his strength, and I didn't want to get hurt. I had been told, just like every girl has been told, that if you realize you're going to get raped, to sit back and relax because it can do a lot of damage to your insides if you don't.

INTERVIEWER: Do you think he had planned to rape you?

Ms. MATHEWS: Yeah, he knew what he was going to do before he even got me into the park. Otherwise he wouldn't have taken me out there.

INTERVIEWER: Did you feel in any way guilty or responsible for what happened?

Ms. MATHEWS: I felt really stupid. And I felt guilty because I had looked attractive. Then I was mad for feeling guilty because I had looked attractive. What kind of a world is this when you can't look attractive? I blamed my naiveté, but I blamed him more, because he knew what he was doing. I guess I was just a sucker because I like to talk to people, and at that time I thought people wouldn't hurt me if I was nice to them. It taught me a little bit more about people.

INTERVIEWER: Did you think about reporting the incident to the police?

Ms. MATHEWS: No. My girl friend didn't think it was rape, and I knew no one else would really think it was rape, because the guy was a TA, and he wore suits to class. He was a respectable person, and nobody would have believed me. I was just a stupid girl.

INTERVIEWER: Can you think of any solutions to the problem of rape?

Ms. MATHEWS: The only solution is to get men in a position where they don't have to show that they're masculine, because that's what the whole problem seems to stem from, that men can overpower women, and that's the sign of masculinity.

INTERVIEWER: How do you think that men can be changed?

Ms. MATHEWS: You have to start when they're kids. If there was more equality between the sexes, there wouldn't be as much rape going on.

In my case, the only problem really was that I was so innocent. I was sexually aware, but I was not humanly aware. It's hard. If you frighten a girl and tell her that a man is just out to rape her, before she's had any sexual experience, she won't ever have any meaningful sexual experiences. So, you have to point out quirks in human behavior, quirks that they should watch to know that someone is basically cruel, and that a cruel person will hurt them.

INTERVIEWER: What sexual experience had you had before you were raped?

Ms. MATHEWS: I had had a lot of sexual experience, and that's why I think my girl friend was shocked that I was upset. I had slept with three or four guys before that, so it wasn't new. She didn't see how it was different than with anyone else. That's what blew my mind, because the difference was that there was no consent on my part.

People tend to behave submissively toward those who have power over them. Given the power John had over Ms. Mathews, as a physically powerful man, as someone ten years older, and as a teacher, there are probably many women who would have been more submissive than she was, or decided to consent, even though they did not want intercourse. In her case, John's power over her wasn't simply in terms of his status in society, it was a direct power over her grades in school.

Rape often affects the victim's life way beyond the psychological trauma of having been violated. For Ms. Mathews, it resulted in her dropping out of school. This is all the more striking since initially she cared sufficiently about her school work to be wary of antagonizing John, who might "blow it for me in the class," even while being raped.

The feelings of guilt Ms. Mathews experienced after the rape are very common to rape victims. In part it may come from the way women are socialized to blame themselves rather than men. They are supposed to try to be attractive to men, but if they are raped by a man, they are held responsible. Ms. Mathews' subsequent attempt to stop trying to look attractive to men is a personal solution chosen by an increasing number of women.

Such a solution will continue to be merely personal as long as men value beauty as the most important quality in women and as long as men's power over women allows them to set the standards for women's behavior. Meanwhile, it seems good for women to show their rejection of the value, but it is not an entirely happy personal solution if the woman continues to want to beautify herself in culturally prescribed ways.

TWELVE

Fathers, Husbands, and Other Rapists

From the time I was, I guess, fourteen till almost seventeen, whenever my mother was gone, I'd find my stepfather by my bed at night. He would make advances, and when I ended up in tears sometimes, he'd say, "Well, what difference does it make? You've had all this before. Why should it bother you?"

Rape of daughters by fathers, and sisters by brothers, is more common an occurrence than we care to believe. Incestuous rape, often referred to simply as incest, is a doubly taboo topic. Julia Downing's stepfather was assaultive in his sexual overtures, but stopped short of rape. However, his behavior suggests that if a daughter has been raped by someone else, the taboo against incest is weakened.

In some circles it is argued that laws against incest should be lifted, and people should be less appalled by its occurrence. I would suggest, however, that the weaker the taboo (it is weaker with stepfathers and stepbrothers), the more instances of daughter and sister rape there would be. For it seems to me that the real "Oedipal complex" is not the child's sexual desire for the parent of the opposite sex, but the sexual desire of the parents for their children, particularly the father for his female children. To relax the incest taboo, then, would increase the instances of fathers raping daughters and brothers raping sisters, and would make it legal, just as it is legal for husbands to rape wives.

Ms. Downing is a forty-three-year-old white middle-class woman who lives in a well-to-do neighborhood with her three children and her second husband. She has been married for nineteen years. Ms. Downing was raped when she was four. Even more traumatic were her experiences with her stepfather, who used the fact that she had lost her virginity to try to get her to have intercourse with him. Grotesque as this is, the attitude that females who lose their virginity outside of marriage are soiled goods remains deeply imbedded in our culture. Few have probably considered what a devastating impact this aspect of sexist ideology can have on child rape victims.

JULIA DOWNING: My parents had taken two eighteen-year-old wards of the welfare department into their home to care for them. They received money from the county for doing this. The boys lived with us about three months. I know it wasn't too long. We lived in a rather small house. If I remember correctly, it had only two bedrooms. I slept in a baby crib, a so-called four-year crib, in my parents' bedroom.

My mother went to the store one day in the afternoon, and while she was gone, these two boys lifted me out of my baby crib and laid me on my mother and father's bed, which was right next to it. I can even remember the pattern of the chenille bedspread. It was a wedding ring pattern. I remember them hurting me and that there was blood. I remember afterward they put me back in the crib. I don't remember too much about it after that. I was told later that the boys ran off after this happened and that no attempt was made to find them.

My parents apparently didn't think that I would remember anything about it, so nothing was said to me, but when I first became aware of what intercourse was, I realized I'd been raped. I'm not sure how old I was when I realized it. I imagine I was around eleven or twelve. I began to ask questions then, and at first my parents evaded them, or said it was my imagination. But I could remember too much detail, and also I had been injured quite severely. A four-year-old child is not constructed to receive a man, and my uterus was pushed very badly out of line.

I started menstruating when I was thirteen, and I had very, very severe problems during my periods, and the doctors finally confirmed that obviously something had happened to me. Eventually it all came out, but in the meantime I had been raised with the idea that you must be a virgin when you marry. You must not get involved like this. Otherwise you weren't a nice girl. Even after I started dating, I always worried about how I was going to explain to my husband that I wasn't a virgin.

INTERVIEWER: And it wasn't reported to the police?

Ms. DOWNING: No. Families hid things like that. When I finally found out, my mother said to me, "Well, we were ashamed, and we just didn't want anybody to know." I took that to mean they were ashamed of me.

INTERVIEWER: What sort of relationship did you have with these boys? Did they play with you?

Ms. DOWNING: I don't know. The only thing I remember is the rape incident. I can remember the first one to touch me, because he stands out in my mind. He was a very husky boy and had blond hair. I can almost see his face. The other one I can't visualize very well. I don't remember much of anything else in my life at that time.

INTERVIEWER: But you remember the pain?

Ms. DOWNING: Yes. I remember crying. The thing that stands out in my mind, maybe more now because of the irony of it, is being lifted out of the crib. To me "crib" means baby, which has no sexuality at all. It is just incredible to rape a baby.

INTERVIEWER: It sounds as if you've never really talked about it with your parents.

Ms. DOWNING: That's right.

INTERVIEWER: It was a taboo topic?

Ms. DOWNING: Right, and I've had nothing to do with my parents in almost twenty years now.

INTERVIEWER: Do you have any ideas about why these boys raped you?

Ms. DOWNING: If I had to guess, I would suppose it was curiosity. They were probably horny and thought that it was safe. Probably they didn't realize they were doing physical or mental harm. After all, they couldn't get me pregnant.

INTERVIEWER: Why, then, did they leave immediately afterward?

Ms. DOWNING: Well, I was obviously injured. I suppose they were scared.

INTERVIEWER: Have you talked with friends about this experience?

Ms. DOWNING: For many years I didn't talk to anybody about it. I was trying to remember if my very closest friend in school knew, and I can't remember if I even told her. I kept it all to myself. I've talked about it more since I was older. I'd say in the last six or seven years.

INTERVIEWER: How have people reacted?

Ms. DOWNING: With sympathy and outrage. Being raped at four years old is shocking to people. If you're raped at eighteen or seventeen, why, that's seen as too bad, but rape of a child is an outrage. Even today I become nauseous when I read a newspaper or an article about a sexual attack on a young child. It happened so long ago, but it still affects me.

INTERVIEWER: How do you see the consequences of your rape experience?

Ms. DOWNING: There were so many other things that happened to me afterwards that reflect the psychological scars. I've had things happen to me that probably wouldn't happen to one out of a hundred people. I don't know how much of it had to do with that incident.

My father died when I was seven months old, and my mother died when I was about a year and three months, so I was adopted. From the time I was, I guess, fourteen till almost seventeen, whenever my mother was gone, I'd find my stepfather by my bed at night. He would make advances, and when I ended up in tears sometimes, he'd say, "Well, what difference does it make? You've had all this before. Why should it bother you?"

It was horrifying to me. I don't know whether his attitude was influenced by my being raped, or whether it was because I was adopted, or whether it would have happened anyway. But all these things build up, and they leave their scars. It really hurt, because up till then I was more fond of my father than I was of my mother, so it was quite a blow.

INTERVIEWER: Could you go into your experience with him a little more?

Ms. DOWNING: Well, he pursued me over a period of three years at every opportunity, until I was afraid to be alone in the house. Pleading didn't do any good.

INTERVIEWER: How far did your stepfather actually go with you?

Ms. DOWNING: Exposing himself. I'd wake up in the middle of the night and find his hands on me underneath the covers and things like that. He asked me to have intercourse, backing me into the corner, fondling me and kissing me and things like that. But there was never any actual penetration.

INTERVIEWER: How often did he do that?

Ms. DOWNING: When we were home alone, every time my mother would leave the house.

INTERVIEWER: Why do you think he came on to you?

Ms. DOWNING: I can remember my mother was always very cold, very unaffectionate. She would not have sex with my father. We had a two-bedroom house, and I can remember sometimes during the night hearing him beg her, but she wouldn't have anything to do with him. I always felt she was at fault an awful lot, but still, it's no excuse for what he did to me. He could have gone out and got a prostitute or somebody else.

I finally had to tell my mother about it, and of course, she didn't believe me. They wanted me to take a lie detector test, which I agreed to do. My father was very humiliated. I finally decided I'd really had it with this family when my mother came to me and said, "Please forgive your father. I want to keep my marriage together."

INTERVIEWER: You had to suffer again in order that the family look all right?

Ms. DOWNING: I hadn't thought about it that way, but I guess it's true. I left home when I got married at seventeen, almost eighteen. My marriage lasted a little over five years. After I was married, the first time my parents were at the house, I asked them why they hadn't been more honest about it. My mother said they thought I wouldn't remember. It was better forgotten. I think they had also gotten the advice from a doctor, so evidently they *did* call in a doctor, that I was so young I probably wouldn't remember it.

At the age of fifteen, they wanted me to have a hysterectomy because my uterus was so badly tilted and I had other internal damage. The doctor that examined me said that I probably would never be able to conceive. I had horrible periods. It was just like having a baby every month. My mother didn't want to allow them to do it, and I didn't particularly want it either, since I wanted to be able to have kids.

I managed to get through it, and after my first pregnancy, why, it wasn't so bad. I had a very rough first pregnancy, but my periods weren't so difficult after that, because things eventually straightened up with the birth. So, I was very fortunate that I had children.

INTERVIEWER: Your mother told the doctors that you had been raped?

Ms. DOWNING: I'm sure she did when I was not in the room. They never discussed it in front of me.

INTERVIEWER: Do you have anything more to say about your feelings about not being a virgin?

Ms. DOWNING: I don't want to use the word dirty, because I don't think I really felt dirty, but I did feel as though at some time or other I was going to have to pay the price for this with a man, and I dreaded this. Each time I would go with someone, if it looked like it was going to get serious, I had in the back of my mind that I was going to have to tell him. It was a big thing with me. Then it turned out that it really didn't mean anything at all, which was a tremendous relief.

INTERVIEWER: They didn't react badly when you told them?

Ms. DOWNING: Well, my first husband and I had intercourse about three months before we were married. I had told him just before, and it didn't make any difference to him. So I felt that I had done all that worrying for nothing.

INTERVIEWER: Was his acceptance of you a factor in why you slept with him and married him?

Ms. DOWNING: I don't know. I think I mostly wanted to get away from home. I think basically the reason that our marriage failed was that I was not prepared for the kind of sex my husband had to offer. I had had too much abuse at that point to handle it in the way he wanted it. I wasn't able to have orgasms when he was in me, and this just drove him right up the wall. He was determined to make me have them, but I couldn't. Probably the more he tried, the less I could. Sometimes he'd force me. He would hold me down on the bed, and sometimes I was raw, and it would really hurt, and I'd be screaming my head off. I guess there is marital rape.

INTERVIEWER: Was he like that when you were first courting?

Ms. DOWNING: No. He was gentle then.

INTERVIEWER: When did he start raping you?

Ms. Downing: We were married five years, so it was probably in the last year of our marriage. It wasn't that I wasn't willing to have sex. It's just that there were times when it was very, very painful. I don't know how much of the pain was due to the injuries that I had, but it was literally because it hurt that I sometimes didn't want it.

Interviewer: How often did it happen?

Ms. Downing: I've really blocked the whole thing out. I couldn't tell you how often. All I remember is that it happened.

Interviewer: Can you remember the first time?

Ms. Downing: Yeah. He was angry because I didn't want to have sex, so he threw me down on the bed and put his knees on my legs and held my arms down.

Interviewer: What happened afterward?

Ms. Downing: He was still angry because I couldn't have orgasms. It was kind of a personal affront to him, the fact that he couldn't do for me whatever it took.

Interviewer: And how did you react afterward?

Ms. Downing: I got more and more resentful. The more it happened, the more resentment built up until finally, that was it.

Interviewer: You were resentful specifically about these episodes?

Ms. Downing: Yes. There wasn't too much wrong with the marriage otherwise. But that ruined everything, because it was a constant battle.

Interviewer: Did you never have orgasms?

Ms. Downing: I could have a clitoral orgasm, but not a vaginal orgasm. I still cannot have vaginal orgasms. I talked to a doctor, and he said it may very well be that the muscle walls around my vagina were very badly torn when I was raped at four, and that it would probably be impossible for me ever to achieve it. The injury is all scar tissue.

Interviewer: But the best research suggests there is only one kind of orgasm.

Ms. Downing: Well, he wanted me to get it from intercourse. It drove him crazy that I couldn't. He felt that it was somehow reflecting on him, that he was inadequate or something.

Interviewer: What did *you* feel?

Ms. Downing: I thought that there was probably something wrong with me physically, that I was deformed or something. I blamed myself for it. I thought I should be able to, because after all, "all women do."

Interviewer: So when he resorted to raping you, did you feel you deserved it to some extent?

Ms. Downing: No. Otherwise I wouldn't have become angry about it, and there wouldn't have been any fight.

INTERVIEWER: Did you perceive yourself as being raped at the time?

Ms. DOWNING: Oh, yes.

INTERVIEWER: Did you tell him you felt he had raped you?

Ms. DOWNING: I don't think so. But in my own mind I considered that he was raping me because he was forcing me against my will, and I tried to fight him.

INTERVIEWER: Did he do this whenever you refused to have sex with him?

Ms. DOWNING: Only sometimes. Then there was also a period for about four or five months when he didn't touch me. He was punishing me. I didn't care, you know, but it was supposed to be punishment. When I finally said that I wanted a divorce, all he said was that I needed a good fucking, and it would straighten me out, and I'd be all right.

Here again, I don't know how much his forcing me had to do with my prior experience of rape, whether the idea that he could take me against my will was OK to him since it had already happened.

INTERVIEWER: Did you tell him about the way your father had treated you?

Ms. DOWNING: Yes. He was the one that insisted we get married so that I could get away from home. He was so outraged.

INTERVIEWER: It seemed from the way you talked earlier that you saw it as some problem of yours that you couldn't respond to your husband's sexual behavior.

Ms. DOWNING: Yes. I always had the feeling that there was something wrong with me that I didn't enjoy it. I thought that I didn't have the same kind of responses as other women. At that time I was extremely naive when it came to sex. At fifteen I was thinking that babies came out of your navel. I read all these books like *Forever Amber* in which women were supposed to be little animals and enjoy it as much as men. I just couldn't do it, so I figured there was something wrong with me.

INTERVIEWER: What sort of personality did your first husband have?

Ms. DOWNING: He came from a background where the man is boss. *He* has the final word. Woman's place is pregnant and barefoot in the kitchen. He wasn't as bad as his father in that kind of thinking, but it was basic in most of his reactions and attitudes. He had very, very set ideas about what a wife should do, the way the house should be run, and the way children should be raised. These ideas just didn't take with me. I've a strong personality in my own right.

INTERVIEWER: Did you tell any of your friends that he raped you?

Ms. DOWNING: Not that I recall. I guess because it's embarrassing to be raped by your husband. Almost none of our friends or the family or anyone knew that there was anything wrong with our marriage. People were shocked when we separated, and they came flocking in saying that something must be done to save it, because it was a good marriage.

INTERVIEWER: Did you ever tell anyone about it?

Ms. DOWNING: Not that I remember. As a matter of fact, I didn't even include that in the divorce proceedings. I guess I was really thinking more about our son, because there were so many things that I could have included and I didn't. I was concerned about the image of his father. These were not things that I wanted my child to know.

INTERVIEWER: Has it also been important for you to not see him that way yourself?

Ms. DOWNING: I can't see him any other way. It kind of blots out the good things that happened, though as a matter of fact, I'm having trouble remembering any of it. At this point it seems like it happened to somebody else. By the way, I used not to believe it was possible to be raped. As a child, yes, but not as an adult.

INTERVIEWER: After he first raped you, did you consent the next time that he wanted it and you didn't?

Ms. DOWNING: Yes. It didn't do any good to resist. I ended up getting hurt worse when I resisted than if I didn't.

INTERVIEWER: What effect do you think your first husband's raping you had on your attitudes toward yourself?

Ms. DOWNING: Had I not left him, I probably would have felt real stepped upon. But the fact that I said, "Enough is enough, I'm a human being, and you don't treat me this way," and that I left him, meant that I felt better about it as a person and as a woman.

INTERVIEWER: Did he realize that this was a big factor in why you were leaving him?

Ms. DOWNING: The only thing that I can remember him saying during the divorce proceedings was, "I don't see how you can leave me. I did everything in bed for you that was humanly possible to do." He just couldn't see anything wrong with what he did.

INTERVIEWER: Did your rape experiences affect your view of men?

Ms. DOWNING: I'm amazed I don't hate men, and people who know about my background are amazed too. Until I got into the women's movement, men were mostly my best friends, and I still have, even today, two or three men that I can say anything to, discuss any subject completely openly with, which I think is kind of unusual in a man-woman relationship. The fact that I was fat when I met them made it possible.

INTERVIEWER: Could you explain what you mean?

Ms. DOWNING: In going back and looking at my life, I've discerned certain patterns. I first noticed about seven or eight years ago that if a man made an uninvited pass, I would get a real panicky feeling I just can't explain. I thought it was a result of having been raped as a child, until I began to talk to other women about it and found out that most women feel the same way. They don't know how to handle this kind of thing either.

What it did to me was that I started eating. Weight became a defense. If you're fat, then you are less attractive sexually, and men more or less leave you alone. Then you can be friends with them. You can enjoy their company. You don't have to worry about sex entering into it. After two or three incidents where a husband of a best friend made a pass at me, upsetting me very much, I put on about twenty pounds in three months. I found that when I got slim again, passes happened more frequently, and I still was not reacting all that well to them.

I was understanding it better, but there's still that funny feeling that I've got absolutely no control over what happens to me, and I get a feeling of panic, still after all these years. I'm sure that it's due to more than the rape. I'm sure it's all the other incidents that happened to me as well.

This last time I was aiming at losing a hundred pounds. I lost about sixty-five pounds in about six months. Then men began to pay attention again. Just men in general, men that I didn't particularly want to pay attention to me. I wasn't interested in them. So over a period of about six months, I've gained almost twenty pounds back again.

INTERVIEWER: Would you say that your experiences of rape really haven't affected your views of men at all?

Ms. DOWNING: Oh, I'm sure they have, but I'm not at all hostile to a man I can respect and trust. But if a man comes on to me, and the only kind of interest he exudes is sexual, he turns me off. I have to have a friendship or something intellectually going with somebody before I would even be willing to consider something like that. Other women look at somebody across the room and say, "Boy, that guy really turns me on." I've never experienced that kind of thing, probably because of all that has happened to me.

INTERVIEWER: Do you have any solutions to the rape problem?

Ms. DOWNING: I would like changes in the education of kids. I think parents have to be prepared for the possibility that their daughters could get raped. They have to develop an attitude toward this from the time they're little, because otherwise, if it does happen, it'll probably be too late. If they've drummed a certain ethic into them all these years, they can't just suddenly say, well, now that it's happened, it's OK that you're not a virgin after all.

Boys should be educated to have a better sensitivity toward girls from the time that they're small. I suppose with the rapist who's mentally ill, it's silly to expect him to think of the consequences of his act, but for the man who thinks that all women want sex, that resistance is just a game, and that women really want to be raped—these men have been miseducated. I sometimes think that if men, not those who are sick but those who think it's a jolly time, realized what rape does to a girl for years and years afterward, they wouldn't do it.

Some men think the woman asks for it, that it's impossible to rape a woman, that a woman shouldn't turn a man on, and that if she does, she's got it coming. After all, women like it, it's probably the best experience they've ever had in their lives!

INTERVIEWER: That sounds like your first husband.

Ms. DOWNING: Very true. He thought everything is solved by sex, that no matter how you hurt someone emotionally, you can fix it all up by a good toss in bed. But it just doesn't work out that way, at least not for me.

Ms. Downing was raped as a child, molested by her stepfather, and raped by her husband. Taken altogether, her experiences challenge a common view, particularly popular with psychologists, that when people seem to suffer more than their "fair share" of victim experiences, they must be victim-prone, or masochistic, or in some way collaborative in the experiences. The alternative hypothesis that emerges from this interview is that, given one victimization, a person is more likely to experience further victimizations, because the very fact of having been victimized provokes aggressors. A rape victim may be more likely than the non-rape victim to bring out the rapist buried in many men.

Ms. Downing's experiences illustrate a number of important points. Her husband's effort to bring her to orgasm was as much a power trip as the more traditional disregard of a woman's pleasure. His inability to recognize his sexual demands as painful suggests his acceptance of the myth of female masochism. He trusted his beliefs about women more than he trusted what his wife said. Perhaps Ms. Downing's experience throws some light on why so many women fake orgasms, whatever kind is required.

Ms. Downing, in answer to a question on how she felt about not being a virgin, said she felt "as though at some time or other I was going to have to pay for this with a man, and I kind of dreaded it." Why, one wonders, didn't she feel that at some point some man was going to have to pay for what happened to her?

Rape and Race

"In order to commit an act one conceives of as degrading and sinful, one must find an object one considers degraded and iniquitous. In the minds of the majority of white men during the era of slavery the black woman satisfied these conditions. The modern white supremacists are little different from their slave holding ancestors.

"To some degree, however microscopic, all white men in America, save a few, carry in their perception of Negro females a dark sexual urge that borders on the vulgar."
—Calvin C. Hernton, *Sex and Racism in America*

"Many whites flatter themselves with the idea that the Negro male's lust and desire for the white dream girl is purely esthetic attraction, but nothing could be farther from the truth. His motivation is often of such a bloody, hateful, bitter, and malignant nature that whites would really be hard pressed to find it flattering."
—Eldridge Cleaver, *Soul on Ice*

"The real problem in America . . . is between black men and white men. Both see themselves as warriors.

"Black men talk about change when what they really mean, I think, is exchange. They want to take over the positions of power white men have . . ."
—Maya Angelou, quoted in the *San Francisco Chronicle*

THIRTEEN

White Man Wants a Black Piece

He said, "Well, I've made it with a black girl. You know, you're the first one I've ever made it with. I feel so good. I was so afraid that I wouldn't be able to satisfy a black woman. But now I know I can."

Few black women who have been raped, particularly if the rapist was white, are willing to talk about it. This form of racism and sexism combined is seen by many blacks as doubly humiliating and degrading, as a brutal reminder of the past when such rape was commonplace.

A seventeen-year-old black woman, who was raped by two white men, broke down in tears during the interview and was too upset to describe the rapes except to say that immediately after being raped the feelings she experienced most acutely were embarrassment and shame. When she was asked if she had reported the rapes, she said, "No. I couldn't go to a white police station and tell the white pigs to look for some white men that raped me. A rape might seem like a trite experience in contrast to all the other injustices. . . . Black women have been raped for a long time, but still I am very bitter about it."

Many black women have a very political perspective on white rapists, which adds to the trauma and makes it much harder for the victims to talk about their experiences. This perspective is also apparent in the interview with Sonia Morrell that follows.

Ms. Morrell's mother is black and her father white. She is very light skinned, and people are sometimes confused about her racial identity. She, however, considers herself black, and that is where her identity lies.

Ms. Morrell was raped in Massachusetts when she was twenty years old. She was first interviewed three or four months after it happened and then again, a year later. At the time of the first interview, it was still too early to know how the rape had affected her, and a second interview provided the opportunity to ask some further questions.

SONIA MORRELL: It was a Friday night, and there was supposed to have been this party on campus. But there wasn't a party, and so about three of my friends and I came back from a God-awful Friday night dinner to the dorm and said, "OK, where are the guys? Where is everybody?" We looked into the living room, and there were these two white guys sitting in there, so we went in, and this girl from our dorm was down there talking to them, and she introduced us to them. It turned out that they were frat guys from X [a prestigious private college].

I was talking to the guy named Vic. The other guy, Bob, was whispering to the girl who introduced us, and they kept looking at me. The girl came over to me and said, "If Bob asked you out, would you go out?" I said, "Who's Bob?" I haven't run into that since high school—where the guy can't even come over and ask you himself.

So he said, "We're having this wine and cheese party tomorrow night at our house. Would you like to come?" I said, "Oh, you have a house?" He said, "Yeah, a fraternity." I thought that my two friends and I could drive to this party, but he said, "Well, I was just inviting you." I said, "Oh, OK." He said, "I'll come and get you and bring you back."

Afterward I panicked, especially considering he was white, and I discussed it with my friends. I have white friends, but never a white fraternity guy. I didn't know how to relate to this guy. Everybody said, "Go, Sonia, because it will be a good experience for you, and you'll learn something." Anyway, it's not every day you get to go to a cheese and wine party, and there was supposed to be a band, so I said, "OK, OK."

Bob came. On the way there we talked about something racial. He said something about this black guy he knew. The way he was talking about him, I really didn't dig it. I thought he's either got a lot of gall or he's ignorant. So I said, "Do you know that I am black?" He said, "Oh, yeah." I figured that the girl he kept talking to the night I met him had told him. I asked her later if she had, and she said that he had asked her, "She's part white, isn't she?"

We arrived, and there were all these white frat people and sorority girls there; everybody there had blond hair. There were no nonwhites there. Just me. The band was really hip. They kept looking at me, and one of the guys in the band turned to me and said, "What are *you* doing here?" I said, "I don't know." He said, "You don't belong in a place like this, because this is the shits." And I said, "What are *you* doing here?" He said, "Well, we're getting paid." I said, "Well, I didn't have anything else to do, so I thought it might be interesting." Then good old Bob came back.

INTERVIEWER: What did he look like?

Ms. MORRELL: He was maybe six one. He was pretty tall and in build a little bit overweight. He was really strong. Really! I'm small, so compared to me he was very big. He was between twenty and twenty-two. He came from a wealthy family. I thought he was really handsome, and he seemed nice except for the racial thing.

We danced, and he kept drinking a whole lot of wine. I had one glass of wine, and after that I drank Seven Up, and I ate a lot of cheese. We danced slow, and he said, "Wow, I've never danced with a girl who could follow me before." He started getting chummy, you know, wrapping his arms around me a little bit more, and I said, "Easy, fella."

We went outside. He held my hand and introduced me to his friends, and his friends were very strange and kept saying, "Wow, you're really hip, aren't you? Wow, Bob, she's hip." I was looking at the girls with their blond hair, and their flower pant suits giving me the eye, like, get out of here. It was pretty bad. But it was interesting because I had never experienced anything like this, so it didn't really bother me.

The party was coming to an end. Bob had been drinking a considerable amount of wine, but I was feeling great. I felt a little bit mellow from the one glass of wine. He said, "Do you want to go upstairs to my room?" and I said, "For what?" He said, "Just to talk." I said, "OK." I wanted to make sure everything was cool. He had been pretty nice, and he was interesting to me.

We went to his room, and I sat down in the chair, and he sat down on the bed, and he was telling me about his life when all of a sudden he grabs my arm and tries to pull me up. I just sat there. I didn't want to get up. He said, "Come on, sit over here on the bed with me. It's hard for me to talk to you in this arrangement." I said, "OK," and I got on the bed with him. He came at me immediately. I figured, OK, one kiss was cool. So he kissed me. It was a crummy kiss, and I was thinking, "Oh, I have to leave."

He kissed me once more, and I looked at my watch, and I said, "Oh, wow, I better get back to the dorm soon. I didn't sign out." He said, "I saw it when you signed out. I've taken girls out from your college before. I know all about the signing-in stuff." I said, "But I really do have to get back because it's getting late, and I'm tired, and I have a lot of studying to do tomorrow." He said, "You can stay a little bit longer." I said, "OK. OK. Then I have to go." He said, "OK." So we talked again.

Then he attacked me again. We started to struggle. I was not responding to his kisses. Then he started with my clothes. I had thought that it was just going to be one of those little make-out sessions, but it was something else. It was terrible. I had these knit pants on, and he kept pulling them down, and I kept pulling them up.

He got my shirt unbuttoned. Then I'd start to button it up, then he'd start to pull my pants down, then I'd pull them up, then he'd unbutton my shirt. It was like a perverted movie.

He was rather large and quite strong, but he wasn't violent. He was persistent. It was this struggle, struggle, struggle, back and forth. I was really fighting him off, but it was not doing much good. I said, "I want to go! Please take me back to school." He said, "No." I said, "Please, Bob, please. Take me back to school. I don't know you, and I'm not the kind of girl who likes to go hopping into bed with people. Please take me back." "No," he said.

So I said, "OK, I'm going to leave then." So he grabbed my purse and said, "You won't get far without your purse." I said, "Oh, come on. You can't be this hard up that you want to go through all this stuff. Give me my purse!" I was really mad. He said, "No." So I thought, "Well, I'll call school and have someone come and get me." But I didn't know where the phone was, and I didn't even think about my best friend who was half an hour away from where we were. I said, "Look. You said you'd pick me up, and you said you'd take me back. Please, please take me back." "No," he said.

"I haven't done anything to deserve this," I said.

"Yeah," he said, "but I've shown you a good time, now I want you to show me a good one." I said, "Look, it was a shitty evening. So now I've given you back your shit. Take me back to the dorm." He said, "No. You know you're lying. You had a good time." It was just terrible. He said, "If you'll make love with me, I'll take you home." I said, "No! Take me home now!" So he continued to fight, fight, fight. He got my pants off. I don't know how he managed that. It was about two o'clock in the morning, and I was getting pretty tired. Then he started with my underpants, and that was a huge struggle. It was incredible. He had taken his own pants off, but still had his underpants on. He pulled my underpants down, and he fell down on top of me, his penis was next to my vagina, but still in his underpants. He started blowing in my ear, because he really thought he was turning me on. He started putting his tongue in my ear and blowing in it and thumping against me with his damn penis. Hell!

So I kept trying to push him and push him and push him, and he kept saying, "What's the matter with you? Aren't I pleasing to you?" He had grabbed my breasts like they were two doorknobs, and he was gripping them painfully. I was getting pretty tired, and somehow he got his penis out and pressed himself inside me. He must have been two inches long, because I didn't even feel it. I just felt this thrust, and I realized he was inside me.

I felt like some huge gigantic vagina. I didn't even feel him. He was thumping up and down, and breathing deeply, but I didn't move. My legs were together, but suddenly he grabbed my legs, and he said, "Spread," and threw them apart. Shit! Then he comes flying out of me and turns me around on my stomach, and he grabs me so I'm on my knees and pushes himself into me again. I guess he really thought he was doing a whole lot. I was like a dish rag. I just had had it. And he just went thump, thump, thump.

All I kept thinking about was how I was going to get to leave. Then he threw me on my back again and came into me from the front, and it's bam, bam, bam. Then suddenly he stopped. And I thought, "My God, now he's had a heart attack." I didn't understand what was wrong with him. Then he just rolled over, and I felt wetness, and I figured, "Oh, that's what it is."

When he was making out with me earlier he had said, "I hope you're protected." And I'd said, "What do you mean?" He'd said, "Well, I would use a condom if you weren't." I'd said, "You're not going to get to use a condom." So I guess he assumed that I was protected. So after lying still, he rolled over and asked me, "Do you have your pills in your purse?" I said, "Oh, yeah, sure. I just carry them around with me daily for exciting adventures like this." Then he fell asleep, just like that. Ka-bam. I mean he "came" just like he went to sleep, ka-bam.

I wanted to go to the bathroom, but it was downstairs. And in this frat house with all these perverted frats, I was afraid that if I got up and went outside, they would attack me. So I lay there, and then I woke him up, and I said, "Please, can we leave." Immediately he started in again. Tha-gump, tha-gump, tha-gump, and I just lay there. This time he didn't try all his little positions. He came, bam, fell out, and then he sloshed over me, and went back to sleep again.

I *had* to go to the bathroom, my bladder was bursting. I put on my long sweater, and I go out in the hall. I felt horrible. I kept thinking that I was like a receptacle for his sperm. I wanted to wash. I went into the boys' bathroom, and when I came out this frat guy who was asleep on the stairs woke up and said, "Hey, do you want to ball? Oh, wow, I see you're already here balling somebody else. Out of sight. Out of sight. Well, when you get done with them, why don't you come with me?" This made me scared to leave the place.

I went back into Bob's room. I felt better. I lay down on the bed. It must have been about 5:30 A.M by that time. I had my sweater on, and my underpants and my bra, and I was just lying there. He woke up, and this claw comes over and attacks my breasts again. I pushed his hand away, and he said, "What's the matter?" I said, "I want to leave." He said, "Why? Didn't you like it? What is it? You don't like white guys? Tell me, what is the difference between black guys and white guys?" I said, "Black guys have rhythm." And he said, "Oh, how do you mean? They move with rhythm?" I said, "Yeah."

So then I guess he had to prove his manhood to me, and he comes flopping on top of me again, and I said, "Hold it, hold it, hold it." I had my underpants on, and here he's going to try to shove himself up through my underpants. I said, "Hold it, hold it, hold it. Forget it. OK? You're an excellent love maker. I want to go home."

He said, "Well, I've made it with a black girl. You know, you're the first one I've ever made it with. I feel so good. I was so afraid that I wouldn't be able to satisfy a black woman. But now I know I can." I felt like throwing up on the bed. I said, "You're really sick!" which was a mistake, because he started on this whole passion thing, that he really dug me, and that he and I could really get it on.

It was day by then, and he said, "Come on. Let's get up and get dressed." He acted like it'd been the love affair of his life. He said, "Come on, I'll take you downstairs, and we'll feed you. You're so skinny." We got down to the little dining room and he said, "OK, what do you want to eat?" I said, "Nothing." "You have to eat something." So I said, "OK, I'll have a cup of coffee." He said, "You've got to have something else." I said, "OK, I'll eat one of these doughnuts." He said, "No, you've got to eat more than that. Take two doughnuts, and you've got to eat some cereal." So I'm eating the stuff, and he's reading the newspaper, and he saw an article. I don't remember what it was, but he made an extremely racist comment. I said, "I'm going to throw up." He got upset. I said, "Don't talk to me, I'm going to throw up. Really. Just leave me alone." I really thought that I was going to lose it any minute. So then he said, "Well, we're going to go."

We got in the car and we're driving along when we saw this girl that I know and that he knows from my school, and so we gave her a ride back. Bob kept putting his hand over and patting my thigh. Back at the dorm he said, "What do you want to do next weekend?" I said, "Anything but be with you!" He said, "Oh, come on!"

INTERVIEWER: Did you see what Bob did as rape?

Ms. MORRELL: No, I didn't feel that I had been raped. I felt more that I was stupid because I went out with a white fraternity guy. I had been bothered in high school by white guys wanting to get a black girl to see what they're like. So I blamed myself for going out with him. Also I didn't think of it as rape because I knew him and because I consented to go. At the time I thought rape was a man coming out of the bushes and attacking you, so somebody you knew couldn't rape you.

INTERVIEWER: When did you perceive it differently?

Ms. MORRELL: When a rape victim told me about her experience, which was similar to mine, I stopped her and said, "My God, that same thing happened to me."

INTERVIEWER: So when she talked about it in those terms, you agreed with her that it was rape?

Ms. MORRELL: Yes. I thought she was absolutely right.

INTERVIEWER: Once you perceived it as rape, did that change how you felt about it?

Ms. MORRELL: Oh, hell, yes! I don't feel I'm to blame at all. I have every right in the world to go out with a man, and I have every right in the world to say no, and my no should be respected. Men can go out, and they don't get raped.

INTERVIEWER: Do you think that the experience affected your sexual relationships with men?

Ms. MORRELL: The rape was a big blow. With my boy friend I always felt like I was going through the routine. You know, I'm supposed to do this, and I do it, because I'm supposed to please him. But I didn't feel anymore that I was getting anything out of it. Then right after talking to that other woman who was raped, I started becoming aware that I had rights as a woman. It's funny, because I've always demanded equality economically and in every other sphere, but sexually my demands were absolutely zero, so I started really thinking about that.

I didn't want to think that all white men were like Bob. In the summer I had a white boy friend, and it was fine. But what I noticed is I have completely rejected traditional ideas of masculinity. I don't want somebody very big or strong, I imagine because of fear. I see a man who's built big, and I immediately become paranoid. And I'm very afraid of older men. Past a certain age, they just really frighten me.

INTERVIEWER: Did your experience affect your attitude toward men in other ways?

Ms. MORRELL: Well, I don't trust men. I went on a date a couple of weeks ago and was absolutely petrified. I was pacing the floors about going. I really am afraid, and I have very little desire to go out and meet more men, because I'm afraid of trusting somebody and having them hurt me.

INTERVIEWER: You feel that it was your experience with Bob that caused this?

Ms. MORRELL: Oh, yeah. I get very nervous when a man tries to talk to me at a party or something. I'm afraid I'll like him. I'll think he's nice, and then he'll push himself on me. Another thing it did was confirm my belief about men who brag about sex being the shittiest at it!

INTERVIEWER: Did it affect your attitude toward yourself at all?

Ms. MORRELL: When it first happened, I thought I was carrying the burden that all black women carry. Now I feel that I'm just taking what all women have to take, but what all women should refuse to take.

INTERVIEWER: Did you find yourself feeling guilty or responsible in any way?

Ms. MORRELL: Immediately afterward I did. Now I feel very guilty that I didn't just go out and hit him really hard in the mouth, because I am pretty strong, and I could have done that. That makes me damn mad. I was still following that feminine role that says I wouldn't be able to do anything. Even if I'd just have screamed!

INTERVIEWER: Why didn't you?

Ms. MORRELL: Because if I drew attention to what was happening, everyone would blame me and say I was stupid. I felt that they would believe him, because he was white, and he was a fraternity guy, and I was just this black girl. I just thought it was useless.

I believe strongly that a black woman against a white man has got very little chance at all. Generally any woman against a man has little. And then I was really afraid to be stuck on that campus in that area, because it was all fraternity houses, and I didn't know where I was.

INTERVIEWER: Can you remember what your predominant feeling was at the time of the rape?

Ms. MORRELL: Well, first I was afraid that he was going to call in his frat brothers and run a train on me, because he said they were in the hall. I remember hearing in high school about girls that had had trains run on them.

INTERVIEWER: That means it's a gang rape?

Ms. MORRELL: Yes. One right after the other.

Also, I really felt hurt, because I had trusted him and thought he was nice. But the feelings of anger and disgust were stronger. I said things to him that were really nasty. I kept putting him down, saying he was really a shitty love maker. I'm using the word *love making* now because that's exactly how I thought of it. Like I said, I couldn't accept that he was raping me. I thought that he was making me make love with him. So I wouldn't move, and I kept faking yawns. But then when he went to sleep, I cried all night.

INTERVIEWER: Did you ever see or hear of him again?

Ms. MORRELL: Yeah. He called me up to ask me out to a play. I hung up on him. I thought he was out of his mind. I never thought he'd ever mention my name again, but he remembered my whole name and asked one of my friends if I still lived in the same dorm.

INTERVIEWER: So is that the only contact you've had with him afterward, indirectly or directly?

Ms. MORRELL: Yeah. Every now and then I think I see somebody who looks like him, and I get really paranoid, and I want to run.

INTERVIEWER: What was your predominant feeling after the rape incident?

Ms. MORRELL: I told my close friend, the girl I live with now, what happened.

INTERVIEWER: Was she the first person you told?

Ms. MORRELL: Yeah. And this interview is the second. I have never told anyone else. I was embarrassed to tell my friend, but I did because I was so upset. I went into a deep depression for a couple of days. I didn't want to do anything. I stayed in my room and watched television and read. I just couldn't handle it, and then when he called a week later, that was too much.

INTERVIEWER: How did your friend react to it?

Ms. MORRELL: She is black, and she reacted by making digs at whites. She said, "All they want is to use us." But she never mentioned the word rape.

INTERVIEWER: Did she blame you at all?

Ms. MORRELL: No, because she's my friend. But there was a hint of "you shouldn't have gone." But she felt guilty because she had told me to go!

INTERVIEWER: How long did your feeling of depression last?

Ms. MORRELL: I think it lasted about four days. I was getting back to normal and feeling pretty good, and then he called, and then it lasted again for about three days. I had broken up with my boy friend, but he came to see me a week afterward, and I didn't want him to touch me.

INTERVIEWER: Did you tell him what had happened?

Ms. MORRELL: Oh, no. I never would have told him, because I think he would have killed me. Black men are pretty heavy about white men messing with black women. I knew he would blame me and say I was stupid to have gone. I also knew that he'd get his friends, and they'd probably go and beat the hell out of the guy.

INTERVIEWER: And you didn't want that?

Ms. MORRELL: No. I didn't want to be reminded of it. I just wanted the whole thing to be buried. I was embarrassed. It wasn't that I thought that my boy friend would get in trouble, because all the black students down there would've rallied around him, and it would've been cool. But I just decided the easiest thing was to forget it.

INTERVIEWER: Why don't you tell people now?

Ms. MORRELL: I don't want my boy friend to know. I think he would generalize about what happened to me and apply it to all whites. I'm sure he would.

We broke up for a while, and he wanted to know if I'd gone out with anybody, and I said yes. And the first question he asked was, "Well, was he white?" I know it'd hurt him too much to tell him, and there is no sense in that. He can't deal with things like that.

Also, I won't tell my mother, because she would be hurt too much. I don't see any reason to cause her pain, and it's not bothering me anymore.

INTERVIEWER: Could you say anything else about how you perceived your rapist's personality and his motivation?

Ms. MORRELL: I definitely think that there was a master-slave thing going on. I think a lot of white men really want to screw a black woman. When I was dancing slow with him, he was making some racial comments, like, "I've always noticed black people dance much better than white people."

He really wanted to be a stud, I think. That's why I started trying to blow his game away. I figured I can't hurt him physically, so mentally I'm going to do him in. I think he believed having a black woman helped him to prove his manhood. Also, I think he knew that if it was somebody white, like most of the girls that he knew from the sororities, he'd just be ruined, because that girl would have more power to do something about it, to cause him trouble. I guess he felt there was no risk with me.

INTERVIEWER: Did he expect you to enjoy it?

Ms. MORRELL: Oh, yeah. He kept saying things like, "Do you like this? How's this position? Well, that was really nice, wasn't it?" and, "How do you like this?" or, "Do this. Don't you like this? This is really good, huh?" And I'd say, "Shit," or something, and then he'd get real upset.

INTERVIEWER: What did you think of his expecting you to enjoy it?

Ms. MORRELL: I couldn't believe it. I thought he was completely fucked.

INTERVIEWER: What would you say his politics were?

Ms. MORRELL: He saw himself as a white liberal, and he thought he was going to help all black people, but he is an extreme racist.

INTERVIEWER: Do you imagine that he had raped other women before you?

Ms. MORRELL: I really doubt it. He was really clumsy. I was equally clumsy because I had never been through it before either. It seemed like the first time for both of us. Now, I know what I should have done. And if he had done it before, he would have been a lot more on his toes, a lot quicker.

He took too many risks. I remember there was a pocket knife on the bedside table, and I thought maybe I could kill him. But I decided I really couldn't handle that. But had he been experienced, he wouldn't have left something like that out. And he even got up and went to the bathroom and left me in the room alone. I could have split and called the police, but I didn't have a dime. Still he didn't know that. So I really don't think he had done it before. He probably is one of those smooth make-out men usually. He's got the kind of label that a lot of girls dig. I know the white girls in my dorm thought he was really hot stuff.

INTERVIEWER: What would you do now if you were in the same situation?

MS. MORRELL: I would hit him. I would really hit him. And I really, really feel stupid that I didn't scream, because I should have screamed. The band was still downstairs, and I could have screamed. I should have just busted out of his room and told him to shove my purse up his ass. I should have gone down and said to the band, "Man, you got to get me out of here. That guy has my purse, and he's trying to rape me." And I know that they would have helped me. Then I could have gotten my purse back.

The thing was, I didn't think about it. I was so involved in the struggle that I didn't reason about what I should be doing. By the time I realized what was happening, it was too late. And then that frat guy was sitting out in the hall, drunk, guarding the stairway. I was pretty much overcome with shock at the time.

You have to be prepared for it, and I was not prepared. But I'm prepared now, and somebody would be in for a definite shock if they tried that on me again. I'd really raise hell.

Many blacks consider white liberals to be as racist as white conservatives. Neither is to be trusted. Bob's actions certainly reinforce this attitude.

In the days of slavery black women were considered to be savage and lustful. This perception of black women rationalized white men's desire to use them to satisfy all their "sinful" sexual urges. At the other extreme, white men placed white women on a pedestal as pure, sexless, virtuous beings. Out of this dichotomization of women into black whore and white virgin arose the belief that to satisfy sexually the black woman, the queen of sex, was proof of true manhood. In addition, many whites view black men as superstuds. The fantasy that they have larger genitals and a greater sexual capacity is widespread. It follows that if a white man can satisfy a black woman, who is presumed to be accustomed to black men as lovers, then surely he must be a stud too.

Ms. Morrell portrays her alienation from what Bob was doing to her so vividly, it should be educative reading for those who think, as did her rapist, that women are always turned on by the old "in-and-out." Men like Bob do not necessarily think women enjoy being raped. They simply do not regard sexual coercion as rape at all.

Ms. Morrell's conviction that her black men friends would have beaten

Bob up had she told them what he had done to her suggests that blacks might be more aware than whites of the political nature of rape, at least when white racism enters into it. In addition, they would know that the chances of obtaining justice through the usual channels are virtually nil when a black woman is raped by a white man. Therefore if they want any justice, they have to make it happen themselves. Black men's rage at their own oppression by whites, as well as their rage at feeling humiliated in their role as protectors, has led some to seek revenge by raping white women.

FOURTEEN

Rape and Black Rage

We're just getting back at you for what happened in the olden days, what the white men did to our black women and the slaves.

In *Soul on Ice* Eldridge Cleaver quotes from a poem of LeRoi Jones: "Rape the white girls. Rape their fathers. Cut the mothers' throats." [1] Cleaver comments: "I have lived those lives and I know that if I had not been apprehended I would have slit some white throats. There are, of course, many young blacks out there right now who are slitting white throats and raping the white girl. They are not doing this because they read LeRoi Jones' poetry, as some critics seem to think. Rather, LeRoi is expressing the funky facts of life." [2]

Similarly, Cleaver's writing about his desire to rape white women presumably is not the explanation for other black men's desire to do so. Rather, the same factors that led Cleaver to decide to rape have led and continue to lead other black men to rape white women. Like Cleaver, the rapists described in this chapter used rape to strike back at whites for their oppression of blacks.

One of the consequences of viewing women as the property of men is that rape can be used to get back at men as well as women. The men who raped Angela Meyers and Roberta Thompson apparently saw themselves as avenging the white man's rape of "their" black women, restoring in the process their masculine image as owners and protectors of black women.

Cleaver is very explicit about this motivation:

Rape was an insurrectionary act. It delighted me that I was defying and trampling upon the white man's law, upon his system of values, and that I was defiling his women—and this point, I believe, was the

1. Eldridge Cleaver, *Soul on Ice*, p. 14.
2. Ibid., pp. 14–15.

most satisfying to me because I was very resentful over the historical fact of how the white man has used the black woman. I felt I was getting revenge.[3]

Remarkably, Cleaver did not appear to see the contradiction between his anger at white men for using black women and his using black women himself. "I became a rapist," he writes. "To refine my techniques . . . I started out by practicing on black girls in the ghetto . . . and when I considered myself smooth enough, I crossed the tracks and sought out white prey." [4]

It should not be forgotten, however, that black females are far more subject to rape by black men than are white females. Furthermore a disproportionate number of rapists also come from the lower class. It is probable that the sexism of black men and lower-class whites is more likely to be expressed in the sexual realm than is the case for middle-class whites, since society restricts their opportunities to be powerful in most other domains. It is also likely, however, that more white middle-class rapists get away without getting caught or reported.

Ms. Meyers was seventeen and a virgin when she and her friend Ms. Thompson were attacked four years ago. She got as far as the eleventh grade in her formal education and described herself as lower class.

ANGELA MEYERS: I was on the beach with my girl friend, Roberta, and a guy named Sam. It was about ten miles away from where we lived, and we were hitchhiking home.

Two rather large black guys in a big blue car stopped and said, "Come on, we'll give you a ride." So the three of us got in the car, and we got as far as Sam's house, and they asked him to get out. I said, "Sam, I want to go with you," but Roberta said, "No, come on over to my house for dinner."

I'd never really had anything to do with black people before, but I thought I could trust them. Still I was kind of torn between going with Sam, like my guts said, and staying with Roberta, like my head said, since I was concerned about her safety and well-being.

It ended up that I stayed with Roberta and these guys, who were supposed to drive us to her house. But they never did. They got onto the freeway and headed downtown. I started feeling kind of scared. I was in the front seat with the driver, and Roberta was in the back seat with this other guy. He was making out with her, and she seemed to be enjoying it.

They took us down to this house where there was an old, old black

3. Ibid., p. 14.
4. Ibid.

woman inside. She looked like a gypsy or a fortune teller or something. There were a bunch of big black guys around there saying, "White pussy, white pussy," so I was really getting scared shitless.

Then these guys said, "Come on, Let's get in the car." So we got in the car since we weren't about to stay there. I'd never been in that area before, and by this time I was pretty scared. We got to an apartment, and we went inside with them. We couldn't really say too much or do too much, and I really didn't think that they were going to rape us, or try to kill us.

What happened was that this big guy, Geoffrey—he was kind of the leader of the two—locked the door, turned on some music really loud, and told me to take off my clothes. I said, "No! Fuck, no!"

He started pushing me around, so I took off my clothes. I had no choice. Roberta, in the meantime, was getting fucked in the back room by the other guy, and Geoffrey was trying to do it to me. He was chasing me around, and I was saying, "No. Get away, get away."

Finally he took me into the bedroom and proceeded to try and rape me. But I wouldn't let him. So he started to strangle me and throw me around. He was strangling me pretty hard. In fact, I lost my breath and almost passed out. The other guy stopped him. He said, "Don't kill her. Just don't kill her."

I kept feeling like I was going to vomit all over the place. I kept running to the bathroom, feeling nauseated and drinking water. I had this really dry feeling in my mouth, and it wouldn't go away. Then this guy and his friend said, "We're just getting back at you for what happened in the olden days, what the white men did to our black women and the slaves." They were just full of prejudice and hate, and I said, "Hey, I'm not even from America. I'm from England. My parents are from Russia and Poland. I didn't have anything to do with slavery." They said, "Well, you're white."

There wasn't really too much I could say. I tried to persuade them by offering them money to stop what they were doing, but they said no. So it ended up that this guy tried to make me blow him. He had a penis about as long as a horse's and as fat as a horse's. It was sickening, you know. It was just really sickening. It was real dirty, and he tried to make me suck it, but I started throwing up. He almost choked me with his cock.

So he tried to screw me again, but I wouldn't let him. I told him I was a virgin, and that I had to have surgery, I had to have myself cut, so that I could have sex, because there was something there. I was really tense and tight and not letting him in. But I didn't want to die, so finally I said, "Well, shit, go ahead." But he couldn't get it in. He tried, but he was so big he couldn't do it. So he got really pissed off and threw me around some more.

I was in a total state of shock and paranoia the whole time. The whole incident lasted about four hours. It was the worst thing that ever happened to me.

INTERVIEWER: So he never had intercourse with you?

MS. MEYERS: No. He gave up and went to ball my friend, Roberta.

His friend came and tried to do it with me. First he tried making me blow him. Again, I just got totally sick, and I wanted to vomit on him. I don't remember if I did it or not. I was pretty much in shock. He didn't try to screw me. It was strange. In fact he's the one that stopped the other guy from strangling me to death. I was pretty lucky that he did. The other guy, Geoffrey, said that what they were going to do was kill us and throw us in some ditch over where the sewers are. I was pretty scared. Roberta was too, but she was just kind of balling them.

Then two more guys came in, and the first two left. They had a bunch of reds. Seconal and grass were lying all over the place. They were really loaded. A big guy named Frank immediately went in the other room and started to ball Roberta. She just let him. She couldn't do much, and she was pretty sick then too.

I talked the guy who was in the front room with me into taking me down to a telephone booth, since there was no telephone there. I told him that I had to call my mother. He was high on reds, and I guess he was kind of out of it, so he took me down. My mother was worried because I was supposed to be home at four o'clock, and it was eight or eight-thirty at night by then. I called her up, and I said, "Mom," and she said, "Where are you?" I said, "I'm in Seabury." She said, "Seabury? What are you doing there?" I said, "I can't say," since the guy was in the phone booth with me.

She said, "Are you in trouble?" I said, "Yeah." She said, "Do you need help?" I said, "Yeah." She said, "Police?" I said, "Yeah." So she said, "Call up Roberta's mother right now," and she gave me Roberta's number. I called up Roberta's house, her mother answered and said, "Hold on a second. I've got a sergeant who wants to speak with you." The guy in the phone booth with me thought I was going to talk with my father.

The cop asked me all these questions, and I couldn't give real detailed answers, but told him where things were at. He asked where we were, and I asked this black guy with me what the address of the place was, and I gave it to the sergeant. He said, "We'll have someone come down there and get you right away." "I hope so," I said. The sergeant wanted to talk to the guy who was with me to stall him, so the cops could get there, so the guy started talking to the sergeant. In the meantime, Roberta was getting balled by Frank.

It took forty-five minutes before the police came. Forty-five minutes! All of a sudden I looked out, it was fairly dark out already, and I saw this police car coming around. The guy who was still talking on the phone was facing toward the wall, so he didn't see the police.

The two cops got out of the car, walked over to the booth, and knocked on the window. I was in there saying, "Come here, come here." The guy I was with made a motion with his hand to say, "Get out of here! Go away!" He didn't even look or see who was there. The cops knocked on the glass again, and he motioned them away again. Finally they just pushed in the door and grabbed him.

I jumped into the back seat of the cop car, slammed the door, and got down real low in case there was any gunfire, because it was a very tense situation. I'm sure they had guns and knives up there in the apartment. The cops were frisking the guy, and I was sitting in the back. Then I saw my friend Roberta come hobbling down, bowlegged. I told her to get in the car, so she did. We both looked pretty bad. We smelled pretty bad, and we felt pretty bad. I guess the reason that she had come down was that they had heard that the cops were there and told her to get out.

A bunch of other cop cars came up. We told them where the apartment was, and they went looking around, but nobody was there. We gave descriptions as best we could—names, the color of the car, and so on. They did get two guys. They got Frank, and they got the guy that was with me. But they didn't get the first guys, the worst ones, the ones that kidnapped us in the beginning.

The first thing the cops did was drive to the hospital. In the meantime they were insulting us, calling us really dirty names, calling us whores, telling us we stank, and really degrading us. We didn't need that! We really didn't. What we needed was some security or trust or compassion or warmth.

The cops were really bastards. It was like getting stuck with a knife and then getting ten more stuck in you all at once. They said, "What are you white girls doing down in Seabury anyways?" They were racists. I mean, they just hated black people, you know.

Before that experience, I didn't have any prejudice against black people, but after it, I don't trust black men. Black women, I can get along with pretty well. So, actually, I don't think I'm prejudiced, really, except with black men.

INTERVIEWER: What happened with the police?

Ms. MEYERS: They got Frank, and they got the guy who was in the phone booth with me. And a couple of days later they did catch up with the two original guys that picked us up.

INTERVIEWER: Were they convicted?

Ms. MEYERS: Yeah. It ended up that Geoffrey, the big tall creepy one that was trying to kill me, had a beautiful wife who was a model. She was telling my mother and myself, "Don't press charges. We'll pay you." I said, "Fuck you! Hell no!"

We pressed charges, sex perversion and rape, and with me it was kidnap and assault with attempt to murder. I don't know exactly what all the accusations were, but they were pretty bad, and the guys got a lot of time. I don't know how much, and I don't really care to know. In fact I don't want to ever hear about them.

Sometimes I fear they're going to come looking for me when they get out of jail. Really, that's a very bad feeling.

INTERVIEWER: Did you feel guilty and responsible in any way? ·

Ms. MEYERS: As far as hitchhiking and getting in the car with them, yes, but as far as anything else is concerned, I didn't feel guilty or responsible for it. They were the ones that were guilty.

INTERVIEWER: Can you describe in detail the degree to which you resisted?

Ms. MEYERS: I totally resisted verbally and physically until he started strangling me. After that I thought, "Hell, what's the use of being a virgin if you're a dead one." So he went ahead and tried, but he couldn't get it in.

By the way, when the cops took us to the hospital, they [the hospital personnel] wanted to check us, but I wouldn't let them check me, because I wanted to go to my own personal doctor. I was really paranoid that night. When I got home, I slept in my parents' room, but my parents didn't give me the security that I needed. They just didn't know what to say. All they said was, "All you do is bring us trouble," and that was it.

INTERVIEWER: Did you tell anyone else besides your parents and the police? Did you tell any of your friends?

Ms. MEYERS: Yeah. I told my best friend. I told my cousin. I told the man I eventually married. I'm now divorced, and I have a daughter three years old. I met my husband three days after this had happened, and I grabbed onto him because I was just really insecure, and I started balling three days later, because I really wanted to do it after that. It was weird.

We ended up getting married. We broke up because he started beating me up and strangling me because I had told him about what those guys did to me. When he started doing that trip with me, I broke up and left him. I couldn't handle him.

INTERVIEWER: Did the experience affect your behavior in any way?

Ms. MEYERS: Yeah. I ended up having two nervous breakdowns as a result and going to three institutions. I suffered for about four years because of it. My daughter suffered for it too. I've been unable to adjust until just recently. I've just recently gotten back my security, at least mentally, not financially.

INTERVIEWER: You said the experience affected your feelings toward black men. Did it affect your attitudes toward white men too?

Ms. MEYERS: Yes. I began not to trust myself and not to trust men. I started dropping a lot of LSD after that. I never have had a decent relationship with a man since then. In fact, for the last year I haven't had any relationship. And I'm very, very sexually hung up.

INTERVIEWER: Do you think it was related to your being a virgin when it happened?

Ms. MEYERS: No, it was because of what it did to my mind, my head. It was a very degrading thing that happened to me, and I didn't value myself anymore. In fact, I sometimes still wonder if I'm worth anything at all.

INTERVIEWER: Did it change your attitudes toward yourself in any other way?

Ms. MEYERS: Yes. I really fell in love with a guy I met. I was using acid, and he was using acid and mescaline, and we would have it together. But I didn't trust him. I told him about the experience with the black guys, and I started to space out when I was with him. I mean, he'd talk to me and try to communicate with me, but I wouldn't be able to communicate feelings back to him because of this thing that happened. I probably ruined one of the best things that I could have had in my life.

INTERVIEWER: What were your impressions of the motivation and personality of your rapists?

Ms. MEYERS: They obviously hated white people. They wanted to get back at the white race, and they said so. I don't think they would have done it alone. It was a group thing. It was a power thing. They were just full of hate and anger.

INTERVIEWER: Besides your shame and disgust at the whole incident, did you feel anger or hate?

Ms. MEYERS: I sure did. I didn't have much time to feel it then. In fact, I was begging for them not to kill me and not to fuck me. I was actually begging! But when I went to court, I felt a lot of hate and a lot of anger. I felt I'd like to kill them. At that time I said to myself that if I had a big knife, a real sharp knife, or a big stick, I'd tie up that guy, big Geoffrey, the one that tried to kill me, and I would take him and clobber him and stick him with knives and gouge out his eyes. That's how I felt. But I'd never *do* that. Another part of me felt that I wanted to excuse them for what they did and put them in jail but not punish them physically.

INTERVIEWER: Do you regret in any way the way you handled the situation?

Ms. MEYERS: No, I don't. I think I handled it the best I could.

INTERVIEWER: Did your experience of rape change your thinking about rape at all?

Ms. MEYERS: Yes, it did. You hear about rape, you hear about killing, and you hear about insane people, and you stereotype these people. Then it actually happens to you. You actually see it first hand, like a live motion picture. It was like waking up into a bad dream. That's exactly what it was like, except that the whole time I was there, I knew I wasn't dreaming. I knew it was real, yet big newspaper headlines kept flashing through my mind, "Two white girls raped and killed and thrown in ditch."

INTERVIEWER: What is your reaction to people who think that rape is usually provoked?

Ms. MEYERS: I disagree a hundred percent. Hitchhiking is a means of getting around. It's not asking for sex or to be raped. If you want sex, you can always get it.

INTERVIEWER: How many women do you know personally who have been raped?

Ms. MEYERS: Two. Both are middle-class Jewish women. One is my best friend. Some guy held a gun to her head. He was a white man. He raped her up in the hills and left her there. And a friend of my parents was raped too. The guy that this girl was going out with ended up taking her and raping her and throwing her into a canyon.

It is significant that Ms. Meyers reacted to her traumatic experience by having intercourse with a man only three days later and then marrying him. Perhaps Ms. Meyers had internalized the view of women as property which, once used, is worthless. Or perhaps the experience intimidated her into feeling that it would be safer for her to give men what they wanted. The fact that Ms. Meyers's husband was inspired by her brutal experience to treat her in similar fashion probably relates to the view of defiled property being disgusting and unworthy of humane treatment.

This is one of the few cases which culminated in the conviction of the rapists. Ms. Meyers suggests that the police were very racist, and the fact that the victims were white and the rapists black probably made it seem more likely to them as well as to the judge and the jury that the women were unwilling participants. In addition, through an unusual set of circumstances, the police were able to arrive at the scene, even though it took them forty-five minutes, while one of the rapists was still there, and while the women were in an obvious state of trauma. Finally, the fact that Ms. Meyers was a virgin and had not been penetrated vaginally might also have helped to convict the men.

Women seem to be more readily believed if rape, as legally defined, is attempted rather than achieved, for if a woman is not successfully defiled, she does not suffer the same stigma of being impure and thereby lose her credibility.

FIFTEEN

White Racism Has Many Faces

He was an extremely dark-complexioned black dude and very hung up about being so much darker than me, or me being so much closer to white. So he called me a "half-white bitch" and a "white-ass whore," and in turn he wanted me to call him things. He said that he knew I didn't like it because I couldn't stand no black niggers. . . .

I felt that this was his way of getting back at white women who he couldn't approach and black women who he felt had rejected him.

The United States, like South Africa, not only has color castes and sex castes, but is essentially a "pigmentocracy": even within castes, people are ranked according to the lightness or darkness of their skin color, hair color, and eye color. At the top of the hierarchy, other things (such as income, occupation, sex) being equal, are blond, blue-eyed, fair-skinned people, and at the bottom are the dark-eyed, dark-haired, darkest-skinned people. Without a strong movement to demythologize this absurd basis for evaluating people, it is impossible to be immune from its psychological effects, to say nothing of the economic and political effects. The existence of racial prejudice within and between minority racial groups should not be allowed to obscure the fact that its origin is in the racism of the dominant group.

Ruth Somers emphasized that she was raped in 1969, which was, according to her, before "blacks were proud of their blackness." Her rapist assumed that Ms. Somers considered him beneath her because of his darker skin color. Angered by assumed rejection, he raped her.

Ms. Somers is thirty-one years old, light skinned, and twice divorced. The mother of two, she is currently on welfare and attends school.

RUTH SOMERS: I was at a neighborhood bar I had been to a number of times. I knew the bartender quite well, so I felt fairly comfortable about going to the bar by myself. I would go in there sometimes during the week and sit around and talk and have a few drinks.

On this occasion I was there for three or four hours, from about 10 P.M. The bartender introduced me to a friend of his, and we sat and talked until about two o'clock. I had not previously met the fellow, but since the bartender introduced me to him, I felt OK about talking with the guy. And after talking to somebody for three or four hours you usually know whether you feel comfortable with them or not, and I felt pretty comfortable with him.

So when the bar closed at two, and he asked me if I could drop him at the bus stop, I said yeah. He seemed to be an interesting fella, and certainly no one I would be afraid to take to the bus station. My car was parked about half a block from the bar, but on a side street, which wasn't very well lighted. The area where I was parked was quite dark, and at two o'clock in the morning there were not many cars parked on that side street. When we got into the car, I still hadn't noticed anything strange.

He commented on the make of the car, and all that stuff, and then he asked if I'd mind if he smoked a joint before I dropped him off. I said, "No, go ahead," but rather than drive through the street with him smoking a joint I preferred to sit there. He asked if I wanted a drag, and I said no, I didn't smoke. When he finished and I was getting ready to drop him off and go home, he made some advances, you know, like where a dude tries to either hug or kiss you and tells you that you are an out-of-sight chick, blah blah blah, the usual kind of stuff.

Like I said before, I had no adverse feelings toward him. He was a nice-looking dude and fairly intelligent, and I didn't have any hang-ups about sitting in a car talking and maybe kissing a fella. So we kissed two or three times. He wanted to know if he could come by and see me and all that kind of stuff. I said yeah, but when I got ready to start the car he made further advances.

By this time it was close to three, and I noticed that when I got ready to actually move the car he would start kissing me. And when he finished kissing, I'd sit back and relax like I wasn't going to start the car, and then he would start talking. If I made a motion to start the car, he started kissing me again.

After this happened twice, I started feeling a little, I wouldn't say leery, but it was just a feeling you get, an odd kind of sixth sense maybe women have, of wariness. At this point he wanted to know, since I was what he called an open-minded person, did I want to go to a motel with him. I told him no, I didn't really want to, it was not my thing that night to jump into bed with him. I said that I enjoyed his company, and that at some future date that might be possible. I wasn't against the idea, it was just that at this time I wasn't interested. I don't know if he thought I was just saying no so that he would say, "Oh, yes," but he didn't take that no as being a very definite no. He felt I was wavering or playing the catching kind of game. So he made some more advances, and I told him that I didn't see any point in us sitting there in the car, kissing and hugging, when it wasn't going to lead to anything. At this point he became insistent.

By this time it occurred to me that I was going to have a hard time getting this dude out of my car. I looked at the situation, being in the car on a dark side street, there weren't people passing by, and I was taking into consideration my situation as a woman. I was ready to get him out right then and there. He could *walk* to the bus , the way I felt about him by then.

I didn't think physically he was that much stronger than me because we were roughly about the same size. He wasn't some huge, overpowering six-foot, six-inch, 280-pound dude. In fact, for a man he was of slight build. So I told him, "Hey, look here, I've got to split, I've got kids at home, and I'm paying a baby sitter, and I don't want to extend the evening any further. I'm willing to drop you off at a bus stop, but that's the extent of the evening."

He wrote out his phone number and address for me to get in touch with him and asked for mine. But I had such a different feeling then than when I first started talking to him that I didn't want to give him my phone number or address, not so much because of his insistence that we go to bed, because I have had people who have been quite insistent and sometimes it worked. It was his lack of concern for my feelings about it.

So I told him I didn't feel it was necessary that he have my number. I had his, and I would give him a call. This seemed to agitate him. He made some comments that I had been leading him on, but I couldn't understand that because he wasn't paying for any of the drinks. The bartender was giving us free drinks, so he hadn't put out any money. In three hours, if I'd wanted to catch him in bed, I am sure I could have had him in bed if it had been my intention to lead him on. In fact, we didn't even discuss any kind of personal things between me and him. There really wasn't anything in our conversation that made him think I wanted to go to bed with him.

By this time it dawned on me that I got a *nut* in the car. I was beginning to feel a little bit afraid because of his reluctance to let me move from where we were. So I got to thinking that maybe if I told him, "Yeah, OK, we'll go to a motel," at least I could get off that street I was on and then maybe if I saw a policeman or something—

At that time I used to carry alcohol in the trunk of my car, so I said,

"Look, I have a bottle in the trunk of my car. Why don't we go some place and have some more drinks and sit around and talk." I think he picked up on what I was trying to do, because he reached over and took the keys out of the ignition. Well, obviously I'm not going *nowhere* if he's got the keys!

Now I *know* I have a problem on my hands. I had safety locks on the car, where you have to actually lift up the door lock in order to get out. You can't just move the handle. I had my back to the driver's door, since I was trying to keep all eyes on him, and I said, "Well, hey, you know, what kind of shit is this? Give me the keys back." I'm still trying to keep it on a light basis, like saying, "Well, I can't hardly drive the car without the keys, so if you want to catch your bus, I'm going to have to have the keys." He said he felt that that wasn't very important.

So I turned around and I said, "OK, *you* take the car. I'll walk if you're going to be that kind of dude. I won't go through no hang-ups about my car or my keys." I reached up to unlock the door, and he grabbed my hand, and he unscrewed the little plastic cover on the door lock and took it off, which meant that when it was recessed, I couldn't pull it up. There I was locked in my own car without my keys with this nut!

By this time it dawns on me that he's going to rape me, and he's going to kill, because he sure can't rob me—I don't have any money. I got angry and said, "Hey, man, what kind of shit is this you're pulling?" At this point the keys were in his jacket pocket. So I got to thinking, well, maybe if push comes to shove, I can get the keys. I cannot get out of the car from my side at all, so I'm thinking, maybe if we switch positions, I'll be in better shape. I figured I'd have to go along with him to a certain point to achieve these things.

He starts kissing and feeling, so I told him that since he seemed to be so intent on what he was going to do, it was really rather uncomfortable, and that I'd prefer to do it in comfort. I suggested that we switch seats. That way *I* wouldn't be under the driving wheel and neither would he. He didn't go for that! I think he knew that what I was trying to do was to get over to his side where I could get out of the damn car. He didn't actually say that it wouldn't be necessary, but he said something to the effect that it didn't bother him.

Then it dawns on me that I'm going to have to shut up and put up, because he isn't listening to anything I'm saying. At that point he had me halfway under him. There was just no way I could get away from him. I started to physically resist his advances, and I kept thinking, well, I'm as strong as this dude is. But I was in such an awkward position that even when I pushed him away, I still couldn't get out of the car, because of the safety lock.

So we go through a good twenty-minutes' scuffle, and he was saying things like, "I don't see why you're resisting so much. You do this anyway." Or, "That's one thing about a bitch. As soon as she has to actually get up off something, then all of a sudden she doesn't want to." At the same time that he's making these kind of weird comments, he has me fairly well pinned.

By this time I'm thinking that I'm in a mess, in fact, one hell of a mess! But I'm still feeling not too super afraid, because he hasn't violently attacked me, and he hasn't pulled a weapon or anything, but I'm thinking that it might get to that point. While he had me down under the steering wheel, and I'm squirming and talking, I got to a point where I really got super pissed off that here's this dude that's going to make me do it regardless of my thoughts or feelings. It hurt because I had been interested in the cat's mind, where he was coming from and all that, and would've enjoyed other meetings with him and probably at some point would have gone to bed with him. So I was pissed off that he felt as a man, as a black man, that he had to lay this kind of heavy forceful trip on me. And I also was feeling, "I sure did misjudge him!"

With all these thoughts running through my mind I was trying in a very strong physical way to get him off. I am in a half-lying position on the front seat of the car between the steering wheel, the seat, and him. There is no room, but I'm really struggling. He had my right arm pinned against the back of the seat, so I had only a free left arm to try to deal with this dude. At this point he made certain motions which indicated he had unbuttoned his belt and unzipped his pants, so I knew time for talk was over with, and that whatever I was saying he wasn't hearing, nor was he going to react to it in any way that I wanted.

I really got super afraid, not afraid so much that he was going to rape me, but more afraid of what he might do in addition, even though he hadn't threatened me with a weapon or anything else. When I heard his zipper unzip, I started struggling as much as I could without having any room to hit this dude. I don't have any fingernails, so I couldn't adequately scratch him. Nor could I kick, because he had his legs wrapped around mine. So I'm trying to use one hand to do something that I always thought a woman could do if she were in this situation, like knee him in his penis. I couldn't knee him because he had my knees pinned down, but I could pull on his ear, which is a source of severe pain, to try to get him to raise up enough so I could get the other arm out.

Like I said, we were about the same weight and build so that it was almost like an equal struggle and, with me having the strong incentive to get him off me, I think I could actually, physically, have done it except that at that point he pulled out a knife and that ended my struggle. I said, "Oh, wow. You've got to be kidding! You're going to sit here with a knife and screw? You've got to be kidding!" It was so far from the picture I had of him two hours before. It was just unbelievable. A knife!

I realized that this kid was serious, and I was in no hurry to get cut or maimed or end up dead. I got to thinking, this fool may decide to do this anyway. You know, this might be some mad-ass rapist who rapes the chick and then does her in anyway after it's over. So I didn't know at that point whether to participate or whether to keep on physically rejecting him. He might harm me even if I acquiesced to what he wanted, or I might get harmed in the process of trying to prevent him from raping me, so I really didn't know what to do.

I'm not the type of woman who can pull the crying jazz, and I don't think it would have worked if I could have. So I got to thinking that maybe at some point he'll put the knife down. Like in the process of intercourse, it would seem logical that since his left arm and my right arm were pinned against the seat, and since the knife was in his right hand, he'd *have* to put the knife down. I couldn't conceive of a dude having intercourse holding a knife in one hand and my arm in the other. That shows you how much I knew.

So I decided that I wasn't going to resist any more because of the knife. That really cowed me. So I just said, "Well, OK, go ahead, and get it over with, I got to go home." I figured he'd think I was going along with it and would put the knife down. The only place he could put the knife down was on the floor of the car, and I had one hand that could reach that far, and I could throw it under the seat, so that he would have to get up off of me to get it. I was figuring I'd try to knock holy hell out of his head when he was looking for it. Anyway, he didn't put the knife down! So that ended that line of thought.

When he actually got to the point of beginning sexual intercourse, I tried to physically resist because I saw he was actually going through with it. When you become physically aware of forced intercourse, I guess regardless of a knife or anything, you make a last effort to try to prevent it. He didn't slap me, because he had the knife in his hand, but he used the butt of the knife to hit me around the temple. I thought, this dude is crazy! So I just lay there and let him go ahead and have intercourse.

At what I would consider to be the beginning of his sexual excitement, he wanted me to use very dirty words. He was an extremely dark-complexioned black dude and very hung up about being so much darker than me, or me being so much closer to white. He called me a "half-white bitch" and a "white-ass whore," and in turn he wanted me to call him things. He said that he knew I didn't like it because I couldn't stand no black niggers, and all that kind of trippy stuff, and I realized that the dude had a very serious hang-up.

This is all happening while he is in the process of having intercourse! He said, "Call me some names." He wanted me to defile his manhood verbally, but I didn't know what to say, to be quite honest, and I wasn't paying much attention to what he was saying. I was figuring I would be glad when this was all over with. He had my left shoulder, and he shook me and said, "You heard what I said." I said, "Yeah, I did, but I don't know what you want me to do." He didn't have a sense of pride in his blackness or my lack of blackness, and he wanted me to use words that had connotations about his color.

Maybe he had a thing against white women, and I was the closest one he could find that night. I don't know. I just know that he seemed to imply to me that it was because of my color and his color that he was doing this as a way of hurting me. This was his way of hurting women, black women who evidently had given him a hard time. I don't know why.

By this time I figured, "It ought to be over with by now." I'm trying to look to when it's over, *then* what am I going to do. Because I'm trying to deal with what is *he* going to do when he's finished? Is he going to get afraid? Is he going to kill me? Is he going to try to physically scare me so bad by beating me up so that I won't tell anybody? Because all along I had intentions of going to the police because I figured between me and the bartender we could certainly locate him afterward. Anyway when he finished, so to speak, it was really a trippy kind of thing because he was back to the sort of person I was kind of digging in the beginning when I was first talking to him.

He still had the knife in his hand though, so he wasn't completely back. When he finished, all I said was, "Can I go?" He handed me the keys, and I said, "Well, aren't you going to get out of the car?" He said, "No, you said you were going to drop me off at the bus stop." I said, "Right, I sure did." I'm thinking, at least I'll get out of this dark street. I still couldn't unlock the door on my side. So we got down to X Street, and it's well lit, so I'm not too afraid then that he's going to do anything, but who knows? At the bus stop, he got out of the car and said, "Well, I'll be seeing you around. Thanks for the lift." By this time, I'm just damn glad he's out of my car.

I go home, and by this time it's about 4 A.M., and I call the police to report a rape. Knowing where I live, I knew that they weren't going to be there like Johnny-on-the-spot. There was about a forty-five-minute wait. Then two officers arrived, and I proceeded to tell them just about what I've told you.

As the conversation went on, it was apparent that they weren't sympathetic to the fact that I had been raped. They asked me, did I frequent bars alone? I told them that I didn't feel I was alone at the bar since I knew the bartender. They asked, "Was someone with your kids?" Then they asked me whether I suspected my underpanties had any semen on them. I said I suspected so, since I had them on during the time, so they asked for those.

Then they asked me to go back over the story. When I said something they didn't feel comfortable with, they would look at me, and then go back to writing. On a number of points, when I was talking about my efforts to prevent it from happening, the officers raised up their eyes to look at me as if to say, "You've got to be kidding." They wanted to know whether or not I had any bruises, and I told them that I didn't suspect so because the blows were in the hairline and I don't bruise easily. I told them that I did not get beat up more because the fella had a knife, and the knife was enough of a threat of violence to me without him actually having to do violence.

They said they didn't feel, based on the information they had, that they would be very successful. They evidently had a low rate of capturing rapists and a low rate of conviction, based on the fact that women didn't want to file suit or press charges. They said that sometimes a woman will have a falling out with her boy friend and accuse him of rape, and the next day everything is smoothed over, and she doesn't sign the complaint. I told them those things didn't apply to my particular case because he was not a boy friend and I was damn sure going to sign the complaint.

I was ready to go to court, and I felt that the information I had given them would make it possible to find the dude. I knew his last name, and I knew the precise kind of job he had in the post office, and I had a good description of him. I didn't know his home address, and I didn't have his first name, but I knew which post office he worked in, and he was a friend of the bartender.

I really thought that since I was giving that much information, it would be cool. I figured that they could go to work and snatch him up after I signed the complaint. The officers said that I had to come down the next morning, which would be the same morning since it was five-thirty, to sign a complaint, and I told them that I would be there.

When I got down there to sign a complaint, they had a young black man who was like an intern in the section where you sign complaints for these types of offenses. This guy was about twenty-six or twenty-five. He quickly looked over the forms, and then he looked at me and said something to the effect, "You don't look as if he gave you such a hard time."

What with the reaction of the police and this on top of it, it started to dawn on me that the type of reception I was getting indicated that I had to prove myself innocent. That it was *I*, not the guy, who was assumed guilty to start with. He said, "You don't have any bruises." So I said, "If you hit me with a truck, I probably wouldn't bruise." Then he said, "You ought to give a brother a break." I said, "*Darn* the *brother!* What about the *sister?*" We continued and he said, "Do you still want to sign the complaint?"

I am down there to sign the complaint roughly six hours after I have been raped, not the next day or twenty-four hours later, and he asks me, "Do you still want to sign the complaint!" I said, "You're God-damn right I want to sign the complaint! Give it here!" So I signed it. He said that they would start an investigation, but that they had various other things to sift through, and if anything came up, they would contact me.

They never contacted me. I don't think that the police officer even went down to the post office. They had asked me if I was quite positive about what I was saying, as if they thought I had fabricated the stuff about him working in the post office. I never heard from them again.

INTERVIEWER: Could you tell me more about the personality of your rapist?

Ms. SOMERS: He had some deep hang-ups about his manhood, or his black manhood. I'm a light-complexioned black, and invariably when I was dating in my teens, those fellas I was dating who would comment on my complexion were very dark-complexioned blacks. There is even this supposed prejudice among blacks that light women like dark men and light men like darker women. I usually don't look at these colors, you know, like green is my favorite color! But this fella, Wilson, repeatedly made reference to my color. It was as if he couldn't deal with me being black, because at first he called me a "half-white bitch" and during the process of the rape a "white-ass whore."

INTERVIEWER: Do you think he would have preferred you to be a white woman?

Ms. SOMERS: I really don't think he'd rape anybody white, to be quite honest. It was strictly a black bar. It wasn't the type of bar that had a mixed crowd. If he were looking for someone white, he damn sure was in the wrong territory. When we got into the car, his conversation changed from the intellectual trip we were on in the bar, and he seemed to think that I didn't dig him because of his color, that I thought I was better than him. I couldn't even relate to that. I didn't want to go to bed with him, because I didn't want to go to bed with anybody. I was ready to go home.

Since then I've been wondering how a young black man, obviously intelligent, got to that point. I figured that, being a black man, he wouldn't be able to have any kind of impact on society because American society does not let a black man be a man. Usually the only way a black man has of proving he's a man is through sexual intercourse. It's sad that he feels he has to *prove* he is a man.

This happened three years ago, prior to the time that blacks were proud of their blackness. So, if he has been made to reject that which he is, black, then it would seem to me that it would really fuck up his mind. It would fuck up mine too. I felt that this was his way of getting back at white women who he couldn't approach and black women who he felt had rejected him.

INTERVIEWER: What were your feelings after the rape?

Ms. SOMERS: I was as mad as hell. I was really, really mad. If I had felt ashamed, I would have felt like shit after I'd finished talking to the police officers. It would have really fucked me up emotionally to talk to those fellas, with the position they took, the inferences they made, those snide innuendoes about frequenting bars. I wasn't crying because I don't cry easily, but it was hard to tell those officers about what had happened. I was trying to be very factual, I was trying not to play the emotional woman, because that ain't my bag. I was trying to show them that I had given due consideration and thought to it, and that I was dead serious about what I was doing.

There ought to be women police officers interviewing women rape victims, because when a woman has just been violated by a male and she has to tell it to another male, that in itself causes a psychological blockage. I think that if I could have told a woman, it would have been much easier. I feel that a woman could be more sympathetic because I doubt if there's any woman who's had sexual intercourse over any period of time who hasn't had to have sexual intercourse when she didn't want to. I think a woman could relate to it better than a man could.

INTERVIEWER: Did the experience of rape change any of your attitudes?

Ms. SOMERS: About the only change it made was that I did a lot of thinking to try to understand why the police, and especially the young black dude, had laid such a trip on me. Even my girl friend, when I told her, made a comment about the fact that I didn't look like I had been raped. So I was thinking, maybe I really wasn't raped. Did I really do everything I could? And after going through that kind of head trip, I decided, hell, yeah, just because I didn't get hit enough for it to show, it sure as hell was a case of rape.

One of the things the experience did was to make me realize how vulnerable a woman is. If my thing is going out at night for walks around the block, or walking to the grocery store, or going out to have a couple of drinks and listening to some music around people, then I'm almost like an ace target for whatever a man might decide he wants to do.

It also made me realize that if I carry a weapon, that in itself invites danger, and I would be put in jail because I am not supposed to carry a weapon—it's illegal. Also, if I get into a situation like I was in before and somebody else has a weapon, I'm not quite sure I could use mine because we both might end up dead.

I had never before been afraid of the dark or being outside at nighttime. I always figured that my senses would be more attuned when I would be out walking around. Naturally, I'd listen for footsteps and sounds, but I was never leery of going out or of sitting and talking with fellas in a bar. You go in, and you sit, and you have a couple of drinks, and somebody will come over to the table.

Once, after it happened, a groovy bunch of people got together at the bar. I didn't know them, but they were going to a party, and they invited me. They decided that everyone was going to ride with everybody in three car loads, and I told them no, I was going to take my own car. When someone said, well, let so-and-so ride with you, I said it was OK but I might change my mind on the way. It made them look at me as if to say, "Wow, what's wrong with that chick?" I think that incident made me realize how unprotected a woman is if she does things that she enjoys doing without having a man stand next to her as a protector.

If you're the type of woman who likes to do things alone, then you are unprotected. I'm quite sure that if I had been in the bar with another man, this wouldn't have happened. In fact, the guy wouldn't have ever said anything to me at all. Even if the guy with me had been there and left, and if Wilson had then come over, and I'd said that the guy was my boy friend and he was coming back, that would have cooled him right there.

INTERVIEWER: If you found yourself in a similar situation again, do you think you would call the police?

Ms. SOMERS: Hell, no. After the kind of reception I got from the police, there's no way in the world that I would call the police if it happened again. I would probably try to call some of my male buddies, or my male cousins, and we'd try to find him ourselves and kick the dude's ass. I wouldn't even recommend anyone else calling the police, unless the victim is a kid. I think the police figure that when you are grown, even if you're only thirteen but look like you're grown, that you enticed the man. It's just a waste of time to call them.

INTERVIEWER: Why do you think some men find it necessary to rape?

Ms. SOMERS: Evidently this is their way of trying to get back at women. I don't see it as normal, but yet there is so much rape. You don't know who is going to be a rapist, until they rape.

In discussing her rapist's motivation, Ms. Somers's suggestion that black men, because of their oppression by whites, are largely restricted to the sexual sphere in their opportunities to prove their masculinity seems reasonable. And black women most often suffer the consequences of this oppression.

The problem of pigmentocracy among blacks is one that has existed since slavery and still continues. During slavery the lighter-skinned slaves were usually children of a slave and her white master. These lighter-skinned slaves were usually house servants, who had a much easier life than working in the fields. After emancipation, the lighter-skinned blacks found it easier to be hired by whites. And, in some cases, if the person was fair enough in complexion and had straight enough hair, he or she would pass as white. The fairest in color tended to clan together because they were accepted more easily by whites and hence had a better life. In order for their children to be able to survive more easily, both parents had to be light. In this way darker-skinned blacks were discriminated against by the lighter ones. There still are many light-skinned blacks who consider themselves to be better than their darker sisters and brothers and don't want to be "bothered" by those darker than they. It is very possible that Wilson encountered this attitude when trying to approach light-skinned black women.

Ms. Somers demonstrated unusual psychological strength in her refusal to be manipulated by the police. She managed not to accept their negative attitude toward her as the rape victim. Instead, she responded to it with the anger it deserved. Similarly, she was able to reject the commonly held view that a woman who goes to a bar alone, and leaves in the company of a man, cannot be raped. She also refused to concur in the attitude of the black police intern, whose concern for "the black brother" was greater than his concern that a black brother would rape a black sister. *"Damn the brother! What about the sister?"*

Ms. Somers mentions that people found it strange when she was cautious about leaving the bar to go to a party with people she had just met. Frequently, when a woman acts suspicious or is slow to trust strange men, this is the case. Yet women who become rape victims because of lack of suspicion are seen as foolish. For example, women who refuse to open doors to strange men are often considered overcautious, particularly if the man has some apparently good reason for wanting them to open the door (a delivery man, a survey researcher, a would-be gardener). Yet the victims of the notorious Boston Strangler were widely judged as very foolish for opening their doors in spite of the plausible reasons they were given. Some suggested they were "careless" because they wished something would happen to them.

Most men expect women to trust *them*, but not other men. *Other* men may be rapists. Unfortunately, it is difficult, as these interviews indicate, to tell which ones. For example, male hitchhikers expect women drivers to trust them enough to pick them up. However, if a woman driver is raped by a hitchhiker she is likely to be seen as having taken an unnecessary risk and immediately suspected of some lurking desire to be violated.

SIXTEEN

The Rape of a White Radical

At first I thought, oh, my God, why did this
have to happen? Why did they have to be
black? Now I'm going to be a racist.... And
every time I'd see a black man, I'd go, "Oh,
God!"

Many white victims of black rapists who consider themselves liberal or
radical share Liz Davis's concern that they will become racist (or more
racist) as a result of rape. For Ms. Davis it seems to have been a major aspect
of the trauma she experienced. But is it racist for a white woman raped by a
black man to be more wary of black men and angry toward them afterward?

Overgeneralization seems to be one indication that an experience has
been traumatic, so it may be that such an overgeneralization is more
indicative of trauma than of racism. On the other hand, perhaps rape is the
kind of traumatic experience that causes or exacerbates racist attitudes
when the rapist is from a different racial group than the victim.

If one accepts the latter argument, does it apply equally to black women
raped by white men who feel more wary of white men and angry toward
them afterward? It doesn't seem reasonable to regard these black women as
racist. Since U.S. history is replete with examples of white men raping black
women, it would seem naive for black women not to be mistrustful of white
men. There are also some indications that black women are more mistrustful of white men than white women are of black men.

For example, there are probably few black women who would accept a
ride with a single white man, let alone two or more. They aren't seen as
racist for this, but as realistic. And if some black men see rape of white
women as an act of revenge or a justifiable expression of hostility toward
whites, I think it is equally realistic for white women to be less trusting of
black men than many of them are.

This is a tremendously difficult thing to say, since many of us have come to see any acceptance of the view that some black men are interested in raping white women as extremely racist. Moreover, data from a study in Philadelphia in 1958 and 1960 suggest that most rape is intraracial and in only three percent of the 646 cases was a black man reported as the rapist of a white woman [1] (compare this with twenty-six percent of ninety-five cases in my study). However, there is some indication that in some areas in this country, the situation has changed.

Recently, for example, I attended a group meeting in Berkeley, California, of sixteen to twenty white women who were there to learn how to be of help to rape victims. Eight of the women in the group had been raped, all of them by black men. But no one wanted even to acknowledge this fact, let alone discuss it.

Similarly, in a study being done by a woman at a nearby university, many of the victims interviewed were white women who had been either hassled or raped by black men. The woman who organized the study said that no one wanted even to report this fact, let alone try to understand it. White guilt also plays a part in the reluctance of many of the white women to report their rapists and to see them jailed. Prisons are not designed to help rapists change, and there is a great deal of racism in prisons. But often there seems to be more sensitivity to the interests of black rapists than to the potential victims on the part of white liberal and radical victims.

Ms. Davis is a middle-class white woman who was raped about a year and a half ago, when she was nineteen. She had been living with a man, Barry, for a few months when she was raped, and she is still living with him now.

LIZ DAVIS: I was living in Boston, and I'd been engaging in a number of activities which were considered quite dangerous, such as driving a taxi. I didn't have a car, I lived in the city, and I got around a lot of the time by hitchhiking because I couldn't always afford public transportation. It's true that the things that I was doing were dangerous, but I didn't want to be oppressed by having to be afraid all the time.

One night I was in a nice, residential area in Cambridge, near Radcliffe, where young women walk at all hours of the night. It was ten o'clock, and I had just been hitchhiking. I got out of the car and started walking down the street. It was a dark street, but it was a very nice neighborhood. A car stopped, and a man got out of it and said, "Excuse me, miss." I turned and stepped toward him, and he grabbed me, put his hand over my mouth, and pulled me into the car.

1. M. Amir, *Patterns of Forcible Rape,* Chicago, 1971, p. 44. Only four percent of the rapes involved white men raping black women. Ibid.

"Now what do I do?" I wondered. "How do I escape from this?" I struggled for a minute or two, but there were three men, and they held me and were rough with me. They said, "Look, we don't want to kill you, we just want to rape you, and that's all that's going to happen to you."

I was relieved to hear this. They said, "Stop struggling, and we won't hurt you." So I did. I realized it was hopeless. They blindfolded me and drove off with me. I was freaked out, but not totally. They were obviously really psychotic people to do something like this.

I was talking to them, saying, "Why are you doing this?" and "Really, isn't this ridiculous?" They would get into talking to me, they would see that I was a human being—and then, all of a sudden, something would click in their minds, and they'd say, "Now wait a minute, we have a knife here. You'd better not say one more word." Then they would go back to their power trip.

Two of them ended up raping me. One of them couldn't even manage to do it. He just didn't have the desire by the time he'd seen the other two go through with it. They really didn't enjoy the process very much, I'm sure of that.

INTERVIEWER: Why do you say you're sure of that?

Ms. DAVIS: Because there was no joy, there was no pleasure in what they were doing. It was just a power trip.

INTERVIEWER: So why do you think they did it?

Ms. DAVIS: First of all, they were black, and they laid a rather heavy trip on me about being a little middle-class white girl. They stole ten dollars and my Timex watch from me, and they tried to make me feel very guilty because they were black and I was a middle-class white girl. And the other trip they laid on me was that I deserved it for walking around alone at night without a man.

They took me somewhere secluded. I was blindfolded the whole time. It seemed interminable to me. My main feeling after an hour or two was, will it *ever* be over?

INTERVIEWER: Did they take that long to get to a place to rape you or did they take that long doing it?

Ms. DAVIS: Both. They undressed me, partly, and there was all sorts of talk going on. They would ask me things like, did I have a boy friend. And they made comments about my body. They said it was nice.

I talked constantly, trying to show them that I wasn't freaked out, that I was a human being and not something that they could just pick up and do this to without any feedback. I tried to reach them, to make human contact with them. I felt that if they were aware I was a human being, they would not be able to do it. But it didn't work. It would start to seep in, and then they would cut it off. They had the knife, and they said, "This knife is one inch away from your throat, and you're going to stop talking." So I stopped talking. But I knew that a few minutes later it wouldn't be one inch away from my throat, and I could start talking until they got uptight again.

I didn't feel I could get through without talking. I felt I would go crazy if I didn't talk. I also wanted to prove that they couldn't destroy me by doing this. So I would talk to them as if I were perfectly at ease. Of course I wasn't, I wasn't fooling myself. I was only showing them that I was not totally destroyed.

INTERVIEWER: You thought that's what they wanted you to be?

Ms. DAVIS: Yes, I definitely think so. I talked mostly about what they were doing to me, and they said, "You're very lucky, you know. You're very lucky. Most rape victims end up knifed or murdered." At the end, I said that I had had a bad day, and that this had just made it a *really* bad day, and they said, "That's your fault." At the time I did accept that I deserved it, because there I was. I must have deserved it! Now I know that I didn't.

They went through my wallet and talked to me about the contents. I was just supposed to answer yes or no. They asked me about my boy friend, possibly because I had pictures of him, but also, I think they wanted to find out if I was someone else's possession. The fact that I dared to walk around without a man was what they focused on. That was what brought it on.

They laughed at my pictures and kept reiterating that I was lucky, that I was something special to be strong enough not to freak out or try to struggle so that they would have to kill me, or hurt me a great deal. They also kept saying, "You have to stay blindfolded. You can't see us, because we know that we can go to jail for many years for doing a thing like this." I said, "I don't believe in sending people to jail. I would never turn you over to the police."

At the very start, when they started to undress me, they kind of touched me, and said, "Wouldn't you really enjoy it?" I said no, there was no way that I could. They weren't violent, but it wasn't particularly comfortable, and I told them that they were hurting me. I thought of telling them that I had VD, or something, but I was afraid that they would kill me if they were not able to rape me. In a way, I'm afraid of learning self-defense techniques for the same reason—that if I can't use them effectively, then the person may get even madder and do something worse to me.

They had trouble working themselves up because I simply sat there being human and wasn't at all into the power-erotic aspect of it. They felt they had to go through with it anyway, because they couldn't pick me up and then not rape me after they'd said they would.

INTERVIEWER: Were they playing for each other's attention?

Ms. DAVIS: No. They seemed to be pretty together with each other. After watching the first two guys go through with it and take so long, the third one just said, "No, I don't think I will do it." It took them such a long time because they couldn't get into it.

They thought that they were horny, because they'd been driving around with no women. I'm sure that they were excited at first, but with all the driving and talking, their desire waned. It was a power trip, basically, so they wanted to go through with it anyway.

INTERVIEWER: Do you think that they were out to find someone to rape, or that they thought of it when they saw you?

Ms. DAVIS: I think they thought of it when they saw me, although I'm not positive. They had not been following me. I'd only been walking down the street for half a block.

INTERVIEWER: Do you think that they'd done this before?

Ms. DAVIS: I asked them, and they wouldn't tell me. Later, they said, "Oh, yes, lots of times."

With me, they didn't seem to think that they were doing anything terrible. Like I said, they thought I really deserved it, and they were only doing what any normal man would do and that they were certainly being very humane about it.

After it was finally over, we had to stop for gas, and they made me keep my head down, so that I couldn't be seen by the gas attendant. I was still blindfolded. After I sat up and was all dressed—there was one man in the back seat and two in the front—I grabbed the guy in the back and held onto his arm, because I needed somebody to hold on to. I was shaking. I think that it bothered them that I was seeking some kind of human comfort from one of them. It was all so crazy. They took me back to where they'd picked me up, and they made me stay blindfolded so I couldn't see their license plate or anything.

I was pretty shaken up. I cried. Then I went to see a friend. I woke Wesley up at three o'clock in the morning. That's how late it was when I got back. He comforted me, patted me on the back, and said, "Well, stay here tonight."

INTERVIEWER: Did you feel that he understood how you felt?

Ms. DAVIS: No, I didn't. But he understood as much as I expected him to. He is not able to give an awful lot, but he does give what he can. His attitude is that the world is a fucked-up place, and that's about as far as I got with him.

Next, I spoke to the woman I was on my way to see when it happened. She went to school at Radcliffe. I had lived with her for a year. She was the first person I tried to see, but she wasn't there for some reason, so I left a note, and then I went to see her the next day. She was black. She helped me a great deal. She said, "I don't see why it should happen to you. You're too nice a person. You're too happy and too good and you don't deserve it." I talked about it with her later during the year, and we got into it more deeply. But at the time, I felt she understood, and it was helpful to talk about it.

INTERVIEWER: Would you say the experience was traumatic?

Ms. DAVIS: Yes, I would. For me the trauma was in the total humiliation of not being treated as a person, not having any respect. No woman can have the right to really love anyone, or make love to anyone, if she doesn't have the right to keep them out, first. This also applies to the lesser kinds of things that men do to women in the street. It's not right that women cannot walk around and do whatever they want to do.

The other night I was walking down the street and three men followed me. They were saying, "Hey, look at her. Wow. Yeah," and getting into this whole thing. I turned around, and they were three nice-looking, long-haired young men, and I said, "What *are* you doing?" They never would have thought of going out and raping a woman, but here I was alone at night, and they were following me down the street, and they really got heavily into it. The whole feel of what they were saying and doing was threatening.

INTERVIEWER: How did they react to what you said?

Ms. DAVIS: Oh, they were quite crushed and seemed really put down. Then I said to them that when I walked around alone, I didn't want to have to worry about whether I was going to be attacked. I like being alone. I don't want to have to hold some guy's hand just to go on the street. They said goodnight to me very respectfully after that. I was lucky that I was feeling strong at that moment and able to cope with it.

When I first started to live in the city, I would walk by the construction workers having lunch and hear all these horrible comments. I didn't quite know how to deal with it. I was embarrassed because I had breasts. I felt it was my fault for having them, and that of course I deserved to be commented upon. Now I know that that's not true. It's *they* who have to change, not me.

Encounters on the street are annoying but not, of course, as serious as actual rape. When I feel strong, when I feel together, I am able to handle them. But when I feel a little bit under, and not quite coping with things, these experiences leave me with a very bad feeling. So to my mind, the solution is for women to become strong, and for us to find ways to help each other be strong, so that when we do have these encounters they won't tear us apart so much.

INTERVIEWER: What effect did the rape have on you?

Ms. DAVIS: It didn't tear me apart. I was able to recover from it, to talk about it with people. It didn't shatter my life. I was very happy at the time, and very secure, and I knew that I had people who loved me.

At first I thought, oh, my God, why did this have to happen? Why did they have to be black? Now I'm going to be a racist. Oh, it's terrible. What can I do about it? I don't want to be a racist. And every time I'd see a black man, I'd go, "Oh, God." I was walking around castigating myself in my mind, saying, "Oh, Liz, you're so awful."

Then I looked at a black woman and said, "Wait a minute, I'm not getting this feeling when I look at *her*. It's not that they were black. It's that they were men." This did a lot to clear my head about the difference between race relations and sex relations. Those black men had oppressed me. I resent the whole trip of having to feel guilty because I'm white or middle class.

I went through a long period of being very, very angry at black men, thinking they were awful and so sexist, and they are, in a very blatant way. But I think that a lot of it's more superficial. They don't have the power that white men do. They may be a little bit more obnoxious on the street, but they're not really the people that control my life.

INTERVIEWER: So, did the experience affect your attitude toward white men?

Ms. DAVIS: I don't think it affected my personal attitude toward white men I know. However, I think it raised my consciousness about sexism. I began to realize that if I went out at night and walked around in the street, I was foolish. I also started to realize why women are important to me. When I'm walking alone at night and I see a woman, I don't have to worry that she's going to knife me or rape me, or whatever. I love her for that, no matter who she is.

INTERVIEWER: Did the rape affect your sexuality at all?

Ms. DAVIS: Yes, it did. I was less able to relax and enjoy myself with Barry, my boy friend, but it wasn't extreme. It only affected me to a small extent. Barry was a little bit freaked out by it. He thought it had given me some fear that I would always have, but this wasn't true.

INTERVIEWER: Have you found yourself more scared after the rape?

Ms. DAVIS: Well, I'm more aware of what can happen. I don't walk around in the streets as much now as I used to before I was raped. And I'm constantly aware of the dangers of hitchhiking.

INTERVIEWER: What were some of your feelings about the rape?

Ms. DAVIS: I'm very angry about it. I thought I had lived out the trauma after a month or two, and then, during the winter, I started to get these flashes of hitting them with my fist. I really wanted to see these men smashed in the face. I felt this tremendous strength, but also frustration, and I kept having these things go through my head, unexpectedly. So I realized that I was not through with the experience. I had to keep dealing with it because it was still there.

And I also had to expunge my guilt at wanting to be violent, at wanting to get my revenge. I don't feel guilty about this anymore, at least so little that it's not significant. I no longer feel the need to find those particular men, to punish them. I do feel the need, if it happens again, not to be afraid to hurt somebody like that, because if you go through this thing of, "Oh, poor men, they're so lonely and messed up and that's why they do it," then you're never going to get strong enough to get back at them.

INTERVIEWER: Why didn't you report the rape?

Ms. DAVIS: Because it wouldn't do any good. The police would only give me trouble. I have some familiarity with the process that usually goes on when you go to the police with a rape. A couple of my friends who were in school said, "You have to take it to the authorities, because there are a number of rapes going on near Radcliffe. It's your duty to report it." But to me, it wasn't worth the pain of having to do that.

I knew that the feeling would be there that I had brought it upon myself. I have a friend who was raped in a house by someone she was on a date with. She didn't realize how the police would see something like that. It was just terrible for her, because she was a very, very untogether person. He harassed her afterward by telephoning her a number of times, and she desperately needed support from people, and none of us were together enough to really give her support.

INTERVIEWER: What do you think should be done with the men who rape women?

Ms. DAVIS: Well, I think they'll die off. But before that, I think the solution is to have some women beat them up. I have read accounts about how a man threatened a woman and ten women physically threatened him back. It worked.

Younger men are more and more sensitive. These things are going on now while they're still young, and they don't have years of it to unlearn. I don't think this growing sensitivity is reversible, though it may take a long time.

Sexual freedom is also a help. When people have been twisted and repressed for many, many years, and when their sexuality starts to emerge, at first it is perverted and twisted. Maybe this accounts for so much rape going on now. But this is no excuse for keeping it repressed. The only way we can become free is to work off some of the sickness that we've accumulated. The answer is not, of course, the pseudosexual revolution, where you're hung-up if you don't sleep with every guy, but true sexual freedom, along with getting rid of sexism, should get rid of rape.

INTERVIEWER: Could you explain what you mean about getting rid of sexism?

Ms. DAVIS: I see rape as the extreme manifestation of sexism. It's just a logical conclusion of it. As you become strong, you become more and more aware of all the subtler forms of rape. I see it, for example, in the way men look at women, and in a great many sexual relationships between men and women. I was reading an article about men's sexual fantasies, and how they do the *Playboy* kind of object trip with women.

I thought about my sexual fantasies, which really do not exist anymore, but what they used to be. It was total submission. No objects were involved, but much more a feeling of surrender, of giving myself over to something else, which was a man, of course. I had a sexual relationship with another man some time before Barry. My concern for his pleasure was so great that I didn't even care about my own pleasure. Then I started thinking about it. Being able to give is all very well as long as you don't give yourself up entirely.

Women know how to give, but they don't know how to *have* for themselves too. This, to me, is like rape, except it's more subtle. In a way it is harder to deal with these subtler forms, because, to many people, your anger seems out of proportion. I think there are many men who are very sensitive to the horror of rape, but at the same time they can't understand how in another situation the woman is being wiped out in the same way.

The reason I don't dig the police thing is because it's such an absurd game. Women seek the protection of certain men from other men, and then if the protection doesn't work, and they get raped, they turn these men over to yet other men. These were black men, and they're oppressed by the police, so for me to turn them over to the police would be contrary to what I feel. It's not going to help them, it's not going to keep them from raping somebody else. Maybe they'll rape other men while they're in jail, but that's no solution. And they'll be treated like animals. You don't make people good by fear.

INTERVIEWER: What do you see as some short-term solutions?

Ms. DAVIS: The first reaction I see in many women is "My God, I'm not going out. People are getting slashed in the streets and getting raped." But that's what men want. They want to keep us in our little houses so we can't ever do anything or get together or be free to walk around.

The only way that I personally can try to help solve the problem is to talk to people about my experience and about the ways that I'm learning to become strong. As far as I can see, there are more strong women now. I've talked about this with other women, and they've said that they, too, have felt much better able to handle the various levels of harassment when they feel strong.

I think that women are potentially very strong physically. I know that when I get angry I feel very strong. As more women get strong, this will raise the consciousness of men, and they'll realize that we cannot be treated as objects. We'll start to get rid of the mentality that women are objects to be raped.

There'll still be women who are raped, and in these cases, we want some kind of physical defense, like the neighborhood whistle and poster thing that they're doing now in a few parts of Berkeley. If you see a house with one of these posters on it, hopefully it will have a whistle hanging near it, and you can run up and blow the whistle, and people who have these posters will be aware that when they hear a whistle they ought to run out into the street. They say that it's worked a few times already. If everybody got attuned to carrying a whistle, that would help, too. And women should come to other women's rescue when they're being harassed.

INTERVIEWER: Do you talk to a lot of women about your rape experience?

Ms. DAVIS: Whenever the subject comes up, I talk about it. I don't like to force it on everybody as *the* oppressive experience, because many of our experiences are oppressive. I don't like to say, "I know all about it, because I've been raped," but a lot of women talk to me about their fear of it, and I think it gives them relief to talk to someone who's survived it. You really do, in a way, think that you would die if it happened to you, but you don't.

INTERVIEWER: Would you handle your rape situation differently now?

Ms. DAVIS: Yes. I was right outside a house. I would probably run up to the house. I am a lot more attuned to what people mean when they say things like "Excuse me, miss," and the way that they say it. I do wish that I had run up to the house that was there, but I in no way blame myself for not having done it. I don't see how I could have foreseen it.

INTERVIEWER: Do you see the rape as being important in your becoming more conscious of the oppression of women?

Ms. DAVIS: Yes, it has played a big part, but not in any way an irreplaceable part. Other things would have made me conscious of these things without it. I'm not exactly glad that it happened, but in a way I do see it as a very valuable experience, because so many women are raped and I identify with the fact that this really is going on.

It really did get me involved and interested in the women's movement, though the process had begun probably six months before the rape occurred. My attitude previous to that time was that I knew that I was a strong person, I've always known it, and I thought I would be able to do whatever I wanted to in spite of what anybody told me. Now I find that's not true. In the past I would look down on other women who could not do as well as me, and say, "What's wrong with them? I can do it. That they can't is their problem." But it's not just their problem, because I can't be free until they are too.

INTERVIEWER: Was there something that you feel you really learned from your experience of rape?

Ms. DAVIS: As I said, it started a whole chain reaction about race. I'd grown up with this liberal guilt, and I had made an attempt when I lived with a black woman to get rid of it. I don't want to carry around hundreds of years of guilt with me. It's not mine, and I refuse to do that. We became very close. I love her a great deal. She's a great person. The rape really unleashed my anger at black men, but then enabled me eventually to get beyond that, and to get back to seeing the black struggle as a very valid one, including the struggle of black men.

And, more important than anything else, it put me in touch with reality.

Ms. Davis's feelings of guilt for being white, and to a lesser extent, for being middle-class, obviously played an important part in the impact the rape had on her, and in her decision not to report her rapists. Her statement that while in prison rapists might simply rape men instead of women, so that prison is no solution, underestimates the importance of getting rapists off the street. This is not to say that there are not often excellent reasons for not reporting rape. Every woman has to determine whether she can handle the additional trauma that reporting rape can involve. A victim may very well feel that she will break down under the strain.

At the same time, if more women realized they could report rape without pressing charges, some police might be on the lookout for the rapist or might be more likely to believe another victim who comes in with a similar story.

One looks forward to the day when victims with the necessary strength and dedication will press charges and refuse to answer sexist questions in court about their past or present sex lives, or that of their husbands, or lovers, or children, questions that are now legally permissible. The first few women who do so will no doubt be convicted of contempt of court, but it will surely be a powerful impetus for change in the laws and their implementation. There is now a whole movement to support such courageous acts.

Ms. Davis's analysis of the relationship between sexism and rape, her perception of the connections between rape and milder forms of harassment, between rape and subtler forms of objectification of women, and between rape and common notions of what constitutes normal heterosexuality (*e.g.*, sexual fantasies, male-oriented sex, sexual liberation) is quite brilliant. And her thoughtful comments regarding the solutions to the problem of rape flow out of her excellent analysis of why men rape.

Perhaps her need to hold on to one of her abductors when she was shaking in the back seat after it was all over was motivated by a desire to normalize the situation. At any rate, some of the behavior arising out of this need on the part of many victims often leads to great skepticism on the part of the police. For example, if a rape victim eats or drinks with her rapists afterward, this will usually be seen as an indication it wasn't rape. The fact that Ms. Morrell, who was raped by the white fraternity man, had breakfast with her rapist (see Chapter 13) does not mean she wasn't raped. Nor does the fact that Ms. Davis needed to hold someone, even if he had just assaulted her, mean that it wasn't rape.

Like many rape victims, Ms. Davis described her rapists as psychotics, and yet their actions seem to belie this. In spite of Ms. Davis's sophistication regarding the cultural roots of rape, she still shares the need with many other rape victims to see her rapists as crazy. It is, after all, more threatening if we have to fear the sane men on the street than if we can restrict our fears to the crazy ones.

SEVENTEEN

Reverse Racism and Rape

My feeling inside was, I don't want him around, and I don't want to talk to him. And there was some fear, but then I shoved that down, and I said to myself, don't be so suspicious. Don't be so distrustful of people. Also, since he was black, there was that trip of, you know, blacks feel inferior, and blacks feel like they're always being pushed around, so try to be nice to this black guy.

The problems of white racism and reverse racism are sensitive issues that must be examined. Gina d'Amico saw herself as racist, and it was in part her struggle not to act in a racist manner that resulted in her being raped.

There are many cases like this. Not all are like Ms. d'Amico in regarding themselves as racist. What is common is the attempt on the part of many white victims to discount their feelings of mistrust for certain black men by seeing their mistrust as racist. Instead of following their feelings, they considered that their fear or lack of trust of the black men was racist, or that it would be seen as such by the men.

"Reverse racism" means that many white women put themselves in situations they would not otherwise enter if the men were white. They assume their lack of trust in black men is racist, when actually it may be quite appropriate. For example, many white women would accept a ride with two or more black men, but not from two or more white men. Others would allow themselves to talk with a black stranger, then go off somewhere alone with him, when they would not do this with a white man. Still others would tolerate more sexist talk from a black man than from a white man.

One white woman interviewed felt compassion rather than anger about black men's sexism because she believed it to be a consequence of the oppression of blacks by whites. She believed that many black men are not more sexist than white men, but they are more blatant in the way they express their sexist attitudes. When she was raped by one of her black men friends, who was offended by her unwillingness to have sex with him voluntarily, and by her statement that she was gay, she did some rapid re-thinking. She realized that even if black sexism *is* due to white oppression, it is no less real or dangerous for women, and that being more blatantly sexist may mean being more willing to act out an impulse to rape.

Ms. d'Amico was a week from being twenty when she was raped. She is now twenty-one. She described herself as from a "Latin family"; both her parents are Italian. Her mother, the chief breadwinner in the family, was a factory worker. Ms. d'Amico's father was unemployed most of the time, though he made some money on odd jobs.

GINA D'AMICO: Last year I worked at a shopping center across the street from X Park. I got to work about an hour early one day, so I decided to go over there and read. It was the middle of the day, August third, so it was really light out. I picked a place where there weren't a lot of people because I wanted to be alone. I leaned up against a tree, and I was reading when a guy walked by. He was black, and he looked tall and young. He just kind of looked at me, and I looked at him, while he kept walking away.

About five minutes later he came back to where I was sitting, and he said, "Do you mind some company?" and I said no. Later I'll get into all the feelings behind what I was saying. So he sat down, and for about fifteen or twenty minutes, we just talked about normal experiences, like do you go to school? Do you work around here? Small talk, like you do when you're getting to know somebody. He seemed kind of young and kind of friendly.

Then all of a sudden he said, "Do you mind if I sit closer?" Inside, I freaked out, and I don't know what made me say OK. He sat closer, and I started to get really scared. We were talking a lot, and then he said, "Can I kiss you?" and I said no, and he said, "Why?" and I said, "Well, because I don't want to do it, and it's not enjoyable unless both parties want to do it." I was getting ready to get up and split, because the whole thing had changed from a casual friendly conversation into this.

Then he reached over, and he touched my breast, and he said, "Do you like that?" and I said no! and I grabbed my purse, and I was going to split right then, but he put his arm around me really fast. He had kept his one hand in his pocket all the time, and he took it out and put something really sharp in my back. I thought it was a knife because that's what it felt like. It was very sharp. It turned out to be a piece of broken glass.

He grabbed my arm, and he had his other arm around my back with what I thought was a knife in it, and he said, "You come along with me, and you won't get hurt." I just froze, you know. Like, my heart just sank. The first thing I thought of was I was afraid I was going to die, and I didn't care about anything else. I looked around, but there was nobody around. It is really strange how you can be in the middle of all these people, but not have any people right there.

I got up, and I kept talking. In the course of the conversation, he told me his name, where he went to school, and his address, which all turned out to be correct. His name was Owen, and he went to X Tech, and he lived on Blank Avenue. I don't remember his last name now.

I kept saying, "Why do you want to do this? What is this? Why do you want to?" And he said, "Well, you wouldn't come back here with me if I didn't do it this way." And I said, "Yeah, well, you're right, but if somebody doesn't want to do something with you, it's not any good for you either." His whole facial expression and his tone of voice and everything had completely changed. It was like he was schizophrenic or something—very strange.

He took me behind an amphitheater made out of stone and cement. There's a wall behind the stage, and then there's a big line of redwoods, so there's really no way that you can see what's going on back there. I was looking around all the time, but there was nobody there. He let go of the hand that he had around me and undid my pants and took them down to about my knees, and then he kind of pushed me down on the ground. He didn't even take his pants off. He just unzipped them and came inside me.

I tried to really tighten up my muscles, so that he couldn't enter me. He could tell I was doing that, and he stuck the glass in me harder, and he said, "You better help." He said, "Kiss me," and I said, "I'm not going to kiss you. There's no way, man, that I'm going to do that. You're doing enough to me. Don't ask me to *kiss* you!"

I never stopped talking. I guess I was maybe talking to myself more than anything else. I said at one point to him, "You're not fucking me. You're fucking yourself." It was over really fast, you know. Afterward he got up and said, "Now, that wasn't so bad, was it?" and just walked away. I lay there shaking my head and saying, "What just happened to me?"

INTERVIEWER: Did he say anything while he was raping you?

Ms. D'AMICO: He kept telling me to shut up.

INTERVIEWER: When did you realize that he had a piece of glass, not a knife?

Ms. D'AMICO: Oh, I didn't realize it until we'd gotten behind the amphitheater, and he had taken his hand from around me to undo my pants, and then I saw it was a piece of glass. Some little kids had been in the amphitheater earlier breaking bottles against the stone.

Evidently, he walked over there, decided what he was going to do, got a piece of that glass and put it in his pocket, and then came back.

INTERVIEWER: Was it pretty lethal?

Ms. D'AMICO: It looked like it could be. I had a flash for a second to run, but he was a very healthy-looking boy. He was tall, and he was young, and I didn't know how far I'd get. I guess right then I was not very worried about getting raped. I was worried about getting my life taken, or getting scarred up. I didn't have the anger to fight. There was a lot of fear, and there was a lot of pity, which was awfully strange, but there wasn't anger, and there wasn't hate.

INTERVIEWER: Why did you feel pity?

Ms. D'AMICO: Because that's part of the thing that I was brought up with. In order to live in my house, I learned at a young age to change hate into pity. My father is a strange man, and he put a lot of strange trips on me and my family. Also, I have a lot of white man's guilt. To this day I think I'm patronizing to blacks.

INTERVIEWER: Could you say what you were feeling when he asked to join you?

Ms. D'AMICO: My feeling inside was, I don't want him around, and I don't want to talk to him. And there was some fear, but then I shoved that down, and I said to myself, don't be so suspicious. Don't be so distrustful of people. Also, since he was black, there was that trip of, you know, blacks feel inferior, and blacks feel like they're always being pushed around, so try to be nice to this black guy. It's hard for me to even say this now, because I really dislike it in myself.

INTERVIEWER: When he asked if he could come closer to you, what did you feel then?

Ms. D'AMICO: There was just a lot of fear at that point. "Oh, oh, what's going on here," that kind of feeling. But I'd learned so well not to act on my feelings, that I suppressed any impulse to act. Right now, I wouldn't hesitate to just get up and run or something, but it's a strange feeling, as though you're in shock, and you can't move. You are glued to wherever you are. It's like you can't act on your feelings.

INTERVIEWER: What was your feeling?

Ms. D'AMICO: My feeling was fear. My feeling was, there's something going on here, and this isn't a good place to be. But at that point, it all started happening so fast. As soon as he moved toward me, he wanted to kiss me, and then he touched my breast, and then it all happened in less than a minute. I had all these conflicting things going through my head, and so instead of listening to any of them, I just sat there.

INTERVIEWER: Were you afraid to run away?

Ms. D'AMICO: I guess I was. I guess my guilt was also pretty strong right then.

INTERVIEWER: Your guilt?

Ms. D'AMICO: Yeah. I don't know. Maybe a feeling of foolishness, you know. When I think about it now, there are still so many things I'm not sure about, and I may not be for a long time yet. But I know now that I could have easily avoided it.

INTERVIEWER: How?

Ms. D'AMICO: Just by following my true feelings. In the very beginning, as soon as he said, "Do you want some company?" I should have said no. But it's taken me a long time to learn how to say no to people. I don't know if it's just being a woman. I'm sure that has something to do with it. You know, you give and give and give of yourself, until you're nothing anymore. Now I can say no to people more easily. I really didn't want his company. I was really into this book, and I didn't feel like getting disrupted. If I had just said, "No, I really don't feel like company, I feel like being alone," I don't think that he would have done it.

INTERVIEWER: You don't?

Ms. D'AMICO: I don't think so, because I think there was a lot of planning involved, and I don't think he was that sure of himself. I think he was scared too, but I think he got his courage up the whole time that we were sitting there talking.

He probably got more sexually excited too, sitting there talking. I was wearing a shirt and didn't have any bra on. It's a strange thing, because now I have a lot more fears about men using me as a sexual object, and I'm a lot more sensitive to it.

INTERVIEWER: What do you think his motivation was?

Ms. D'AMICO: I think he just wanted to have an orgasm. It turned out that I was the first of three girls that he raped. At any rate, I was the first that reported it. He may have raped many more, but there were three of us that finally went to court. During the summer, he raped two other girls, both white. And I feel that was the motivation for it. I think there was an insecurity, both in his malehood and in his race, a really deep insecurity.

INTERVIEWER: What made you feel that?

Ms. D'AMICO: I mentioned love to him at some point when trying to talk him out of raping me. I said, "This is no substitute for love," or something to that effect. And it was almost as if he kind of sneered at that bullshit remark. And that was the feeling that I got when he asked me to kiss him. It was as if he wanted to make love, but didn't know how to do it.

INTERVIEWER: How old do you think he was?

Ms. D'AMICO: He's seventeen.

INTERVIEWER: How long did the actual rape part of it last?

Ms. D'AMICO: Oh, four or five minutes. It was very short. He was very hard when he came inside me, and he climaxed in no time at all. Then he got up and put it inside, zipped his pants up, and walked away.

What really blew my mind was the changes I saw in him. I saw him as very young, very scared, and very insecure when he was talking to me at the beginning. Now I'm remembering things I said to him after this point. I kept telling him to look at me, because I thought that would bring him back to the conversation we had had, but he wouldn't look at me. He wouldn't make eye contact. He seemed very young and scared.

But later, he had the determination of a madman. I couldn't talk to him at all.

When he got done, he said, "Ah, that wasn't so bad, was it?" He was like a dapper type, you know, "Look at me, man, I'm a big bad tough" type of thing. It was like he was very satisfied with himself then. That remark was a very masculine type remark to make. I think that he probably got a lot of masculine ego fulfillment from it.

By the time he walked off, it was time for me to go to work. I worked with all young girls about my age or a little older, and I walked in there, and I said, "Rita, I'm not going to come to work. I've just been raped." I was spaced out and bleary eyed, and she didn't know what to do. She hugged me and sat me down and said, "Don't worry about a thing. I'll stay here tonight and take your place." It was just a part-time job.

I didn't know what to do, and she asked me if I wanted her to call Jake, who was one of the security guards there. For some reason I didn't want any male that I knew to know. Especially him, because I guess I'd always felt sexual overtones in his rapport with me, and he was also black.

I was also working at a drug house. I was volunteering there, and also going to groups there and stuff, and I thought those were the people I wanted to talk to.

INTERVIEWER: You didn't think of calling the police at that point?

Ms. D'AMICO: No, I didn't. In fact, I wouldn't have called them at all. What happened was I tried to get hold of the guy that ran this group, the guy that was the head of the place, but he was in a group, and they don't disturb them when they're in a group. So I just sat there for about half an hour, and then I said OK, I'm going to drive over there. So I drove over, and I just broke into the group. That was when I let it all out, you know. I said, "I got to talk to somebody." I was almost yelling. I said, "I've just been raped in a park."

It just really blew their minds. Then I started yelling. I don't even remember what I was screaming, but I was yelling something about civilization. I was putting it off on the world.

Then this guy talked to me, and he said, "I think you should call the police," and I said, "I don't want to." And he said, "Well, why?" I said, "I don't feel like it's going to do him any good, and I don't have any trust or faith in how the police would handle a situation like this, or handle a guy like that. He'd just be ill treated." He said, "Well, it could happen to other women, and other women that wouldn't accept it like you did. A lot of women would fight, and they'd get hurt, and a lot of women would be virgins, and it would really screw them up." I thought about that, and I said, "Yeah, you're right. I hadn't even thought about that." And so he called the police.

This guy went with me to the police station, and the police came and picked me up. They took me to the hospital first. They have to take a sample to see if you have any sperm in you before they'll believe you've been raped. They got me in this little room, and they took a report.

These two policemen had really come to the conclusion among themselves that I knew this guy, so they tried to get that out of me. They kept saying, "Are you sure you didn't know this guy already?" And they told me that they have a lot of women who come in and say they've been raped just to get men in trouble. Their attitude was, here's this woman trying to get this guy hooked. They said lots of women know the man, and it comes out later.

INTERVIEWER: As if that means they weren't raped.

Ms. D'AMICO: Right. It really bugged me. I said, "I don't know this guy. I've never seen him before in my life!" They couldn't believe, I guess, that I didn't fight at all, which is what I had told them. They couldn't believe that I sat there and talked to him for fifteen minutes. What really bothers me is that when you tell the truth, people don't believe you. They'll say, "That's bull shit. You're not telling the truth."

So, at first they were very suspicious, and really, really giving it to me, really trying to make me break down and say something that I hadn't told them. I kept repeating the same thing over again, and getting more and more pissed off. Finally, they accepted what I said, and then their attitudes changed a bit, and they became more friendly and more helpful. I talked to them for about two hours. They wanted to know every little detail, you know, *everything*. Was the piece of glass colored, the thickness, the size, and what did he look like, what was he wearing? The next thing I had to do was go look at mug shots.

Things were kind of quiet until he'd raped the third girl, and they caught him right after, because immediately after she was raped, she went and called the police. They were almost on the lookout by this time, because two of us had been raped within one block of the same area. So was the third girl. She had fought, and she had been hurt. He used pieces of glass every time. They found the glass, and they got his fingerprints, and so there was really a lot of evidence.

INTERVIEWER: But you also had quite a lot of evidence. You knew the school he went to, you knew his name, you knew the street he lived on. Why do you think they weren't able to trace him from this information?

Ms. D'AMICO: That's a good question. They would have been able to. All they would have had to do was get an X Tech yearbook, and let me look in it, and I would have found him. But I guess they didn't believe that it was possible that this guy would have told the truth in all these instances.

I got the feeling that they felt that one report from one woman wasn't substantial enough. The policemen also said that so many women get raped that don't bother to report it, whatever that was supposed to mean.

The worst part of this whole thing was going to court. That was just unbelievable. After he was caught, this sergeant, who was one of the nicest people that I had contact with throughout this whole thing, had six pictures, and he told me to look through them. I saw his picture, and immediately I said, "This is the guy that raped me." And he said, "Are you sure?" and I said, "Yeah." So he set a date for the hearing. It was to be a preliminary hearing for them to decide whether there needed to be a trial or not. I think it was on the day of the hearing that they shuffled me into the D.A.'s office, and this stranger I'd never seen before reads my report to me, just to freshen my mind, and he prepares me for being smeared all over the place.

INTERVIEWER: Had you not been prepared before for the kind of questions you would get?

Ms. D'AMICO: Not to this extent, no.

The judge was a *fucker!* God, he was a cold man. I was the first one. They did it in order of how we had been raped, and since it was a preliminary hearing, the other girls had to wait outside while I was testifying. Apparently, the last girl who had been raped was really affected by it. She came walking up to the courtroom, clinging to her husband. They had just been married. Apparently, she had been a virgin before the rape.

But I wasn't allowed to hear their testimony, just as they couldn't hear mine. Owen, the guy that had raped us, was in the courtroom. So were his mother and some of his family, which was really hard. I looked at his mother. She fascinated me. She was a little, very frail woman, and very, very anxious, wringing her hands. We all had to stand together outside the courtroom and wait for it to open. Owen kept looking at his mother, who had to wait out there with us. Neither one of them would look at any of us. It was very uncomfortable and awkward.

Finally everybody was let in except the other two girls and their husbands. First of all, the D.A. asked the judge if all unnecessary people could be cleared out of the courtroom. There were a lot of observers, and he pointed out that it was going to be a very sensitive topic. The judge said, "No, I don't feel that's necessary."

The first thing he asked was my name, my address, things like that. Then they asked me things like, was I a virgin when this happened? and when was the last time I had sex? how many men approximately had I had intercourse with before this happened? And then he asked me how it happened.

They tried to make it sound like I was responsible for it. It was the judge's tone of voice that was so incredible. He said, "Do you wear a bra?" but it sounded like, "You pig, do you wear a bra?" He should have put "pig" in front of his questions, because that's how he was saying it. And he wanted to know "was he hard?" and "was I wet?" He wanted to know if I was wet! It really blew my mind. It was hard for me to yell these answers out, but the judge kept saying, "Speak up, speak up." I feel like punching him now, but I didn't then. Right at that time I was almost crying, and I was scared. I wouldn't speak up to his satisfaction, so finally he had a microphone put under my mouth. Right now, while I'm thinking about it, I would like to beat him. Finally I got off the stand.

Later the district attorney questioned me, but of course, he was trying to prosecute this guy, so he didn't go through the same trip as the defense attorney had. When I left, I just ran out of that place. It was really bad. I was thinking about the trial and how I didn't want to have anything to do with it. I didn't want to go through all this again. They told me when the trial was going to be. It was a couple of months later.

But apparently Owen pled guilty because of all the evidence against him. So I didn't have to go down there again. Apparently, the judge had really given the other girls a very bad time. I talked to the girl who was raped right after me. I'm sure she really, really got ripped apart, because she had just gotten out of a live-in community for drug addicts. She had been addicted to heroin, and she had gotten out of there the day that it happened. Owen had accused one of them, I think it was her, of trying to sell him dope. I don't know how he could have possibly known that unless he had talked to her too, and she had told him she'd just left the place. I'm sure that they just ripped her apart. The D.A. told me when he called me up afterward that he'd put something in the record about the judge, because he was unnecessarily cruel to the women.

INTERVIEWER: Did you hear what happened to the last woman?

Ms. D'AMICO: I heard something about her husband trying to jump over the rail to either attack the defense attorney or the judge. I could see that this last girl was ready to break down when she was walking up there. She was really, really on the edge, and I'm sure it didn't take much. She seemed to be the one who was most psychologically affected, outwardly at least. But then again, there's no way of really telling that.

INTERVIEWER: Was it reported in the paper?

Ms. D'AMICO: It may have been, but I didn't see anything in the paper.

INTERVIEWER: What was the outcome?

Ms. D'AMICO: He pled guilty, but I never found out what happened to him until the other day when I got hold of the sergeant, because I really wanted to know. He said he remembered me, and he said that since Owen was only seventeen, he had been given to the California youth authority. They don't give them a sentence for any specific length of time there. He said it's an institution where they get a lot of psychiatric help. He said that sometimes they'll keep them in until they're twenty-five. Or they'll let them out, and they'll have to come back and report—a parole type thing—until they're twenty-five.

INTERVIEWER: How does that make you feel?

Ms. D'AMICO: I just hope that there's a lot of psychiatric help, because I feel he really needs it. But I'm kind of pessimistic and negative about government institutions.

INTERVIEWER: How did you feel about the trial?

Ms. D'AMICO: I felt like I was the one that was being tried. It just pissed me off. After I left, I cried for a long time, because that was how I got all that anger out. That has been my way traditionally of getting all my anger out, which is really fucked, because you don't deal with anything that way. I felt like being on trial was worse than being raped. I felt like that was the true rape. Man, *that was the rape of my soul!* I hated the judge, and I hated that defense attorney. He was an older middle-aged, long-haired, mod attorney, and I felt like he was just a big dick walking around. I really did. It really bugged me.

INTERVIEWER: Did the rape experience affect your attitude toward men at all?

Ms. D'AMICO: Yeah, I think it did. I had had an IUD in, and I had had a little bit of trouble with it. When I went to the hospital that night, the doctor who had to tell them if there was sperm in me or not happened to be a really, really fine person. He told me that I also had an infection of some kind and to come to his office. I must have gone there five times after this happened, and he never charged me a cent for it. Shortly after that, I had the IUD out, because I felt turned off to having sex. I really did. I didn't have any for quite a while. It must have been about three or four months before I did anything else again.

INTERVIEWER: Was the infection caused by the rape?

Ms. D'AMICO: No, the doctor didn't think so. I went to the hospital six hours after I was raped, and the infection was one that looked like it had been around awhile, because I was having a lot of discharge. I'd noticed it before, but I'd kind of gotten used to the fact that if you're a woman you've got to fuck up your body in order to be with men. I had already gone through two kinds of pills that had screwed my body up. And I tried the IUD, and it hurt, but I thought, oh, well, it's not as bad as the pills. But after all that happened, I didn't care about sex anymore.

The experience seemed to numb me. I could talk to other people about it and laugh and say, "I'm still alive. It's no big thing," but the changes that happened were so gradual, I didn't see them until a long time after. My ability now to get angry at people, for example, because there was so much anger from that experience. I was even angry at myself because of the realization that to a certain extent, I'd let it happen. Understanding how and why it happened made me change.

INTERVIEWER: But it seems that it did actually affect your attitude to sex pretty immediately.

Ms. D'AMICO: It really did. And I was worried because I hadn't had a period for about three or four months. So then I went through this traumatic thing of worrying about being pregnant. I didn't get my period for about six months, and the only way I could start it again was to go back on pills. As soon as I got back on the pills, I started having sex again. It's almost a kind of logic like, if you're going to be fucking up your body, you might as well be out screwing while you're at it.

INTERVIEWER: So, did it affect your attitudes toward men in any other way?

Ms. D'AMICO: Yeah. It made me very aware of being manipulated. I'm not flattered anymore by sexual compliments or overtones of any kind. In fact, that turns me off. I'm better able to recognize a man's motivation to want to know me and able to tell somebody, "No, I don't dig where you're at, and I don't want any part of you."

INTERVIEWER: Did it affect your attitude toward yourself at all?

Ms. D'AMICO: I think it did. I'm from a Latin family and my father's a chauvinist. He's an insecure male who's dominated my mother and his family his whole life, and that's where he gets his balls. I could see that it was so important to him, that I came to fear hurting him for fear that he would fall apart. That was where the guilt came from. It's still hard to deal with the guilt, but the anger is almost as strong.

I still have a lot of anger for myself, but I'm learning to like myself better all the time. I'm learning to be able to free myself to the point of throwing things around, or being angry. And I realize what I was trying to do before. I was seeing so much hassle, and so many bad vibes around, that I was trying to absorb them all within me to make everything right, like a good little mother should do, or a good little woman.

INTERVIEWER: In some ways it seems as if the effect of the rape was to put you in a better, rather than a worse, place.

Ms. D'AMICO: Yeah, right. Exactly. I think it helped.

INTERVIEWER: And what effect did the trial have on you?

Ms. D'AMICO: That was really hard, because I felt like I'd been through a really hard experience. And I really had believed that I was going to be treated with some kind of respect. Maybe I wanted some sympathy. But instead, I felt like I was kicked around like a piece of shit. It made me see the whole thing about justice as just a complete farce. Now here's this judge, and he won't even clear the court of all these men. I don't know what they were doing in there.

INTERVIEWER: Was it mainly men in there?

Ms. D'AMICO: Maybe I was just more sensitive to the presence of men, but it seemed that there were mostly men in there. There was this one young guy in there, and I remember him laughing at a lot of parts of it, and it was really hard to take.

INTERVIEWER: How did the people you told about it react?

Ms. D'AMICO: I didn't tell too many people, mostly because I didn't want to be viewed as, "There's the one that's been raped." I told a few very close friends, and they were surprised and shocked, and then they were curious and wanted to know how it had happened.

One friend told me that she always had a feeling that something like that was going to happen to me. She's the type of person who's very self-protective. She'd never peep her head out after dark, and things like that, and she's very guided by her fears. She always felt I was too trusting.

INTERVIEWER: Did you notice any difference in the reactions of men and women?

Ms. D'AMICO: Well, the women were the ones that usually had the curiosity about the details. The men would express some kind of sympathy, or some kind of horror, and that would usually be it. They wouldn't try to understand the whole thing—except for one guy with a lot of sexual problems. He reacted with the most interest of everybody. He wanted to know how I was taking it, how I was feeling about it, if I felt scared of men in general.

But I really didn't tell that many people. I didn't tell any older people that I knew. I definitely didn't tell my parents. They probably would have packed me up and dragged me home. They live just a few miles away.

INTERVIEWER: That must have made it harder not to let them know.

Ms. D'AMICO: It did. It was hard going over there. It's like a whole part of my being that I just leave outside the door.

INTERVIEWER: Did you get much support while you were going through the trial?

Ms. D'AMICO: No, I didn't. I didn't know anybody who could really give me any support. I just did it by myself. The only person I could talk to was the guy I mentioned, David. Sometimes I felt I just wanted to hold somebody, but there wasn't anybody there that I could do that with. It was like learning to hold myself.

INTERVIEWER: Did your experience of rape change your attitude to rape at all?

Ms. D'AMICO: I guess it did. I guess it had always been like a monster story in my head, or something very terrifying. But it's really two humans, you know. I've always wondered how my experience compares to other women's experiences who've been raped, because I'm sure there are a lot more terrifying experiences.

There's still a lot of fear in me of being attacked. One thing that I would like to do is to have some self-defense lessons that won't cost too much money.

Aside from the part Ms. d'Amico's struggle not to be racist played in her getting raped, her conditioning as a woman was also very important. She suppressed her impulse to act, had difficulty in saying no, had difficulty in expressing anger, and had feelings of guilt about being raped. Since she brings out the connection between these feelings and her socialization as a woman so clearly in the interview, it requires no further elaboration here.

Very few rape victims manage to grow as a result of the experience and turn it into something positive, but Ms. d'Amico was able to do this. She was able to see that her concept of the female role made her ineffectual in dealing with her rapist, and this helped her be more assertive and open with her anger. In turn, this has made her feel much better about herself.

As long as rape victims are put on trial, rape will rarely be reported, and when it is reported, the victims will often decide against pressing charges. An attorney who had been practicing in the Bay Area for ten years has said that unless the circumstances are particularly grisly, or the man is witnessed or caught in the act of intercourse, the case won't have a chance of reaching court. A doctor who had been assigned by the city of Oakland to examine rape victims was asked why so few rape cases got as far as the courts. His response (paraphrased) is illuminating:

We try to discourage the women from going through with it because it's such a strain and often an embarrassment. All the defending lawyer has to do is establish a "reasonable doubt" in the jury's mind. This is easily done by bringing in her whole sexual history. If a woman has been with more than ten men before she's

thirty, she doesn't have a hope. A woman who was attacked early
one Saturday morning in her own house reported it to the police
with a positive test, went home, and was attacked the following
Saturday morning by the same man. The police *knew* it wouldn't be
worth even attempting to take it to court. The jury wouldn't believe
anything like this.

The doctor was then asked, "Would you recommend that rape victims
report to a city doctor like yourself afterward?" His reply was, "No, not
really. There's really no conclusive evidence in a pelvic examination except
the fact that she did have intercourse with someone. Moreover, it's a terribly
embarrassing procedure for a woman to go through, filing complaints, the
trial, etc. I know of a case where the fact that the woman had been raped was
used against her, enabling her parents-in-law to gain custody of her children."

The doctor mentioned that he had heard of one successful conviction
about three years ago. Someone had made the mistake of assaulting a
state attorney's daughter. The authorities did everything but bring in the
FBI. Fingerprints were checked, photos taken, and practically the same
procedure as for a murder case was followed. In the end, someone was
convicted.

When it is one woman's word against one man's, the woman will rarely
be believed, unless she is the equivalent of the state attorney's daughter.
The word of three women against one man is more likely to be taken
seriously. In some states the law actually requires that there be a witness to
corroborate the victim's story in order for a woman to press charges against a
rapist.

The American system of justice provides the vast majority of rape
victims with no redress. Even if we recognize the importance of protecting
the rights of the innocent, and the difficulty of proving guilt in cases of rape,
these factors do not adequately explain the gross treatment so many victims
receive. Why, for example, wasn't the information given by Ms. d'Amico
followed up by the police? Why did they assume she knew her rapist and
imply that she was reporting him in order to get him into trouble? The
answer may well be that police, as men, are more concerned that a man
might be falsely accused than that a woman may have been raped.

However, the attitudes of police and the legal system are no different
from those of most people in this society, and we fool ourselves if we think
that if it weren't for nasty policemen and judges, rape victims would get a
fair deal.

Rape and Society

Only 4% of reported rapes involved any precipitative behavior on the part of the victim.
—*Federal Commission on Crimes of Violence*

"The newspapers print only what they want to. I tell them about little girls of seven or eight who come up with venereal disease inflicted on them by male members of their own families. An appalling number of 11- and 12-year-olds are giving birth after being raped by their own fathers. But they won't print things like this. They're only heartbreaking and horrible—not sensational."
—Lieutenant Robert Caldwell, Chief of the Sex Section, Police Dept., Washington, D.C., quoted by Peggy Alderton, in "Rape!," an unpublished paper written in 1972

"During 1970, in San Francisco, there were 621 reported cases of rape. Fifty-nine cases of forcible rape actually reached Superior Court. There were 27 convictions and three acquittals or dismissals. The remaining 32 cases were still pending at the end of 1970. Out of 27 convictions, six men were sent to State prison, one to the California Youth Authority, six were put on probation, thirteen were given probation on the condition they serve approximately a year in the county jail, and one man was referred to a narcotics rehabilitation center."
—Gail Bernice Sullivan, "Rape and Its Neglected Victims," *San Francisco Chronicle*, April 9, 1972

EIGHTEEN

Keep It to Yourself

> I had tried to talk to people close to me about it, but I couldn't, because nobody would listen.... When I tried to talk to other people about it, I felt like I was talking about something I wasn't supposed to be talking about.

Rape has only recently been recognized as a widespread and serious problem. People haven't wanted to know about it before. Many are still unwilling. When Betty Duncan was raped three years ago, for example, rape was still a taboo topic for discussion. Other things being equal, the more taboo it is to talk about an experience the more traumatic it is likely to be. As a result of this reaction from family, friends, and police, Ms. Duncan tried to repress her ugly experience, and the price she had to pay for that was high indeed.

Thanks to the growing numbers of rape victims who are now willing to speak out, it is becoming impossible for people to bury their heads in the sand and continue pretending that rapists are the crazy few and rape victims the provocative few who deserve what they get.

Ms. Duncan is a twenty-six-year-old black social worker, recently married, who describes herself as "middle class or upper middle class." She was unmarried at the time of her rape experience three years ago.

BETTY DUNCAN: I had been dating a guy for about three months, and we were in the middle of breaking up. I was really upset the weekend this happened. I went over to a girl friend's house and spent several hours with her, talking and trying to get myself together. But I was still very upset when I got home about nine or ten on Sunday night. I must have gone to bed about midnight.

At about two in the morning I was awakened by someone holding a pillow over my face. He did it very lightly, but enough to make me wake up. I remember being really confused. I couldn't understand how the guy had gotten into my apartment. I lived on the second floor of a modern apartment building because it seemed safer than living on the first floor. I had put a chain on my door and locked the door before I went to bed. I had left the sliding glass door to my balcony open, but the screen door behind it was locked, and to get to it you had to climb over a couple of fences. Anyhow, the guy had unlocked the screen door by cutting a hole in it.

I must have been in a really deep sleep, because I didn't hear him at all until he had this pillow over my face. He pressed it down a little bit and told me not to scream. Then he took the pillow away and told me not to move or he'd kill me. He was fully clothed, but he then took down his pants, and that's when I realized what was going on. I started to fight, but it's hard to do that when you're flat on your back, and somebody's holding you.

There was no physical violence to me other than being raped. He spoke very softly. I never could see his face. It was pitch black in the room. I don't know whether he had a mask on or what, but I could not see the features of his face. He got into bed with me, and I tried to fight. I was very tempted to try to kick him in the balls, but I couldn't figure out how I was going to get out of bed after doing that, to get to the door and get out.

I tried to struggle, but he said again, "Don't fight, or I'll get my knife out and kill you." Another time he put his hands around my neck. I found out later he was wearing gloves. So, he had his hands on my neck, his thumbs on my windpipe, and again he said, "If you move, I'll kill you."

He wasn't aroused at all at first. He had to play with himself to get a hard on, and again I had to lie there feeling very helpless, feeling like I ought to be fighting. I remember thinking that I ought to be doing something, but then I thought, "I'm not going to risk getting myself killed. I'm just going to gamble that this guy's not going to kill me. And I'm not trying to save my virtue, so there's no point in fighting."

I moaned in a very disgusted way, which apparently bothered him. He told me to cut it out. Then I made myself relax physically. I had had a lot of training in dance, and I made myself relax as completely as I could physically, because I thought if he's going to do this, he's not going to enjoy it. That was the only form of fighting I could do at that time.

Before I had realized what he was going to do, I had asked him, "What are you here for? Are you here for money?" Apparently that gave him the idea that maybe he should rob me too. So after he raped me he asked me where my purse was, and I told him, and he took all my money, about ten dollars. He told me he was going to be nice and leave me my credit cards. He told me to stay still and to not move until he left. I heard him take the chain off the door, so I knew he hadn't come in that way, and then he left.

I got up and went to the balcony. I could see him leaving, but I could only see his back. It's making me kind of sick to think about it now. First I called my older sister, but her line was busy because she had taken the phone off the hook. Then I called the police. Then I called my mother. It was 2:30 in the morning. I was crying by this time. I told her what happened, and she screamed and said, "I'll be right over." She got there at the same time that the police did. The police got there pretty quickly, in about ten or fifteen minutes.

The two officers were pretty nice, but I don't think they believed a word I said. By that time I was in a state of shock. I had really gone into traumatic shock, but I *sounded* very calm. I kept shaking, but I wasn't hysterical, and I wasn't screaming. I appeared very calm. I felt very, very detached from myself. I told them what had happened. They took the report, and then they told me that they would have to take me to the hospital to get evidence. That was the way they put it. It wasn't really to see if I had been damaged at all, but to get evidence!

So we went there, and my mother went with me. My mother was very concerned about whether it would get in the papers or not, which made me extremely angry with her. When I went into the examining room, the nurse who was preparing me said something like, "What's wrong with these guys tonight? There's been three rapes this evening. Must be a full moon or something." It was really a callous kind of attitude. She might have been trying to help me, but that just wasn't what I needed. I didn't need to know I was the third one that night!

I stayed home from work the next day, and I stayed in a state of shock for two months. I wandered around like it hadn't happened to me, feeling like there was a numb spot in my brain. Finally, my supervisor, who's really beautiful, said, "Why don't you go downstairs and see one of the counselors and maybe they can help you." He'd noticed that something was not right. So I saw a counselor, and that helped some. But I happened to know the guy, so he didn't want to get into a therapeutic thing with me. He told me that I should go see someone else, and gave me a name, but I didn't go right away.

At that time I was the kind of person who would hold in everything. I remember getting a rash on my hands, like water bubbles or something. Every time I got nervous, the palms of my hands and my wrists would break out. I didn't connect it with anything. I thought it was some strange disease, but it was clearly a stress reaction. I also got a severe pain in my hip for about two months. I could walk, but it was really painful, and that too, I think, was a stress reaction.

I stayed in the same apartment because I decided that if I didn't think about it, it would go away. I had tried to talk to people close to me about it, but I couldn't, because nobody would listen. I didn't even talk to my mother because she had made it very clear that she didn't want to deal with it. That's her philosophy—if you don't think about it, it will go away. My older sister listened, but then she said, "Oh, yeah, well, that kind of thing happens." And my closest girl friends got freaked by it. When I tried to talk to other people about it, I felt like I was talking about something I wasn't supposed to be talking about.

INTERVIEWER: Did you get any support from anybody?

Ms. DUNCAN: No, not at that time. I understand that it's just too close to women to want to hear about it. I can rationally understand this, but emotionally I can't.

I began to go out with a man shortly after that. He went into a big protection thing, you know, "Boy, I wish I had been there. I would have killed him." That wasn't what I was asking for. I was asking for somebody to tell me it was OK, to just be there with me, but that's not what men seem able to be when it comes to rape.

I went out with him for about two months. Then I came up here for Memorial Day weekend with some girl friends, and when I went back to Los Angeles, the guy had married somebody else. He hadn't bothered to mention that little fact to me. I got home and hadn't heard from him for a couple of days, so I called, and his number had been changed. So I called the other number, and he answered and said something like, "Oh, I happened to get married last weekend."

That's when it really all came down on me. I got really upset, I mean, hysterically upset. Nobody thirty-one years old just happens to get married, but I couldn't say anything to him. I was just stunned. All I said to him was, "Oh." Then I hung up, and I started crying. I called my sister, and she came over. She was trying to be helpful. She brought a bottle of tranquilizers with her, and we talked for an hour or so, and then she left.

I tried to go to bed, but I couldn't sleep because I kept crying and being really upset. All these awful things were happening to me. Finally I went to get one of the tranquilizers that my sister had left, and I sat for an hour staring at the bottle of pills, trying to figure out why I shouldn't take all of them. I literally went through a whole battle with myself about how come I shouldn't kill myself. There was a part of me that kept saying, "Come on, that's silly. You don't want to do that." And another part kept saying, "Why not? There's nothing left."

What finally got me out of it was that it suddenly occurred to me that if I killed myself, this guy that had just gotten married would think it was because of him. He was such an egotistical bastard, he'd probably think, "Wow! Some girl killed herself for me." I wasn't going to give him that pleasure! That was the first healthy thought I had—it wasn't me I was mad at, it was him. But I had scared myself, so I went into psychotherapy and was in therapy for two years. I still haven't completely gotten over all those things happening to me like that.

INTERVIEWER: Did anything eventually come out of your meetings with the police?

Ms. DUNCAN: No. About two days after I reported the incident, the police came to my apartment, looked at the screen, and saw that it had been cut open. They figured that he was wearing gloves. And later, when I wanted to wash the dishes I realized that my gloves weren't there and that he must have gone into the kitchen and taken them. So I called the police who were supposed to be in charge of my case, because this meant that there should be fingerprints on the screen door, which he'd have touched before he'd put on my gloves. They said that, well, if there were fingerprints on the door, they were probably gone by then, and not to worry about it. That was the last I ever heard from them. I checked later with some friends of mine who were deputy sheriffs, and they told me that fingerprints stay for a long time. They just didn't want to be bothered coming out to take fingerprints.

One of the first questions the police had asked me was, "Did you know him?" I said, "No, I couldn't see his face," but I knew that I didn't know his voice, so it wasn't somebody I knew. But something kept going through my mind, and I didn't know what to do with it. There had been a guy who lived in the building who had moved right around that time. He was about the same height and build as the rapist, and I remember that he used to stand in front of his apartment and look down from the balcony at me as I would go in. Sometimes I would say hello to him, and he would kind of smile. It was obviously a leering kind of look.

About three weeks after I was raped, I happened to be going out to my car on my way to work. This guy was sitting in his car, and he called across the street, using my name, with this big smile on his face. He could have gotten my name from the roster on the apartment building, which I had taken off after I was raped, but he had never said anything to me before, and there was this big smile on his face. I remember going to work wondering if he had done it, and then not knowing what to do about it.

I couldn't identify the rapist, because I couldn't see his face. By that time I had figured that the police really didn't care anyway, so I didn't know what to do with the idea. I thought if I called the police and said, "Well, I think that it was a neighbor because he smiled and said hello this morning," that just wouldn't sound reasonable. But that was something that I always kept thinking about.

INTERVIEWER: What were your impressions of the motivation of your rapist? Did you think that he came in with the sole intention of raping you?

Ms. DUNCAN: Yes, I think he did. As I said, I think robbery was a secondary thought. I remember trying to convince myself that he was a very sick individual, and therefore that I shouldn't be angry at him. I'm sure he was sick.

INTERVIEWER: Besides his verbal threats, how forceful was he?

Ms. DUNCAN: He wasn't very forceful except when he put his hands on my throat and squeezed. Even that wasn't very forceful, but it was frightening.

INTERVIEWER: Did you say anything?

Ms. DUNCAN: I remember telling him, "Please don't," and "Get away from me," but that was all. I remember thinking that if I screamed no one would come.

INTERVIEWER: What sort of emotions were you in touch with during and after the rape?

Ms. DUNCAN: The main feeling during the rape and right after it was fear. I was also very disgusted. And I was angry. I got disgusted and angry at the point where he had to play with himself. During the rape I felt fearful, and I felt shame.

INTERVIEWER: Did the experience affect your behavior in any way?

Ms. DUNCAN: I don't think it affected it very much outwardly at the time. It was mostly an inside thing. I got literally numb. Nothing affected me. The physical reactions that I described were the main things that happened right after the rape. When I got into therapy, a lot of other things started to happen, but my behavior didn't change a great deal.

INTERVIEWER: Did the experience affect any of your attitudes toward sex or toward men?

Ms. DUNCAN: For a while it did. Again, that was mostly kept inside. I remember being very, very fearful around men. I was in a job where I interviewed people, and I would see men, and it would flash in my head, is that the guy? I was much colder sexually for quite a while afterward. It got much harder for me to be aroused or turned on.

Aside from sexually, it mainly added to the feelings I was already developing. At that time I had been going through a number of bad experiences with men, and it mostly made me more cautious and more withdrawn. It took me a while to work through these feelings.

INTERVIEWER: Did it affect any of your attitudes toward yourself?

Ms. Duncan: Very much so. I thought that I must have done something to deserve it. For a long time I thought that I should have fought, and I felt badly that I hadn't put up a valiant effort to do something or other. And I felt ashamed.

Interviewer: Did your experience of rape change any prior notions that you had had about rape?

Ms. Duncan: Yes, it did. I hadn't thought very much about it before. I thought a lot about it afterwards. I can better understand now how things like that happen. I've talked with young girls who have been raped, and their emotional reaction is much the same as mine was. I've gotten a lot angrier.

Interviewer: Do you regret in any way the way you handled the situation?

Ms. Duncan: When it comes down to it, no.

Interviewer: Would you handle it in the same way if it were to happen again?

Ms. Duncan: I really don't know. I think that I would be much more tempted to fight. I think that would be my first reaction. It would be hard for me not to. That's what scares me. If it happened again, I'd probably want to kill whoever tried.

One thing that I became very much aware of after the rape was how much magical thinking I do. I was living on the second floor because that was safe, and I was locking my door and putting a chain on it, because that was safe too. The lock was on the screen even though the glass door was open a little bit. But I have become much more aware of the fact that all of those things don't guarantee anything. And I've become more comfortable in living with the fact that I don't have control over everything.

Interviewer: What is your reaction to those who think that rape is usually provoked?

Ms. Duncan: I think most people who say that are just protecting themselves against dealing with the fact that there are violent people, there are sick people who want to rape women.

Ms. Duncan told many people about her experience, but none seems to have been willing to really hear her, let alone give her emotional support. Her mother made it very clear that she didn't want to deal with it, so Ms. Duncan didn't talk about it with her. Ms. Duncan's sister seems to have been no more willing to get involved. Her closest girl friends "got freaked by it." Her counselor suggested she see someone else. Finally, the police and the hospital personnel also weren't interested in hearing about the rape. Wherever the responses came from, it was apparent that solitary confinement is not limited to prison.

The contrast between Ms. Duncan's and Ms. Fujimoto's (see Chapter Three) experiences is striking. Ms. Fujimoto's hysteria after the rape, in the presence of the police, seemed to enhance her credibility with the police, and also seemed to leave her free of trauma five months later. Ms. Duncan, on the other hand, tried to suppress her distress and subsequently developed several psychosomatic ailments.

Ms. Duncan now believes that were a man to attempt to rape her again, she would probably want to kill him. One of the consequences of her not fighting was that she felt partially responsible for having been raped. This is a common reaction and seems to occur even when the victim has no regrets about the way she handled the situation. Perhaps it is precisely this feeling of responsibility that leads to the compensatory fantasy of trying to kill any future would-be rapist rather than let it happen again.

NINETEEN

Warning: Men Are Dangerous—on the Road and in the Police Station

They [the cops] said I would have to take a lie detector test and that I had to have a doctor's examination and semen had to be found in me before they could swear out a warrant to go look for the man. . . . Then I said, "I'll take the lie detector test as soon as possible. . . . When is the soonest time that you can schedule it?" He said, "A week from today."

Relating to a rape victim seems to turn some men off and some men on. Joanne Kelly experienced both reactions. One of the policemen on her case appears to have hoped for some sort of gratification from the shyness he assumed she would feel about going into the details of what happened. Another seemed to identify directly with the rapist: "I know how serious this is, little lady. This is as serious as if I forced you with a gun into my car, and I took you out in the woods, and I forced you to have sexual intercourse with me." For Ms. Kelly, his words were as upsetting as the rapist's pulling a gun on her. Such sexual overtones on the part of law enforcement personnel who handle rape victims are not unusual.

In general, the treatment of Ms. Kelly by the police is another example of how the victim is treated as the criminal. In this case she was tried by police whose incompetence and inefficiency were as noteworthy as their hostility.

Ms. Kelly is a white, single, middle-class woman, twenty years of age. She was attending college when she was raped six months ago. Her feelings and reactions are more confusing than those of most of the women interviewed, but it is precisely her complexity that makes this case so interesting.

JOANNE KELLY: I was hitchhiking in a small town to get out to my college when he picked me up. He was kind of weird, but I've been picked up by weird guys before, and nothing had ever happened. He took a route that I didn't know, but I didn't want to say anything for fear it would give him an idea to go off with me.

Then he spoke, and I turned to look at him, and he had this big gun pointed at me. I just freaked. I think he was either on heavy drugs, or he was crazy, because he was whispering, and his eyes were almost shut all the time. He said, "Do what I want and you'll be all right." I said, "Do you want my money? I just got paid. You can have my money." He said, "Shut up."

It was really freaky. The rape was nothing. It was the gun and the man and the car that scared me. He kept driving, and I kept trying to talk to him so that he would look at me as a person, a nice person, and he kept telling me to shut up. I was trying to talk to him and get him to realize exactly where I was at, so he would understand and take pity on me. I said, "Look, I'm really scared. Can you understand that?" He said, "Why?" I don't think he was putting me on. He really meant the question. I said, "Because I'm alone in a car with a man that I don't know, and he's got a gun, and he's taking me somewhere. Do you understand?" My approach was to try to make him understand how scared I was. I kept saying, "Look, I'm really terrified, and I want to know what you're doing. I'm really scared. Can you understand how I want to know what you're doing?" At that point I thought that he probably wanted sex, since he didn't want my money, and the next thing, after that, would be to cut me up.

Then he pulled me over to him on the seat, and put his hand between my legs. It was like he was acting out a role. There was no passion. It was just automatic. Then he took his hand away and put his arm around my shoulder and pulled me over and put my head on his shoulder and started stroking my hair. His body movements were very gentle, and it was very freaky. A lot of different vibes were going on. He had the gun. He was forcing me to do something, but his body was gentle.

We kept driving and driving and driving, and I would say stuff like, "Where are we going? Why don't we stop at a hotel? Let's stop right here," but he wouldn't. He wanted me to keep talking at this point. He kind of enjoyed my chattering on. He drove way up into these logging roads that you hear about. It was at noon so that was better than it being night.

I was trying to flatter him and make it easy for him in all ways that I could, because I know that I'm such a bitch, and I make men really mad, and I didn't want to make him mad! Like, he put on shaving cologne, and I said, "Oh, your cologne smells nice. What is it?" And he said, "Hai Karate." It was awful! And I questioned him about the gun. I said, "Why are you doing this? Did you get the gun out and then go driving to look for a woman?" He said, "Yes." I said, "Well, why?" and he said, " 'Cause I haven't had a woman for two months." To flatter him, I said, "Oh, well, most men wouldn't think that's a very long time." And he said, "Well, I do."

It was really funny. I was hating him so much, but playing it like I dug him. It was a blatant farce. I had told him I was having my period, hoping that would stop him, and he said, "Oh," really deep to himself, and I said, "Well, would that matter?" and he said, "Yes."

Then he stopped the car and turned to me and started kissing me. He put his hand on my breast and his tongue in my mouth. It was like a corpse doing it. I have never been kissed and not responded, even though many times a guy would kiss me and I didn't want to kiss him, I'd always respond. I put my tongue in his mouth because that's what I always do, and then I thought, "No, I'm being raped, I don't have to do anything." It's so automatic to me to respond when somebody's touching me. So I just sat there, and then he picked up my arm and put it on the back of his neck.

Then he said, "Take off your pants," and I took off my pants, trying to be very clumsy, trying not to be graceful or sexy at all. He put his hand on my leg, and I said, "I have my Tampax in, remember?" So he leaned across me, rolled the window down without saying anything. Then he said, "Throw it out, baby." I said, "Don't look," and so he turned away, and I pulled my Tampax out and threw it out the window.

Then he put the seat down lower and took off his clothes. I was afraid he was going to pull the gun, which he had put down next to him on the left-hand side between himself and the door. He opened the car door, and I thought, "Oh, now he's going to drag me out into the woods," but it turned out he did it so that when he laid down, his feet would stick out.

He got on top of me, and he tried to put his penis inside me, but he missed, or it didn't work, or something. So he said, "Put it in." I did it, and then he was moving, and he said, "Oh, baby, you're so good." The guy didn't appear to come. He pulled out really quickly. Like the whole thing took about ninety seconds.

Then he got out of the car, and he still had his erection, so I knew he hadn't come. He got back in the car and then sat hunched over the wheel without fixing up the back of the seat. It was very frightening, because his behavior was very weird. And I thought, "He's going to shoot me now." I just sat there, and didn't say anything. Then I started talking in a soft voice, and I said, "Do you feel bad?" and he said, "Yes." And I said, "About what you did?" and he said, "Yes." Then I said, "Could we please go back now? I have a class at the college."

Then I touched his arm, and I knew that had to get to him. I couldn't get to him another way. Either he would explode and hit me, or that would touch him. And it touched him. He drew out his cigarette and smoked it, and then he moved the seat back so it was upright. I never saw the gun again, but I knew it was there.

Then he started driving me back. I was still pretty freaked, and I thought, I have twenty dollars in my purse. I can offer it to him. And then I thought, I'm not going to give him my money. Fuck! And then I was talking to him in a very slow voice like you talk to a retarded child, saying, "I don't think you should do this again, because it really scared me, and you could really scare a girl this way. Do you understand?"

It was like I was his mother talking to him in a very slow way. I was really being very patronizing, but he was accepting it and saying, "Yes, I understand." He took me back to the college, and I said, "You can let me out here." Just before he stopped the car, he said the same thing that he had said when he was screwing me, and in the same way. He said, "Oh, baby." It was so weird that I said, "What did you say?" And he repeated, "Oh, baby." Then I got out of the car, and I turned around, and I said, "I don't think you should do this to anybody again." He nodded, and I slammed the door, and that was it.

INTERVIEWER: Did you report the rape?

Ms. KELLY: Yes. I called the cops, and they interviewed me, and they were horrible. They were really upsetting to me. It was a totally and completely bungled affair. And they didn't get him either.

As soon as I got to school I started to cry. A girl friend took me up to the counselor's office. I phoned the police from there. They sent a policeman out who was not versed in the law. He said that I did not have to have a doctor's examination, which is not true. You're supposed to have one. He asked me to describe it, and then he went away.

I phoned up the police about a day or two later and asked if the man had been caught. They had my phone number and everything, but they had not contacted me, and they said, "Oh, well, you were supposed to come in right then. You were supposed to come in to speak to the chief sheriff." I said, "The policeman didn't say that." And he said, "Well, he didn't know." It was really stupid.

They said, "Well, come out this afternoon," and I said, "How am I supposed to get out?" There were no buses going from the college to the town. So I had to get a cop car to bring me out and bring me back, because I wasn't going to hitchhike. To hitch there was against the law anyway.

So I arrived there, but I had to wait a long time. I had given a complete description of the man, and where he worked. He had told me where he worked, but I think he lied about that. Anyway, I said, "What has been done on this?" and a policeman said, "Nothing. Perhaps you would like to go out and arrest this man before a warrant has even been sworn out. Would you like to do that?" I couldn't believe it.

I shook my head, and I said, "Well, he's very dangerous, and there are other women hitchhiking right now, and he has a gun, and he's crazy." And he said, "I know how serious this is, little lady. This is as serious as if I forced you with a gun into my car, and I took you out in the woods, and I forced you to have sexual intercourse with me. That's how serious this is." I was starting to cry and thinking, I'm going to phone mother. The two times that I was the most upset during this whole experience was when the man pulled the gun and when that cop said that to me. That cop was just horrible.

He asked me to describe the rape, and when we got down to the physical thing where the guy stopped the car and turned to me, he said, "Now, I want you to describe this part in great detail." It was like he thought that I would be very shy, like he was *hoping* that I'd be shy, and he'd have to pry it away from me, and take pleasure in exposing me. But I wasn't shy, and it wasn't exposing me, so I don't think he got off on it as much as he could have..I said, "The man put his hand on my breast," and he said, "Now, was this over the sweater and the bra, or between the sweater and the bra, or under the bra next to the skin?" And I said, "Oh, well, I don't wear a bra." And he said, "Oh!" and this just blew his mind for a minute, and then he forgot that he had wanted to have me describe it in detail, and he didn't ask me to again. So evidently it wasn't of importance.

They said I would have to take a lie detector test and that I had to have a doctor's examination and semen had to be found in me before they could swear out a warrant to go look for the man. That's what the cop told me at the beginning of his interview of me when he didn't like me. Then at the end, when I was acting more friendly, more like a sweet little girl who had recently been raped and needed protection, he said, "Well, we don't need a doctor's examination. We can go out and get this man." I said, "But I thought you said legally you had to have that as evidence?" and he said, "Well, not necessarily. You see, this man could confess, and then we would have him." Then I said, "I'll take the lie detector test as soon as possible, because you say that you can't go out looking for the man until the test has been taken. When is the soonest time that you can schedule it?" He said, "A week from today."

The lie detector test was incredible. The man was asking me all these stupid questions, like, "Have you ever had an argument with your father?" I said no. Another was, "Have you ever done anything that you felt was perverted sexually or anything that was illegal sexually?" And, "What is your opinion of lie detector tests?" I really got on to that one because I had just been speaking to my father about that. I said to him, "I think they are a great invasion of privacy," and he said, "Then why are you taking this?" And I said, "Because I was told by the chief sheriff that I had to take the lie detector test before a warrant could be sworn out," and he said, "No, that's not true." So I was just fucked over, and then they never found the guy anyway.

INTERVIEWER: Who did you tell besides the police about the rape?

Ms. KELLY: All my friends and my parents, though I didn't go shouting about it. There were about six or seven people that I would see every day at school, and I told them. And their general reaction was one of shock, like, "Oh, Joanne, that's awful!" They were protective of me. I was acting hard and sarcastic about it, like, "This bastard, he didn't even come!" Then people started to react to me in different ways. Most of my women friends were really cool. They understood how I was taking it.

But I found that men reacted to me in two ways for the most part. One, they thought that I was a dirty slut, and they thought that I was lying, that I hadn't really been raped, that I had led this man into some kind of sexual trip. And the other kind of man wanted me to talk about it. They wanted to help me, and then they would put their hand on my thigh and pat it and say, "It's going to be all right." I don't think they were aware of what they were doing—any of them.

INTERVIEWER: Do you think the experience affected your behavior in any way?

Ms. KELLY: I know it did. I used to be really uptight when I was standing in an elevator, and there were three men standing there in a group. Sometimes they stopped talking, and just gave me a look. It made me very uptight and scared. I'd turn my back to them.

Then right after the rape, I wasn't as scared of it. I felt like I'd gone through it all the way. I knew what can happen. I was not as afraid. I was more relaxed for about three or four days afterwards. I didn't care anymore if they looked at me. But then, and this is still with me, and it's been about six months since it happened, I am still terrified of walking home alone. Also, I don't hitchhike anymore, ever. I'm scared to hitchhike when I'm with a man too.

And whenever anybody jokes about rape, I just freeze up. It's not fucking funny! It's like joking about murder when somebody's murdered my mother or something. When I'm writing or reading in a café and a man walks close to my table, I flinch sometimes, like he's going to hit me.

INTERVIEWER: Has your attitude toward men changed?

Ms. KELLY: Yes. I feel a little bit sorry for them. If it had been a brutal physical rape, I wouldn't, but that man was so helpless and stupid and blind. I feel a kind of pity. They have this dumb little sexual need. Part of their body has to be rubbed really hard, and then they groan. It just seems kind of stupid to me.

INTERVIEWER: Did the experience affect any of your attitudes toward sex?

Ms. KELLY: Yes. I had been extremely promiscuous about three months before it happened, thinking that there was a kind of a personalness to my promiscuity. But then I realized with the rape that the feeling of that sexual intercourse was not as painful or as repulsive as other intercourses I've had, and I realized then that the other intercourse I've had must have been really impersonal. So I realized how very impersonal sex is. How you can come, and the man can moan, "Oh baby, baby," but yet it can be completely impersonal.

So now I haven't been sleeping with men. I slept with one man once, but aside from that, I haven't slept with anybody since the rape, which has been about five months, I guess. I feel like a person's caress has to be very personal now.

INTERVIEWER: Did you feel guilty and responsible in any way?

Ms. KELLY: Yes. I feel guilty very easily. If I hadn't been hitchhiking, if I hadn't gotten into his car, it wouldn't have happened.

INTERVIEWER: Do you regret in any way the way you handled the situation?

Ms. KELLY: Yes. I do. I regret it because I had to kiss so much ass. But I would be willing to kiss that much ass again in the same situation. I resent being a simpering little flower waiting to be plucked, allowing a man to do whatever he wants to me. Yet I would handle it in the same way again, because I would be terrified again, and I think that's the right way to handle it with somebody like that. I've been hit by men because I sassed them, so I know that I would handle it that way again.

INTERVIEWER: What advice would you give to other women regarding how to avoid being raped?

Ms. KELLY: Don't hitchhike alone, period. If somebody has a weapon, don't fight them. Don't consider your body something inviolate. I spoke to a woman, a newlywed, a very good friend of mine, and she said that she would have told him that he would have to kill her, that she wouldn't make it with him. And I told her that I thought she was stupid. The gynecologist can get his instruments inside of you. You think nothing of it. That's what it's like. You should want to keep yourself unharmed. Don't let it get violent. Talk to him, so that he will look at you as a nice person caught in a bad circumstance rather than as an enemy. Let him rape you, and then get away. That's what I think a woman should do.

INTERVIEWER: Can you think of any solutions to the rape problem?

Ms. KELLY: Having legalized prostitution. Having all women learn how to defend themselves physically. And then, of course, having people brought up in a different way, so that rape is not a normal thing in society.

I think there will always be rape in society, just as there will always be murder in society, but it doesn't have to be a status symbol. I sit with a guy at a café sometimes, and I look very pretty, and he said one time, "You look very nice, very pretty," and I said, "Thank you." And he said, "I'll walk you back if you're leaving." I said, "OK, but I can't ask you up," and he said, "OK. But you're so beautiful, I might have to rape you." He was only kidding, but the idea that somebody would even think like that is incredible. It's like saying, "Your flesh looks so taut and fresh that I might have to stick a knife into it." That's what it sounds like to me, now that I've been raped. I go cold, and they don't understand. We could raise them so they'd understand.

INTERVIEWER: What is your reaction to people who think that rape is usually provoked?

Ms. KELLY: I think that people who make that statement not only are prejudiced against women, but have no conception of how horrible rape is. That's like saying, "You were trying to attract that murderer."

Ms. Kelly's response to her experience of rape was ambivalent. On the one hand, she seemed to take the rape fairly casually. On the other hand, it seems to have had a tremendous impact on her: she stopped hitchhiking, she radically changed her sexual behavior, and her attitude to rape was completely transformed. When asked about her reaction to people who think that rape is usually provoked, Ms. Kelly's reply was unequivocal.

One fascinating aspect of Ms. Kelly's experience is that she found herself automatically responding to her rapist's kiss and his gentleness until she remembered that she didn't have to respond. Responding to a rapist's kiss does not, of course, indicate sexual desire on a woman's part, but may be a result of fear, or an attempt to pacify the man and so avoid greater harm, or conditioning. In Ms. Kelly's case, it appears to have been the latter.

The trauma of rape for Ms. Kelly, and probably for most victims, comes not so much from the physical unpleasantness of the experience as from the fear or terror that often accompanies rape, the humiliation and outrage at being used as a mere receptacle, or the transformation of what is for many women an intimate act into a completely impersonal one, used for the expression of hate, conquest, or contempt.

Ms. Kelly's view that a woman should never risk physical harm to herself in order not to be raped is held by many victims. There appear to be diametrically opposing viewpoints on this issue. Some women believe that the more liberated women became (in terms of sex roles and sexuality), the less traumatic rape will be, at least for postadolescent females. This viewpoint assumes that as a culture becomes less sexist, the stigma will disappear, making rape a relatively untraumatic experience, unless additional brutality and threats or dangerous weapons are involved. Believing rape to be a fate worse than death, they say, is a symptom of sexist thinking, by which the woman is transformed from "good" to "bad" by virtue of being raped. It follows from this that it isn't worth a great deal of struggle and pain to avoid being raped.

The opposite view is that the more liberated women become, the more humiliating and traumatic it is for them if men subject them to the supremely sexist act of rape. More liberated women are likely to resent most the political nature of the act and experience it as a new kind of violation, a violation of their will as well as their bodies, rather than of their virtue.

Since it is often recommended as a partial solution, Ms. Kelly's idea that legalizing prostitution would aid in the solving of the rape problem needs to be considered. While some rapes occur because some men simply want a vagina to empty themselves into, and a prostitute will do very well, I think many men would not be diverted from rape. Their sexual need is usually not the primary one. And just as masturbation is often seen as a poor substitute for a woman, having to pay for intercourse is seen by many men in this culture as humiliating. It should also be pointed out that proposing legalized prostitution as a solution is like trying to solve one problem that arises out of sexism by resurrecting an institution that is equally sexist.

TWENTY

Sexual Liberation without Sex-Role Liberation Can Get You Raped

> Then there's the question of can a hippie prosecute a rape? All hippies believe in free love, so, you know, who cares if someone rapes a hippie?

Women who accept common cultural notions of sexual liberation will still be rape victims. Many people assume that men are more sexually liberated than women, and some who subscribe to the position that women should become sexually liberated believe this means women should become more like men in expressing their sexuality. Getting rid of the double sexual standard, then, is seen to involve accepting that women can be as casual about sex as many men, as interested in multiple relationships, as able to separate sex from feelings of affection, respect, romanticism, and loving, and particularly as able as many men to separate sex from any kind of commitment to a relationship. Based on this assumption, sexual liberation for women requires no changes on the part of men except that they should be able to accept sexually liberated women and not feel threatened by them.

By the criteria mentioned above, Chris Roberts is a sexually liberated woman. At eighteen she describes herself as "fairly close to being a virgin" since "at that point I had kept track of who I had slept with. It was thirty guys." Her casual attitude toward sex may help explain her casual attitude toward being the victim of gang rape. This is not to suggest that all women who have a casual attitude toward sex will take rape casually. But the difference between choosing to have sex and not being given the choice is experienced as more salient by some people than by others.

"Sexual freedom" usually does *not* mean equality in sex, but rather, that men expect more women to cater more readily to their sexual needs with no strings attached. Women like Ms. Roberts who buy this male notion of sexual freedom often experience so many situations of having sex with men where their own needs and wishes have to be suppressed, that rape is hardly a special case.

Sexual liberation without sex-role liberation can actually result in greater oppression of women. There seem to be two ways in which sexual liberation without sex-role liberation can lead to rape. First, when men who are not free of sexist desires to dominate and conquer women are freed of internal constraints by a philosophy of supposed sexual liberation, some are likely to become active rapists.

Second, a woman who chooses the male model of sexual liberation must still function as a woman in a sexist society where men call the shots. Ms. Roberts, for example, is aware of the fact that a "promiscuous" woman is commonly regarded as unrapable, and that hippie women are automatically seen as promiscuous. In a sexist society a promiscuous woman means a "bad" woman, hence one that a man can feel less guilty or even righteous about raping.

Ms. Roberts is a white woman, now twenty-two years old. She was single at the time of her two rape experiences, but subsequently married. She was separated at the time of her most recent attempted rape experience, shortly before the interview, and described herself as a "welfare mother."

CHRIS ROBERTS: It happened in a college community called Denton, which is about forty miles north of Dallas, Texas. Today it is a very hip place, but then it was still tremendously full of rednecks. It was in the fall of 1968. School had just started, and I guess everybody was pretty high-spirited. I was living up there with a man, and I needed to hitchhike into Dallas to get some birth control pills.

I got a ride from a man. After a while he said he needed to stop at an apartment house to say something to one of his buddies, which he did. We were getting ready to leave the apartment when the next thing I knew, he was trying to make it with me on the couch. His buddy was there, and I was dragged into the bedroom, and I was raped. I'm not really sure whether it was the guy I was hitching with or the roommate who did it first. But by the time both of them were through, I could hear cars pulling up outside, and I could hear people coming into the front living room. Apparently they had called all their fraternity brothers to come over. I'd say there were about twenty men in the living room when I looked out the door.

Two more men raped me. The next one in line was a little short blond, and he looked really timid and shy. All his brothers were putting him up to it. I figured this was my key out, and I pulled a knife on him, and I said that until his buddies went away, the knife was going to stay at his throat. He began talking to his buddies through the door, saying, "Hey, this chick has got a knife on her, and you guys gotta leave, 'cause if you don't, this knife is gonna be in my throat." And I'm saying, "Yes it is! See, here it is." It took a little bit of doing, but they left, and I was the last one out the door, with the exception of the little blond guy. It was a case of threatening my way out of the situation.

INTERVIEWER: Why didn't you use your knife before this point?

Ms. ROBERTS: The other four guys were all bigger than me. The fifth guy was my size, and he was a very mellow type of person. I could have probably talked him out of it anyway, but talking him out of it wouldn't have solved the other twenty persons, so he was a good victim to hold hostage.

INTERVIEWER: You were alone with each guy in a private room?

Ms. ROBERTS: Yes, I think it was because they were probably afraid that they couldn't function without privacy. They'd be under too much pressure.

INTERVIEWER: Could you tell me more about the degree to which you resisted?

Ms. ROBERTS: There's not much resisting when there's that many people. When there were just two men, I tried physically to push him away, and I yelled no and stuff. There was no knife drawing. At that point, I couldn't even get to my knife. There wasn't a lot of fighting, because I knew I wasn't going to win anyway, unless I got super violent. But I wasn't into a really violent stage then.

INTERVIEWER: Did you report the fraternity guys to the police?

Ms. ROBERTS: No. In no way would I have even thought of reporting it.

INTERVIEWER: Did the rape affect your behavior, or did your attitudes toward men and sex change at all as a result of it?

Ms. ROBERTS: Every time I've been in Denton, I've avoided that apartment complex. I can say that much. And I've had a very definite suspicion that I shouldn't get in a car with a fraternity rat.

INTERVIEWER: Was the gang rape a kind of initiation for members of the fraternity?

Ms. ROBERTS: I think so. Certainly, they do this kind of thing for initiations.

INTERVIEWER: You mentioned that you had another experience of rape when you were eighteen.

Ms. ROBERTS: Yes. I was hitchhiking between Dallas and Houston in Texas. It was a really cold, dark night, and I was having trouble hitching to Houston. I waited there a long time. I had started out at dusk, and I had to get there. There was important business I had to attend to, and I was desperate for a ride, but no one would stop. I was on a pretty bad stretch of road.

Finally a green pickup truck pulled over. I didn't like the looks of the truck, but it was the only chance I had for a ride in at least twenty minutes, so I accepted it. We drove along, and I don't recall making small talk or anything. He said he was going to X [a small town], and I said I was going to Houston. He said he could take me as far as X. I noticed that he went past X. This happens a lot when I'm hitchhiking. People go on and take me to the other side of town, just as a courtesy. I thought he was probably going to drop me off and turn right around.

So we got to the edge of X, and I mentioned in passing, "Oh, this is the other side of X. I guess I'll get out." He said he would drive me further, but asked what I would give him, or some such rap that I'd heard a million times before from a million other people while hitchhiking. He pulled into one of these roadside parks, and he tried to get me to make love to him. I refused, and he said OK, he'd take me back out to the highway. He went back out to the highway and went on down a little way. Then he turned into a little country road off the highway, and I knew I was in trouble. He went out into the middle of a field somewhere. I have no idea, even to this day, where it was. I recall something about a billboard. That's all I really remember. I wanted to get out of the truck and split and run. I realized the chances were slim, but I was still willing to try.

I tried to jump out of the truck, but he grabbed me back, and he was starting to unbuckle when I managed to work out my knife. I didn't think he had seen the knife, but he had, and he grabbed for it and threw it out of the truck. So that was the end of my great escape attempt.

I also noticed that he had a knife, one a little larger than a hunting knife, on the dashboard of his truck, so it dawned on me that it was probably not too swift an idea to try anything more. I tried reasoning with him. I said I was pregnant, and that I was having trouble with the pregnancy anyway. I asked him, "Why are you doing this to me?" He was really a dumb-dumb, to put it mildly. And he said that he didn't have any girl friends. And as to why he was raping me, well, he said, just to find out what it felt like.

INTERVIEWER: Did he threaten to use the knife at all?

Ms. ROBERTS: He didn't have to. Its very presence was enough to let me know that it was not a very swift thing to fight him. He was also considerably larger than I was, and I realized that my chances of running away in a dark field were pretty slim. So it was either staying in the truck and getting raped there, or running out into the field and getting raped there, and then having to find my way back to the highway.

INTERVIEWER: Could you describe the amount of force he used?

Ms. ROBERTS: He really had the weight advantage over me. Once he was able to get himself on top, that was the end of the fight. I weighed 105 pounds, he probably weighed at least 200 pounds. It was sheer force. He didn't have any mind, it must have been all body. So there was no way of fighting my way out of that, and I knew it. There was no reasoning with him because he didn't have any mind to be reasoned with.

When we were driving back to the road, I asked him again why he had done it, and he said it was to find out what it felt like. So I said, "Well, would you *kill* someone to see what it felt like?" He got really quiet for about ten seconds or so, and it scared the daylights out of me. Then he said, "Yeah, I'd like to try that too." I knew right then and there that I had just had it. It was all over. There was no chance that I was going to live through the experience, and I was really terrified.

We got back to the road, and he must have had some kind of wit, some kind of brains after all, because he decided it was safer for him to find me a ride all the way through to Houston, so I wouldn't run into a highway patrolman and report the rape. It was a very cold night, and he got out his flashlight, and he flagged down a trucker who would take me all the way into Houston.

Since I was in no shape to keep hitching at that point anyway, this was just as well. I didn't know what to do. I was eighteen years old, away from home for the first time, and I actually didn't know much about even doing my own grocery shopping. I managed to deal lots of dope and dodge the cops and go to school, and that was it. I was just goofing off. Actually I was going between cities to deal dope, so if I had to deal with the police about the rape, I knew they would ask a lot of questions. That's why I really didn't feel like reporting the rape. So I let it ride.

I found out I had a miscarriage when I got to Houston the next morning. That miscarriage hung over me for two years. When I would think about having a baby, I would cry. I never got a D and C after it. I had no sex education and didn't know I was supposed to. When I got married, I didn't get pregnant. I hadn't used birth control, and hadn't gotten pregnant for many years, and I figured something had happened as a result of the rape. I figured I'd probably never have children, and I was very upset about it. I was forced into changing my whole outlook in a lot of different ways, and it was a really miserable experience.

I was hitchhiking one night to the underground flicks in Dallas with some friends, and we got a ride with a nice person, and he dropped us off at the flicks at the parking lot. Everyone had gotten out of the car, and I was getting out when he asked casually, "Do you hitch a lot?" I said, "Yeah, it's the only way we have of getting around." And he said, "Don't you ever have bummer experiences?" I said, "Yeah, sometimes people really hassle me."

We started talking, and I found out he was a police officer from a private force in my part of the city. He asked me if I had ever had any *really* bad experiences. I told him I was hitchhiking down by X, that a guy in a green pickup truck picked me up, and he was a real dumb-dumb who raped me. I described what the guy looked like, and so on, and finally he said, "Stop, I don't believe you." I said, "Why not?" He said, "You must have been reading the papers." I said, "I don't know what you're talking about." He said that another woman had been hitchhiking in that area, and they found her body in X, raped and stabbed eighteen times. And it all flashed back to me, how he had wanted to kill someone just to see how it felt.

From that time on, I held myself responsible for that woman's death. If I had gone to the police and identified him, we could have found that man, and he could have been stopped. I didn't go to the police because I was involved in drugs at the time, and I was afraid to go to them. Also, I wasn't sure of the laws on hitchhiking, and being a hippie I was afraid that if I went to the police with a problem, they would probably arrest me. Because harassment of hippies at that time was pretty heavy.

Then there's the question of can a hippie prosecute a rape? All hippies believe in free love, so, you know, who cares if someone rapes a hippie? I don't know whether we could have gotten him or not, but I realize now that it was a tremendous mistake not to report it. I didn't follow the trial, but I know that he is serving a life sentence now in a Texas penitentiary.

INTERVIEWER: Did the experience affect any of your attitudes toward men?

Ms. ROBERTS: It's not just this experience that did it. It's also the guys that do gang bangs in Texas, and it's my women friends who have gone through similar experiences. A lot of things have made me down on men, including a real bummer of a marriage.

INTERVIEWER: After this rape experience, could you see any noticeable change in your attitudes?

Ms. ROBERTS: I was more suspicious, more filled with hate. I frankly wanted to go back to X and kill him, and at times I'd say, "Yeah, yeah, let's go get him." Then I would cool myself off not to. It was lacking control of my own fate that bothered me so much. It seemed to me that men assumed the right that they could have any woman that they wanted. It doesn't matter who you are or anything else. If the man wants to rape you, he is probably going to do it. I began resenting being a woman, because I had to go through that, and I had really no means of retaliation or revenge. I felt an immense sense of frustration.

INTERVIEWER: Did the experience affect any of your attitudes toward sex?

Ms. ROBERTS: At the time, it did make me think that men were very brutal and animalistic. I don't think it was a very long lingering feeling, though. I don't think it was really responsible for any major changes.

INTERVIEWER: Whom did you tell afterwards?

Ms. ROBERTS: Well, when I got to Houston, the people I was living with knew what had happened. I was very upset, and in Dallas a lot of people knew, because I had just had my pregnancy confirmed not an hour before I had left Dallas, and when I arrived back in Dallas not pregnant, just about everyone that I knew learned about it.

INTERVIEWER: How did they react?

Ms. ROBERTS: Well, it was a pretty mixed crowd. It was the hippie hangout. Some of the people were very upset. You know, the peace and love thing and all of that. And then there was Killer Sam, who was going to go down to X to kill him, just for the sheer fun of it. Nobody approved of what happened, but I think that most people were concerned with the rawness of what had happened rather than with my own feelings.

INTERVIEWER: Do you suppose their feelings might have been different if you had not had a miscarriage?

Ms. ROBERTS: Oh, yeah. *My* feelings would have been different too. At the time there was a total of six of us who had gotten pregnant at the same time, and all of us were happy with our pregnancies and looking forward to our babies. It was like the murder of an unborn child. If he had been charged, he would have been charged with that too. The fact that I had been pregnant made it doubly bad, and the fact that I had a miscarriage as a direct result of the rape made it just almost incomprehensible to everybody. It was just too much.

INTERVIEWER: What feelings did you have during and after the rape?

Ms. ROBERTS: *That fucker!!* Not only does he rape me, but he expects me to give him a fine performance. I mean like, do this, do that. I wouldn't do shit for him. My total response was one of a complete dead fish, and he was bitching because I wasn't trying to give him the super fuck of his life. If he had been Prince Charming, maybe I could have gotten into it or something, but he was Mister Slob, Mister Short Peter, Mister Lousy Lover, and Mister Poor Bedside Manners.

If I had been a girl from X, and had I gone out with him, I wouldn't have considered going to bed with him. And had I been in bed with him, I'm sure I would have been bored stiff. If that comes from a woman who had liked him, imagine how I felt getting raped by him. Total numbness of sensations.

It was a feeling of pressure, and a constant movement, and it hurt. But as far as any penis, I don't even remember him having one.

INTERVIEWER: And what emotions were you in touch with?

Ms. ROBERTS: Total fear and hatred. And total upset about what was going to happen. Disgust too. My main fear, the main thing on my mind, was worrying about the baby.

INTERVIEWER: How upsetting would you say the experience was? Would you call it traumatic?

Ms. ROBERTS: The one reason that I didn't volunteer to go to court when they found him for stabbing the other woman eighteen times was that it was still too recent. It happened only three months after he raped me, and I don't think I was in any shape to get on the judge's stand, and go through the whole gory thing of what had happened. I think I would have cracked up and had to be hauled away. At least two and a half years after it happened, every time I thought about what had happened—[Ms. Roberts broke down and cried at this point.]

INTERVIEWER: Did your prior notions about rape change due to your own personal experience of it?

Ms. ROBERTS: I never really contemplated being raped before it happened. It was a foreign thing to me. I could imagine being knocked down or being thrown to the floor, but rape, I couldn't even imagine.

INTERVIEWER: Would you handle the rape situation in the same way if it were to happen again?

Ms. ROBERTS: If it was 1969, and my fingerprints were not on file at the FBI in that year, as they are now, I would probably leave the suitcase and jump out at a roadside stop, and just take my chances from there.

INTERVIEWER: Have you had any other experiences with rape?

Ms. ROBERTS: Yeah. About nine weeks ago, I was hitchhiking with my baby to a friend's house. She was going to take care of my baby since I was having surgery the next morning and had to get a good night's sleep and get to the doctor early. I was in a rush, and this guy pulled around the corner. I needed a ride pretty desperately as I was running on a tight schedule. I had to meet someone back at my place for an appointment in half an hour, so I took the ride although I felt suspicious of him.

The minute I touched the door knob the word "rape" just went echoing through my head. I knew what was going to happen. I just knew. I said, "Oh, this is silly. I'm projecting my own fears onto this man. It's just my paranoia coming up, and I'm psyching myself out." We rode a bit, and I told the man I was going down towards Y Street. I never tell a man exactly where I'm going. I give a nearby cross street. If I'm going to visit another woman friend who lives alone, I won't even give the right cross street. I always get off at the wrong place and walk it.

He said, "Are you from the South?" and I said, "Yes, I'm from Texas." I guess I still have my Texas accent, and I don't know whether that played a part in it, whether, being black, he thought he was going to get revenge on a Southern white woman, or whether he was out in the neighborhood to rape anyway. Aside from that, we didn't really talk. We got within two blocks of my friend's house, and he said, "I'm going to rape you." I couldn't decide whether he was for real, or whether he was going to see what my reaction was just for the pure fun of it. There are some guys who will just shake you up a little bit.

But he made a corner, and I knew that was it. I decided to jump out, but he was going too fast, so that was out of the question. I didn't know exactly where he was going, but I figured we were going into the Berkeley hills, and I knew up there I wasn't going to have much of a chance to fight. But really there was no way I could jump out of a speeding car. I thought maybe I could catch a red light, but we didn't even get over a block and a half further, when he pulled over.

I didn't know exactly what street I was on, but the building on the left appeared to be deserted. The building on the right was a housing project that was also completely deserted. There were families living opposite but there was no chance of being heard if I screamed. I didn't even really believe I could run and get away from him, since he said he had a gun. I figured he might shoot me for the pure fun of it.

He stopped the car, and he said, "Roll up your window." I recall saying no, and so he reached over and rolled it up, which was the only time that he touched me and the baby. And I said, "Why are you doing this? As long as I'm going to get raped, I want to know why." I was really terrified. This was the most terrifying situation I've been in so far, because this guy apparently had it a lot more together than the guy in X. I was really, really afraid of him. I thought the chances of psyching him out were really slim, but it was worth a try, just to stall him for a time.

I said, "I'm a mother, and I know I've got gonorrhea," but he wouldn't believe that. I said, "Look, man, when you take off my panties, you're going to know I've got the clap." I really had a bad discharge, and it really did look like the clap. I started to get a trembling in my voice, and he knew I was fixing to cry. He said, "Listen, man, don't pull any of that shit with me! Don't pull any of that shit. It makes me angry." I said, "In front of the baby! You're really going to be damaging her whole psyche." And I said, "As long as I'm getting raped, do you really have a gun?" "Yeah, I really have a gun," he said. "Well, can I see it?" "Oh, no. Why do you want to see?" "Well, if

I'm getting raped, and you say you've got a gun, and I tell my friends later that I got raped, I want to know whether there really was a gun or not." "Yeah, there's a gun," he said, "but I don't want to get it out." So the chances of his having a gun dropped by about fifty percent in my mind. That was the first break I'd gotten.

At this point, a man walked by on the other side of the street. I didn't know whether he'd see me, but I decided this was the only chance I was going to have. So I talked to the guy in the car and rolled the window down, and waited until the other guy was really close by, and then screamed like a bat out of hell. And the guy just walked on like nothing was happening. But the guy that was trying to rape me didn't know that the other guy hadn't seen what was going on, and he panicked. He opened the car door and tried to push me and the baby out, and as he was doing that, he managed to get it together to start his car and yell, "Get out! Get out!" But I couldn't jump out with the baby from a car that was moving, so I said, "I'm not going to get out unless you stop," because I didn't want the baby to get hurt. Me getting raped is one thing, but her getting hurt is another.

He slowed down just enough to let me hop out of the car. I was shaking, the baby was crying. I never heard any baby cry like that. She was horrified. I was horrified that he really might have a gun and might come back by for the pure hell of it and shoot me. I went over to a man I saw coming from a house, and I said, "Could you help me, please?" And he did.

INTERVIEWER: Did you call the police?

Ms. ROBERTS: I did finally call the police, and they sent over an officer. He handled himself quite well. He did not ask any embarrassing questions. I was very surprised after everything I've heard. The next day, I saw the guy who tried to rape me again and got his license number. I phoned it in to the police, who were going to put out an all-points bulletin and try to pull him in that day. But they didn't do it.

I called Inspector X two weeks later to ask what was going on. He said he had read about the case and would send a man out to talk to me. The guy showed up here at midnight on a Saturday night, a routine call, and scared the hell out of me, because he even looked a lot like my assailant. I was trembling, and I had a knife in my pocket when I answered the door.

He said that he had located this guy from the license number, and they would go over and check this guy in police files and CID files and Sacramento. If nothing else, they could get his driver's license picture, and other mug shots that they'd like me to identify. That was about seven weeks ago now.

Last week I called Inspector X again to ask what was going on, and he said, "Oh, well, I was on vacation." And, "Oh, yeah, we had a guy on your beat that quit, but I'll get things started again.'' We talked for a while about the rape situation in Berkeley, but nothing's been done. It's the usual. They don't care. They just don't give a damn.

INTERVIEWER: How many women do you know personally who have been raped?

Ms. ROBERTS: Virtually every woman I know in Berkeley has been raped. There are two exceptions. Every one of us is so down on men since we came to Berkeley, you know, going through some kind of hassle with them every day. I was hitchhiking home the other day, and a Chinese-American guy picked me up. He said, "I pick up girls hitchhiking because I think maybe they will go home with me and make love to me." And he said, "How do you feel about rape?" I said, "I feel very strongly about rape. I tend to become very violent with anything like that." And he didn't bother me after that. After that he was going back down to Grove Street to pick up someone to prostitute for him. At least he wasn't the violent type.

Every day there is some sort of a sexual hassle hitchhiking. And just walking from here down to the corner, I can get hassled three times on the street. I'm so down on men out here.

INTERVIEWER: What advice would you give to other women about how to avoid getting raped?

Ms. ROBERTS: Number one, before you get in the car, size up the person who's in the car. Almost one hundred percent of the black men whom I've tried to hitch a ride with have tried to harass me. I was brought up in a very polite home, and I found it very difficult to hurt someone's feelings, even when in a situation where I should. Someone offers me a ride. Obviously I am standing out there hitchhiking. I feel stupid saying, "No, I want to wait for somebody else." However, if it's a man I can usually say, "I'm sorry, I only ride with women," and I haven't had any hassles with that, except one black man saying, "I'm sorry, baby, but I don't pick up no homosexuals." If it's a group of men, I say, "I'm sorry, I don't ride with more than one person."

In Berkeley, people don't even bother to go out of the city to rape. They simply make the next corner and pull over to the side of the road. I guess because they know they won't be hassled by the police even if they are reported, so they're very, very bold here.

INTERVIEWER: What advice would you give to other women on how to handle a rape situation?

Ms. ROBERTS: I usually tell them that I've got the clap. And if he's one of the scroungey types who wouldn't mind getting it for a piece, I tell him I've got syph. People sometimes have never heard of it, so I explain it's a lot like the black plague, and for the next five years I can't fuck, and it's very contagious, and I've got to get it treated, and I was on my way to the hospital when he picked me up. I go through a big bunch of bull shit, and about half of them believe it.

I'd say, size up the situation. Decide how big a person he is in comparison to how big you are. If he has a weapon, size it up, and decide whether or not you really think he is going to use it. Is he the kind of man who is willing to stab you or shoot you, or is he going to let you go rather than get into that much trouble? And if possible, I'd say carry a weapon yourself, and know how to use it.

INTERVIEWER: What do you see as the solution to the rape problem?

Ms. ROBERTS: The police and court system have got to be improved. Unfortunately, the chances in some places of the police ever doing anything about rape is practically nil. Here in Berkeley, they sure don't care. Men here have the attitude that the police won't arrest them, and if they do arrest them, they're going to get off super light. They just get away with it over and over and over again, and they realize it thoroughly, and they take advantage of the situation. It's a free piece of pussy is the way some men look at it. If they knew that women were going to report it, and that it was going to go to court, I think it would cut down on a lot of rape.

I think after a man has raped two or three women, it's time we castrated him. I think if they're going to get into raping women that much, something ought to be done to them on a very permanent, irreversible basis. I also think women should resist and fight rapes more. Men know that women are going to be afraid to fight. I think that the more women who actually do fight and create one hell of a battle and then storm into the police station and report the rape, the better. I think women have to organize and get together and take action ourselves and be a collective pressure on politicians to do something to stop rape.

INTERVIEWER: What is your reaction to people who think that rape is usually provoked?

Ms. ROBERTS: They are ridiculous. I don't dress provocatively anymore, and I get plenty of harassments.

My final statement of my feelings right now is of disgust and contempt for men. Men comprise the police force, and they are all chauvinist pigs down there, because they won't do shit to help their sisters. That's my feelings towards men right now.

Being a welfare mother, I'm frightened because I have heard through the grapevine that if a welfare mother is raped, they can take the child from her. I recently read that in the paper.

It is extremely common for rape victims to fear for their lives. This fear often cancels out the anger and is one reason many women submit without great struggle. Such fear is often highly unfortunate. Presumably many men who rape would not kill to get what they want. But it appears that Ms. Roberts's second experience of rape did involve a killer.

On being asked how many other women they knew personally who have been raped, several of the women in the study, especially those who hitch-hike, replied, as did Ms. Roberts, "Virtually every woman I know in Berkeley has been raped." The perspective of these raped women clearly involves a very frightening world.

Ms. Roberts's suggestion that confirmed rapists should be castrated is rather extreme, though I do think that confirmed rapists should be indefinitely confined until there is a sound basis for believing that they will no longer be a danger to women or girls. Perhaps such rapists should have the option of being castrated in order to gain their freedom. Many women are tired of the view that castration is a deadly sin, whereas a blind eye is turned against rape.

TWENTY-ONE

Psychiatrists, Husbands, and Others Find the Victim Guilty

> My husband took it [the rape] very badly and was unable to understand. I think that was as much of the grief as any of it. The day that I was first home from the hospital, right in front of the children, he just threw me on the bed, and he said, "If that's what you wanted, why didn't you come to *me?*"

Given common cultural prejudices, Margaret White should have been able to expect sympathetic treatment when she was raped. She is white, the respectable wife of a military officer, and of mature years. In addition, she had obviously struggled against the man who raped her. There was skin under her fingernails and blood on her torn clothes. The semen in her vagina was identified as recent, and she was conspicuously traumatized by the experience. She did not delay in reporting the rape. She was not high on any kind of drug. She was raped by a complete stranger who was lower class. The small degree of trust she showed in him seemed justified on the basis of his behavior. And her rapist was caught.

But "society," in the form of Margaret White's husband, the police, and the hospital psychiatrist as well as other hospital staff, all appear to have blamed her for being raped.

Ms. White was thirty-eight, married, and the mother of four when she was raped seven years ago in a small midwestern town where she was living with her family. She has been married to her husband for eighteen years.

MARGARET WHITE: I was driving home from the officers' club, where I'd been playing bridge with friends of mine, women friends. I guess it was about eleven or eleven-thirty. Driving back to my quarters I had to go out onto the main highway, and I ran out of gas. I pulled over to the side of the road and sat there trying to think what to do.

Very shortly a car pulled up alongside of me with two men asking if they could help. I said, "I appear to be out of gas," and the man that was driving said, "Aw, go on. Leave her alone." He seemed to be drunk and rather incoherent. But the man who was riding with him said, "No, I'll help her." He seemed very refined and very nice. He had workman's clothes on, but appeared clean and polite.

The other man who was driving just zoomed on down the highway, muttering to himself. The one who offered to help said that he would walk the mile or mile and a half up the highway to get a five-gallon can of gas, which he did. I sat in the car waiting. I sat with it locked.

Pretty soon he came back and poured the gasoline in the car and came around to my side. I was still sitting in the driver's seat, and he said, "Well, move over, and I'll see if I can start it." The car was on a slight incline, and he said it would take a while for the gas to reach the engine from the gas tank, or something technical like that. Something told me this wasn't right, and that I shouldn't let him in the car at all, but what does a woman know about getting a car started?

He was very insistent, though still in a nice way. He said again, "Well, move over so I can get it going for you." So I moved over, and it did take a minute or two, but very shortly it started. So I said, "Fine, thank you very much," and indicated that I would like him to get out, and I would go on my way. He said, "Well, aren't you going to drive me back to the gas station so I can return the can?" The awkward part of it was that this was one of the few times that I had forgotten my wallet, and I didn't have a cent on me, so I felt doubly indebted to him. Also, he was very pleasant, a good Samaritan, really. He was a very charitable, nice-appearing man.

We drove to the gas station, and he got out and paid the man for the gasoline and gave him the can. Then he asked if I'd mind going down the road to a little road house. He said, "I think that I'll find my friend down there." I really couldn't see anything too harmful in that. Since he was still in the driver's seat, he drove. He started asking me about my children, their ages and their names. He seemed very quiet but very interested.

Then all of a sudden, absolutely without any provocation, he gunned the motor and started down the highway at about ninety. It seemed like we were flying! I said, "Slow down, slow down! Don't drive so fast. We're going to be getting to my quarters very soon. Stop! Stop! What are you doing?" He swung left and took a country road and continued to just fly that car. I knew I was in trouble.

I started begging and crying and saying, "Please don't. Please. Stop. Take me back. Please don't hurt me. I have a family." While I was crying and begging for him to stop, his attitude changed, and he started describing all the juicy things that he had planned for me in very explicit, shocking terms. I kept saying, "I have on white gloves. I have on white gloves. I'm a lady," as though the white gloves would somehow make me immune—that I wasn't the type that you go around raping. I wasn't a sex object. I wasn't aware that even at this point, I was not a person to him. It was pointless to argue, but it was also pointless to just sit there. Nothing would have saved me from that point on.

I didn't consider jumping. We were going too fast. I had a sprained ankle that was in an ace bandage, and I didn't struggle physically with him at this point for fear of causing an accident.

He turned off the highway onto a country road that soon turned into a dirt road that turned into woods that wound deeper and deeper into farmland and woodland. I was becoming completely disoriented. It was an extremely remote area. Then he stopped the car and lunged at me, and I immediately started resisting him.

Although I had a sprained ankle, I fought and kicked and scratched and bit and hit. I guess what I did must have been the worst thing I could possibly have done, because the fight just incensed him more. He was more enraged. I raked my fingernails across his face, which later helped to identify him. He took out a knife, held it first at my throat, and then actually drew it across the back of my hand, cutting the veins. I was bleeding profusely. The blood got all over his clothes, which also helped to identify him. I still have some scars. And he threatened to cut my throat and all that sort of thing.

I had a rather intricate underwear arrangement with a girdle and one thing and another. It would be very difficult to imagine the fierce struggle necessary to get them off. But the very large car gave him a great deal of room, and he tore my hose and panties off. I was pretty well immobilized even though he wasn't a huge man.

After raping me, he started crying. He didn't realize that he'd had an ejaculation.

INTERVIEWER: Did he complete intercourse?

Ms. WHITE: Yes, he did, although, I suppose because of the car, he didn't penetrate me very far. His saying that nothing had happened, that he couldn't come because I wouldn't let him, indicated how ill he was. He became enraged, saying, "If you'd just let me. If you'd just let me, I could have come."

He had his hands on my neck and shoulders, and he started banging my head on the side of the post of the car as though he was going to throttle me.

He hit my head so hard and so many times that as a result I had a concussion. Meanwhile he continued to describe what he had planned to do to me, but finally it came to an end. He nearly fell from the car, exhausted, still sobbing and crying and incoherent.

I noticed a farmhouse in the distance, and I said, "Is that where you live?" He then became very, very defensive and said, "Now, get out of here fast, and if you ever say anything to anybody about this, I'll find you and kill you." Then he said my children's names and that he'd kill them too. Then he left.

I was bleeding, I was wounded, I was in dreadful shape. I moved over to the driver's seat, sat stunned for perhaps a moment or so, thinking, "Get out of here, get out of here." I was able to start the car, drive perhaps a mile, but I found myself only deeper in the woods, more lost, not having any way of knowing how to get out. Then I saw some headlights in the rearview mirror, and it was as though hysteria started coming from my stomach. I thought I was going to throw up, and everything sort of rose and gorged me. I was afraid that it was the man coming to get me again, or maybe it was somebody else. I was hurt and so beaten, and I leaned on the horn with all my weight and started screaming at the top of my lungs. I couldn't stop. I was hysterical. Just this awful scream.

And of all things, it was the police. I don't know what they were doing patrolling out there where I was, but I was so thankful. I thought, help at last! And I told them what had just taken place, and to please take me to the hospital, that I was seriously wounded in a number of ways. They drove me to the hospital, to the emergency entrance, and I rode along with them, sitting up and talking coherently. They were skeptical.

INTERVIEWER: How do you know?

Ms. WHITE: Their cross-questioning. They repeatedly asked, "What were you doing on the highway? Why were you out at eleven-thirty? Why would you let him in the car? Don't you know better than that? You look like a mature grown woman who should certainly know the facts of life," and, "What were you doing out alone?"

I asked to see a doctor, and I told the story to him once very calmly and very coherently with more detail than I am telling it now. Many of the injuries were visible. My clothes certainly indicated that I had been through some sort of terrible struggle that I had hardly inflicted upon myself.

Then I went into shock and couldn't talk anymore. My blood pressure dropped, and they immediately took me up to the intensive care unit, where I stayed for about three days. My mother had passed away at that very hospital just three months before, and I had had some minor surgery there, so I knew many of the staff.

I felt as though I was safe at last, and yet I was met with such hostility, such skepticism. Blood samples were sent to the state for possible evidence of narcotics. Blood samples were taken for alcohol. There wasn't a positive on barbiturates or anything. Everything came back negative. But still they pressured on, "Well, now you can tell us what *really* happened."

The interrogation never stopped, day and night. Of course in intensive care the lights are on, and everything is busy all night long. The OSI, the military version of the FBI, and all the authorities of every description from every agency, questioned me day and night.[1]

INTERVIEWER: You were interrogated by some of the law enforcement people or by the staff or by both?

Ms. WHITE: By both. The first staff member who saw me was a psychiatrist. His first words were, "Haven't you really been rushing towards this very thing all of your life?" He knew nothing about me, nothing! I had never been to a psychiatrist.

INTERVIEWER: This was before he had a chance to hear a word from you?

Ms. WHITE: Yes. He had just heard of the case. I was dumbfounded.

INTERVIEWER: You had been physically examined at this point?

Ms. WHITE: Oh, yes. I suffered a number of very serious lacerations, and my head needed to be X-rayed because of the side where I'd been hit on the car.

INTERVIEWER: And your story had been verified?

Ms. WHITE: The superficial wounds had been taken care of, and everything had been verified. Every scrap of clothing had been sent to pathology for evidence of his blood, of my blood, of any discharge. These verified that the rape had occurred. The semen was identified as recent. But the psychiatrist said, "You know, things don't just *happen*. You *make* them happen."

INTERVIEWER: This was prior to having listened to the details of your story?

Ms. WHITE: That's right.

INTERVIEWER: Were you afraid of being pregnant?

Ms. WHITE: No. At that time, if you got pregnant from having been raped, it was not legal to get an abortion. It was a very bad time in my cycle, so they decided to give me a D and C before they even found out if he had impregnated me. This was the one very good thing they did for me. I didn't have to face the possibility of being pregnant.

INTERVIEWER: Did they ever catch the rapist?

1. The OSI was involved presumably because Ms. White's husband had a job requiring maximum security clearance.

Ms. WHITE: Yes. The OSI found a man by the description I'd given them. He was easily identified by the scratches on his face. But despite all their coaxing and saying it would save other women, I chose not to press charges. I was put in a very strange position of ambivalence. While being urged on the one hand to prosecute, to take this whole thing to trial, at the same time, being an officer's wife, there was a good deal of implication that it should be hushed up to avoid the dreaded transfer. My husband was threatened with a transfer to X, which was the worst place that you could possibly be sent. And indeed, as soon as I recovered we were transferred, but not to X.

Also, my decision [not to prosecute] was influenced by my being a mother and a psychology student. I'd majored in psychology. Having three sons, I was afraid that due to the publicity, they'd find out what had happened to me, and I didn't want them to grow up with bad, negative attitudes about sex. In that very small community it would have been impossible to have kept the publicity down. I felt that they were not up to handling it at that very impressionable teen-age time.

And so, even though they identified him, they couldn't lock him up or anything as long as I wouldn't press charges. And now, of course, every time I read of an attack in that area, I have misgivings. I sometimes wish that I had gone ahead with the trial, that I had had the courage to take a chance with my boys. They would have eventually understood. I'd have been able to be helpful in stopping at least one of these people. He undoubtedly went on to get other women into serious trouble.

INTERVIEWER: Did the experience affect any of your attitudes toward sex, or men?

Ms. WHITE: Oh yes. It took me quite a long time to get over my negative feelings about sex, about intercourse. I couldn't be touched for quite a long time. And of course I'd had the D and C so I couldn't have intercourse for some time after that anyway.

My husband took it very badly and was unable to understand. I think that was as much of the grief as any of it. The day that I was first home from the hospital, right in front of the children, he just threw me on the bed, and he said, "If that's what you wanted, why didn't you come to *me?*" He couldn't accept it. I guess it was just too traumatic for him too, and he didn't know what he was saying.

I could have hated him. But every time I would think about this, I would think, well, I have three sons, and they're nearly men. If I categorically hate men, I hate my sons too, but I don't, and I never will, so I can't say that I hate men.

INTERVIEWER: What effect did the rape have on your marriage?

Ms. White: Our marriage really deteriorated after it. It was the end of my pedestal days. He approached me sexually when I was still very injured, and I said, "No, please don't. Not now. I'm not ready. It's going to take me time. I'll be able to accept this one day, but I'm not ready now."

At that point I didn't want it even if he would have been very loving, kind, and gentle. A man's body just—it was so reminiscent of what I had recently been through. His reaction was, "I have rights, and you're my wife, and as long as you're my wife, it is my conjugal right. So don't fight me."

Well, I certainly wasn't going to go through a physical rape attack again, so I didn't fight him. When I saw that he was determined to go ahead, I really couldn't believe it, and I started crying. He proceeded, and when he was finished he left the room and slammed the door. There was no loving, tender kindness there. He was just ventilating his anger about the whole thing, which was the only emotion that he seemed to feel. And I think that he still feels it. It destroyed our marriage because of his inability to accept it. He has always seen me as his possession, not as a person. And you don't take his possessions and do anything to them. You don't hurt his car. You don't do anything to his wife.

That rape attack seemed to let down the barriers completely to another side of his personality that I had only had glimpses of before.

Interviewer: What was your sexual relationship with your husband prior to the rape?

Ms. White: He had a problem of premature ejaculation. He made very few sexual demands on me, but this meant he also denied me any sexual gratification, which I later came to view as being a sign of his hostility toward me. He'd approach me Saturday nights with the lights out, and it would be very cursory.

I went to a doctor, and he asked how long it had been since I had been able to achieve an orgasm in sex, and I said, "Eighteen years," and he almost collapsed. He said, "Oh, my God, I thought you were going to say eighteen days, eighteen weeks, or eighteen months! But you mean you've gone eighteen years and put up with it?"

But my husband wouldn't do anything about it. He said that I should be able to keep up with him, though sometimes he'd ejaculate before he'd even penetrated me. And there'd be very little foreplay. Also he didn't like the idea of any variety or experimenting. He especially did not like for me to take the initiative by snuggling up and reaching out to him. He'd be repelled by such overtures. He viewed me as very aggressive when I did that, and he'd call me a slut. So slowly over time I got to feel that I had no sexual rights anymore.

Regarding fidelity, I never doubted that he was faithful to me, as I was to him all the time he was overseas.

INTERVIEWER: Why do you still live with your husband?

Ms. WHITE: I felt while the boys were at home, a bad father was better than no father. My father left when I was four and a half, and my stepfather left when I was seventeen, and my father remarried when I was thirteen, and that was a dreadful experience. The loss of my father was one that I never really got over.

So there was this long chain of women in our family who had been abandoned by their men, and I was committed to the idea that I was going to be different. I have been very reluctant to give it up. It's very hard to do after all these years. I remember the good times and the good memories. And I feel sorry for him, knowing his background.

And I have to take some responsibility for the way our relationship has turned out, because I could have established, perhaps in the first week of our marriage, that I was not a possession of his. I accepted that I was because this is the way we were brought up in our time. We were to serve and please our husbands passively and put up with everything, and divorce was the absolute last resort.

I have asked him for a separation. I wanted it to be amicable, but he said, "I think that it behooves you to stay with me," and, "Before your attorney would ever get me to court, I'd be so far out of the country that they'd never find me." But I still intend to end our marriage.

INTERVIEWER: Did the experience of rape by the stranger affect your attitudes toward yourself?

Ms. WHITE: My self-image was rather obscure at that time. I didn't see myself in any particular light, as either sexy or provocative. I knew that I hadn't done anything to bring it on, so it didn't really have any effect on my feeling about myself. I didn't feel that I was bad.

INTERVIEWER: Do you regret in any way the way you handled the situation?

Ms. WHITE: I don't know. So many people have asked, "Well, don't you think that if you had been absolutely passive that maybe nothing would have happened?" It seems to me that if I had not fought, but simply let him have his way with me, he still wouldn't have thought that anything had happened. And he would have indulged in all those practices that he talked about, which would have been repugnant.

Anyhow, I didn't have time to think. I was acting on reflex and instinct, and fight was all I knew. Looking back, I can't see how it could have been avoided, although I can see that the fight enraged him more and stimulated him more.

INTERVIEWER: Did you feel guilty or responsible in any way?

Ms. WHITE: No. Except after seeing the psychiatrist. Another psychiatrist told me later that what the first psychiatrist said was supposed to shock me, as it did. Evidently, it was an attempt to bring me out of the deep shock that I was going into. He said it could have gone two ways. I came out of it fine, but I could have retreated too far into myself. Apparently he knew this, and he used this device as a means to get me to fight back and to come alive again.

But now I feel no guilt. Our husbands were flying or overseas so much of the time that women being out alone in the early evening was nothing unusual in that community. And we came and went to dinner or bridge, and there were always activities at the club, and it wasn't thought to be out of line at all to go out alone at a reasonable hour if we didn't go alone into bars and places like that.

INTERVIEWER: Can you think of any solutions to the rape problem?

Ms. WHITE: I don't know. If the man who raped me was a psychopath and had a record, and chances are he had, and if I'd identified him and gotten him committed, he would have only gotten out or have been paroled in a very short time. He would have been further enraged by his incarceration and have gone on and done the same thing again. He should be treated like a sick man, not a criminal. It was a criminal act, but done by a sick person.

I think about all the controversy over prostitution and whether it should be legalized or not, but it doesn't seem to be the solution because it's the overpowering need for some men to overpower a woman. He was a sadistic brute, and my fighting him gave him the opportunity to use all of his hostility. So if he had found a prostitute who would have simply complied, I don't think he would have been interested. I truly can't think of a solution except that when men are known rapists I think they should be sent to a medical prison facility where there's some attempt to rehabilitate them.

INTERVIEWER: What is your reaction to people who think that rape is usually provoked?

Ms. WHITE: I think the people that theorize on something like that are very pompous, because they can't possibly know what you did, and what you said, and what your body language was saying. They haven't been raped, or they wouldn't say it.

The reactions of the psychiatrist and Ms. White's husband are the most devastating aspects of this case. Rather than a ploy designed to bring her out of shock, it seems likely that the first psychiatrist's accusation, and its timing, would have further traumatized her. The view that victims of rape must want it is commonplace in conventional psychiatric dogma.

Mr. White's reaction was extreme. Prior to the rape, he apparently held his sadistic urges in check, but when his wife was raped by someone else, he was no longer willing or able to do so. His belief that his wife had finally shown her true colors, after eighteen years of marriage, and that she actually desired her horrendous experience, dramatizes the power of the myth of the rape victim's culpability.

Crazy as Ms. White's rapist seems to have been, the case makes it clear that not all rapists appear or behave as if they are insane. How many of us would not allow ourselves to trust an ordinary-looking, pleasant-speaking, apparent good Samaritan who offered to help us out in a jam? How would it be to live in this world if one suspected every male stranger, no matter how kind he seemed to be, of being a possible rapist?

TWENTY-TWO

Get Back Down Under, Uppity Woman!

He said, "Listen, any time any man wants to
rape you, he can, and I'm telling you this for
your own good."

Nan Murray's experience illustrates rape as a political act perhaps more
vividly than any of the other cases. The masculine ego of her rapist was
apparently so threatened by her sexual rejection of him, by her verbal
deflations of his sexist assumptions and comments, that he raped her to "put
her back in her place." This was his way of asserting that he belonged to a
caste superior to hers by virtue of his power to rape. In a matter of minutes
he reduced her from a strong, assertive woman to a pleading, sobbing,
hysterical one. Since she refused to defer to him as a woman should, he
forced her to. And in the short term, at least, it was a successful political act.
He won the power struggle he had constructed. She was beaten into submission, her confidence was smashed, and another uppity woman had been
shoved into her rightful place.

Just as lynching may be seen as the supreme political act of whites
against blacks, so rape may be seen as the supreme political act of men
against women. And just as poor whites often initiated lynchings, so it is
disproportionately lower-class and black men, who feel powerless in a society that defines masculinity in terms of power, and who have less access to
nonphysical means of asserting their power over women, who are directly
involved in rape.

At the time of her rape five months ago, Ms. Murray was a twenty-
seven-year-old junior in college, who had spent many years working between
graduating from high school and attending college. Her background is
working class.

NAN MURRAY: I was at home at my apartment where I lived with three other people. It was a Friday night, and I was by myself. Two of the people in the apartment were out of town, and one of them, Steve, had gone to a dance. I was expecting him back around ten or ten-thirty.

I was talking on the telephone to a friend when someone came to the door. A black man was there, and he introduced himself to me as Rick and told me that he had been at a party we had given at the house a couple of weeks ago, that he was a friend of Steve's, and that he was in a therapy group with Steve at X College. He said that he was on his way home, and he thought he would drop by to see Steve. I said, "Well, Steve isn't here, but he should be back soon, if you'd like to come in and wait." Rick said OK, and I said, "I'm on the telephone, and I'm going to continue talking." He said OK, and I shut the door to my room and continued on the telephone.

I guess I may have been on the telephone another fifteen or twenty minutes. I could hear him roaming around the rest of the house, putting on the stereo and things of that nature. When I got off the telephone I went into the kitchen, and I said that I was going to have some tea and asked him if he wanted some. I believe he said yes. I also asked him if he wanted to smoke any grass. I'd been working for a couple of days, and I was really tired and exhausted and wanted to relax. Rick said that he'd been drinking, but he smoked grass with me too.

Almost immediately from the time we sat down at the table together, he started coming on to me in a very sexual way, asking if I was involved with a man. I said no. He made some sort of comment, like, "Well, free, willing, and ready, huh?" I said, "What are you talking about!" I couldn't believe anybody would say anything like that. To just assume that because I wasn't involved with a man, I was ready to go to bed with someone, was so totally off the wall, I laughed it off.

But his remarks kept going on that way. I would be either laughing at what he said, because it seemed so absurd, or periodically getting really pissed off and coming down really hard about what he was saying. When I would react in this manner he would say, "You're really defensive," and, "Why are you so defensive?" At another point in the conversation he said that he would like to sleep with me. I said, "You're crazy! I mean do you think someone just walks into my house, and that I'm immediately attracted to him and hop into bed with him?! Where are you coming from?" It was all very strange.

With my women's liberation approach to what he was saying, I really came down on him very hard a lot of times when I got particularly angry with him. At one point he responded by saying that any time that any man wanted to rape me, he could, and I should not forget that. It was obvious that he was almost threatening me with what he was saying, but what he said was so ridiculous, I didn't have any other recourse except to laugh, because I knew it was pointless to argue with him, so I really laughed a lot.

It became clear to me as the discussion progressed, that he was very threatened by my strength, and by my lack of interest in sleeping with him, or having anything to do with him. I was just sitting there calmly smoking my joints, and I wasn't in the least bit swayed by anything that he was saying. And it became obvious to me as the discussion continued that this really made him uptight. It was when I was unconcerned about what he was saying that he would accuse me of being defensive, and he'd sit back in his chair and shake his head, as if I were this really pitiful creature.

I guess we talked for an hour, maybe an hour and a half. I was getting bored with the whole thing. He made several attempts to get up and go. He would say he was going, but then he'd start back into a conversation. I still didn't perceive that there was anything really wrong or really unusual about the whole interaction. He was saying some really, really sexist things, but it wasn't that much different from the sexism that I often experienced except that he was really being very blunt about it, which I was unaccustomed to hearing in a place like Berkeley.

He got up to leave again, then came back in to talk, and then came over to me and tried to reach out to touch me, and I said, "Listen! Keep your hands off me! I don't want you to touch me!" He backed away and then came back again and reached out and tried to hug me or something. I'm really very definite about that, that I don't want people to touch me when I don't want them to touch me, and I said as much to him.

Then there was this scene in which I was backing away from him and he was sort of coming at me more, trying to reach out to me. There was a time where it was almost a chase scene around this big kitchen table. I was on one side of it and he was on the other, and we were going back and forth. But finally he grabbed me. I was really pissed at that point and started fighting. I realized right then that he wasn't going to let me go, that he was totally serious about what he was talking about, and I started struggling. He started hitting me around the face and yelling at me and telling me I had better do what he said.

At that point I completely froze. I was so frightened. This wasn't a simple thing of verbal sexist statements being made to me. This was really an attack on me, and I became totally frightened, and just froze up. My body went absolutely stiff. I was bent over holding my head because he had been hitting me in the face. He picked me up and threw me into my bedroom, which was right off the kitchen. At this point I couldn't even scream. I was just pleading, "Please, leave me alone." He started tearing at my clothes. I heard my clothes tearing, and I realized that I was going to be raped.

I was too frightened to do anything about it. At this point I was sobbing hysterically. I was afraid to fight anymore with him, and so I was just laying there, completely stiff and numb and thinking, oh, God, it will be over in a few minutes. But it wasn't over as quickly as I thought it might be, because he kept insisting on trying to penetrate me although he was having trouble keeping an erection.

My hysterical sobs had decreased to a sort of moaning and steady sobbing. I was just so blown apart by the experience. Then he pulled out of me, and said, "Well, if you *really* don't want me to—" And all the time I had been crying! There was *nothing* in my behavior to indicate that I wanted to sleep with Rick, but now he was acting as if the reason that he had stopped was because I didn't want it.

He must have had an orgasm at some point, because when I was cleaning myself up afterwards, there was all this semen inside of me. He then started saying, "Please, please don't cry. Please. I like you. I'd like to come back and see you. It's not that bad. What are you making such a big thing over?" I was aware that unless I quit crying, he wasn't going to leave. I made a conscious effort to stop crying, but I wasn't able to hold back the tears. They just came out in big sobs again.

At this point I was lying down on the bed, and he was sitting on the bed and patting my head. I kept saying, "Please go." He would look like he was ready to go until the sobs would come out again. But finally he did leave. I got up immediately and sort of staggered around. I called a friend to come get me. I was in the bathroom trying to get myself cleaned up. I knew that I would stay with this friend, and so I was trying to think of what things I would need, like a toothbrush and stuff. But I was really very much dazed.

It occurred to me that my friend was coming to pick me up, and the front door would be locked, so I had better go unlock it so she would be able to get in, because I might not hear the doorbell while in the bathroom. So I did that. I was getting myself together in the bathroom, when I heard someone come in. I thought it was my friend, so I walked out into the living room. But it was this man coming back.

When I saw him again, I started crying. He started reaching out to me again, and I said, "You should go. There's someone coming over here, and if you don't want trouble, I think it's better you leave." He looked at me and said, "So you had to resort to that!" There was nothing I could say to that. He had come back because in the scuffle that took place, he had dropped his ring, so he came back to get it.

After hearing that someone was coming, he did leave, but not in any great panic. In fact, when my friend came in a few minutes later, she said that she saw him walking sort of casually and nonchalantly down the street as she was driving up.

INTERVIEWER: Did he hit you pretty hard?

Ms. MURRAY: Not hard enough to bruise me, but he slapped me around in the general area of my head and face enough for me to know that he wasn't playing. It was obvious right away when I started struggling with him that he was much stronger than me. He had me in an absolute hold in which I couldn't get away from him.

INTERVIEWER: What can you say about his personality?

Ms. MURRAY: In the next couple of days a lot was found out about him, with the help of friends of mine who were so enraged they wanted to do something about it. The thing that I can see most clearly is that he really does have an awfully big problem with sexuality. Steve, my roommate who knew him, talked to Rick on the telephone, and Rick insisted that I wanted it, that I had smoked dope and I really wanted it.

Steve would push him and say, "Listen, Nan didn't tell me that, and I believe what she says." Rick said, "Well, she's completely wrong. She wanted me to fuck her." Steve said, "No, Rick, it's not like that." And Steve kept being very firm about it. Then Rick would break down in tears and sobs and say, "Oh, I just don't know. I don't know what's happening. My head hurts." It was obvious to anyone who had any kind of interaction with him in the next couple of days that he was very, very screwed up.

INTERVIEWER: Why do you think he raped you?

Ms. MURRAY: I don't think he came there with any intent to rape anyone. But in thinking about the situation afterwards, it seemed evident to me that everything that I had been that night, and everything that I had said, and the fact that I was not in any way impressed with the kinds of things that he was saying, did nothing but threaten his ego. I think this was clearest when he said, "Listen, any time any man wants to rape you, he can, and I'm telling you this for your own good." It seems that the longer the discussion went on, the more threatening I was to him, and the only way that he could get back at me was by some sort of physical assault. I definitely think it was a political act.

INTERVIEWER: Did he seem very sexually excited?

Ms. MURRAY: No, not really. I don't think he was.

INTERVIEWER: How long did the actual rape take?

Ms. MURRAY: It's hard to estimate the time. Maybe around five minutes. I don't think it was any longer than that.

INTERVIEWER: So what happened afterward?

Ms. MURRAY: First of all, I told my women's group. They were terribly,

terribly upset about it and wanted to take some action right away. Also I told Steve, who was really upset about it.

We found out that there had been similar incidents with other women, but that it had never gotten that far before. One woman was really afraid of him, and had gone out and bought herself a gun, and told him that any time he came near her house again, she would kill him. Another woman had gotten very funny vibes from him. She had been out with him and felt very peculiar about him, but she didn't want to talk about it.

We were trying to get together people to go to the therapy group to confront Rick with what he had done. Steve was encouraging both of these women who had had these experiences with Rick before to go to the therapy group too, but both of them were too afraid of him to go. We also talked to the leader of the group, who apparently was one of the people who was closest to him. He had been working with him individually. The group leader said that Rick was psychotic. He said that his grandmother, whom he lived with, had talked about getting him committed, but that she didn't want to have to do that to her grandson.

So it seemed apparent that he had a long record of psychological disturbances and went in and out of the psych emergency center a lot. But because he would have these really lucid moments at times, they would usually dismiss him down at the psych emergency center. And then he would be back in. It seemed clear that jail certainly wasn't the place for this person.

Everyone felt that the best way to deal with it was to recognize that this man needed to be off the street, especially since this thing had happened with more than one woman, and there was no telling what he might do next. People thought the best way to deal with it was to see if they could get him to commit himself. They pointed out to him that he really had problems and needed help.

Eventually enough people put pressure on him, particularly Steve, that this did happen, and he went into the hospital, which had a three-day hold on him. After that time, he could either commit himself for a longer period voluntarily, or the hospital could decide to keep him if they wanted to. I don't know actually how long he did stay in the hospital. This incident happened toward the latter part of May, and I do know that he was out of the hospital in July, because Steve ran into him in the street.

INTERVIEWER: It was mainly Steve who was responsible for what happened to Rick?

Ms. MURRAY: Yeah. Though he also got some cooperation from the man who led the therapy group, but not an awful lot. This man was overly concerned with whether we were concerned for Rick's best interests.

INTERVIEWER: The first person you told was the woman friend that you called?

Ms. MURRAY: Yes. She was in my women's group, and she and the man that she lives with came over and picked me up immediately, and I went over to stay at their house. They were really shocked. They seemed to recognize that the most important thing at that time was to get me out of there. We didn't even discuss whether or not we should report it.

INTERVIEWER: You didn't?

Ms. MURRAY: No, not on the Friday night on which it happened. I guess I didn't even think about it. I was just so totally hysterical about it, it didn't even occur to me. I stayed with my friends the whole of the next day, and went out with them that night to the house of another woman in my group. Everybody was really upset. The concern was more for me, rather than what we were going to do about it.

Then the next night, Sunday night, I went to my women's group. The other three women in the group had all, by this time, heard what had happened. They were talking about what kind of tactics they could use to deal with somebody like this, and they were really, really angry.

So it was at that women's group meeting that we really began thinking of what could be done. My burst of anger about the situation had happened as soon as he had grabbed me, and I had started fighting against him. But then when I realized that fighting was useless, I was no longer in touch with the anger that I felt about the situation. I was just too hysterical to think about that.

So a couple of days later, when people were talking about what could be done, I didn't know what to say. I was just too shaken up by it. The whole incident had come to represent something much more to me, in that all during the time that I had been having the conversation with this man, I had felt that I was really asserting myself, and making it clear what I didn't want, and what offended me about the things he was saying.

I consider my whole behavior throughout the discussion as being very, very strong. I was not being manipulated into any kind of compromising position. The fact that the rape followed all that symbolized to me what happens when women are really particularly strong in a relationship with men. I felt completely kicked in by that. My confidence in myself and self-assurance in walking down the street or in any kind of unfamiliar situation immediately left me. And I noticed from then on, whenever I would go places in which I wasn't familiar, I would get very, very nervous and very, very unsure of myself, particularly around black men. I've become totally paranoid about relating to black men. It seems clear to me now that there's an awful lot of bitterness of black men toward white women, and I'd never really realized that before.

INTERVIEWER: Has it affected your attitude toward men in general, or is it just black men?

Ms. MURRAY: I guess men in general too. I have an awful lot of anger about the fact that men don't realize, and a lot of women too, that rape is a real thing, that it happens, and there are situations in which people can't do anything about it. I've become enraged about the attitudes toward rape in society.

Even when friends of mine would hear about it, the first question they would ask is, "Well, did you resist?" as if it's not totally valid at all unless I did resist. This kind of insensitivity to the whole problem really infuriates me. I do find myself generally more hostile. The hostility is there, but I'm afraid to let men see it, so I've drawn away from men.

INTERVIEWER: Did it affect your attitude or feelings about sex?

Ms. MURRAY: Very definitely. I didn't want to sleep with anybody for weeks, but I finally did sleep with this black friend of mine. I'm sure it was the fact that he was black that made it so heavy for me. It was a really traumatic experience in which I started crying and really couldn't deal with it. It's hard for me right now to see how sexual relations between a man and a woman can be anything but rape.

INTERVIEWER: Is that what it felt like when you slept with your friend?

Ms. MURRAY: Not really. It wasn't what he was doing that bothered me. But I was just much more conscious of the fact that he was a black man, and that black men seem to be totally insensitive to me as a white woman except to vent their hostility on. I've been a friend of his long enough to know that he wasn't venting his hostility on me, but simply that the dynamics of the situation made a sexual experience with him seem very, very weird and very, very heavy.

Every now and then I find myself getting sexually attracted to men, but I find myself much less willing to pursue it, because I feel that invariably what will happen is that my strength will become obvious to them, and I am afraid of men's reaction to it. Either they have raped me, like Rick, or they have drawn away from the relationship in some way or another. It's been my experience that men find it difficult to deal with the strength in women.

INTERVIEWER: How did it affect your attitude to yourself?

Ms. MURRAY: It was like getting used to a whole new person in a lot of ways. I would not think anything about doing something like, say, walking down Telegraph Avenue, and then I would immediately realize that it was not a situation I wanted to be in, that the heavy street scene, and the way that black men in particular come on to white women on the street, I could do without. I wasn't sure what kind of situations were going to bring about this sort of panicky fear in me.

There was one time a couple of days after the rape in which I found myself doing my laundry in a laundromat. The people that managed the laundromat were a couple of black men. It got to be late in the afternoon, and I found myself being totally terrified by that situation, and I left before I had finished my laundry. So basically the overall reaction was being very, very unsure of myself.

INTERVIEWER: And do you still feel that?

Ms. MURRAY: I think it's improving somewhat, but then again, I'm much more cautious. I don't walk down Telegraph Avenue without thinking about it. And I think it has affected me in other situations. I'm just generally not as sure of myself in unfamiliar kinds of situations, whether it be with men or with women. I find a lack of confidence about myself and what I'm doing, and how I'm appearing to other people.

In relationships with men, the fear comes from knowing that even if I were strong enough physically to resist, I'd have the psychological fear that I now have of men to get over. I've thought about learning some form of self-defense since then, but although I think it is a really valid thing to do, I also know that for me, and I assume that this is true for a lot of women, the fear has to be overcome before you can defend yourself. And I don't know how to go about doing that. I don't think learning karate would give me that confidence.

INTERVIEWER: It seems in general that your friends reacted very supportively. Was there any exception to this?

Ms. MURRAY: Oh, yeah. There were exceptions. One friend of mine had called me up at my house on the day after it happened, and talked to Steve. He told her that I was not there, and that I had been raped, and he told her where I was. She called me at my friend's house, and said, "How are you?" I said, "Well, I'm sort of freaked out," and she said, "Yes, I know. Steve told me." I said, "Well, what did he tell you?" She said, "He said that you had been raped," and I said, "Yes, that was it." And her first response was, "Oh, Nan, you should try to get into therapy." I felt totally ripped off. I said, "Someone rapes me, and *I* should get into therapy!" I mean, it just doesn't follow.

In talking to people about it there was an awful lot of insensitivity to my feelings, particularly from men. I found it hard to communicate with them at all. The result was that I moved out of the house I was living in, because I felt the men there, although they empathized with me, really had no realization of the kind of fear I felt. I think men can't understand that physical kind of fear of someone else, and also the psychological kind of fear that completely paralyzes you. And then I have also picked up in men that although they may be friends of mine, and can sympathize with the situation, deep down inside they *do* think, even if it's on a subconscious level, that somehow I did bring it on, or that subconsciously I really wanted to be raped.

INTERVIEWER: Did the experience of rape change your thinking about rape in any way?

Ms. MURRAY: Very definitely. Like a lot of other people, I thought in some way that a woman really couldn't be raped unless she wanted to be. I can remember that was an attitude that I had several years ago. In the last couple of years since I've been involved with the women's movement, it was not something that I had really thought about, but I'm sure that attitude was down deep inside. When I would hear of other women getting raped, I really couldn't conceive of that happening to me. Somehow, I figured, they must have put themselves in compromising situations.

INTERVIEWER: Did you find yourself feeling any guilt about being raped?

Ms. MURRAY: Yes, I did. Particularly right after it happened.

When my friend came over to the house and made me tell her what happened, I kept being very confused. I kept saying, "I don't think there was any way I could stop it." And she would immediately reassure me, "*You're* not guilty! Quit doing that to yourself!"

That really felt very good, but in the couple of days afterwards, particularly with all the contact that we still had with Rick, I kept thinking, is there any way I could have stopped it? I knew that there wasn't, but I was constantly reevaluating my behavior.

INTERVIEWER: Did you regret the way you handled the situation?

Ms. MURRAY: My reactions to this particular black man, and the strength that I displayed verbally in letting him know that I was not interested in him in the slightest, was a reaction to an experience I'd had with another black man several weeks before. He had come to the house through friends to see other people in the house, and we'd got into a discussion. I had been pretty passive, and not really very up front about my strong woman's views and stuff, and it had gotten very complicated. Not that he was about to rape me or anything like that, but he perceived that I wanted a relationship with him when I didn't. This experience was very much in my mind when Rick dropped by. I didn't want a similar situation to build up in which he would think, simply because of my passivity, that I was interested in a relationship with him.

INTERVIEWER: Do you regret not reporting the rape to the police?

Ms. MURRAY: I don't think so. Knowing how hard it's been to deal with psychologically, I can imagine how much worse it would have been if I had gone to the police. I think that, at that particular time, it may have succeeded in convincing me of my own insanity.

INTERVIEWER: Have you seen Rick since he raped you?

Ms. MURRAY: Yes, I saw him a couple of weeks ago. I was with Steve. He saw Steve, then turned away. Presumably, he identifies Steve with a bad experience in his life. He didn't see me, but I felt pushed into a corner again, even though I was twenty or thirty yards away from him. I kept wanting to get out of there. I felt really enraged that he was walking around in the park enjoying himself.

INTERVIEWER: Have you had any other experiences similar to being raped?

Ms. MURRAY: I know there have been a lot of times in which I've been with men, and if I've been very firm and said, "I don't want to sleep with you. I'm just interested in talking to you," they either got angry at me and wouldn't have anything more to do with me, or they tried to coax me into it and argue with me and say, "Why not?"

When they do the arguing bit, and the coaxing and the pleading, there have been times when I've slept with men that I wasn't particularly interested in sleeping with at all. But I just felt like I didn't have my argument articulated as to why not to sleep with them. In a lot of ways I can't see where there's that much difference between this kind of thing and rape.

Did Ms. Murray "collude" in the rape because she smoked grass with her rapist and stayed in a social situation with him in spite of his obvious sexual interest in her? Absurd as it may be, when a woman's judgment that a particular man can be trusted to respect her physical autonomy turns out to be mistaken, this is the way most judges and juries appear to think.

It is interesting how much Rick changed once he had raped Ms. Murray. Back on top, in his eyes, he even became solicitous: "Please don't cry. Please. I like you. I'd like to come back and see you. It's not that bad." Once his ego was restored by smashing her ego, he appeared to have felt guilty enough to pretend that he hadn't raped her. He also tried to belittle what he had done: "What are you making such a big thing over?" Why should a woman be so upset by being used or put down by a man? If a man is put down by a woman, that may justify threats and rape. But it's part of a woman's lot to be beneath men anyhow, so what's the big deal here?

Ms. Murray was merely asserting her right to do as *she* wished, not as *he* wished. But he felt put down by her not allowing him to dominate, to have his wishes prevail. If male domination is accepted as the proper relationship between men and women, as it is in our culture, then women's demand for equality becomes a threat.

As a result of being raped, Ms. Murray felt that being a strong woman was dangerous with men. But so was being weak and passive. The solution? To be strong, but not show it? But these are the old devious ways of the past. These are some of the dilemmas that are shared by women, even if not all of us are fully conscious of them.

While Ms. Murray was not willing to become a victim of the misnamed system of justice, the way that she and her friends dealt with the rapist was definitely not passive. If more rapists were confronted in this way, the incidence of rape would probably decrease, but the confrontation required the kind of support for the rape victim that is still rarely found.

With the growing influence of the women's movement, more rapists will be confronted, sometimes compassionately as was done in this case, sometimes vindictively in a desire for retribution. These confrontations will occur because the system of injustice to rape victims will not become a system of justice overnight. Such confrontations will probably serve to speed up the changes needed, because they demonstrate so powerfully the inability of the present system to deal adequately with the problem of rape.

TWENTY-THREE

Rapists Speak for Themselves

By Jack Fremont

INTERVIEWER: Do you think that many men commit rape?
JIMMY: Oh, yes, I know damn well they do! With no more feeling involved and no more neurosis than just, "I want you, and I can't have you, so I'll take you."

As a boy I was trained to fear girls, fight boys, hide emotions, and get ahead. It was a normal childhood.

I've spent many years trying to unlearn what parents, teachers, peers, television, history, and art taught me, and I've been fortunate in finding people willing to struggle along with me. I don't think I've ever raped anyone, but like most men I've played the coercive sexual games that border on rape. My men's group experience has taught me that many men harbor rape fantasies, just as they harbor fantasies of wealth and glory, but most men keep their fantasies under lock and key or channel urges into socially accepted pastimes like wife beating and football.

Perhaps the reasons why some men rape while others make do with poker, pornography, or political aspirations has to do with fear, hatred, the need to conquer, or the need to humiliate or be humiliated, but this chapter cannot pretend to offer insight into so complex an area. Nor should the rapists interviewed for inclusion in this chapter be regarded as typical. In fact, they are probably atypical. The average rapist doesn't respond to newspaper ads or call radio talk shows as did the four rapists whose experiences follow.

The four rapists included here are probably different from many rapists by dint of their class, race, and disposition. They are all white. Three are middle-class. Two were caught and convicted. None approached hitchhikers.

No one really knows what most rapists are like. There is no satisfactory way to conduct a study of rapists, no way of obtaining a statistically valid cross section. What follows are four cases of a class of men whose parameters remain unknown. Given this, I should still like to hazard one generalization: most rapists seem incapable of viewing women as people.

JIMMY

Jimmy is a white male, forty-nine years old. Recently released from jail after serving nine years for burglary and attempted rape, Jimmy believes he raped women in order to compensate for feeling inadequate about his social position. Of lower-class Southern background, Jimmy was twenty-six and working as a shipping clerk in Boston when he raped his first victim.

An illegitimate child, he was raised by his grandmother and saw his mother only rarely. Jimmy has never been married. He claims his sex life outside of the four rapes he committed was satisfying and normal and that, in fact, sexual desire was not what motivated him to rape.

INTERVIEWER: When did you last commit rape?

JIMMY: It was a long time ago, in 1962. The funny thing is that the one I did time on was an attempt not a completed thing. But I have committed rapes before that particular incident that I didn't do time for.

INTERVIEWER: How do you feel about having committed rape?

JIMMY: Oh, it's an awful thing, taking advantage of anybody, taking away their right to say yes or no. But at that particular time it gave me a sense of power, a sense of accomplishing something that I felt I didn't have the ability to get. You see something or somebody that you want, and you know that under normal circumstances you wouldn't be able to attract this person, so you take her.

INTERVIEWER: Could you tell me a little bit about that first rape, what your motivations were, and what went through your mind?

JIMMY: It happened in Boston. The chick was a white girl. I'd seen her around, from afar, followed her home, and peeped in her window. This was something I wanted, and I felt that I would never be able to make this, and I've always been told that this was the thing to have, you know. I wanted this particular kind of person—she was a college girl—but I felt that my social station would make her reject me. And I just didn't feel that I would be able to make this person. I didn't know how to go about meeting her. Anyway, I waited one night until she had gone to bed. After the lights were out I just went into the window. She was frightened, of course, and I took advantage of her fright and raped her.

INTERVIEWER: Did you use a weapon?

JIMMY: No. I didn't threaten her either, but she was frightened and said she'd do what I wanted. I told her what I wanted, so she said, "I'll do what you want. Just don't hurt me." I was in a high state of anxiety, but I accomplished what I wanted to accomplish. I was only frightened afterward, afraid that she might report it. I think that had she reacted differently it might have turned me off completely. Had she yelled or screamed or struggled, I would have split. It might have shocked me into the realization of what I was doing. I mean, all a girl has to do is turn around and point a finger at you and laugh and that would put you down so badly you wouldn't have the courage to do anything.

INTERVIEWER: How did her fear affect you?

JIMMY: I wasn't concerned with her fear. I was only concerned with her body and being able to accomplish something that, given my upbringing, I couldn't accomplish any other way. I felt elated that I was able to accomplish what I wanted. It gave me power over her. Her feelings didn't mean anything to me at all. The thing that mattered was the thrill. I wasn't interested in whether someone else felt, or what they felt. I was only interested in a selfish thing. All I wanted was a convenient place to get rid of my thing.

The conquest is in the accomplishment. The easier the better. The only feeling I had is that I wanted this beautiful fine thing and I got it.

INTERVIEWER: Why did you choose her?

JIMMY: Because of the way she looked and the way she carried herself.

INTERVIEWER: How did you feel about what you'd done?

JIMMY: Well, at the time, I was frightened, naturally. But the feeling of accomplishing what I wanted was uppermost, and I didn't give it any other thought except for the fact that I didn't want to be detected. I knew the consequences of what I was doing, but I did things in spite of the consequences, because the feeling far outweighs the consequences.

INTERVIEWER: How long after that first experience did you rape again?

JIMMY: Well, it wasn't long, I'll tell you that. I've raped about four chicks. They were all about the same as far as bodily makeup. They all had a certain self-assurance, a sarcastic way about them, as if they were thinking, "I look good, and I know you want me." It used to be threatening to me. They don't need you, there's the rejection thing, but you want this, and you don't see why you can't have it, so you take it.

INTERVIEWER: In each case, did you break into someone's apartment?

JIMMY: Yeah. I'd either wait for them in their apartment or go in once they'd gone to bed. I've never gone up and jumped on anyone. I've never used weapons. I smacked a girl once. She resisted, and I smacked her, but that's the only violent thing I've ever done. I would never grab someone off the street or drag anyone into an alley.

INTERVIEWER: Did some resist more than others?

JIMMY: Yeah, some had to be coerced, but I didn't enjoy doing it. It wasn't a turn-on. I wanted things as easy as I could get them. And if they didn't give in, I would threaten, and if I had to go through a big hassle, or exert any kind of violence, well, that was nothing for me then, but I didn't like it.

They'd try to talk me out of it. I've had them even tell me, "I'll introduce you to a doctor," you know. "I'll have you talk to my psych." But I didn't rape because I couldn't make a girl. I don't have any difficulty at all expressing myself with a woman, or making her. But somehow it didn't have the same intensity as when I would reach above myself. I grew up believing you didn't reach above yourself socially. You stayed where you were. But I couldn't accept that.

INTERVIEWER: So going to a prostitute, for example, would not have satisfied your need?

JIMMY: Exactly. Making a girl wouldn't do it either. In other words, if I were to run across a certain person that I didn't have the ability or the expertise or the balls to approach and hit on because I didn't know how to go about it, it made me want her. It was the unattainable that I wanted. I couldn't go up and say, "Hey, I'd like to take you out," or, "Hey, I desire you." I could do this with certain people. It wasn't that I was unable to perform, or felt threatened, or felt unable to respond.

INTERVIEWER: Was sex any different for you when you raped and when you were with a woman who was willing?

JIMMY: No, there was no difference at all.

INTERVIEWER: How did the women you raped respond?

JIMMY: They didn't get into it, and I didn't expect them to get into it. I didn't *care* whether they did or not. I really didn't give a damn.

INTERVIEWER: Were you remorseful afterwards?

JIMMY: No, I had no remorse. I wasn't elated either. I didn't feel, "Hey-hey, look at me, see how strong I am, feel my muscles." My feeling was only that I've rid myself of the anxiety and tension that I felt as a result of not being able to express myself. Once that was relieved, I felt exhaustion.

INTERVIEWER: What happened with the attempted rape?

JIMMY: I turned it into a burglary, but that's not what it started out to be. What happened was that she became terribly upset, crying and screaming and everything like that. I wasn't going to hurt her, so I just split. I was identified later by someone who saw me flee, and I was busted for burglary and attempted rape. That's what I did time for.

INTERVIEWER: In what way have your feelings changed in the past ten years?

JIMMY: Well, I'm able to express my feelings. I've had enough rape. I've gone through the gamut now to such an extent that I've learned there's more to sex than just the bodily expression. I learned this in the joint in therapy groups. That was the first time I was able to look at what I'd been doing. They force you to look at yourself and talk about it. When I admitted to myself what I had done, I was able to get a whole different attitude about the whole damn thing.

INTERVIEWER: Do you think that rape is damaging for the women?

JIMMY: Definitely. Whenever you take advantage of someone and take away their right to say yes or no, it's damaging. Women really have no defense once a person overpowers them. Everyone stands in awe of being hurt. I've had many tell me, "Don't hurt me." The first thing on their minds is the fear of pain. Who wants to experience pain?

INTERVIEWER: Did you see a difference between making love and raping at the time?

JIMMY: No, I didn't. I didn't care either. Love itself meant nothing to me. All I cared about was this tension I felt, and I had no other way of getting rid of it.

INTERVIEWER: Were there many people you met in jail who were there for rape?

JIMMY: Oh, yes. But I was different because I didn't have a desire to maim anybody, so my desire for power and possession wasn't the same as theirs. The only similarity is a feeling of inadequacy.

INTERVIEWER: Sexual or social inadequacy?

JIMMY: Both, but I think basically it all comes from social inadequacy. I think that's the key. Most of the rapists there felt one-down in some way and had to try some way to get back in a position of power, either socially or sexually. Some of them had homosexual problems, and they had trouble accepting themselves. Some of them just didn't give a damn. To them it was just a selfish kick. Some of them have found it was easy to rape so they kept doing it. I can't speak for a person who is really a psychotic. I'm just talking about normal everyday people who do this thing.

INTERVIEWER: Do you think that many men commit rape?

JIMMY: Oh, yes, I know damn well they do! With no more feeling involved and no more neurosis than just, "I want you, and I can't have you, so I'll take you."

INTERVIEWER: What was your general attitude towards women at the time?

JIMMY: I've always felt good about women generally, but my only consideration was being able to get this thing I couldn't have. In other words, if a girl was in college, if she was a nurse, or a schoolteacher, or something like that, these were things I couldn't get. If she wore clothes that showed any sorts of affluence, man, I had to possess that!

I believe that rape gave me some sort of greater satisfaction than getting it freely. I had a low opinion of myself. I felt as though these women weren't for me. If one of these girls had said, "Well, OK, I dig you too. Let's go," I couldn't have handled it.

INTERVIEWER: When you were in jail, were any men raped?

JIMMY: Yeah. But it wasn't for sex. There might have been an occasion that it was, but usually it was a power thing. I was in Soledad for three and a half years, and they had two or three occurrences in the same wing I was in. It was a thing like, "We're going to show you what we think of you, and we're going to take your manhood away from you."

INTERVIEWER: How did you feel about that?

JIMMY: I felt bad because it is always bad when someone takes away your right to say yes and no. People have been making their own decisions for millions of years and that is as it should be. But once someone usurps your right to say yes and no, then I think it's unhealthy and I think it's wrong. That's how I felt for the men who had their manhood taken.

INTERVIEWER: How about your feelings towards men. Do you look at men in competitive terms?

JIMMY: I think all men do to a degree. I wanted to be like Rubirosa,[1] and I wondered what was wrong with me, why I couldn't be like him. I wanted some of the trappings that he had. The trappings were the type of things I couldn't get.

INTERVIEWER: Like the women he was with?

JIMMY: Right. So I got the women.

Perhaps the most interesting aspect of this case has to do with Jimmy's rehabilitation. Many victims, particularly if they are liberal or radical in their political outlook, refuse to report their rapists on the grounds that prison fosters criminal behavior and punishes rather than reforms. Jimmy's experience contradicts this belief. He felt group therapy sessions in prison helped him to understand and change his ways of relating to himself and others.

He admitted he couldn't distinguish between rape and love making. Love, itself, was no more than a sexual tension, something to be discharged into the most convenient receptacle. And yet Jimmy also claims that he's always liked women, and many other rapists concur, denying they harbor feelings of resentment or hatred. That Jimmy found himself attracted to

1. Porfirio Rubirosa, a playboy frequently mentioned in the press in the fifties.

women he felt would reject or put him down is interesting in light of his avowed good feelings. Rather, rape seems Jimmy's way of striking back at society and women for actual or potential rejection.

Because Jimmy was too poor to afford counsel, the state appointed a lawyer, who talked Jimmy into pleading guilty. In a deleted section of the interview, Jimmy refers to his counsel as "Cop-out Murphy," and his bitterness may be due to the fact that lawyers generally have an easy time winning rape cases. In the courtroom, the rapist is often treated with kid gloves. This was true with Roger, an upper-middle-class white male, who was seventeen years old when he attacked a nurse in a doctor's office.

ROGER

ROGER: In Florida in 1964, I was charged with assault with intent to commit rape. The way I was treated by the police was incredible. It was as if I was a new recruit on the force. A captain in the sheriff's office took me into his office and gave me a cup of coffee, then took out his handkerchief and wet it in the sink and helped me clean my face, which was scratched. He looked at me and said, "Damn women always causing trouble for everybody." He did not treat me like a criminal at all.

My lawyer kept asking me, "Are you sure she didn't do things to encourage you?" When I was brought into court, the woman started crying. My lawyer attacked her with his questions: Did she touch me first? Had she had sexual intercourse before she was married? Had she had sexual intercourse outside of marriage since she'd been married? He attacked her for being older than me, even attacked her for being British.

I wasn't about to object openly to what was going on. In Florida, the sentence is five to fifteen years for this particular offense, and I wasn't looking forward to that. But I wanted to say something to her, to tell her that my attack on her was nothing personal.

I never thought, well, I'm going to rape somebody. It was an instantaneous decision. She was a nurse in a doctor's office, and we found ourselves alone one noon. I was seventeen, and I was trying to prove that I was a man. I didn't fit into a John Wayne image, so I had to do something to prove my manhood. I grabbed her from behind, turned her around, and pushed her against the wall. I'm six foot four, and I weighed about two hundred and forty pounds. She didn't have much chance to get away from me, but she tried. I pulled her back and hit her several times in the face quite hard. She stopped resisting and said, "All right, just don't hurt me." When she said that, all of a sudden it came into my head, "My God, this is a human being!" I came to my senses and saw that I was hurting this person, that it was not an actress in a movie. It was difficult for me to admit that I was dealing with a human being when I was talking to a woman, because, if you read men's magazines, you hear about your stereo, your car, your chick.

When I released my grasp on her, she went for my eyes. I jumped back, but she got me right below my eyes and raked downward with her fingernails. It was extremely painful, and I put my hands to my face and felt blood. That took everything out of me, and she was able to run out of the room. It's very traumatic for a man who has never felt violent toward women to realize that down inside him somewhere it's something that can suddenly erupt.

Because I was an upper-middle-class white, my case was handled very delicately. I was adjudged "insane" at the time it happened and the charges were dropped. I went to a mental institution, and as anybody who's ever been in a mental institution knows, all you have to do is be a good boy and they let you go. They don't care what you did outside, as long as you're a good boy inside. That's what I did, and they let me go. I spent a total of sixty days in custody.

Three months after I got out I was so obsessed with myself as some sort of maniac that I actually became one. I remember walking up to a neighbor woman's house with my father's pistol in my pocket. As I approached her house, I thought, "My God, what am I doing?"

I thought of myself for a long time as a monster, a complete monster. My self-image changed when I met a woman I could talk to about my experience. She helped me see that, because I wasn't John Wayne, I had to do something to prove that I was really a man. The image of a man in this society is violent and hypersexual, so I just put those two things together.

I had never been violent before this happened, and I haven't been violent since. The attack took everything out of me, in almost all ways. I had to interrupt my schooling, and I never went back. You might say it ruined my life. It was my doing, but I was also a victim. I had no image of a man who could be gentle and kind and still sexual. The emphasis was always on being superaggressive. If that's what you believe you should be, you're going to end up committing some act of violence. Violence exists on all levels, and one is rape, but the instincts of a ruthless businessman could be almost the same as those of a rapist.

When I tell people of my experience, men and women react differently. Men want to know all the details. They say, "You should have gone ahead and done it." When I tell a woman about my experience, she'll tell me hers. She'll say, "Well, a man pulled me into his car," and it's like trading stories.

I didn't have any sexual relations until I was twenty-four, just last year. And in the sexual relations I've had recently, I guess I'm gentle. I don't have any sadistic instincts.

If it weren't for women, the police captain implied as he offered Roger aid and comfort, the world would be a better place. This attitude is tied in with feelings of inadequacy and fear of women's sexuality. Hostility results.

Like Jimmy, Roger was able to act out his fantasies only so long as his victim remained a nonperson. Had the nurse not struggled, Roger would probably have completed the rape. Jimmy, too, was only thwarted when his last victim refused to submit passively. Of the rapists interviewed, only Roger suffered trauma. In this respect he resembles rape victims, and it is not strange that he "trades stories" with women rather than align himself with men who customarily engage in sexual boasting.

By virtue of his membership in the middle class, Roger fared better than Jimmy in court. His lawyer used sexism in an attempt to discredit Roger's victim and succeeded in minimizing Roger's punishment. Contrary to the masculine mystique, Roger's real hope resulted from his failure, not his success. Had he succeeded, he might have continued to rape and continued to judge himself a failure unless he could delude himself into thinking he was John Wayne.

Roger finally recognized his victim's humanity and, in the process, salvaged his own. The next rapist, however, is still incapable of such recognition and remains a distinct threat to women.

ROY

Roy is an aggressive salesman, thirty years of age and "going places." A middle-class white man, he has had two years of college. Presently divorced, he was still married three years ago when he raped a sixteen-year-old white middle-class girl in an apartment that "by a fantastic stroke of luck" was unlocked.

Like many of the rapists who called in response to the newspaper ads, Roy was disappointed at finding his interviewer was male. He broke off the conversation in midinterview, and many questions were left unanswered.

INTERVIEWER: You have committed rape?

ROY: Yes. Technically, twice. The first was four years ago when I was twenty-six. I was working as a salesman, and I was in a town in California which will remain nameless. We were staying in a motel, and we got very, very drunk, and I wandered off from the other men. It was strange—the odds would say that it couldn't happen this perfectly—but I wandered around town, and I was really smashed out of my mind and knew I wanted a piece of ass. So I went into this apartment building. The front door was unlocked, and I just went upstairs to the second floor and tried an apartment door. It was locked, so I tried another one and it was open and I just went in. It was a fantastic stroke of luck. By fate, the only person in there was a young girl. Talking to her later I found out her mother worked at night, so the girl was in there alone. I just commenced to rape her.

INTERVIEWER: Did she resist?

ROY: At first she did. There was a little light so I could see my way around, and when I opened the bedroom door the girl sat up in bed and said something like, "Where's my mother?" And I said, "Oh, she's out here." She yelled and jumped from the bed and started to run, and I grabbed her around the neck and choked her a little. I told her she was stupid to resist, and I threatened her with great harm if she didn't shut up. I implied I'd kill her, and she became passive after that. Then I told her to get on the bed. I took her nightgown off, got undressed, and got with it.

INTERVIEWER: Would you describe her?

ROY: I'd say she was roughly sixteen. She was a virgin, and that excited me. She was white, fairly attractive, frightened.

INTERVIEWER: Did her fear turn you on?

ROY: Yes.

INTERVIEWER: How did you feel about her becoming passive? Would you have preferred her to resist more?

ROY: I have ambivalent feelings about that. Resisting is exciting, but submission is exciting also. After I finished I asked if she had ever done that before. She said no, and later on that was confirmed because there was blood all over the place.

INTERVIEWER: Was there any other conversation?

ROY: Yes. After I raped her, and while I was resting up, I asked her about her mother. Her mother worked at night and was supposed to be home pretty soon. I asked her what her mother looked like, was she good-looking? The girl answered my questions. I thought about waiting for her mother, then decided to split. I wondered if she'd report it, but there was no mention in the papers I read the next day. I tried to think how I could be linked up with it, and I did have quite a bit of apprehension for about the next week or so, and then it just went away.

INTERVIEWER: Did you tell anybody about it?

ROY: Yes. I told a friend about a year later. He also thought it was very interesting that it just seemed to happen. It was like an instinct took me to the right place. I mean, the odds would say that you would not find an apartment unlocked, the odds would say if you did there would be a man and a woman in there. It was quite a coincidence to find a girl alone.

INTERVIEWER: Do you think she got turned on at all?

ROY: No. I think that my grabbing her and threatening her with harm if she resisted put her in a state of shock. Her only reaction was pain. I know that she was hurt when I first went inside her, whether because she was a virgin or because I was a bit rough, I don't know.

INTERVIEWER: How did you feel about her being hurt?

ROY: That was exciting. It gave me a feeling of power. Afterward I felt a bit of apprehension about the possibility of getting caught. The next day I had a horrible, horrible hangover, and there was blood all over my shorts. And I felt something like, "Boy, you'd better stay away from the booze!" But I didn't feel guilty.

INTERVIEWER: What about the other time you raped a woman?

ROY: It was about two years ago. It was an entirely different thing. I met a girl at a party, and I considered her snobbish and phony. She latched onto me at the party, and we laughed and had a good time and went somewhere else. She was an attractive woman in her thirties, but she irritated me. When I took her home to her apartment she was telling me goodnight and I raped her. I really didn't feel the urge. As a matter of fact, I had a hell of a time getting an erection. Once again, I'd had quite a bit of booze. But I forced myself to do it to prove a point to her, to prove that she wasn't as big as she thought she was.

INTERVIEWER: Did you think that she might report it?

ROY: No. It would be very difficult because she was seen at a party hanging all over me so it would be very difficult for her to say that I raped her.

INTERVIEWER: Did you have to use any force?

ROY: A little bit, combined with a threat of harm. [Break-Off]

Roy's viewing the first rape as a stroke of fate, implying the gods approved, is an interesting example of an egocentricity that is found in many males. His cavalier attitude, his admission that power, not sex, motivated him, his lack of guilt, and his coldness are horrifying. Women are depersonalized and exist only for his use and pleasure. That other people have feelings, will, thought, is irrelevant. Only Roy counts. Only what Roy wants matters.

What motivated Roy to rape the first time? "I wanted a piece of ass," he says, employing a familiar term of objectification. Apparently, then, his desire outweighed all other considerations, and yet he later admits that the basis for his satisfaction was not sexual but the feeling of power he derived from forcing his victim to accede to his will. The second rape appears also to have been primarily a power trip.

Roy's hatred of women is demonstrated by the second rape, accomplished despite a lack of desire in order to prove his superiority. Probably, Roy's second victim would have had sex with him willingly, but Roy wasn't interested in that. He wanted to show his victim she had no power. Even if Roy's assessment of her character as "snobbish and phony" were valid, his decision to punish her by raping her is horrendous. Most frightening of all is Roy's lack of guilt, conscience, or feeling. There is little doubt that he will rape again.

Moreover, there is little chance he will be caught and, if caught, less chance he'll be convicted. He's a "regular guy," not a criminal. He's white, makes good money, has an active social life. He has the support, the mentality, and the consciousness of millions of men.

FRED

Unlike Roy, Fred is not the guy next door. Fred is a thirty-six-year-old business executive who enjoys being humiliated by women, especially with regard to his sexual performance and genital size. He admits to committing rape twice, thirty and ninety days prior to being interviewed.

A white college graduate, Fred is married.

FRED: The only aspect of my marriage that's not good is that I have a very unhappy sex life. The reason for this is that I'm endowed very small, and this has been a source of embarrassment to me because I've never been able to perform properly, in my estimation. Women go crazy about men who have big cocks and being small has made me feel inadequate. A lot of my gratification is self-gratification, and I spend about three days a week sitting in my car and checking out the supermarkets for women. Hopefully, when they bend over to put groceries in their cars, I can look up their skirts.

INTERVIEWER: Tell me about the first time you raped a woman.

FRED: It was ninety days ago. It was after a grocery parking-lot episode. I happened to see a woman get out of her car. She had on a garter belt and stockings, which drives me up a tree. I haven't seen them in years because of the popularity of panty hose. Anyway, I was waiting when she came out. This wasn't an isolated area by any means, but there was no one else around at the time, and I managed to watch her bend over. I could see the top of her stocking and her actual thighs. This turned me on no end.

I got out of my car, and when I went by, she was pulling her stockings up a little bit, adjusting them or whatever the terminology would be. I stopped and looked, and she saw me and kind of smiled at me. It kind of embarrassed me, and I walked away. Then I came back around on the passenger side and looked down again. I asked her if I could help her, and she said, no, she was capable of doing it herself. Well, I had an erection that just wouldn't quit, so I unzipped my pants and showed her. She immediately rolled up her window and drove away.

Three days later I saw her again. This time I followed her home. She lived not too far from the supermarket and was carrying some groceries into the house. She left the door open, and I just walked in. I took a chance on nobody being there, and nobody was. She recognized me, but I grabbed her and that was it.

INTERVIEWER: Did you exert any force?

FRED: To some extent, yes. I held her so she couldn't get away. She tried to struggle, but she didn't seem very frightened. I don't think I would've gone through with it if she'd screamed. Anyway, the whole thing was over very quickly. Afterwards, I asked her what she thought of the size of my cock. She said I was small and that stimulated me. Later on, I was scared. I didn't know if she'd report it or not, but I was scared for several weeks afterwards, and I didn't go anywhere near the area.

INTERVIEWER: Have you committed other rapes?

FRED: Yes, about a month ago. It was basically the same type of thing. Again I was in a parking lot. Only this particular girl had on panty hose and no panties. Again, I followed her home, and the door was left open. Actually, the second one didn't really come off. It was just an oral thing on my part. I told her I wanted to eat her first, and she said, "Would you do that only?" I said OK if she wouldn't fight. So that's what I did. She was very cold about it. Afterwards, I asked if she would give me an honest opinion. I showed her myself and asked if in her opinion, I was average or smaller or what. She said small. That turned me on. Afterwards I felt tremendously guilty but ultimately it went away.

INTERVIEWER: Is there any particular type of woman you look for in a parking lot?

FRED: Yes. Women with short skirts and nice legs.

INTERVIEWER: What do you think women should do if confronted by someone who wants to rape them?

FRED: Shoot them. If they don't have a gun I think they should have some type of weapon to ward them off, a spray of some type or some type of acid, though that could backfire and go on them just as easily.

INTERVIEWER: Do you think that the police or the courts deal fairly with rapists?

FRED: No. I don't think that they are severe enough. Castration is an extremely severe, rather barbaric method, but by the same token, a lot of women are extremely affected by being raped. In my case, I honestly believe that if the individual would have put up a heavy fight, I would have walked away from it.

Although it's easy to dismiss Fred as a nut, a pervert, a sadomasochist, he holds much in common with the "normal" rapists previously encountered. In one respect he is more "normal" than the others: his motive for raping is based in part on sexual desire.

"I don't think I would've come through with it if she'd screamed," Fred says, and in this respect he is similar to Jimmy and Roger. And like Roger he is motivated by feelings of inadequacy. It is not John Wayne who represents masculinity to Fred. It is his perception of a symbol of maleness that represents power and masculinity: a big cock. Fred punishes women whom he believes venerate that which he feels he is not: a complete man. In effect, Fred has constructed his own world and barred himself from it. And, Fred's belief that rapists should be shot and that castration is, as it were, meet punishment, indicates the extent of his self-hatred and his desire for punishment.

Built on the lie of unattainable strength, will, cool, desire, and self-realization, many men's egos are understandably fragile. Because of this, most men prefer passive women and find aggressive women sexually threatening. Rape is then the logical expression of the stereotypical male. Obviously, solutions to what is not yet seen as a problem must go beyond therapy, imprisonment, or castration, and attack the cultural acceptance of male supremacy where aggressive, depersonalized power ploys are hallmarks of masculinity. While equality may appear threatening to many men at first, it would probably in fact reduce the fear, the feelings of inadequacy, and the compensatory drive under which so many men labor. No longer forced to perform, no longer aspiring to emulate this hero or that playboy, perhaps men would learn to integrate sex and emotion, discover sensitivity, communicate deep feelings honestly, and experience joy.

TWENTY-FOUR

Rape and the Masculine Mystique

Many people continue to believe that a woman cannot be raped. Many years ago Clarence Darrow allegedly attempted to demonstrate this in court by holding a cup in a mobile hand and instructing someone to try to insert a pencil into the cup. I was subjected to the same game on a TV program in 1972. Of course one could easily get the pencil into the cup if one were armed, or if one were to beat the person in the face so that he stopped focusing on moving the cup away, or if one twisted an arm behind the cup holder's back until pain achieved the same end. But these points were missed, presumably because they contradict the myth that women cannot be raped.

It is remarkable that so many people retain that myth in the face of the increasing incidence of reported rape, and despite bloody cases of rape that make headlines. It may be that people cannot contend with the enormity of such a crime and prefer to believe, on the same principle as "you can't cheat an honest man," that rape only happens to victims who ask for it.

But it should be noted that men benefit from the wishing-away of rape. For if women cannot be raped, it must mean that women really want intercourse with men whenever men want it, in spite of any woman's claims to the contrary. Ultimately the penis is irresistible. This fantasy is expressed in movies like *Hospital*, *Straw Dogs*, or *Little Sisters*, to say nothing of standard pornography.[1] But most women require more than the old "in-and-out," as the hero of *A Clockwork Orange* calls it, in order to enjoy sex.

---

1. Aljean Harmetz points out that "at least 20 films during the last two years served rape to their audiences," and quotes the explanation of MGM's vice-president in charge of production, Daniel Melnick: "It has something to do with the fantasy life of the men who make movies. They seem to want to believe that at some point the woman stops struggling and starts moaning, that all women really love it, really want to be raped." "Rape: New Hollywood Game—An Ugly Movie Trend," *San Francisco Examiner*, October 28, 1973.

Ignorance and the force of sexual myth prevent many men from realizing this fact.

If women cannot be raped, it is not surprising that men who rape often see themselves as lovers, not as rapists. They believe so strongly that women really want intercourse with them, that they are unable to hear women's protests to the contrary. Women's physical and verbal resistance is seen as part of the female game of pretending reluctance, or as an expression of a desire to be overcome. For example, one woman reported that her date finally succeeded in raping her after a two-hour struggle, but he could not understand why she was so upset, and he was unable to comprehend why she accused him of raping her. He considered himself a lover in the tradition of forceful males and expected to have a continuing relationship with her.

This expectation is quite common when rape occurs in a dating situation and is apparent sometimes even when the rapist is a complete stranger. Two victims reported receiving marriage proposals from their rapists. Some of the men who raped women they knew apparently *were* able to see their acts as rape, though most were not. But even then, the victims report that some rapists did not appear to think that the act of raping would necessarily count against them. After all, since the man had felt sexually turned on to the victim, hadn't she provoked it? Wasn't she asking for it? In any case, don't women like to be raped?

After being raped by two men, a few victims, for example, were asked by their rapists which of the two they enjoyed most. Another woman reported that her rapist was "furious because I wasn't getting turned on." One woman who was raped by one of her best friends, whom she had known for over a year, but with whom she had never related sexually, reported that he had to beat her up to achieve his goal. That was the end of their friendship, but a year or so later she reported that he expressed resentment toward her for not having had more compassion for the "forceful trip" he had been into.

The reader may recall how Ms. White, who was hospitalized for three days after she was attacked and raped by an apparent good Samaritan, was asked by a male psychiatrist at the hospital, "Haven't you really been rushing toward this very thing all of your life?" and then on returning home from the hospital she was asked angrily by her husband, "If that's what you wanted, why didn't you come to *me?*" The myth that women who are raped must want it appears to have been so powerful for this man that he subsequently raped her himself.

In a society dominated by men, it would be difficult for women's view of rape to differ greatly from that of men. Therefore it is not surprising that many women also accept the myth that there is no such thing as rape. But it serves a different function for them. Women have always been dependent on men. It is much more comfortable for women to deny that men are really brutal toward women.

One of the consequences of accepting the myth that there is no such thing as rape is that in situations which fit the definition of rape used in this study, many women, like many rapists, do not see themselves as rape victims. For example, it was only several months after a woman had been working on this study that she reevaluated earlier experiences and realized that she had been raped twice.[2] The difficulties of realizing that rape has occurred are clear for women who accept the myth. For if rape cannot happen, then the experience of forcible intercourse must be something else. I have come across many such cases, particularly when the woman was not subjected to much violence, or if her rapist was not a stranger.

Unfortunately the myth that women cannot be raped is far more dysfunctional than functional for women. While the myth generally protects men's image in the eyes of women, one of the consequences is that women, like men, often "put down" raped women by disbelieving them, or by seeing them as responsible for their victimization. (The increasingly popular field of victimology contributes to this view.) And if these unbelievers themselves are raped, they have to struggle with the incredulity of others and their own sense of guilt at somehow having caused it. Often it seems easier to deny the whole experience, but this is hardly a healthy way to deal with the problem.

Even most of those who do realize that they have been raped do not report it, as they do not expect to be believed. Several women, for example, stated that they had always believed that it was impossible for a woman to be raped until it happened to them, and they were convinced that if they told their friends, their colleagues, or the police, they would not be believed, since the victims expected others to subscribe to the myth as unquestioningly as they had done. Unfortunately, this conviction is often borne out. If the woman was raped by a friend, a date, a lover, an ex-lover, an employer, a teacher, a doctor—in fact, if the rapist was not a complete stranger—the

2. Briefly, one of her experiences was as follows: A man she had met once recently at a social gathering turned up uninvited to see her. It was obvious that she was ill, and at first he seemed solicitous of her health. Then, realizing she was alone in the house, he made some sexual advance toward her. She made it clear that she had no desire in that direction. Not discouraged, he picked her up, carried her to a bed, and pulled off her pants. She had very little strength and was unable to push him away. After an initial attempt to do so, she just lay back motionless. He had a hard time getting an erection and became very annoyed that she was so unresponsive. He finally was able to work himself up to a weak erection. He entered her, but could not ejaculate. This made him very angry, and he finally left in disgust. Though intercourse had certainly been imposed on her against her will, and her lack of interest in having intercourse was obvious, she did not see this as an experience of rape until very recently.

police and many other people are unlikely to believe the victim's story. In my study, with three exceptions, only victims who were raped by strangers reported it to the police.

Fortunately, the myth of unrapable women is not as popular as it once was. A less extreme and more widely held belief is that rape *does* happen, but very rarely. This view is supported by the fact that most people have read about the odd case in the newspaper. But few have ever wittingly associated with a woman who was raped. Most people believe that the women they know have never had such experiences. Another myth is that the few rapists who exist are crazy, sadistic psychopaths—freaks of society. This myth is perpetuated by the fact that these are largely the kinds of cases we read about in the newspaper, and we don't hear of any others.

One function of the myth that rape is only perpetrated by society's freaks is that rape then appears to have no further implications for the rest of society. All the sane men must protect "their" women from the few insane ones, and women without men must watch out. Yet rape is *not* exclusively the act of sadistic psychopaths and is much more widespread than most people realize. Indeed, the view that emerges from this study is that rape is not so much a deviant act as an overconforming act. Rape may be understood as an extreme acting out of qualities that are regarded as supermasculine in this and many other societies: aggression, force, power, strength, toughness, dominance, competitiveness. To win, to be superior, to be successful, to conquer, all demonstrate masculinity to those who subscribe to common cultural notions of masculinity, i.e., the *masculine mystique*. And it would be surprising if these notions of masculinity did not find expression in men's sexual behavior. Indeed, sex may be the arena where these notions of masculinity are most intensely acted out, particularly by men who feel powerless in the rest of their lives, and men whose masculinity is threatened by their sense of powerlessness. Perhaps this peculiar relationship of powerlessness and undermined masculinity explains why rapists are disproportionately black and lower class.

The desire to prove oneself is very different from a desire for enjoyment. Several of the victims commented that their rapists didn't seem to be enjoying themselves. Some were reported as having difficulty getting erections. These observations suggest that some rapists are not motivated by a sexual urge; the assertion of power over a woman seems more important. At least two of the rapists interviewed by Jack Fremont are cases in point. It is in this sense that rape is sometimes referred to as a political act. A compliant woman doesn't satisfy some men's desire for power, which can only be exercised when there is opposition. Sometimes, then, rape is intended to keep women in their place—beneath men. The men who raped Ms. Davis, for example, told her that she was only getting what she deserved for walking on the street without a man at night. They saw themselves as decent for letting her get away so lightly. She felt they did not particularly enjoy the rape, but were behaving in a way they saw as natural to men when women give them the opportunity, by being unprotected, that men are not supposed to be given. And Ron, one of the rapists interviewed, explained his decision to rape a woman as follows: "I really didn't feel the urge. As a matter of fact, I had a hell of a time getting an erection. . . . But I forced myself to do it to prove a point to her, to prove that she wasn't as big as she thought she was."

The view of rape as the natural outcome of opportunity is even more clearly revealed where rape of enemy women is seen as natural soldierly behavior. This view indicates a widespread acceptance of men's capacity to express aggression and hatred through sex. The recent behavior of soldiers in Bangladesh, where an estimated 200,000 Bengali women were raped, may have received more publicity than the rape of women by American GIs in Vietnam because the rapists were not Americans.[3] In Vietnam, according to Smail, one of the few members of Charlie Company who talked frankly about rape, "That's an everyday affair. You can nail just about everybody on that—at least once. The guys are human, man." [4]

If men can express their hatred and aggression through wartime rape, it would be remarkable if they could not do it at home too. For many men, it seems, aggression and sex are closely related. The unconscious thinking seems to go as follows: being aggressive is masculine; being sexually aggressive is masculine; rape is sexually aggressive behavior; therefore, rape is masculine behavior.

Of course, the connection that exists between sex and aggression does not necessarily express itself in rape. Conscience gets in the way for some. Less extreme ways of expressing the connection are more common. For example, some men prefer women to be passive, leaving all the action to them. These men *do* things *to* women; it is not a mutual act. The men have the power. They are the boss. They do as they will, using women. This is not rape. It is a different kind of power trip. But if one were to see sexual behavior as a continuum, with rape at one end, and sex liberated from sex roles at the other, the classic pattern just described would be near the rape end. The similarity is clear.

An interesting study by Kirkpatrick and Kanin at Indiana University illustrates the commonness of male sexual aggression. Of the female student respondents, 20.9 per cent reported that they had been offended by "forceful attempts at sexual intercourse in the previous year," and 6.2 per

3. "Women of Bangladesh," *Ms.*, August 1972, p. 84.
4. Seymour M. Hersh, *My Lai 4: A Report on the Massacre and Its Aftermath* (New York: Vintage, 1970), p. 185.

cent by "aggressively forceful attempts at sexual intercourse in the course of which menacing threats or coercive infliction of physical pain were employed." [5] The incidence may be even higher than these percentages indicate, since the authors report that "there is no reason to think that offended girls had merely a single unpleasant experience with one partner." [6] It is interesting that seven out of the ten most violent episodes involved girls in "regular dating, 'pinned,' or engaged relationships." Comparable figures for seniors at high school were obtained in a later study by one of the same authors.[7]

It could be argued that since it is customary for males to take the initiative sexually with women, it is to be expected that they will often go beyond what the woman wants and "offend" her in this way. In other words, these studies simply reveal the hazards accompanying men's role as initiators. While it seems to me that the traditional masculine role is burdened by such hazards, such a view does not fully explain the findings of these studies. Taking the initiative but being even minimally sensitive to the other person's wishes would not, I believe, result in so many "offensive" experiences, particularly not at the more extreme levels of aggression nor in the more intimate relationships.

Gagnon's work on female child victims also illustrates the commonness of male sexual aggression. Gagnon says that in the course of gathering data for *Sexual Behavior in the Human Female*, women were asked whether they had ever experienced sexual contact or approaches as a child by an adult male (defined as a person at least five years older and postpubertal while the female was prepubertal).[8] Twenty-four percent of the 4,441 women reported having been so victimized.[9] Referring to these data in his study of female child victims, Gagnon concluded that "it is possible to estimate that between twenty and twenty-five percent of children reared in a middle-class environment will experience a victim experience in childhood and that the bulk of these will be minimal in character such as exhibition and genital touching," [10] and that children in a lower-class environment will be exposed to a higher risk of such experiences, probably between one in three and as high as two in five, and the higher risk of exposure will include offenses of greater seriousness. "If these crude estimates are correct," Gagnon continued, "the number of

5. E. J. Kanin and C. Kirkpatrick, "Male Sex Aggression on University Campuses," *ASR*, 22 (1953): 53.
6. Ibid.
7. E. J. Kanin, "Male Aggression in Dating Relations," *AJS*, 63 (1957): 197–204.
8. J. Gagnon, "Female Child Victims of Sex Offenses," p. 179.
9. Ibid., p. 180.
10. Ibid., p. 191.

children exposed will be in the range of 500,000 per year." [11] It is common, then, for females of all ages to be subjected to the imposition of male sexual desire at varying degrees of intensity. Imposition is necessarily aggressive. But to be aggressive, domineering, controlling, and powerful is considered masculine.

There are many ways in which the sexual socialization of males predisposes them to rape. That is to say, beyond the masculine mystique, there is a more specific *virility mystique*, which focuses on the sexual domain. For example, males are expected to be able to separate their sexual responsiveness from their needs for love, respect, and affection. They are expected to be able to get an erection in the presence of an attractive "sexy" woman or upon seeing pictures of naked female bodies. A man is not supposed to be impotent if he is with a prostitute, if he is a participant in a gang rape, or if he is angry with his wife or lover. He is supposed to be able to perform despite any chilling circumstances. One of the reasons why some men are so threatened by women who take the initiative in sexual relations or who want a lot of sex is that it forces men to realize that they *can't* perform whenever the opportunity arises. This fact is less apparent if men always take the initiative. Hence many men feel "castrated" by women who demand equality in making sexual overtures.

The experience of a woman who was the victim of an attempted rape makes the point. Her would-be rapist felt very embarrassed when he could not get an erection. "Play with me," he commanded, to which she contemptuously replied, "Who's raping who here? That's ridiculous, man!" According to the informant he then felt very foolish and ashamed. "I had the upper hand from then on. . . . I gave him a hell of a time. He drove me to town. He was very frightened that I would phone the police, and I told him I sure would, and that if he ever did it again, I'd find out. He had to swear many times that he'd never do it again." Since he had had the physical strength to pin her down and remove her pants, he could also have made her "play" with him. But it seems that she was able instead to play on his feelings of being unmanly for not being able to rape her without assistance. It is a sad commentary on the consequence of subscribing to the virility mystique that a man feels bad about not being brutal enough to rape a woman.

One of the consequences of being trained since childhood to separate sexual desire from caring, respecting, liking, or loving is that many men regard women as sexual objects, rather than as full human beings. And since the virility mystique stresses the importance of having access to, and keeping score on, many women, the more the better, this approach dominates the

11. Ibid.

perspective on women. Indeed, simply viewing women in this way, and making it clear to male companions that he does, is important for the man who wants to appear virile. One of the rapists interviewed said, for example, "It was a difficult thing for me to admit that I was dealing with a human being when I was talking to a woman." After she requested that he not hurt her, "All of a sudden it came into my head, my God, this is a human being!" Subsequently, he wished he could tell her that his desire to rape her was completely impersonal, as if that would somehow make her feel better.

Many of the rape victims expressed the feeling that they were viewed by their rapists simply as available cunts. As Roy, another of the rapists interviewed, put it when asked why he had raped his first victim: "I wanted a piece of ass." Such observations suggest that if men were not taught to separate sexual feelings from feelings of warmth and caring, rape would be unthinkable, and fewer men would impose their sexuality on unwilling women in other less extreme ways too.

The virility mystique, expounded by magazines like *Playboy*, has no place for the inexperienced or virgin male, when experience is determined by the number of partners and their attractiveness as sexual objects rather than the attractiveness of their personalities and the quality of the total relationships. The crux of the would-be rapist's explanation of his desire to rape the nurse (described in Chapter Twenty-three) was that he felt bad about being a virgin at the age of seventeen and wanted to prove that he was a man. According to the virility mystique, until a man has "made it" with a woman, his manhood is in question. How he "made it" is not so important. And a man must continue "making it" with women. "It's better to commit rape than masturbate," said Norman Mailer,[12] while according to Ogden Nash, "Seduction is for sissies. A he-man wants his rape." With such values to guide men, it is not surprising that so many are strongly tempted to rape, and that more than we may care to believe succumb to the temptation.

The virility mystique, then, predisposes men to rape. If women were physically stronger than men, I do not believe there would be many instances of female raping male, because female sexual socialization encourages a woman to integrate sex, affection, and love, and to be sensitive to what her partner wants. Of course, there are many women who deviate from this pattern, just as there are men who have managed to reject their socialization for virility. But cultural trends make these cases exceptional. If our culture considered it masculine to be gentle and sensitive, to be responsive to the needs of others, to abhor violence, domination, and exploitation, to want sex only within a meaningful relationship, to be attracted by personal-

12. *The Realist*, 1962, p. 20.

ity and character rather than by physical appearance, to value lasting rather than casual relationships, then rape would indeed be a deviant act, and, I would think, much less frequent. Among the Arapesh of New Guinea, males are reared to be gentle and nurturant, and according to Margaret Mead, "Of rape the Arapesh know nothing beyond the fact that it is the unpleasant custom of the Nugum people to the southeast of them." [13]

If lynching is the ultimate racist act, rape is the ultimate sexist act. It is an act of physical and psychic oppression. It is an act in which a woman is used against her will sometimes because she is seen as just another piece of ass, and sometimes because the act of dominating her provides a sense of power. Like lynching, it is cowardly, and like lynching, it is used to keep individual women, as well as women as a caste, in their place. And finally, as with lynching, the rape victim is blamed for provocation.

Rape is an abuse of power, and the increase in rape shows that men are increasingly unable to handle their excessive power over women. As one of the rapists, Jimmy, says, men rape "with no more feeling involved and no more neurosis than just 'I want you, and I can't have you.' " Ray, another of the rapists interviewed, revealed his willingness to take advantage of his physical capacity to rape merely because a woman irritated him. He was also taking advantage of the freedom society gives him by making it virtually impossible for a woman who had behaved toward him as she had to press charges of rape. Eradicating rape requiries getting rid of the power discrepancy between men and women, because abuse of power flows from unequal power.

I have argued that rape is consistent with the masculinity and virility mystiques and, in fact, is promulgated by them. Intrinsic to these mystiques is the sexist notion of the biological superiority of males, which justifies their domination of women. Since concepts of strength and superiority are relative, the notion that men should be strong, independent, superior, and domineering implies that women should be weak, dependent, inferior, and submissive. If women were also strong and independent men would presumably regard them as masculine, which would undermine men's own sense of masculinity. The fundamental notions of masculinity and femininity are therefore part of the sexist ideology of this culture. Hence, it would be as accurate to relate rape to sexism as to the masculine mystique, for the masculine mystique is a sexist mystique that serves to maintain the power of men over women.

13. *Sex and Temperament in Three Primitive Societies* (New York: Dell, 1935), p. 110.

TWENTY-FIVE

Rape and the Feminine Mystique

Freud held the pessimistic view that men are inherently sadistic while women are innately masochistic. The application to rape is obvious. Men like to rape and women like to be raped. Unfortunately, Freud's idea outlived him and is reflected in much of the literature on rape. While it is true that some women do appear to get some kind of gratification from *fantasies* of being raped, *it does not follow that it is part of women's nature.* It is more likely that it comes out of women's situation.

While it is often seen as wrong for a woman to desire sex, it is not seen as wrong for her to be desired. In fact, women are taught to be desirable in much the same way men are conditioned to be sexually aggressive. Hollywood and Madison Avenue conspire with parents to convince a girl that her goal in life should be marriage and that the path to that goal lies in packaging herself to be desirable, if not downright irresistible.

Similarly, while it is often seen as wrong for a woman to touch, it is less wrong to be touched, especially if she has no choice in the matter. Women have been taught to be passive and submissive, and what more passive, submissive role can be imagined than the rape victim?

Finally, women have been taught that sex is bad. Guilt frequently accompanies sexual stirrings, and in many rape fantasies, by imagining physical or mental pain, a woman can punish herself for having forbidden sexual desires. In this way she can atone for her guilt about feeling sexual.

For example, a married friend, strongly committed to maintaining a sexually exclusive relationship with her husband, experienced strong sexual feelings toward her therapist. This conflict resolved itself in a fantasy in which the therapist was forced by a gunman to rape her. The fantasy allowed her to come to terms with the three elements in the situation: her strong desire, her commitment to monogamy, and her desire to see her therapist as a decent and responsible person.

The point is that women are likely to have rape fantasies to the extent they are sexually repressed. But it cannot be overstressed that *having voluntary fantasies of being raped, and wanting to be raped in actuality, are two entirely different things.* First, people are in complete control of their fantasies, even if the fantasy involves a situation in which they are out of control. A woman is hardly in control when she is raped. If she were in control, the act would not be imposed, and it would not be rape. Second, a person is rarely likely to feel fear in a fantasy which *she* has constructed. But in a real rape or attempted rape situation, unlike the fantasy version, women are usually afraid and often terrified.

This does not apply with equal strength to men who have fantasies about raping women. It is true that a man is in control in his fantasy, but not necessarily if he rapes in reality. Not all rapes, after all, are successful. However, most would-be rapists presumably hope to be in control, so there is no discrepancy in this regard between the fantasy of raping and what they would like to happen in reality. However, guilt, for those who feel it, is the factor that makes the fantasy and reality situation most different for men. This is where ideologies play a part, since these can sometimes be used to justify rape and absolve the man from feeling guilty, or at least, diminish his guilt enough so that he can do it. White racism has served this function for centuries, and some black men now use the notion of rape as "an insurrectionary act" to ease their guilt about raping white women. A sexist ideology helps to free men of guilt feelings about raping women in general, as well as particular categories of women, like those seen as "belonging" to other men, or those seen as "loose," or the "uppity" ones who need to be put down.

So the relationship between fantasy and what a person actually wants in reality is more complex than many people seem to realize. In fantasy, precisely because it *is* only fantasy, one can allow the expression of feelings which might be incompatible with one's conscience, or with another set of feelings. For example, a woman might fantasize being raped as an expression of a passive desire to be overwhelmed by a man so that she doesn't have to take responsibility for her own sexual feelings. But this might conflict with another feeling of mistrust about how men who overwhelm women use the power they have over them. This might be expressed in the fantasy of being completely independent of men. To conclude that this woman wants to be raped would be false for two reasons: one, on the fantasy level itself, what she wants is contradictory, and two, fantasy and reality, when it comes to being a victim of rape, are so entirely different. Two women who were raped in their early teens, for example, have had rape fantasies subsequently. However, they maintain that rape was a horrible experience in reality, and that they definitely would not want their fantasy of rape to happen in reality again.

Some women also have dreams about being raped, as they do about being murdered or betrayed or deserted or seeing their child hurt or killed. However, it seems to be only with rape that people are so ready to see the dream as an expression of a wish. When myths are strong, logic goes by the board.

Fantasies and dreams aside, if we examine the cultural notions of what constitutes femininity, we see that "feminine" traits like submissiveness, passivity, and weakness make women more subject to rape. This is not to say that strong, assertive, aggressive women are not raped, as the interviews show. Indeed, it may even take some assertiveness to be raped. After all, the rape victim is saying no to a man. Some very oppressed women may not be rape victims only because they don't clarify their desire not to have sex. For example, a woman who had lived for about a year in a hippie commune in Sonoma County, California, said the men there assumed that the women they came to for sex would oblige them. She felt she had been raped by her "old man," who would not accept her refusal to sleep with him one night. However, like many of the other women, she was so oppressed that she had frequently slept with men without wanting to. And it was not absolutely clear that on this particular occasion it was reasonable to expect her "old man" suddenly to understand, even if resistance were expressed a little more strongly than before. The females in this sexist utopia had become communal sex objects rather than the private sex objects of particular men typical of women in the "straight" world. For the most part, it seems, they are too oppressed to be raped.

Without denying that it takes some assertiveness to be raped at all (as opposed merely to being used), it seems that conformity to traditional notions of femininity makes women more vulnerable to rape, at least once they are in a situation where an unarmed man intends to try to rape them. On the other hand, women who reject traditional notions of femininity are probably more likely to find themselves in rape situations in which the rapist is a stranger. The price of greater freedom is a greater risk of rape. When rapists are armed, notions of femininity probably have very little significance. In many cases, however, the victim seems to be unduly intimidated by her would-be rapist through lifelong conditioning to behave submissively toward men, and to think of herself as weak and men as strong. Paula Scott, who was raped in a car by a man who offered her a ride, commented: "I hated myself for not being able to take a stand in the situation. He wielded his power with such confidence, and there I was, feeling absolutely helpless. I shouldn't have to feel that helpless even though I am small and less muscular and all that. . . . But it's like once you're in there, you become paralyzed with this feeling that he's a man, he's got muscles, and he knows about things like guns."

Many women, particularly those from middle-class backgrounds, have not had the opportunity to develop their strength (or even to know it) by fighting. Whereas male sports are designed to require and develop strength, this is less true of female sports. Women's gymnastics in this country often merely help women lose weight rather than develop strength. And there are female push-ups that won't develop the biceps, since females are not supposed to develop muscles that show.

Not only are women not taught to fight, they are discouraged from learning. It is unladylike. Even anger is unladylike, as the following case illustrates. Gretchen Townsend was a twenty-one-year-old virgin when she was raped by a man she met in a coffee house on Telegraph Avenue in Berkeley. After talking for a while, the man invited her to his place for a beer. She describes the scene in this way: "He pushed me into his bedroom, got on top of me, and he was really strong. I held my knees together and buckled them up in front of me. I was really terrified, and I kept saying, 'I'm a virgin,' and he kept saying, 'Oh, shut up! Bull shit, you aren't.' I could have fought harder. I know that now, and I still kick myself for that sometimes. But I finally gave in."

The traumatic experience affected her feelings about sex and men for many years afterward. "A friend asked me why I didn't fight. The answer is that I didn't know what to do, and I was afraid to fight back as hard as I could have, because I've never had experiences that would prove to me that that was a good thing to do. I wasn't allowed to fight at home."

Later she explained further how she felt in the rape situation: "I was scared, and I was mad, but I was also afraid of my own anger, which comes from having a father who beat me up. I wasn't allowed, when I was little, to express my anger at all. I got hit for clenching my teeth or my fists. So after years of that I wasn't in much of a position to fight back very hard, especially physically, against anybody who aggressed on me." Like Ms. Townsend, most middle-class women have had either very little experience with fighting or none at all. Though most do not have such violent fathers, it is common for women not to be allowed to express their anger in any direct way.

Whatever the cause, many raped women who did not respond as aggressively as they could have feel that they would act quite differently if it were to happen again. Ms. Townsend, for example, said, "I think now if I were in that situation, I'd probably fight like bloody murder, and I'd kick, and I'd bite, and I'd scratch like hell. I'd do anything I could to stop it."

Not all rape victims struggle even as much as Ms. Townsend did. The physical behavior of many of the preadolescent victims and many of the older women could be categorized as "submissive" rather than as resistant. Sandy Rogers's experience illustrates this point, and also illustrates that such behavior should by no means be taken to mean that the victim has a casual attitude toward being raped.

Ms. Rogers, an eighteen-year-old woman, was hitchhiking with her boy friend, George. The man who picked them up got lost. They stopped at a restaurant, and George got out to get directions. "Next thing I know, good old driver is speeding up the car, and down the road we're heading, without George." She realized the man was going to try to rape her. (Earlier when George was out of earshot, he'd asked her if she wanted to "ball" him.) Her immediate reaction was: "I knew I had no chance physically, because even for a girl, I have no strength at all." Then the car got stuck in the mud. Sandy actually got out "to help push the car," but it was hopelessly stuck. They got back in, and he proceeded to rape her. "I didn't hold out much hope for not getting fucked," she wrote, "and sure enough, he insisted. I relaxed my body as much as I could and took my mind to other places—Frisco, for example. I made sarcastic cracks to myself. I even began to ego trip on how some girls would have been gone by now. Physically, I did nothing. The man kept fucking me—forever, it seemed. It was getting very painful. I asked him to stop twice.

"Afterwards we went about half a mile down the road to get some help in towing the car. I know it is very strange that we were acting like friends. The worst strangeness is that when we finally found an old farmer to help us, I did not try to escape my assailant. This is the part that really scares the shit out of me. I like to rationalize it and say I was too scared to try anything. I think I just wanted to die subconsciously or something like that. The whole thing began to be like a dream. I guess after a certain period of time, my mind just kind of conked out and started floating away."

After the rape she wrote, "The first day was the worst, because I wondered if I deserved to live. . . . A difficult thing is thinking of all the things I could have done. Like I could have taken the key out of the ignition right at the beginning, or I could have tried something physical like hitting him with my purse. . . . My statement to the world is this: I don't know why I acted like I did, and I don't know why I didn't fight him off, and I don't know why I'm alive." And she kept asking herself: "Would it have been better to struggle and die, or to give in and thus have words like 'you really wanted it, didn't you?' and stuff like that to plague me."

There is nothing in her five-page description of her experience to suggest that the man was a killer, nor did Ms. Rogers express a fear of being killed when describing how it happened. Part of the trauma of her experience seems to be that it forced her to confront her own passivity and submissiveness. But this could hardly have been so upsetting if she'd had a casual attitude toward being raped.

While not all women are subjected to the same societal pressures, and while not all women uniformly conform to these pressures, passivity and submissiveness are regarded as typical female behavior, particularly in relation to men. And yet, when these acculturated patterns are operative in a rape situation, victims are castigated for this behavior and, often, the incident is regarded as something other than rape. Like Ms. Rogers, many women who behave the way they've been trained to act, castigate themselves afterward.

Passivity also plays a part in many women's feelings and actions after they have been raped. Having been overcome by a rapist left some of the women with a feeling of having been conquered. Virgins are especially susceptible to this feeling, which explains why a few of them consented to see their rapists again. The fact that they did so does not mean that the experience was not very upsetting to them. Rather, feeling conquered, they no longer acted on a principle of self-determination. Many men share this view of rape. The belief is similar to the view that once a woman has consented to intercourse, she will, indeed, must, continue to consent. Of course, many women want to do so, but of those who don't, many still feel obligated. Petting works in a similar way. If a woman allows a man to reach a particular point of physical intimacy one time, he does not expect to lose ground the next time. Even if she goes further than she intended to, or feels comfortable with, her momentary "weakness" has implications for what will be expected in the future. It would be surprising if women were unaffected by this strong male expectation. This explains the docile behavior of some rape victims after the rape. It is as if they had been broken.

When rape occurs within a dating relationship, particularly one in which some petting has occurred, the woman is especially likely to be seen as partially or wholly responsible. But it does not follow that because a woman engages in sexual foreplay, she has acquiesced to intercourse, although the very notion of "foreplay" assumes it is preliminary to penetration. This assumption indicates the extent of male domination of sexuality. Women's sexuality, particularly at the virginal stage, is very different from men's, and it is common for women to desire sex that does not culminate in penetration. Men tend to be penetration-oriented. This orientation is oppressive not only to women but also to men, for exclusively goal-oriented pleasure underemphasizes the pleasurability of the means.

Ideally, men would accept that a woman is entitled to respond only to the point desired by her. She should not be made to feel responsible for satisfying a man once he has been aroused. But in fact many women, wishing to avoid constant pressure and insults, give in and accept this responsibility, yielding to the "all-or-nothing" standard of sexuality. Many a woman accepts that she has "asked for it" if she has allowed herself to engage in what might be for her a preferred way of being sexual, cuddling and petting but not necessarily culminating in intercourse. Such sexual behavior might be preferred if intercourse is not particularly enjoyable to her, or if intercourse might make her feel more vulnerable to the man than she cares to feel, or if it might go against her sense of morality. Rather than experience the unpleasantness, which may include rape, of asserting her unrecognized right not to engage in sexual acts that she doesn't wish, many a woman will accede to this implicit male rule.

Assuming that a man's sexuality should have priority over a woman's is, of course, highly sexist. To argue that, if a woman gets what she wants, it is only fair for a man to get his wants met is unreasonable if his doing so would be at her expense. If a man prefers no contact to petting without intercourse, he can choose that.

Aside from being submissive, passive, and weak, women are supposed to be kind, compassionate, patient, accepting, and dependent. They are also supposed to take the primary responsibility for problems in their relationships with men. These traits also make women more subject to rape. For example, Daphne Fujimoto, although angry with her date, decided to help him take the picnic things up to his apartment, where he raped her (see Chapter Three). Alicia Gomez was raped by her drunk friend after walking him home (see Chapter Five). Helen Rawson forgave her friend after he attacked her, only to be attacked more forcefully, and raped, the next time (see Chapter Nine). And these so-called feminine traits are even more important in explaining why women put up with lovers or husbands who rape them. Jean Michel, who was raped in front of a group of people by her hippie husband (see Chapter Seven), and Margaret White, who is still living with her husband who raped her after she returned home from the hospital where she had been treated for shock because of an attack by a stranger (see Chapter Twenty-one), are apt examples here.

This is not to say that women should not be kind, compassionate, and patient, although these qualities certainly can be overdone. It is to point out that such traits can contribute to women's victimization, as in the case of Gina d'Amico, who was raped by a man whose company she could not allow herself to reject, even though she didn't want to be disturbed by him (see

Chapter Seventeen). Many women need to put more effort into protecting themselves rather than men's egos.

However, there certainly are ways in which women contribute to their vulnerability to rape. The most obvious is an ambivalence about being treated as sexual objects. On the one hand women have learned that it is very hard to get any benefits from men if they don't play into this aspect of male sexism. On the other hand, they feel depersonalized by it. In addition, many women have internalized male notions of attractiveness, and so in order to feel good about their appearance, they have to pile on makeup, and display their breasts, legs, or behinds. This need contributes to their own objectification, which in turn contributes to the rape problem.

The issue of attractiveness is a source of much ambivalence in many women. After being raped, Ms. Towsend, for example, said, "It made me think I've got to minimize my physical attractiveness, and my feeling of attractiveness." On being asked how she felt about having to do this, she replied, "If somebody told me I had to minimize my attractiveness, I'd tell them to go take a flying fuck. I'd get mad, and I'd say, 'Who in hell are you to tell me to do that!' Because I like being attractive, and I like looking pretty. I like expressing myself, and I don't want to be a dummy. But I want to be respected, too." On the one hand she feels that looking attractive makes her more vulnerable to being raped, and on the other hand she really wants to be attractive.

Paula Scott's feelings show the degree to which women internalize the view that they provoke rape by looking attractive. "I was wearing a white blouse and a skirt and a pair of stockings and a pair of dressy shoes. I was very conscious of feeling very female, you know, crossing my legs and talking kind of coyly. . . . So, when I thought about it afterwards, I thought that maybe I did egg him on in a way, because I had been feeling very conscious of being female." Here again the notion is expressed that if a woman is feeling sexual (in this case, merely feeling "female") she is somewhat responsible if the man reacts by raping her.

But saying that women, by dressing up to excite men, contribute to their own objectification, which contributes to the rape problem, should *not* be interpreted as agreement with the view that women who do this are provoking rape. I am merely saying that by doing this we cooperate with rather than discourage men's ability to separate sexual desire from desires for affection and friendship, and that it is men's ability to do this that is one of the factors enabling them to rape strangers and acquaintances.

The solution is not for women to dress in drab, shapeless clothes and hide their faces. The change has to come in the way men view women, the excessive value placed on female beauty, and contemporary notions of femininity. It is paradoxical indeed that women are regarded as the beautiful sex, yet many cannot bear to be seen unmasked, and so much time, emotion, and money is invested in beautifying them still more. In much the same way, the fact that men are seen as more aggressive than women leads to the absurd expectation that they ought to train themselves to be even more so.

Males are brought up to be very much in touch with their sexual needs ("Boys will be boys," and if they won't be, they'd better pretend) and out of touch with needs for love, romance, and affection. In order to be regarded as successful, males must satisfy their sexual needs with females rather than by masturbation. Females, in contrast, are discouraged from being sexual. For example, they masturbate less. They are supposed to be virginal, or at least, to confine their sexual relations to males who really care about them, and about whom they really care.

At all costs, females have to be careful of their "reputations." The same behavior that gives status to males (promiscuous sexual relations) endangers it for females, yet it is very important for females that they are attractive to males and sought after by them. Females are also supposed to be submissive toward males. With such a bundle of contradictions, it is a wonder that people talk about males and females being "made for each other." With these basic incompatibilities in socialized needs and expected behavior, it is not surprising that there is often hatred between the sexes. And it is no wonder that there is rape. It is a logical consequence of the lack of symmetry in the way males and females are socialized in this society. Indeed, the remarkable thing is not that rape occurs, but that we have managed for so long to see it as a rare and deviant act, when it is, in fact, so embedded in our cultural norms, as a result of the clash between the masculine and the feminine mystiques.

If males and females were to be liberated from their sex roles, the rape situation would change dramatically. I believe that male sexuality would become more like female sexuality, in that males would value sex within relationships more than sex for its own sake, and would respond to women more as people than as sexual objects. And female sexuality would become more similar to male sexuality, in so far as women would become more in touch with their sexual needs and less apt to obscure the real person and the true nature of the relationship with their romantic fantasies. In short, I believe sex-role liberation would result in a mix of the male sexual and the female romantic elements in both males and females, so that there would no longer be a war between them. But we have a long, long way to go. And rape will be with us as long as these contradictions exist.

As emphasized earlier, there cannot be sexual liberation without sex-role liberation; nor can there be sex-role liberation without sexual liberation. And so the problem goes beyond unfortunate socialization, because the socialization is what it is because males and females are being trained to take their unequal places in the society. The changes needed do not merely require parents to socialize their children differently. This change is important, but it's not enough. Men have to give up their monopolization of power in the society as a whole, and in more than token ways, for the problem of rape to be solved. And for this to happen does not only mean that as many women must have power as men. The structures, the values, the processes, all have to change too, since sexism is inherent in them. To achieve this end will require the most total revolution for which people have ever struggled.

TWENTY-SIX

Solutions: Female Rage and Other Alternatives

> Henry was trying to get up and get out because he was obviously in pain. . . . I told him and the rest of them why I did it. I said it was for the women that he'd raped in Mexico, it was for the *macho* pig trip about the acid he laid on Franny, it was for physically attacking another woman when they were having an argument during a house meeting, and it was for thinking he could get away with telling a hideous story like that about brutalizing women.

While the purpose of this book is to learn about the experiences of rape victims, it also seemed necessary to include a chapter on ways to avoid victimization and how to deal with rape when attempts to avoid it fail. Very little has been written or done to prevent rape that doesn't put women in a restrictive or inhibiting position. Most advice, including some offered here, sounds like a list of behaviors for women *not* to engage in, but it is also realistic under present circumstances.

The issue at hand seems to be that if the institutions we rely on don't protect us, we must protect ourselves. Since the system of justice does not begin to deal with the problem of rape adequately, and since women are relatively powerless in this society, and therefore in a poor position to change laws, it seems justifiable to deal with the problem in extralegal fashion. Those who see such a statement as condoning violence should remember that violence against women is already condoned without stirring much concern.

There is no way that women can exempt themselves from the terrifying threat of rape, since females of all ages, races, classes, and marital statuses are potential prey for rapists. But it is equally true that there will be fewer victims of sexual assault when women are less victimlike.

When I had an opportunity to interview a woman who is definitely not victimlike, and who took it upon herself to make a rapist suffer for his brutal behavior, for which, like most rapists, he had never been apprehended or been made to suffer, I took it. After reading twenty-two accounts of how women were raped and how others reacted to their experiences, the reader may find it an interesting contrast to learn of a situation where a man became the victim of a woman as a consequence of being a rapist.

Ann Fisher, a thirty-two-year-old woman, is five feet five inches tall and weighs 125 pounds, though according to her, "my best fighting weight is 120 lbs. I'm lighter and quicker then." Ms. Fisher has had no training in street fighting or any kind of self-defense.

ANN FISHER: I went to visit a friend and one of the men that was in her house was an admitted rapist. His name is Henry Millar. He had been telling my friend Franny and other women around town that he had raped women in Mexico. He said he was with a gang of teen-age boys who left Phoenix and went to Mexico for a few days. They got drunk and supposedly held the café at knifepoint for three days and three nights and raped the women in it. He obviously thought it was a far-out thing to do.

It's one of those groovy little memories he had, and he'd tell this story to women mainly, and occasionally to men. He'd get off on it. He presumably had a particular reason for telling women. I think he expected them to be impressed, and I think at times he expected them to be intimidated.

One night, two or three weeks ago, he was tripping on acid with a friend of his, and he went into his Mexican rape trip, and his friend talked about beating up queers in the park. Then they tried to force my friend to take some acid against her will. They didn't succeed, but they frightened her, and she had to hide in her room to get away from them. I think he was talking at that time about the violence of the rape to intimidate her, because they weren't getting along. In talking about their violence, the men were trying to get themselves revved up to do something to her, I think, and that's why she refused to trip with them. It was really a relief to her when other people came home that night. When I went up there she told me about it, and I was furious.

I felt furious with Henry and also with the women for allowing him to get away with bragging about rape to them. Apparently, nobody questioned him, nobody punched him. He should have been punched out. So I decided to do it.

INTERVIEWER: Could you describe him?

Ms. FISHER: He was white. He was about forty years old, an Okie. He thought he was pretty smooth. He has a pretty high opinion of himself. He's very masculine, very male. He looked like a mountain man, talked like one, acted like one. He was a real pig, very objectionable.

INTERVIEWER: What was he like physically?

Ms. FISHER: He's probably about five feet eight inches or five feet nine. He's pretty strong. He had a big torso, big hands, and big arms. I had been measuring his strength all day because I knew I was going to have a confrontation with him. I knew that if I was to succeed, I was really going to have to incapacitate him fast, because he could really hurt me. I had to really surprise him and incapacitate him immediately.

INTERVIEWER: How did you go about punching him out?

Ms. FISHER: Well, after Franny told me about his bragging and also what he'd done to her, I thought all day about it, trying to decide how to get him to tell me, because I obviously couldn't just start attacking him. Also, I wanted the attack to be witnessed by other people, and I wanted everyone to understand why I was doing it. So I had to get him to tell me about the rapes in front of everybody. We started this stupid sex survey game the household played occasionally in which everyone is supposed to tell about their sex lives and tell the truth about it. After dinner, at about eight-thirty, I suggested that we start playing that game, and I added the question, "Have you ever raped anyone?" to the sex survey. There were four men and two women besides myself at this point. And I specifically asked Henry if he had raped anyone, and he said yes. He admitted that he had, and he repeated the story. But this time he said that he really didn't consider it rape because they were prostitutes and they only took what the women expected to be paid for, so it was just a disagreement over price. I said, "But if you forced them it was rape, wasn't it?" I said, "You've been telling other women in town this story, and I just wanted to hear it from you." And he said, "Well, yeah, I guess it was rape." And that's when I started verbally assaulting him.

Earlier in the day I had asked him what he would consider the greatest insult to him. He said that he could take any insult to him personally, but he would not stand to have his mother or father insulted. I asked him, "Oh, you mean if I were to call you a son of a bitch and a bastard that would be terrible?" And he said, "Yes, that would be pretty bad. I wouldn't put up with anything like that." So I shouted, "You're a son of a bitch and a no good bastard and a rapist pig." I was in such a rage.

Then he called me a whore, and that's when Franny, who was sitting next to him, threw beer in his face. Then they started grappling, and that's when I jumped on him, and we started fighting. I got on top of him, and somehow he was bent over backwards with his head on the floor in the corner, and his groin was exposed, and I punched him in his groin as hard as I could. I punched him in the balls because I wanted to render him completely inoperative.

After I punched him in the balls, I grabbed his glasses and broke them and started choking him. And he was trying to push me off with his hands but the blow in the balls was pretty effective, and he didn't have much strength at that point. I had him bent over backwards, and I was on top of his body, straddling him and choking him. I got my knees up on his stomach, and I was sort of jumping up and down on him, and also continuing to try to knee him in the groin. And I choked him, and I was gouging his eyes—anything I could do. I was trying to destroy him.

I think the suddenness of the attack took his strength away. I mean, at one point we were just sitting there after dinner, and I was asking him a question, and the next minute I was on top of him, and I think he was really surprised. I think everyone was really surprised. And hitting him in the balls really did incapacitate him, I know it hurt a great deal.

INTERVIEWER: Were the other people just standing around and watching?

Ms. FISHER: No. His friends, the other men in the house and one woman who apparently was in league with these men, were trying to rescue him. When I punched him in the balls the people in the room gasped. Rose screamed that it was a dirty rotten thing to do, and the men were pretty angry and outraged. I could hear all this activity going on behind me, because they were trying to get at me, and Franny was fighting with them. Rose was the one who was originally trying to get me off him. She was protecting him. So Franny was slugging it out with her, and Rose was in the way so the other men couldn't get around her because Henry was wedged in such a peculiar place that I was protected by all this massive furniture. They had only one way of coming at me to get me off of him, and Franny was blocking that way and defending me. She wouldn't let them pull me off.

INTERVIEWER: Was that because she was that strong or was it because they weren't actually trying very hard?

Ms. FISHER: Well, she did get a big sock in the jaw. She got hit a couple of times and had a puffy face, but she kept at it. But finally one of his male friends came around the table from the other side, got around Franny, pulled the table out, grabbed me, and pulled me off of him. Henry was trying to get up and get out because he was obviously in pain but he didn't want to show it. He didn't want to lie there and moan and groan in pain.

Then I told him and the rest of them why I did it. I said it was for the women that he'd raped in Mexico, it was for the *macho* pig trip about the acid he laid on Franny, it was for physically attacking another woman when they were having an argument during a house meeting, and it was for thinking he could get away with telling a hideous story like that about brutalizing women. It just infuriated me.

INTERVIEWER: Were you at all afraid that you wouldn't be able to pull it off?

Ms. FISHER: No.

INTERVIEWER: What was the basis for your confidence?

Ms. FISHER: My rage. I had no physical fear for myself at all, but I think one of the reasons I attacked Henry so fast was that he was grappling with Franny, and I felt that he was really going to do her in. She was in a very awkward position and he was getting on top of her at the point that I jumped over the table.

INTERVIEWER: Do you think this is something that women in general should do to rapists?

Ms. FISHER: Yes, I would like to see women deal with their own personal rapists. I would like women not to listen to crap like Henry's bragging. I told him, and I told the rest of the house, that I hoped that the day would come when a man wouldn't dare say what he said and expect to live.

INTERVIEWER: Were you actually trying to kill him, or punch him out?

Ms. FISHER: I think if they hadn't gotten me off of him, I probably might have gone on to kill him. It wasn't a conscious desire to kill, it was just something very instinctual and primitive.

INTERVIEWER: How did people react afterwards?

Ms. FISHER: Well, there was one Chicano who was probably angrier than anyone else. His face was very red and he was trembling, and he helped Henry outside, and he was probably giving him first aid or whatever they do to men when they get their balls kicked. Then he came back in and started giving me a lot of bull shit about what I had done. I said, "Listen, let's even look at it from your chauvinist point of view. How do you feel as a Chicano about this honky Okie going with his friends across the border into Mexico to rape Mexican women because they're not white and they can get away with it? Now how do you feel about *that!*? Where are *you* at politically? What are *you* doing with your life?" And he looked at me and said something about how glad he was he was leaving, and he was particularly glad he wasn't going to have to see *me* anymore. And I said, "I wonder how many rapist fantasies *you* have had, you asshole." And he walked out and his seventeen-year-old brother followed him.

Then Henry, the rapist, came in and disappeared into his bedroom, and the other guy, Dave, disappeared into Rose's bedroom and left the rest of us out in the living room. I think that the men really were blown away by what happened. I don't think they knew how to handle a woman who physically attacks a man. I think it really blew Henry away that I attacked him like he would expect a man to attack. He was lying in bed hollering through the walls that he had held back his strength because he didn't want to hurt me. But in fact he would have killed me if he had a chance. I had blown his trip. I had humiliated and exposed him. I told him that I had told all these women in town that I was going to do this to him, so I blew his trip everywhere. I kept an eye on him because I thought he might attack me, and I didn't have surprise on my side anymore. I had lost the advantage. I guess in a regular test of strength he would have won.

INTERVIEWER: Did other people in the house know of your plan?

Ms. FISHER: Only Franny and Sara, another woman they had all been trashing in the house. Sara said that she would meet us later back at the house, but didn't show until the whole thing was over. She chickened out because she was too fearful. But Franny was always ready. She said she'd give me a hundred percent support. In fact she said, "Let's go do it," and we had one more drink, and we went and did it.

INTERVIEWER: What did you actually experience when you were beating him up?

Ms. FISHER: Oh, I felt good. I especially felt good when I punched him in the balls. I was sort of amazed because I had wondered what it would feel like. It felt like punching a feather pillow. There isn't anything there, really. It really felt good.

I don't think he's going to tell another woman his story again.

INTERVIEWER: It sounds as if you're pretty much in touch with your strength. Have you had many fights before?

Ms. FISHER: Well, I guess kids fight when they grow up, but I haven't had any real fights in a long time. Oh, I punched a man in the jaw a couple of months ago. He made a rude remark about my friend. She was drunk and he was standing there laughing and he said that what she needed was the prick of a donkey. And I went up to him, and I said, "What did you say?" I was smiling at him so he'd tell me, because I wanted him to know that I knew what he said. When he repeated it, I hit him. He was shocked. Then one of his friends restrained me. He was standing with two other men.

INTERVIEWER: You haven't had any karate or judo training?

Ms. FISHER: No, and not any street fighting either. But I do know where to go and what to go for.

INTERVIEWER: And do you feel strong?

Ms. FISHER: I'm healthy. I'm not superstrong. I think a righteous anger helps a lot.

INTERVIEWER: And how do you manage to not feel afraid?

Ms. FISHER: Because I have never let a man pig on me. That's why. I have never let a man beat me. Men have tried. A man has never raped me, but men have tried. I have never allowed them to succeed. I imagine if I got a really good beating from a man one time, I would think about it before I attacked. Maybe some day I'm going to get it. I could see that hitting that guy who insulted my friend in the street was foolish because the men could have beaten me up rather badly. But I just can't tolerate that kind of insult.

I'd like to see more women hit back or hit first. I think hitting first is best.

Don't give them any leeway. Don't let them make snide remarks about women, insulting your people. Nobody else lets it happen. I mean, even a racist doesn't talk about niggers in front of a black man, because he knows he's probably going to get punched. If enough women can defend themselves and their sisters, I think that men will really think twice. Now they think that they can get away with it, and they *do* get away with it. They get away with insults all the time, why can't they get away with rape?

INTERVIEWER: It seems from what you say that you feel that women shouldn't only defend themselves but they should defend each other, too.

Ms. FISHER: Of course. Letting someone insult another woman is insulting you too. Listening to a man smugly recount his rape experience or talk about the last time he beat up his old lady, without saying anything about it, is an attack on you. It's as much of an attack on you as it was on his old lady, and if you do nothing, you are letting him get away with it.

INTERVIEWER: What do you think about weapons?

Ms. FISHER: I think women should learn how to use guns, and I think they should carry them in the streets. And if they are harassed, they should pull them out, and if that doesn't work, and a man continues to harass them, then they should shoot him.

INTERVIEWER: But first of all, many men are armed. And secondly, wouldn't they arm themselves pretty fast?

Ms. FISHER: I think they'd stop harassing women faster than arming themselves. If they thought that it was going to come to a fifty-fifty chance of them getting hurt, they're not going to press it too much. Because most men doing these assaults and harassments on the streets are in the habit of doing it. But if they met pretty stiff resistance, if a woman pulled a gun on one of them, he'd run. I'm pretty sure he would. And if he didn't, then that's a potential rapist that's dead and who cares, you know. I certainly don't.

INTERVIEWER: Have you done anything about arming yourself?

Ms. FISHER: No, I haven't. I think when I do, I'll probably stop talking about it. I expect I'll do it pretty soon.

INTERVIEWER: And do you believe in learning self-defense?

Ms. FISHER: I'm more inclined to favor arms because it takes years to learn self-defense well enough to be able to overcome a really much more powerful foe than yourself. You have to consider also that many of your potential attackers have been trained to kill with their hands by the armed forces. They are trained killers, so you really have to get to be pretty damn good, especially since a lot of times they have the element of surprise on their side because they are doing the attacking.

I don't favor knives, because men really know how to use knives, and they have a much longer reach, and they can disarm you. A gun pulled at the right moment, so that there's enough space between you so a person can't lunge at you, is much safer. And if this happens enough, I think men are really going to be a little more cautious about who they approach, and who they assault in the street.

INTERVIEWER: Do you see this as something that is happening?

Ms. FISHER: Yes, I think so. I know from the women who have gotten off on my story that there are a lot of angry women around. Because there certainly is an epidemic of rape.

It feels so good to actually have done what I did, because I've been ranting and raving about rape for a long time and sitting around talking with women about how they should defend themselves and be more aggressive. So that one rapist, Henry, paid for a lot of sins. I had a lot of hostility, a lot of rage about rape. It felt really good to do it.

When confronted with a threatening situation each woman must choose her own alternative, and in anticipation of the possibility of such an experience, every woman has to work out her own methods of dealing with it. However, it seems to me that Ms. Fisher, who believes in carrying and using a gun, expresses a dangerous view. For one thing, carrying a gun (as well as many other weapons, if concealed) is a punishable offense and involves the risk of being caught. Second, there is a danger that the weapon will be used against the armed woman. A woman would have to be a practiced shot to use a gun effectively since men are more likely to be familiar with guns, and the same applies to knives. An error in assessment is more likely to lead to the woman being killed or maimed than if she is unarmed. Any weapon a woman carries should not be lethal nor easily used against her. Carrying a can of Mace, although also illegal, may be worth the risk of being caught. The laws should be changed to permit women to carry it legally.

Finally, while violent tactics that involve loss of life are sometimes expedient as well as justified, they are not, I believe, the most expedient for dealing with rapists. There seem to be other ways of trying to change the situation that should be tried first. It is only in the last two or three years that some women have made concerted and organized attempts to bring about change in attitudes toward rape and rape victims, and receptivity to these attempts is increasing almost visibly, so that the time for implementing radical changes on this issue is better now than it has been previously.

The male-dominated structure of this society fosters the masculinity mystique as well as the femininity mystique, and this hierarchy has to be completely restructured so that sexual caste systems are eradicated. The masculinity mystique is clearly a mystique of people with power, and it is unlikely to disappear, or even substantially to lessen while the power discrepancies between men and women remain as they are now.

Really to solve the rape problem, then, the male-dominated social structure has to go, together with its sexist ideology, and the psyches of men and women, particularly men, have to change. Unfortunately, few men have so far shown any interest in changing, so women are going to have to continue to take the initiative in forcing changes in men and the structure they control. This is why the women's movement is so relevant to dealing with the rape problem.

But what can women do about rape in this still very sexist society? Many participants in social movements are too apt to think in terms of there being only one right way. In the case of rape there is room for many different tactics. Those in a position to take the risks involved or who feel strongly enough about rape to take any risks, may opt for militant actions. Others who do not believe militant actions justified, or who think other less militant actions preferable, may try more moderate tactics. Tactics should not compete but complement one another. Anyone who wants to put energy into solving the rape problem should be able to find some tactic that suits her particular situation and beliefs.

Many of the rape victims made excellent suggestions for solving or alleviating or dealing with the problem of rape. Most of the following ideas have been mentioned by other feminists as well as by some of the victims who participated in this study.

LEARN SELF-DEFENSE

Self-defense is an important way for women to appreciate their strength, whatever it may be, and a way of keeping fit as well. According to the booklet, *Stop Rape*, karate is the best of the Oriental methods of self-defense for women. Judo and jujitsu apparently require more weight and aikido too much intensive training.[1] However, the authors argue that ideally women should devise their own methods of self-defense, "culling what they have found to be the most useful from many different sources."[2]

Learning self-defense, of course, doesn't mean that women can get themselves out of all ugly situations, or that using the techniques learned will even be wise in every situation. However, women with this skill will at least have a choice, and often a higher and more appropriate level of confidence. An argument often used against self-defense is that a woman will develop an excessive degree of confidence and will therefore so enrage a rapist that she will end up in an even worse situation than if she simply submitted. On the basis of this study, it seems that many women seriously

1. *Stop Rape*, p. 32. This booklet was published by Women Against Rape in 1971. Copies may be obtained for $.95 from Detroit Women Against Rape, 1821 Patton Street, Detroit, Mich. 48219.
2. Ibid.

underestimate their physical capacities, and that self-defense training may help women to evaluate themselves more realistically.

It is truly peculiar reasoning that because men are generally larger and hence stronger than women, men are the ones who should develop their strength still further. If equity were given more than lip service in this country, then it would be women, rather than men, who would be given the opportunity and encouragement to develop their strength.

RESISTANCE

Even without learning self-defense, women need not be helpless, unless they decide submission is the best tactic. Jerrold Offstein reports that, "According to our research, in 100% of the cases in which the woman *successfully repelled or escaped from* the assault, there was one common element: *resistance* by the attacked woman; whether the making of noise or physical resistance or a combination of the two. *No one* that we could find got free by compliance with the attacker." [3] However, as we have seen in many of the previous chapters, some victims prefer to submit rather than risk what they see as almost certain defeat. They feel that to fight and lose is more dangerous and will be more traumatic for them than submission. This decision is certainly understandable, but it also appears that many victims too readily feel intimidated by a man. This conclusion is supported by some of the victims' accounts, but it emerges even more clearly in the chapter on rapists. The ease with which two of the rapists accomplished their goals is quite striking, as is their insistence that they would not have been able to go through with it had the woman screamed and struggled. And in the two cases of substantial resistance, the men did not achieve their goals.

However, there are also some cases where rapists are stimulated by resistance. There are women whose resistance cost them their lives or serious injury. Yoshika Tanaka of San Francisco, for example, bit her would-be rapist severely on the tongue when he tried to kiss her, and was stabbed by him with four knives, the blades of two of them breaking off in her body.[4] Every woman under attack has to judge whether her attacker is such a man or the probably more common type who does not want to contend with a violent or screaming woman.

According to Offstein, "in the primary data source used, 60% of all the successfully repelled assaults were accomplished by the presentation of loud noise alone." [5] Offstein goes on to recommend: "Practice your yell. It is a very

3. *Self-Defense for Women* (Palo Alto, Ca.: National Press Books, 1972), p. 2. Author's italics.
4. "Bite Stops Rape, Sparks Stabbing," *San Francisco Examiner*, March 29, 1973.
5. *Self-Defense for Women*, p. 4. Unfortunately it is not clear what Offstein's "primary data source" consists of.

effective weapon for you to have available for your self-defense." [6] Since some women are unable to scream when they are very afraid, it would be wise for women to carry whistles in their purses. A good whistle can be even louder than a scream, and is less likely to be interpreted as "merely" a marital fight, and therefore to be ignored.

WOMEN AGAINST RAPE ACTION GROUPS

Georgia State Representative Julian Bond has advocated that black people should take the law in their own hands and inflict physical punishment, if necessary, on drug dealers who sell dope to black youngsters. "I'm not advocating murder," the civil rights leader said. "I'm advocating community action. Drug dealers act outside the law and the police seem unwilling or incapable of dealing with them. The pusher needs to know that it's dangerous for him not just in terms of sanctions of the law, but in terms of sanctions by the community. If they catch the pusher in action, they should inflict immediate discipline." [7]

With the same arguments in mind, I would like to see women treat in a similar manner rapists whom they have good reason to believe will not be found guilty in courts. Beating up a rapist (many particularly angry women who have developed a strong desire for retribution favor buggering rapists with some foreign object) is the most obvious tactic here. But there is room for more imagination. For example, a man held a stag party the night before he was to be married at which a dancer was invited to perform. After her performance, she was raped. A group of women wrote up what had happened and went to the church the next day to leaflet the wedding guests.

If a woman is raped by a man in his home or place of work, she could inform his wife or girl friend (if he has either), as well as his employer or employees. She could mention bodily peculiarities he may have, or describe the room in such a way that it is clear at least that she has slept with him, if this information would be damaging for him. A group of women could also picket outside his home or outside his place of work. He could be harassed on the phone at all hours, or at work, and anyone who answers his phone could be informed that he is a rapist. Quite often, victims strongly want to avoid seeing their rapist a second time, but of course there is no need for the victim herself to participate in these actions, though it is important that her consent is obtained.

Another tactic, one that has actually been used by women in some communities, is to post pictures of a known rapist around the community warning women to watch out for him and giving him some publicity that he'd no doubt prefer to avoid. If no picture of a rapist is available, a

6. Ibid.
7. *San Francisco Chronicle*, February 4, 1972.

description of his physical appearance, his name, address, place of employment, and whatever other information about him is available could be posted. In addition to this information, a leaflet might be prepared describing the rape incident, and women could distribute the leaflet at the rapist's home and place of work. If he is a well-known person, the press might also be successfully involved.

Difficult as it is to do, women should try to find out when trials of rapists are scheduled and attend them. If trials are conducted in a sexist manner, women should object by leafletting outside of the courtroom, or, if they are willing to be arrested for contempt of court, by disrupting the proceedings.

Ideas for other actions should be shared. The reader might send suggestions to one of the many rape crisis centers that have sprung up all over the country. There are many possibilities. Unfortunately most require knowing the rapist or where he lives or works.

Some Los Angeles women successfully intimidated a particular man about whom they had no information. He had been following a woman for several days when they "turned the tables and followed him around until he became frightened and disappeared." [8] Street patrols have been attempted in many places, though most, to my knowledge, seem to have been abandoned. The action, namely persuading the rapist to commit himself to a mental hospital, taken by the friends of Nan Murray is a good example of an *ad hoc* group determining the best way of dealing with a rapist (see Chapter Twenty-two). Such *ad hoc* groups of friends of rape victims would probably be even more effective than permanent antirape groups as the personal involvement might be greater. Exactly what action a particular group takes will depend on the politics and values of the members.

Such actions will, no doubt, receive much criticism and perhaps provoke a libel suit here and there, but they will focus attention on the problem and should help to hasten the implementation of improvements in the way rape victims are treated. With some issues, confrontation tactics are far more effective than using the "traditional channels," and when the traditional channels are so unfair to rape victims, they certainly seem justified.

RAPE CRISIS CENTERS

Rape crisis centers have emerged all across the country in the last few years. These centers aim to help the rape victim in whatever way they can. A typical description of the services offered by one such organization follows:

> Usually, rape victims are isolated and without support. . . . A group of concerned women has formed a Community based organization called *Bay Area Women Against Rape*. Our main purpose is to try

8. Martha Shelley, "How it works in L.A. . . ." *Ms.*, Sept. 1973, p. 16.

and lessen this isolation by offering support and assistance to the rape victim. We provide rape counselling services, emergency support, escort services to police and hospitals by women advocates, and basic legal and medical information concerning rape.... A woman can call a central number and be placed in contact with an advocate from *Bay Area Women Against Rape,* who will listen to her situation and offer support and assistance in whatever she decides to do.

In addition, information on self-defense training, therapy, or consciousness-raising groups is also available at these centers.

Such centers are additionally useful in so far as they serve as a kind of lobby to police, legal, and medical personnel on behalf of rape victims. In Berkeley, for example, the police seem to have become more conscious of and sensitive to criticisms of their sexism in the handling of victims because of the presence of the Bay Area Women Against Rape (BAWAR).

These centers serve a very important function and should receive substantial community support. Until enough women impervious to the sexist brainwashing which turns victims into culprits are employed in the police departments, hospitals, and judicial institutions, such centers will be necessary. But with proper funding these centers could do far more than they are now doing. For example, they could offer a place for rape victims to stay overnight if they are afraid to return home alone; they could undertake more extensive educational campaigns about rape; and they could offer self-defense classes and rap groups for rape victims. Even without funds, some groups are offering these services.

Just as AAA members are able to call a number whenever they are having difficulties with their cars, so there should be an emergency number that women can call whenever they are being harassed by men. Since women don't always want to report such incidents to the police for various reasons, it would be preferable that such a service be provided by a rape crisis center. Once again, some groups have tried to offer such a service, though usually it is rather limited. Unlike the police, a Los Angeles group bravely accepted requests from women "to interfere in 'domestic quarrels.' Sometimes this service enabled a woman to escape a violent and unwanted boyfriend." [9]

Three information and suggestion leaflets put out by BAWAR appear in the Appendix. They offer many practical suggestions for how women can better protect themselves at home, in their cars, in the streets, while hitchhiking, what objects they can use as weapons, and what women can do should they become rape victims. They also give a more concrete idea of the work that rape crisis centers are doing.

9. Ibid.

The Washington, D.C., Rape Crisis Center has made available a booklet called *How to Start a Rape Crisis Center* for a donation of $2.50.[10] They also publish a bimonthly newsletter and distribute a pamphlet called "Protection Tactics." [11] The emphasis of the Washington, D.C., Rape Crisis Center is now on reaching potential victims (*i.e.*, all females) and educating them about the problem, as much as on offering services to rape victims.[12] They feel it is important that rape crisis centers get beyond an exclusive service-to-the-victim orientation.

NEIGHBORHOOD ORGANIZATION

Ms. Davis, who was grabbed off the street in Cambridge, Massachusetts, by three men and raped by two of them, mentioned the whistle system that operates in parts of Berkeley (see Chapter Sixteen). More communities should organize such a system, which might even help to create real communities where none previously existed. Ms. Davis also suggested that women should intervene and help other women who are being hassled on the street. Concerned women should meet to consider what can be done in their community to help alleviate the rape problem.

GUN AND OTHER WEAPONS CONTROL

Generally it is men who are armed and women who are unarmed in this society, and it is chiefly men who know how to use arms and are willing to do so.

While I think Ms. X (Chapter One), who was imprisoned for two days in her own home, acted sensibly and commendably in arming herself after she was raped, women would probably be less vulnerable if rigorous gun and other weapon control laws were passed and implemented.

So long as this is not the case, women who feel comfortable owning a weapon should consider arming themselves, but stricter controls on guns and other lethal weapons is a more desirable alternative. Women are much more likely to resist rapists successfully if the latter are not armed. Fear of being killed plays an enormous part in the submissive behavior of many rape victims. This fear is not absent when there are no weapons, but it would be lessened in many instances.

10. Their address: P.O. Box 20015, Washington, D.C. 20009.
11. The cost of the bimonthly newsletter is $3.00 a year, and the pamphlet is free if you send a self-addressed, stamped envelope. Additional publications are available from this center.
12. Darlene Cole, personal communication.

ELIMINATION OF SEXISM FROM THE LAWS AND THE LEGAL SYSTEM[13]

After extensive examination of the laws relating to rape, a woman lawyer concludes that "rather than protecting women, the rape laws might actually be a disability for them, since they reinforce traditional attitudes about social and sexual roles. . . ." [14] She goes on to say, "Although societal attitudes no doubt are responsible for the present construction of rape laws, it is also true that this construction serves to reinforce those attitudes. *If the laws were changed to relate more rationally to the reality of the crime and to the goal of sexual equality, attitudes about the crime might also change.*" [15]

Though it is rare for the law to be ahead of public opinion, it *has* happened, and it could happen in regard to rape, if women apply sufficient pressure.

There should be more women judges and attorneys, and when selecting a jury, the district attorney should have the right to disqualify potential jurors who subscribe to the common myths about rape and who reveal sexist attitudes in general.

The difficulty with making recommendations in this area is the nature of the whole judicial system. Attorneys are required to be combative verbally and to develop extremely competitive personalities if they are to succeed. There must be another way to determine guilt and innocence, but right now this seems too hypothetical to warrant further thought.

Compensation should be made by the government to rape victims who apply for it.[16] This is not only a humane and desirable policy for victims of all crimes, but would also serve as an incentive for rape victims to report. In many cases a victim knows that she will not be able to identify a rapist, and so doesn't report the incident. If victims could apply for compensation, more would report, more rapists would probably be caught, and we would get a more accurate picture of the size of the rape problem. And since rape victims are disproportionately poor black women, financial compensation would be helpful in a very practical way.

13. The City Council of Washington, D.C., recently held hearings on rape at which women testified about the need for revision of rape laws and made recommendations as to what these might be. Those interested should write to the Rape Crisis Center, P.O. Box 21005, Washington, D.C. 20009, for information on how to acquire this report.
14. Camille E. LeGrand, "Rape and Rape Laws: Sexism in Society and Law," p. 919.
15. Ibid., p. 919. Italics mine.
16. A very limited form of compensation for victims of violent crimes has been available in California since 1971. However, it is dependent on the economic need of the victim, and compensation is only offered for expenses directly related to the injury. While better than nothing, my proposal would not limit compensation in either of these ways. Trauma does not always incur medical expenses, but it surely deserves compensation.

The penalty for convicted rapists is often extreme, particularly in the South, where racism is often the primary motivating influence. When race is involved, a double standard often operates. If the victim is white and the accused is black, the rigorous requirements of proof that exist when the rapist is white are lifted, and the rapist is more likely to be found guilty. However, if the victim is black and the rapist is white, the victim is likely to be subjected to a far harsher and more unfair trial than her white sister.

According to a recent study:

> The death penalty's apparent hit-and-miss nature has actually been only a matter of hitting blacks while missing whites. . . . Of 1,265 cases of rape in southern areas where that offense is punishable by death, seven times as many blacks were executed as were whites. When the races of both the rapist and victim are considered, the pattern becomes even more clear. The most deadly combination, of course, is black rapist-white victim. Such defendants were found 18 times more likely to be executed than the defendants in cases involving any other racial combination of victim and defendant.[17]

When sexism and racism are combined, it is extremely unlikely that a white man will be convicted for raping a black woman. However, in the North today reverse racism sometimes operates, usually at the expense of a white woman, not a white man.[18]

Not only is the penalty for convicted rapists often extreme, but there is a tremendous range in the possible sentences, often from one year to life. While I am not opposed to such a range, it has made it easy for racism to enter the sentencing, with one year for a man who rapes a black woman, and life for a black man who does exactly the same thing to a white woman. The Federal Bureau of Prisons' national statistics for executions during the period from 1930 to 1970 report four hundred fifty-five execution penalties for rape. Four hundred five of those men receiving the death penalty were black, although the numbers of blacks and whites executed for murder were almost identical.[19]

17. *Human Behavior*, November 1973, p. 35.
18. For example, a black man was sentenced to spend fifty-two weekends in the county jail for raping a white cocktail waitress. *San Francisco Chronicle*, April 24, 1971. Describing the sentence as a "wrist-slap," the D.A. filed an appeal, and on retrial, the accused was found guilty of three counts of rape and one of kidnapping, for which he was sentenced to serve two consecutive three-years-to-life terms in State Prison. Ibid.
19. *National Commission on the Causes and Prevention of Violence*, 1969. These data were brought to my attention by Barbara Fagan.

Racism is not the only explanation for the extreme penalties for rape. Hypocrisy is involved as well. It would make sense if the small percentage of men who are convicted rapists were totally different from the huge majority of men who are either not rapists or not caught. But rapists are not necessarily extreme psychopathic sexual deviants. Many rather ordinary men have raped women.

Aside from eliminating the racism in sentencing, rapists should receive an indeterminate sentence, with the length of time served dependent on how rapidly and successfully they are resocialized to become nonrapists, or at least, non-acting-out rapists. Such a sentencing procedure would provide an incentive for rapists to examine their *macho* attitudes.

CHANGE THE PENAL SYSTEM

As with the judicial system, it seems useless to suggest one or two reforms in the penal system, when the whole is in such need of restructuring. Rape victims in this book who feel pessimistic about the rehabilitative job prisons do for rapists are generally justified. On the other hand, the fact that rapists know that in many situations there is little or no danger of their landing up in prison encourages them to go ahead. Hence it is important not only that more rapists are imprisoned, but also that more serious attempts be made to rehabilitate them while there.

Very little thinking appears to have been done on how rapists might be rehabilitated or treated. There is a great deal of literature on how to treat phobics or alcoholics but not rapists. An understanding of the connection between rape and sexist attitudes in the society at large suggests that it is difficult to treat rapists without treating the society. Still, programs could surely be developed that would resocialize some rapists to have less sexist attitudes, and to discourage them from acting out these attitudes. But this resocialization would be difficult if not impossible when rapists are surrounded by equally *macho* prison personnel. Those working with rapists would have to have some resocialization training themselves.

CHANGE HOSPITAL PROCEDURES

Rape victims often receive callous and sometimes even punitive treatment by doctors and other health care personnel, for which they are often billed large amounts of money. The Palo Alto Rape Collective makes the following recommendations for improving this treatment.

When possible, the rape victim should be given priority treatment in the emergency room.

She should be attended by a nurse in a private room rather than in the public waiting room.

A rape victim should have the option of being examined by a female doctor.

She should be offered use of the telephone, shower, mouthwash and tranquilizers if desired.

A rape victim should be advised about and offered anti-V.D. tests and anti-pregnancy treatment.

She should be allowed to have a friend or relative stay with her throughout the medical examination.

Hospitals should maintain referral lists for supportive counseling services.[20]

RESEARCH

So much of the research on rape has been done by men who subscribe to the common cultural myths about it that we need to start almost from scratch with the research. The sexist notions that many clinicians, doctors, policemen, and attorneys have about rape need to be refuted through extensive documentation to help convince many who require this kind of evidence before they believe what they would rather not believe. In addition, there is need for nonsexist research to discover the best methods of resocializing and treating rapists, the resistance tactics that seem to work best for women who are attacked, the ways women might more easily identify their rapists, weapons that women can carry and use without endangering themselves, and the best way of helping rape victims recover from their experience, to mention but a few examples.

GENERAL

In general, women must start *talking* about rape: their experiences, their fears, their thoughts. In talks I've given on my research with rape victims, I've sometimes pointed out that we keep talking as if no rape victims are in the room; it is always our "friends" we talk about. My saying this often causes an abrupt change of subject, but sometimes women have felt safe enough to share their experiences with the group when invited to in this way. The difficulty they have indicates what a long way we have yet to go. This wall of silence about rape must be broken. Hopefully, this book will be a push in the right direction.

20. *The Rape Handbook*, p. 18.

Appendix

Rape Prevention Tactics and Advice on What to Do if You Are Raped

*By Bay Area Women Against Rape * *

BE SAFE AT HOME

Use initials on your mailbox—never first name (the same goes for listings in the phone book).

Never leave a key under your doormat, in the mailbox, or any other place where it might be found by the wrong person.

Have good lighting at all entrances—front and back.

Have good strong locks on all doors—deadbolt locks are the best—they are virtually pickproof. Most doors have spring latch locks—these can easily be opened by sliding a credit card or thin sheet of metal between the door and the wall. Try it—you can probably break into your own house very easily.

Make sure all windows are well protected—there are rubber stoppers that make it impossible to open windows from the outside—there are other devices that do the same thing. Or you may want to put objects such as flower pots, decorative bottles or rocks on all your window sills—these will create quite a racket if someone should try to climb in. You might try bells or something similar actually affixed to the windows that will make noise when windows are opened.

* P.O. Box 240, Berkeley, Ca. 94701 (415) 845-RAPE.

Sliding doors are not very safe—you can insert a broom handle or large stick between the door and the track—this will prevent it from being opened from the outside.

Don't have dense shrubbery around your windows—this offers good concealment to someone trying to break in—he will spend more time if he is hidden from view.

If you live in an apartment house here are some things to look into: If there's an intercom system, make sure it is in good working order. Never buzz someone in unless you are expecting someone or have some way of checking who's there first. Make sure your landlord keeps the front door locked and that only tenants have a key. Know the other tenants—at least those on your floor—that way you will have some idea of who belongs in the building and who doesn't. Report any suspicious persons that you may see hanging around in the halls if you don't think that they belong there. Make sure there is good lighting—in all hallways, stairwells, and entrances. If there is a garage, it should be locked, and again only tenants should have access to it. Check out elevators, stairways, fire escapes—make sure that they are adequately protected. If you feel that your building is unsafe, get together with the other tenants to demand that your landlord do something. Draw up a list of changes that need to be made and stick to it until you get some action.

If you're home alone—never open the door unless you're sure who's there. Don't hesitate to ask for identification from repairmen, salesmen, etc. before opening the door. If you have any doubts, make them wait outside and make a quick phone call to their company—if they are legitimate they will wait—do the same if someone comes around and says they are taking a survey—check to make sure that it's legitimate.

Don't make appointments over the phone with someone you don't know. If a person calls and says they're from such-and-such company and want to come over to demonstrate their product or tell you about their insurance policy, always take the phone number and call back—speak to the supervisor—check with the Better Business Bureau if you have any doubts. Make sure this isn't a come on—it is a very common way of operating in order to get into someone's house.

Never have things around that could be used as weapons. Most intruders (rapists included) don't enter a house with a weapon—they often will rely on there being kitchen knives or other potential weapons readily available.

If you're going out for the day and will get back after dark, leave some lights on. This will undoubtedly increase your electric bill, but may prevent someone from breaking in if he thinks people are home—also, you will not have to fumble around in the dark for your key. Some people leave a radio on when they go out.

If you're home alone and someone is at the door, you can yell out in a strong voice, "I'll get it, John."

If you're home and want the door to be unlocked (if your kids are playing outside, for instance)—attach something to the door that will make a noise when it is opened (bells, or a door opener). This will eliminate the possibility of your being taken by surprise—the sound of the door opening will register in your mind, and you will at least know that someone has come in—be it your kids, your neighbors, or an intruder.

The Berkeley Police (and probably police departments in other communities) will come to your house and check it out for safety against intruders. They will thoroughly inspect all possible entries and advise you on how to make your home safer. Check with your local police department about this service.

BE SAFE IN YOUR CAR

Always lock your car doors.

Try to park in well-lighted areas at night—also, avoid parking in deserted places.

Have your key in hand when you are going to your car (especially at night).

Always check the back seat when you get in.

If you think you are being followed by a car, change directions, make a U-turn, speed up—ascertain whether or not you are being followed.

If you are, keep your hand on the horn and speed up—do whatever you can to lose him. One thing always to keep in mind is the location of the nearest police station—if you're being followed you can drive there with him right behind you. If you are in the country, drive to the nearest home, keeping your hand on the horn all the way.

PICK UP WOMEN HITCHHIKERS, NOT MEN.

BE SAFE ON THE STREET

Wear long hair up—long hair worn down can too easily be grabbed and pulled.

If at all possible, wear comfortable pants and good running shoes. It's too hard to run away while wearing long skirts, clumsy shoes, etc.

Don't load yourself down with packages or books. It is a good idea to not even carry a purse when you are walking alone at night.

Always have a whistle with you—a good police whistle is the best—they cost about seventy-five cents at most sporting goods stores. Wear it around your wrist or have it on your key chain and carry keys and whistle in your hand. (Never wear anything around your neck—necklaces, chains [even thin ones], and scarves can be used to choke you if you are attacked).

Walk in well-lighted areas. Walk down the middle of the street in dark or deserted neighborhoods. Don't walk close to bushes, alleys, etc.

Know your route home from school, work, and friends' houses. Notice locations of stores, especially those that stay open late, buildings with doormen, police and fire stations. Also familiarize yourself with those areas where men hang out, alleys and unlit parts of the street.

If cars pull up slowly or start to hassle you, cross the street and walk in the other direction.

If you feel someone is following you, do not hesitate to turn around and check. Be aware. It is neither silly nor cowardly. To verify suspicion, try changing your pace or crossing the street. If the other side of the street looks unsafe, walk down the center of the street. Use car windows as mirrors.

Once you have determined that someone is following you, look for a safe place—an inhabited or lighted area. Assess the distance from where you are to the nearest safe place. Consider your clothing. Should you shed anything in order to run faster? All this while, increase your walking speed. Make sure that if you are going to run, then do it as fast as you can, all of a sudden, yelling or blowing your whistle every step of the way.

If you are in a populated area and in trouble, don't yell "Help"—yell "FIRE." This will get a much better response.

Remember, if you do make it to a house, that you are not just stopping by for a visit. Ring the bell, bang on the door, and if no one answers immediately smash the glass. Your life is at stake. It's no time for social convention.

Should running not be the wisest option at first, you have two others. Remaining calm and collected, you can try to psych out the would-be rapist. Is he likely to fall for a sob story? Could he be intimidated if you acted very strong and sure of yourself? Would he believe your roommate or someone is expecting you? You can try acting crazy, fainting, or saying that you have a contagious disease (V.D. for example). Such excuses have worked for women before; they may work for you. (However, please don't rely on the idea that you can talk your way out of anything—some women really believe that they can and don't take any measures to protect themselves. You should always try to be careful and alert—some self-defense training is a good idea if you can manage it. We suggest the above-mentioned tactics only to be used in an emergency.)

Your other alternative is fighting back in order to gain time to run. Don't fling your foot or arm at the man's groin. It is very difficult to be effective and a miss will only anger a man to more violent action.

Your attacker will be expecting a passive victim so any effort will surprise him, giving you time to flee.

WEAPONS

Remember, any weapon you have can be taken from you and used against you. You must always have a good grip on any weapon. Accessibility is also important. Keep the weapon in your hand, in a pocket, or some other handy place—not at the bottom of your purse.

1. *Lighted cigarette*—smash out in the eye or area surrounding the eye.
2. *Pen or pencil*—holding securely, stab at face or neck.
3. *Corkscrew*—jab quickly and directly, then twist. Particularly effective on face, neck, abdominal region.
4. *Plastic lemon*—can squirt juice up to 15 feet. Aim for eyes. Juice can be replaced with ammonia.
5. *Aerosol can*—spray directly into eyes. Use any with "caution" contents, "flammable" warnings—for example, spray oven cleaners, small perfume atomizers.
6. *Keys*—carry a good heavy key ring with lots of keys—these can be used by holding onto the ring and swinging the keys hard and fast—aim for face, neck.
7. *Umbrella*—Use with quick jabbing motion like a bayonet—don't use as a club—it is not as effective and can easily be taken from you.
8. *Stiff hair brush or steel comb; high heels or wedge shoes; hat pin*—can all be very effective.
9. *Tear gas*—This is illegal in California—check in your own state.

Remember that these weapons should be used to provide an opportunity to flee from the attacker. Unless you are trained in self-defense, it is absolutely senseless to stick around. If faced with a gun, forget using weapons. The attacker might still be able to shoot after your effort. Probably your best defense in such a case is to remain calm and try to talk him out of his intentions. This should be an individual woman's decision.

If there is no weapon and you think you have a chance to do something to get away, a good tactic is to stamp down on his instep with all of your weight—or deliver a good hard kick to the shin. These are two very painful tactics and may give you time to run.

If he grabs you from behind, bend over quickly: come back up quickly and slam your head against his chin (the back of your head is very hard and this should not hurt).

If he grabs your arms with his hands, pull your arm away in the direction of his thumbs; this will quickly loosen his grip.

These are only a very few of the many tactics that women can use to defend themselves. If there is self-defense training available to you, by all means take advantage of it. If there are no classes in your area, pick up a copy of Jerrold N. Offstein's *Self-Defense for Women*, published by National Press Books. It is the best work of its kind: eight lessons that can be easily followed.

Some of these tactics may sound very repugnant to you. We agree that hurting another human being is a repugnant idea. It seems to be even more so to women who have been raised to create life, to nurture, to heal the sick and to sustain life. We must realistically assess this type of conditioning so that it no longer immobilizes us from protecting ourselves. *Remember*, you are being attacked through no fault of your own. You did not ask for a fight. If someone's intention is to do you harm, you must take whatever steps are necessary to protect yourself.

SISTERS: IF YOU SOMETIMES HITCHHIKE, PLEASE READ THIS!

HITCHHIKING ISN'T AS SAFE AS IT USED TO BE, BUT SOMETIMES IT'S NECESSARY. WE DO HAVE TO GET PLACES, AND MANY OF US DON'T HAVE CARS OR ANY OTHER MEANS OF TRANSPORTATION. WE RECOMMEND THAT IF YOU CAN GET A RIDE FROM A FRIEND, BORROW A CAR, OR TAKE THE BUS—BY ALL MEANS, DO SO. BUT IF YOU ARE HITCHING PLEASE READ THE FOLLOWING INFORMATION AND KEEP IT IN MIND—IT COULD KEEP YOU OUT OF DANGER AND IT MAY SOMEDAY EVEN SAVE YOUR LIFE.

1. CARDINAL RULE #1: Never accept a ride from a man who has stopped if you did not have your thumb out (i.e., if you were just standing by a bus stop, on the corner, etc., and we were not actively seeking a ride).
2. Try not to hitch alone.
3. Try not to hitch at night.
4. Never accept a ride if there is more than one man in the car. Don't put yourself in a position where if something should happen you would be outnumbered from the beginning. Say "No thanks" to larger groups and stay away from the car door when refusing the ride.
5. If you get a ride from a woman, thank her and encourage her to keep picking up sisters.
6. When you get a ride from a man, check out the following when you get in:
   Look in the back seat—it's a great place for someone else to hide.
   Make sure there is a door handle on your side that works. This is crucial if you should for any reason want to get out in a hurry.

Make sure he has both hands on the wheel or one arm leaning out the window—not out of sight.

Make sure the man is not exposing himself and is fully clothed.

Don't accept a ride if you see beer cans or liquor bottles on the floor of the car—he may be drunk. (Needless to say, if he appears to be strung out on anything, don't accept the ride.)

Don't accept a ride from a man who was driving very fast and slammed on the brakes when he saw you.

Don't accept a ride if he changed directions when he saw you, for instance, if he went around the block and came back, or made a U-turn.

Always ask where he's going before he asks you. If he says, "Oh, I'll take you wherever you're going" or something like that, don't accept.

7. Once you've accepted a ride and are in the car, keep these things in mind:

Always keep the window on your side rolled down, in case you have to yell for help.

If you are carrying something (a package, etc.) keep it on your lap and hold it with your left hand—always keep your right hand free. If he starts to hassle you, you may be able to use the package to ward him off while you use your right hand to open the door and get away. (Also, the left elbow can be used for a good hard blow in the ribs—this hurts and may stun him long enough for you to get away.)

If you smoke, always have a cigarette lit while in the car. If you're in trouble, jab the cigarette in his face.

Another tactic to remember is this: If he tries to start something and the car is not moving very fast, you should reach over and turn off the ignition—then throw the keys out the window. This will definitely draw attention from other motorists and passersby.

Also, if you are on a busy street, you can throw your door open (use your judgment—you wouldn't want to cause an accident or hurt someone). Again, this will draw attention.

If he says he wants to make a quick stop and will then take you where you're going, get out as soon as possible.

ANOTHER CARDINAL RULE: Always know exactly where you are going and how to get there. If he starts going in the wrong direction, or says he knows a quicker route, insist on being let out.

NEVER get dropped off exactly where you are going, especially if you are going to your house.

There may be a time when you have to jump out of a moving car. If this happens, remember the following: Make sure that you roll to a clear spot—away from other moving cars. Throw your shoulders first with your right hand near your body. Tuck your head in and keep your body curved —let your feet follow. It'll hurt, but if you fear danger and you aren't near any stop lights or in traffic, this may be your only chance to get away.

8. A few additional pointers are:

Always wear a whistle around your wrist (not your neck)—A metal police whistle is the best—they cost about seventy-five cents at any sporting goods store. If you sense danger and there are people around, blow the whistle or scream as loud as possible. Most men don't expect women to try to defend themselves in any way—this tactic will probably startle him and may enable you to get away.

Bear in mind that the way you are dressed may affect a man's behavior. Don't wear "sexy" clothing when you are going to be hitching.

9. If you are raped or assaulted, get as good a description of the man as possible. Try to remember any outstanding characteristics, such as scars, etc. Also, leave your fingerprints on the windows of the car and perhaps a small item that you can later identify as yours (but never leave anything with your name or address). (Start practicing now to recognize makes of different cars—it may help you out later.)

10. Also, get the license number of the car and make a mental note of the direction he drives, when he takes off.

11. If you should get hassled and there is no way to escape—use your own judgment to assess the situation. If you are trained in self-defense and really believe that you could successfully deal with the man in this way, do so. But if he has a weapon, or is obviously more powerful than you, don't try to resist. Remember, your life is the most important thing—it must be protected in any way possible. You may be dealing with a very *sick* individual—don't do anything that would fire him up more than he already is—such as cursing at him, arguing, etc. Most rapes do not involve serious violence or harm to the woman. None of us wants to be raped—but we must first guard our lives in a dangerous situation.

REMEMBER: You are in a weak position when accepting a ride from a man. If something happens to you and you report it, a lot of the blame will be laid on you if you were hitching. Hopefully this attitude will change in time, but for now, we must realize that police (and others) don't take a kindly view toward hitchhiking.

REMEMBER: As long as the man is driving and doesn't have a weapon, chances of your getting away are fairly good. You might try yelling "Let me out" in a loud voice before trying anything else. Attracting attention may be your best defense.

IF YOU ARE RAPED....*

1. Get to a safe place immediately.
2. Call a friend or a rape crisis center for support. You will have to decide whether you want to report the rape to the police or not.
3. Go to a hospital, clinic, or your doctor for V.D. and pregnancy tests. Gonorrhea is sometimes treated immediately (usually with penicillin), but this is not always effective. You should have another test for gonorrhea in 2–3 weeks. (The incidence of V.D. from rape is high.) Syphilis cannot be detected until 6–8 weeks later. For pregnancy, the morning-after pill is generally available—or an abortion later.
4. Find out what medication you are given and any possible side-effects (e.g. with the morning-after pill). Be sure to let the medical people know about any allergies or reactions you have to medication.
5. Remember, you can make an anonymous report to the police without getting involved, just so they will have the case and perhaps a description on record, in case he rapes again.

If you are thinking about or definitely decide to report the rape:

1. Call a rape crisis center or a friend for support FIRST. In some cities you are entitled to have a friend, relative, or a rape victim advocate with you throughout the entire police questioning, hospital procedure—except the pelvic exam—and at the preliminary hearing and trial.
2. Do NOT shower, douche, or change clothes. This destroys evidence.
3. Call the police as soon as possible. If you do not call right away they will ask you why you didn't, and may assume it wasn't a "real" rape.
4. It is advisable to bring along a change of clothes as the police may want yours for evidence.
5. Do NOT carry anything incriminating to the police station. Also, you will automatically be checked for any outstanding warrants, e.g. traffic tickets, when you report the crime.

* Adapted from a Bay Area Woman Against Rape Leaflet.

6. If you are under 18, your parents can be notified WITHOUT your consent.

7. Your lifestyle may affect how you are treated by the police, but remember that you can have a friend, relative, or rape victim advocate with you.

8. You can request that a policewoman question you on personal details.

9. Make sure you read over the final police report before agreeing to it. If you don't agree with it, but they won't change it, you are entitled to make your own report and have it attached to the police copy. If you are not positive about exact times and words, be sure to have them labeled: "approximate."

10. The police will probably ask you for the address of where you work and have been known to come and question a woman further at work (even when specifically asked not to).

11. Either before or after questioning, the police will take you to the hospital. It is best to go as soon as possible. If you have insurance elsewhere you will have to INSIST to go there. (You must report the rape and go to the hospital of the city in which it occurs.)

12. At the hospital, they should comb for pubic hairs, photograph bruises, and check for sperm (all may be used as evidence at the trial).

13. They should give you V.D. and pregnancy checks and treatment: immediate and follow-up.

14. The hospital or rape crisis center should give you information on abortion counselling and therapists in general.

COURT PROCEDURE

15. If the police and District Attorney decide that you have a good case, it will go to court—if you cooperate.

16. You have the right to back out any time before the preliminary hearing. After that, women can—and have—been subpoenaed as witnesses.

17. In court, the District Attorney represents you. You cannot choose your attorney. If you can afford it, you can have your own attorney on the side to counsel you. Try to get information on sympathetic women lawyers.

18. You should ask that your address NOT be read at the preliminary hearing and trial. Otherwise, it is read automatically, and rapists sometimes have vengeful friends.

19. The court is open to the public. You cannot have a closed hearing unless the defense attorney agrees. This very seldom happens.

20. In the preliminary hearing, a judge decides whether or not there is enough evidence to warrant a trial. If so, the case goes on to a jury trial. Your past sexual history is considered admissible evidence and the defense attorney will be sure to research it. Your "reputation" is often attacked. The defense attorney's usual ploy is to make the woman the defendant. He will attack you verbally on the witness stand and try to "prove" that you "caused" or "provoked" the rape.

21. If you are beaten, kidnapped, or assaulted, it is sometimes better to prosecute those crimes since convictions are easier to obtain in those cases than in rape cases. (A rape victim—especially a young one—is seldom tried by a jury of her peers.)

Since these procedures tend to be very harrowing, many women find emotional support imperative. Try to have a friend or rape victim advocate with you throughout the reporting and trial. The decision of whether to report a rape or not is yours. You can weigh the possible trauma of reporting it against the possibility that he might rape again. You can also consider reporting anonymously.

Bibliography

Compiled by
Barbara Fagan, Diana E. H. Russell,
and Margaret Stone

Much of the relevant writing on this subject derives from unconventional sources, such as "underground" newsletters, unsigned and undated. Including this material, so different in approach and attitude from either scholarly or mass-media treatments, has made it impossible to compile a formal bibliography. Authors, publishers, and publication dates have of course been cited whenever available.

"Admissibility in a Rape Trial of Testimony of Defendant's Prior Rape Victims." *Maryland Law Review*, Spring 1960, p. 180.

Alderton, Peggy. "Rape!" Mimeographed, n.d.

Amir, Menachem. "Forcible Rape." *Sexual Behavior*, November 1971, p. 25.

———. *Patterns in Forcible Rape*. Chicago, 1971.

———. "The Role of the Victim in Sex Offenses." In H. L. Resnik and M. E. Wolfgang (Eds.), *Sexual Behaviors: Social, Clinical and Legal Aspects*. Boston, Mass.: Little, Brown, 1972, pp. xiii, 448.

———. "Victims Precipitate Forcible Rape." *Journal of Criminal Law, Criminology, and Police Science*, 58 (1967): 493–502.

"Anatomy of a Rape." *It Ain't Me Babe*, July 1970.

Angelou, Maya. *I Know Why the Caged Bird Sings*. New York, 1969.

Anonymous. *My Secret Life*. New York, 1966.

Astor, Gerald. *Rape Squad: The True Story of Nine Policewomen in Their Fight Against the Unspeakable Crime.* New York, 1974.

"Atrocities at Home." *The Ladder*, April-May 1972, p. 12.

Aurthur, Robert Alan. "Hanging Out." *Esquire*, July 1973, pp. 64 f.

Bengis, Ingrid. *Combat in the Erogenous Zone.* New York, 1973.

Biderman, A., et al. *Report of a Pilot Study in the District of Columbia on Victimization and Attitudes toward Law Enforcement.* Field Survey I of the President's Commission on Law Enforcement and the Administration of Justice, 1967.

Blanchard, W. H. "The Group Processes in Group Rape." *Journal of Social Psychology*, 49 (1959): 750–766.

Bornstein, F. P. "The El Paso County Program for the Medical Investigation of Sexual Offenses." *Journal of Forensic Sciences*, 3 (January 1958): 123–130.

———. "Investigation of Rape: Medicolegal Problems." *Medical Trial Technique Quarterly.* March 1963, pp. 61–71.

Boston Women's Health Collective. "Some Myths About Women"; "Anatomy and Physiology"; "Sexuality."—*Our Bodies Our Selves.* 1971, pp. 25–31, 4–9, 9–24.

Brown, Julia S. "A Comparative Study of Deviations from Sexual Mores." *American Sociological Review*, 17 (April 1952): 135–146.

California Sexual Deviation Research. Sacramento, Calif.: State Department of Mental Hygiene, 1954.

Casida, June Bundy and Joseph Casida. *Rape: How to Avoid It, and What to Do About It If You Can't.* Books for Better Living, 1974.

Chappell, D. "Forcible Rape." *Studies in the Sociology of Sex.* 1971, pp. 169–190.

Chesler, Phyllis. *Women and Madness.* Garden City, N. Y., 1972.

Chriss, Nicholas C. "Can a Black Be Acquitted?" *The Nation*, December 18, 1970, pp. 690–91.

Cleaver, Eldridge, *Soul on Ice.* New York, 1968.

Cohen, Murray L., et al. "The Psychology of Rapists." *Seminars in Psychiatry*, 3 (August 1971): 307–327.

Cohen, R. "Sexual Molestations in Hospitals." Philadelphia: *Clin. Pediat.*, 3 (1964): 689.

Cohn, Barbara N., et al. "Succumbing to Rape." *Lavender Women, Chicago Lesbian Newspaper.* Also in *Second Wave.* 1971, No. 2, pp. 24–27.

"Comment: Police Discretion and the Judgment That a Crime Has Been Committed—Rape in Philadelphia." *University of Pennsylvania Law Review*, 117 (1968): 277–322.

Connell, Evan S., Jr. *The Diary of a Rapist.* New York, 1966.

"Corroborating Charges of Rape." *Columbia Law Review*, 67 (1967): 1136–1148.

"The Corroboration Rule and Crimes Accompanying Rape." *University of Pennsylvania Law Review*, 118: 458.

Davis, Angela. "On Black Women." *Ms.*, August 1972, p. 55.

Davis, Elizabeth Gould. *The First Sex.* Baltimore, 1972.

DeRiver, D. *The Sexual Criminal.* Springfield, Ill., 1956.

Devereaux, G. "The Awarding of the Penis as a Compensation for Rape." *International Journal of Psychoanalysis,* 38 (1957): 398–401.

Dictor, Renee. "Rape Squad: Women Avengers Take the Law into Their Own Hands." *Coronet,* October 1972.

"Disarm Rapists." *It Ain't Me Babe,* December 1, 1971.

Dworkin, Roger B. "The Resistance Standard in Rape Legislation." *Stanford Law Review,* 680 (February 1966).

Eidelberg, L. *The Dark Urge.* New York, 1961.

Ellis, A., and Brancale, R. *The Psychology of Sex Offenders.* Springfield, Ill., 1956.

Ennis, Philip H. *Criminal Victimization in the U.S.: Report of a National Survey.* Field Survey II of the President's Commission on Law Enforcement and the Administration of Justice. Washington, D. C., 1967.

Evrad, John R. "Rape: The Medical, Social and Legal Implications." *American Journal of Obstetrics and Gynecology,* September 1971, pp. 197–199.

Factor, M. "A Woman's Psychological Reaction to Attempted Rape." *Psychoanalytic Quarterly,* 23 (1954): 243–244.

Fanon, Frantz. *The Wretched of the Earth.* New York, 1963.

Fettamen, Ann. *Trashing.* New York, 1972.

"Forcible and Statutory Rape: Exploration on the Consent Standard." *Yale Law Review,* 62 (1952): 55–83.

Fox, S. "Crisis Intervention with Rape Victims." *Social Work,* 17 (January 1972): 34–43.

Frank, G. *The Boston Strangler.* New York, 1966.

Friday, Nancy. *My Secret Garden: Women's Sexual Fantasies.* New York, 1973.

Gagnon, J. "Female Child Victims of Sex Offenses." *Social Problems,* 13 (1966): 176–192.

Gebhard, Paul. *Sex Offenders.* New York, 1965.

Geis, Gilbert. "Group Sexual Assaults." *Medical Aspects of Human Sexuality,* May 1971, pp. 101–113.

Goode, William J. "Violence between Intimates." In *Crimes of Violence,* edited by D. J. Mulvihill and M. Tumin. Washington, D.C.: U.S. Government Printing Office, 1969.

Greer, Germaine. "Seduction is a Four-Letter Word." *Playboy,* January, 1973, p. 80.

Griffin, Susan. "Rape: The All-American Crime." *Ramparts,* September, 1971, p. 26.

Gorham, C. "Not Only the Stranger." *Journal of School Health,* (1966).

Gornick, Vivian. "Woman as Outsider." *Woman in Sexist Society: Studies in Power and Powerlessness,* edited by Vivian Gornick and Barbara Moran, 1971, New York.

Graves, L. "Medicolegal Aspects of Rape." *Medical Aspects of Human Sexuality,* April 1970, pp. 109–117.

Halleck, Seymour. "Physicians Role in the Management of Victims of Sex

Offenders." *Journal of the American Medical Association*, Vol. 180, pp. 237–238.

Hariton, E. Barbara. "The Sexual Fantasies of Women." In *Female Experience*, edited by Carol Tavris, *Psychology Today*, 1973.

Harkowitz, Judy. "Rape." *Baltimore Woman's Liberation Newsletter*.

Harmetz, Aljean. "Rape: New Hollywood Game—An Ugly Movie Trend." *San Francisco Examiner*, October 28, 1973.

Haymen, Charles, et. al. "Consent in Sexual Offenses." *Modern Law Review*, 25 (1972): 272–286.

———, et al. "Public Health Program for Sexually Assaulted Females." *Public Health Reports*, 82 (June 1967).

———, et al. "Sexual Assault on Women and Girls in the District of Columbia." *Southern Medical Journal*, 62 (1969): 1227.

———, Lanza, Charlene, et al. "Rape in the District of Columbia." Adapted from a presentation to the American Public Health Association, October 12, 1971.

Hernton, Calvin C. *Sex and Racism in America*. New York, 1965.

Herschberger, Ruth. "Is Rape a Myth?" In *Masculine/Feminine*; Betty and Theodore Roszak, editors. New York, 1969.

Holmstrom, Lynda Lytle and Burgess, Ann Wolbert. "Rape: The Victim Goes on Trial." Paper delivered at the American Sociological Association Annual Meetings, 1973.

"I Never Set Out to Rape Anybody." *Ms.*, December 1972, pp. 22–23.

Jenkins, R. L. "The Making of a Sex Offender." In *Criminology*; Clyde B. Vedder, Samuel Koenig, and Robert E. Clark, editors. New York, 1953.

Kanin, E. J. and Kirkpatrick, C. "Male Sex Aggression in University Campuses." *American Sociological Review*, 22 (1953): 52–58.

Kanin, E. J. "Male Aggressions in Dating Relations." *The American Journal of Sociology*, 63 (1957): 197–204.

———. "Sex Aggression by College Men." *Medical Aspects of Human Sexuality*, May 1971, pp. 28–40.

Kanowitz, Leo. *Women and the Law: The Unfinished Revolution*. Albuquerque, 1969.

Karpman, Benjamin. *The Sexual Offender and His Offenses*. New York, 1954.

Kearon, Pamela and Nearhof, Barbara. "Rape: An Act of Terror." *Notes from the Third Year*, 1971, pp. 79–82.

Kluckhohn, Clyde. "Sexual Behavior in Cross-Cultural Perspective." In Himelhoch and Fava, *Sexual Behavior in American Society*, pp. 332–345.

Lake, Alice. "Rape: The Unmentionable Crime." *Good Housekeeping*, November 1971, pp. 104–105.

Landis, Judson T. "Experiences of 500 Children with Adult Sexual Deviation." *The Psychiatric Quarterly Review Supplement*, 30 (Part 2, 1956): 91–108.

Lanza, Charlene. "Nursing Support for the Victim of Sexual Assault." *Quarterly Review*, 39 (No. 2, Summer 1971).

Lear, Martha Weinman. "Q. If you rape a woman and steal her TV, what can they get you for in New York? A. Stealing her TV." *New York Times Magazine,* January 30, 1972, pp. 22–23.

———. "What Can You Say About Laws That Tell a Man: 'If You Rob a Woman You Might As Well Rape Her Too—the Rape Is Free.'? " *Redbook,* September 1972.

Lee, Al. "Ways to Protect Your Home." *Better Homes and Gardens,* June 1972, p. 16.

Lee, Betty. "Precautions Against Rape." *Sexual Behavior,* 2 (No. 1, January 1972): 33.

Legman, G. *Rationale of the Dirty Joke: An Analysis of Sexual Humor.* New York, 1968.

LeGrand, Camille E. "Rape and Rape Laws: Sexism in Society and Law." *California Law Review,* 61 (1973): 919–941.

Lély, Gilbert. *The Marquis de Sade: A Biography.* Translated by Alec Brown. New York, 1961.

LeVine, Robert. "Gusii Sex Offenses." *American Anthropologist,* 16 (1959): 965–990.

Lindsey, Karen, et al. "Aspects of Rape." *Second Wave,* 2 (1972): 20–28.

MacDonald, John M. "Castration for Rapists." *Medical Aspects of Human Sexuality,* February 1973, pp. 12–27.

———. "False Accusations of Rape." *Medical Aspects of Human Sexuality,* 7 (No. 5, May 1973): 170–193.

———. *Rape: Offenders and Their Victims.* Springfield, Ill., 1971.

McGeorge, J. "Sexual Assault on Children." *Medical Science Law,* 4 (1964):245.

Maslow, A. H. "Self-Esteem (Dominance Feeling) and Sexuality in Women." *Journal of Social Psychology,* 16 (1942): 259–294.

Massey, Joe B. "Management of Sexually Assaulted Females." *Obstetrics and Gynecology,* 13 (1971): 190–192.

Medea, Andra and Thompson, Kathleen. *Against Rape.* New York: Farrar, Straus & Giroux, 1974.

———. "Woman's Body/Woman's Mind: How Much Do You Really Know About Rapists?" *Ms.,* July, 1974, p. 113.

Mehrhof, Barbara and Pamela Kearon. "Rape: An Act of Terror." In *Notes From the Third Year: Woman's Liberation.* Notes from the Second Year, Inc., 1971, p. 79.

Mendelson, B. "The Origin of the Doctrine of Victimology." *Excerpta Criminologica,* 3 (1963): 229–240.

Meyer, Judith. "Comparative Rape Laws." Mimeographed, January 30, 1972.

Meyers, L. "Reasonable Mistake of Age: A Needed Defense of Statutory Rape." *Michigan Law Review,* (1965): 105–136.

Millett, Kate. *Sexual Politics.* Garden City, N. Y., 1970.

Moore, Robert. *The Rape Conspiracy* (pornography). New York, 1971.

Murphy, Robert F. "Social Structure and Sex Antagonism." *Southwestern Journal of Anthropology*, 15 (1959): 89–98.

Norman, Eve. *Rape*. Los Angeles, Calif.: Wollstonecraft, Inc., 1973.

Offstein, Jerrold N. *Self-Defense for Women*. Washington, D. C., 1972.

Paulshock, B. Z. and Anderson, M. V. "Estrogen Therapy After Rape?" *Annals of Internal Medicine*, 72 (1970): 61.

Ploscowe, Morris. "Rape." *Problems of Sexual Behavior*, pp. 203–240.

"Police Discretion in Rape Cases." *University of Pennsylvania Law Review*, 117 (December 1968): 272ff.

The President's Commission on Law Enforcement and the Administration of Justice. Washington, D. C., 1967.

Praz, Mario. *The Romantic Agony*. New York, 1951, 2nd ed.

"Protest." *Glamour*, April 1972, p. 56.

Randal, Judith. "Rape: An Analysis." *The Washington Evening Star*, November 12, 1971.

"Rape and Its Consequences." *Medical Aspects of Human Sexuality*, February 1972, pp. 12f.

The Rape Center Women. *How to Start a Rape Crisis Center*. Washington, D.C., 1972.

Rape Collective. *The Rape Handbook*. (Student Workshop on Political and Social Issues.) Palo Alto, Calif., 1973.

"Rape, Combat Training." *Every Woman*, 1 (No. 14, February 5, 1971): 8.

San Francisco Neighborhood Legal Assistance Foundation, Women's Litigation Unit. "Proposed Amendments to the Rape Laws." Mimeographed, June 22, 1973.

Schmidt, Peggy. "How to Make Trouble: Rape Crisis Centers." Ms., September 1973, pp. 14–18.

Schurr, Cathleen. "Rape: Victim as Criminal." Pittsburgh, Pa.: Know, Inc., reprint, n.d.

Schwartz, Barry. "The Effect in Philadelphia of Pennsylvania's Increased Penalties for Rape and Attempted Rape." *The Journal of Criminal Law, Criminology, and Police Science*, 59 (1968): 509–515.

"Sex Offenses—Credibility of Complaining Witnesses." *Iowa Law Review*, 43 (Summer 1958): 658ff.

Shaffer, Helen B. "Crime of Rape." *Editorial Research Reports*, 1 (No. 3, January 19, 1972).

Shah, Diane K. "Women Attack Rape Justice." *The National Observer*, October 9, 1971, p. 21.

Sheehy, Gail. "Nice Girls Don't Get Into Trouble." *New York*, pp. 26–30.

Sheldon, Ann and Margolin, Debbie. "Rape: The Experience"; "Rape: The Fact"; "Rape: A Solution." In *Women: Journal of Liberation* (Sexuality Issue), Vol. 3, No. 1, 1972, pp. 18–23

Shelley, Martha. "How It Works in L.A. . . . ." *Ms.*, September 1973, p. 16.

Shulman, Alix Kates. *Memoirs of an Ex-Prom Queen.* New York, 1972.

———. "The War in the Back Seat." *Atlantic*, July 1972, pp. 50–55.

Shultz, Gladys Denny. *How Many More Victims? Society and the Sex Criminal.* Philadelphia, 1965.

———. "Society and the Sex Criminal." *Reader's Digest*, November 1966, pp. 139–146.

———. "What Sex Offenders Say About Pornography." *Reader's Digest*, July 1971, pp. 53–57.

Simon, William and Gagnon, John H. "On Psycho-sexual Development." In *Handbook of Socialization: Theory and Practice*, David A. Goslin, editor. Chicago, 1969.

Slovenko, R., editor. *Sexual Behavior and the Law.* Springfield, Ill., 1965.

Slovenko, Ralph. "Statutory Rape." *Medical Aspects of Human Sexuality*, 5 (March 1971): 155–167.

"The Story of Morris Kent—Rapist." *The Washington Post*, June 18, 1967.

Sullivan, Gail Bernice. "Rape and Its Neglected Victims." *San Francisco Chronicle*, California Living Section, April 9, 1972.

Sutherland, Sandra and Scherl, Donald J. "Patterns of Response Among Victims of Rape." *American Journal of Orthopsychiatry*, 40 (No. 3, April 1970): 503–511.

Svalastoga, K. "Rape and the Social Structure." *Pacific Sociological Review*, 5 (1962): 48–53.

Tegner, Bruce. *Complete Book of Self-Defense.* New York, 1968.

———. and McGrath, Alice. *Self Defense for Girls: A Secondary School and College Manual.* New York, 1969.

Thompson, Hunter S. *Hell's Angels: A Strange and Terrible Saga.* New York, 1966.

Uniform Crime Reports. Washington, D.C.: United States Department of Justice. Issued annually.

Van Heller, Marcus. *Rape* (pornography). San Diego, Calif., 1971.

Von Hentig, Hans. *The Criminal and His Victim.* New Haven, 1948.

Wheeler, S. "Sex Offenses: A Sociological Critique." *Law and Contemporary Problems*, 25 (1960): 258–279.

Willie, W. P. "Case Study of a Rapist: An Analysis of the Causation of Criminal Behavior." *Journal of Social Therapy*, 7 (1961): 10–21.

Wolhofen, Henry. "Victims of Criminal Violence." *Journal of Public Law*, 1959.

Women Against Rape. *Stop Rape.* Detroit, 1971. (Obtainable from Detroit Women Against Rape, 1821 Patton St., Detroit, Michigan 49725.)

Women's Crisis Center of Ann Arbor. *Freedom from Rape.* 306 N. Division St., Ann Arbor, Michigan 48108.

Wood, Pamela Lakes. "The Victim in a Forcible Rape Case: A Feminist View." *The American Criminal Law Review*, 11 (Winter 1973): 345–347.